# UCFB

# SPORT AND COMMUNICATION

As such a major source of passion and influence throughout the world, sport represents a fascinating area of research for academics from a broad range of disciplines, including sociology, politics, economics, history, and media and communication.

The **SAGE Library of Sports Studies** demonstrates the wide scope of this ever-expanding field and charts the rapid development of intellectual interest over the last few decades. Each multi-volume set represents a landmark collection of the essential published works collated from the foremost publications in the field by an editor or editorial team of renowned international stature.

**Raymond Boyle** is Professor of Communications at the Centre for Cultural Policy Research at the University of Glasgow. He has published widely on sport and media for over 20 years. His books include *Sport and National Identity in the European Media* (1993 with Blain and O'Donnell); *PowerPlay: Sport the Media and Popular Culture* (2000 and 2009 with Haynes); *Football in the New Media Age* (2004 with Haynes); *Sports Journalism: Context and Issues* (2006); *The Television Entrepreneurs* (2012 with Kelly) and *The Rise and Fall of the UK Film Council* (2015 with Doyle, Schlesinger and Kelly). He sits on the Editorial Board of *Media, Culture and Society* and the Advisory Boards for *Communication and Sport* and *Leisure Studies*. He also delivers the *Communication, Media and Public Relations* module on the UEFA Certificate in Football Management programme which is taught with national football associations across Europe.

SAGE LIBRARY OF SPORTS STUDIES

# SPORT AND COMMUNICATION

## VOLUME I

*History and Context: Heroes and Villains*

Edited by

Raymond Boyle

Los Angeles I London I New Delhi I Singapore I Washington DC I Melbourne

Los Angeles | London | New Delhi
Singapore | Washington DC | Melbourne

SAGE Publications Ltd
1 Oliver's Yard
55 City Road
London EC1Y 1SP

SAGE Publications Inc.
2455 Teller Road
Thousand Oaks, California 91320

SAGE Publications India Pvt Ltd
B 1/I 1, Mohan Cooperative Industrial Area
Mathura Road
New Delhi 110 044

SAGE Publications Asia-Pacific Pte Ltd
3 Church Street
#10-04 Samsung Hub
Singapore 049483

Editor: Mila Steele
Assistant editor: Matt Oldfield
Permissions: Km Ranjana
Production controller: Bhairav Dutt Sharma
Proofreader: Vaibhav Bansal
Marketing manager: Kay Stefanski
Cover design: Wendy Scott
Typeset by Chennai Publishing Services, Chennai
Printed and bound by CPI Group (UK) Ltd,
Croydon, CR0 4YY [for Antony Rowe]

MIX
Paper from
responsible sources
FSC   FSC® C013604
www.fsc.org

At SAGE we take sustainability seriously. Most of our
products are printed in the UK using FSC papers and
boards. When we print overseas we ensure sustainable
papers are used as measured by the Egmont grading
system. We undertake an annual audit to monitor our
sustainability.

**Library of Congress Control Number: 2015955440**

**British Library Cataloguing in Publication Data**

A catalogue record for this book is available from the
British Library

ISBN: 978-1-4739-1306-6 (set of four volumes)

*To Noelle, Lauren and Liam*

# Contents

## Volume II: Sport, Media and Communicating Identities

# Volume III: The Sports Communication Industries

## Volume IV: Sports and the Digital Age

# Appendix of Sources

All articles and chapters have been reproduced exactly as they were first published, including textual cross-references to material in the original source.

Grateful acknowledgement is made to the following sources for permission to reproduce material in this book.

1. '"They Play in Your Home": Cricket, Media and Modernity in Pre-war Australia', *Frazer Andrewes*
   *The International Journal of the History of Sport*, 17(2/3), Special Issue: Sport in Australasian Society Past and Present (2000): 93–110.
   Reprinted by permission of Taylor & Francis Ltd, http://www.tandfonline.com via Copyright Clearance Center's RightsLink service.

2. 'Long Before Arledge . . . Sports & TV: The Earliest Years – 1937–1947 – as Seen by the Contemporary Press', *Dave Berkman*
   *The Journal of Popular Culture*, 22(2) (1988): 49–62.
   Reprinted with permission from John Wiley and Sons Ltd.

3. 'Media Sport: Hot and Cool', *Susan Birrell and John W. Loy, Jr*
   *International Review for the Sociology of Sport*, 14(1) (1979): 5–17.
   Published by SAGE Publications Ltd. Reprinted with permission.

4. 'From Our Gaelic Fields: Radio, Sport and Nation in Post-Partition Ireland', *Raymond Boyle*
   *Media, Culture & Society*, 14(4) (1992): 623–636.
   Published by SAGE Publications Ltd. Reprinted with permission.

5. 'Drama in Sports Commentary', *Jennings Bryant, Paul Comisky and Dolf Zillmann*
   *Journal of Communication*, 27(3) (1977): 140–149.
   Reprinted with permission from John Wiley and Sons Ltd.

6. 'Sport and the Media in Ireland: An Introduction', *Seán Crosson and Philip Dine*
   *Media History*, 17(2), Special Issue: Sport and the Media in Ireland (2011): 109–116.
   © 2011 Taylor & Francis. Reprinted by permission of Taylor & Francis Ltd, http://www.tandfonline.com via Copyright Clearance Center's RightsLink service.

7. 'A Speculative Paradigm on the Birth of the Modern Sport
Spectacular: The Real Madrid and Eintracht Frankfurt European
Cup Final of 1960', *Scott A.G.M. Crawford*
*The International Journal of the History of Sport*, 9(3) (1992): 433–438.
Published by Frank Cass, London. Reprinted by permission of
Taylor & Francis Ltd, http://www.tandfonline.com via Copyright Clearance
Center's RightsLink service.

8. 'Sport on Commercial Norwegian Radio 1988 to 2003', *Peter Dahlén
and Ragnhild Thomsen*
*Trends in Communication*, 12(2/3) (2004): 117–130.
Copyright © 2004, Lawrence Erlbaum Associates, Inc. Reprinted by
permission of Taylor & Francis Ltd. http://www.tandfonline.com

9. 'Local Radio Sport from the Producer's Point of View', *Peter Gilmore*
*Sport in History* (formerly *The Sports Historian*), 13(1) (1993): 26–30.
Copyright © The British Society of Sports History. Reprinted by permission of
Taylor & Francis Ltd, www.tandfonline.com on behalf of The British Society
of Sports History via Copyright Clearance Center's RightsLink service.

10. 'How Should We Theorize Sport in a Capitalist Patriarchy?', *M. Ann Hall*
*International Review for the Sociology of Sport*, 20(1/2) (1985): 109–115.
Published by SAGE Publications Ltd. Reprinted with permission.

11. 'A Pageant of Sound and Vision: Football's Relationship with Television,
1936–60', *Richard Haynes*
*The International Journal of the History of Sport*, 15(1) (1998): 211–226.
Published by Frank Cass, London. Reprinted by permission of
Taylor & Francis Ltd, http://www.tandfonline.com via Copyright Clearance
Center's RightsLink service.

12. '"Lobby" and the Formative Years of Radio Sports Commentary, 1935–1952',
*Richard Haynes*
*Sport in History*, 29(1) (2009): 25–48.
Copyright © The British Society of Sports History. Reprinted by permission
of Taylor & Francis Ltd, www.tandfonline.com on behalf of The British
Society of Sports History via Copyright Clearance Center's RightsLink
service.

13. 'The BBC, Austerity and Broadcasting the 1948 Olympic Games',
*Richard Haynes*
*The International Journal of the History of Sport*, 27(6), Special Issue:
Europe and the London Olympic Games 1948 (2010): 1029–1046.
© 2010 Taylor & Francis. Reprinted by permission of Taylor & Francis Ltd,
http://www.tandfonline.com via Copyright Clearance Center's RightsLink
service.

14. 'BBC Radio and Sport 1922–39', *Mike Huggins*
    *Contemporary British History*, 21(4) (2007): 491–515.
    © 2007 Taylor & Francis. Reprinted by permission of Taylor & Francis Ltd,
    http://www.tandfonline.com via Copyright Clearance Center's RightsLink
    service.

15. 'The Interdependence of Sport and Culture', *Günther Lüschen*
    *International Review for the Sociology of Sport*, 2(1) (1967): 127–139.
    Published by SAGE Publications Ltd. Reprinted with permission.

16. 'Hero Crafting in *Sporting Life*, an Early Baseball Journal',
    *Lori Amber Roessner*
    *American Journalism*, 26(2) (2009): 39–65.
    Reprinted by permission of the American Journalism Historians
    Association, www.ajhaonline.org via Copyright Clearance Center's
    RightsLink service.

17. 'Making Soccer a "Kick in the Grass": The Media's Role in Promoting
    a Marginal Sport, 1975–1977', *Thom Satterlee*
    *International Review for the Sociology of Sport*, 36(3) (2001): 305–317.
    Published by SAGE Publications Ltd. Reprinted with permission.

18. 'Assessing the Sociology of Sport: On the Mediasport Interpellation
    and Commodity Narratives', *Lawrence A. Wenner*
    *International Review for the Sociology of Sport*, 50(4/5) (2015): 628–633.
    Published by SAGE Publications Ltd. Reprinted with permission.

19. 'The Unholy Alliance: Notes on Television and the Remaking of British
    Sport 1965–85', *Garry Whannel*
    *Leisure Studies*, 5(2) (1986): 129–145.
    © 1986 E. & F.N. Spon Ltd. Reprinted by permission of Taylor & Francis
    Ltd, http://www.tandfonline.com via Copyright Clearance Center's
    RightsLink service.

20. 'Pregnant with Anticipation: The Pre-History of Television
    Sport and the Politics of Recycling and Preservation', *Garry Whannel*
    *International Journal of Cultural Studies*, 8(4) (2005): 405–426.
    Published by SAGE Publications Ltd. Reprinted with permission.

21. 'From Plantation to Playing Field: Historical Writings on The Black
    Athlete in American Sport', *David K. Wiggins*
    *Research Quarterly for Exercise and Sport*, 57(2) (1986): 101–116.
    Reprinted by permission of the Society of Health and Physical Educators,
    www.shapeamerica.org via Copyright Clearance Center's RightsLink
    service.

22. 'Selective Representation of Gender, Ethnicity, and Nationality in American Television Coverage of the 2000 Summer Olympics', *Andrew C. Billings and Susan Tyler Eastman*
    *International Review for the Sociology of Sport*, 37(3/4) (2002): 351–370.
    Published by SAGE Publications Ltd. Reprinted with permission.

23. '"The Grand Old Game": Football, Media and Identity in Scotland',
    *Raymond Boyle and Richard Haynes*
    *Media, Culture & Society*, 18(4) (1996): 549–564.
    Published by SAGE Publications Ltd. Reprinted with permission.

24. 'Italian Television Sport Coverage during the 2000 Sydney Olympic Games: A Gender Perspective', *Laura Capranica and Fabrizio Aversa*
    *International Review for the Sociology of Sport*, 37(3/4) (2002): 337–349.
    Published by SAGE Publications Ltd. Reprinted with permission.

25. 'A Content Analysis of News Coverage of Asian Female Olympic Athletes',
    *Chia-Chen Yu*
    *International Review for the Sociology of Sport*, 44(2/3) (2009): 283–305.
    Published by SAGE Publications Ltd. Reprinted with permission.

26. 'Women Play Sport, But Not on TV: A Longitudinal Study of Televised News Media', *Cheryl Cooky, Michael A. Messner and Robin H. Hextrum*
    *Communication & Sport*, 1(3) (2013): 203–230.
    Published by SAGE Publications, Inc. Reprinted with permission.

27. 'Gendered Narratives in Spain: The Representation of Female Athletes in *Marca* and *El País*', *Liz Crolley and Elena Teso*
    *International Review for the Sociology of Sport*, 42(2) (2007): 149–166.
    Published by SAGE Publications Ltd. Reprinted with permission.

28. 'Which Nation, Which Flag? Boxing and National Identities in Ireland',
    *Mike Cronin*
    *International Review for the Sociology of Sport*, 32(2) (1997): 131–145.
    Published by SAGE Publications Ltd. Reprinted with permission.

29. 'The Power of Stereotypes: Anchoring Images through Language in Live Sports Broadcasts', *Fabrice Desmarais and Toni Bruce*
    *Journal of Language and Social Psychology*, 29(3) (2010): 338–362.
    Published by SAGE Publications, Inc. Reprinted with permission.

30. 'Liberal and Radical Sources of Female Empowerment in Sport Media',
    *Margaret Carlisle Duncan and Barry Brummett*
    *Sociology of Sport Journal*, 10(1) (1993): 57–72.
    © 1993 Human Kinetics Publishers, Inc. Reprinted with permission from Human Kinetics, Inc. via Copyright Clearance Center, Inc.

31. 'Separating the Men from the Girls: The Gendered Language
of Televised Sports', *Michael A. Messner, Margaret Carlisle Duncan
and Kerry Jensen*
*Gender & Society*, 7(1) (1993): 121–137.
Copyright © 1993 Sociologists for Women in Society. Reprinted by
permission of SAGE Publications, Inc. via Copyright Clearance Center's
RightsLink service.

32. 'Women's Boxing and Related Activities: Introducing Images and Meanings',
*Jennifer Hargreaves*
*Body & Society*, 3(4) (1997): 33–49.
Published by SAGE Publications Ltd. Reprinted with permission.

33. 'Sport, National Identity and Public Policy', *Barrie Houlihan*
*Nations and Nationalism*, 3(1) (1997): 113–137.
© ASEN 1997. Reprinted with permission from John Wiley and Sons Ltd.

34. 'Race Relations, Sociology of Sport and the New Politics of Race and Racism',
*G. Jarvie and I. Reid*
*Leisure Studies*, 16(4) (1997): 211–219.
© 1997 E & FN Spon. Reprinted by permission of Taylor & Francis Ltd,
http://www.tandfonline.com via Copyright Clearance Center's RightsLink
service.

35. 'The Death of a Female Boxer: Media, Sport, Nationalism, and Gender',
*Roy Dereck McCree*
*Journal of Sport & Social Issues*, 35(4) (2011): 327–349.
Published by SAGE Publications, Inc. Reprinted with permission.

36. 'Sports Spectacle as Drama: Image, Language and Technology',
*Barbra S. Morris and Joel Nydahl*
*The Journal of Popular Culture*, 18(4) (1984): 101–110.
Reprinted with permission from John Wiley and Sons Ltd.

37. 'Dallas with Balls: Televized Sport, Soap Opera and Male and Female
Pleasures', *Barbara O'Connor and Raymond Boyle*
*Leisure Studies*, 12(2) (1993): 107–119.
© 1993 E. & F.N. Spon. Reprinted by permission of Taylor & Francis Ltd,
http://www.tandfonline.com via Copyright Clearance Center's RightsLink
service.

38. 'Mapping the Mythical: A Geopolitics of National Sporting Stereotypes',
*Hugh O'Donnell*
*Discourse & Society*, 5(3) (1994): 345–380.
Published by SAGE Publications Ltd. Reprinted with permission.

47. 'Twenty20 as Media Event', *Nick Anstead and Ben O'Loughlin*
    *Sport in Society: Cultures, Commerce, Media, Politics*, 14(10), Special Issue:
    Twenty20 and the future of Cricket (2011): 1340–1357.
    © 2011 Taylor & Francis. Reprinted by permission of Taylor & Francis Ltd,
    http://www.tandfonline.com via Copyright Clearance Center's RightsLink
    service.

48. 'Be Like Mike?: Michael Jordan and the Pedagogy of Desire', *Michael Eric Dyson*
    *Cultural Studies*, 7(1) (1993): 64–72.
    Reprinted by permission of Taylor & Francis Ltd, www.tandfonline.com via
    Copyright Clearance Center's RightsLink service.

49. 'The Hungry Games: Television at the Atlanta Olympics', *Seth Feldman*
    *Queen's Quarterly*, 103(3) (1996): 461–469.
    Published by The Quarterly Committee of Queen's University. Reprinted
    with permission from Seth Feldman.

50. '"You Gotta Appease the People Who Run This Place": Corporate
    Ownership and Its Influence on Sports Television Production',
    *Jason Genovese*
    *Electronic News*, 7(3) (2013): 141–158.
    Copyright © The Author(s) 2013. Reprinted by permission of
    SAGE Publications, Inc. via Copyright Clearance Center's RightsLink
    service.

51. 'The Globalization of Sports, the Rise of Non-Western Nations,
    and the Impact on International Sporting Events', *Amit Gupta*
    *The International Journal of the History of Sport*, 26(12), Special Issue:
    South Asia (2009): 1779–1790.
    © 2009 Taylor & Francis. Reprinted by permission of Taylor & Francis Ltd,
    http://www.tandfonline.com via Copyright Clearance Center's RightsLink
    service.

52. 'Assessing the Sociology of Sport: On Media, Advertising
    and the Commodification of Culture', *Steven J. Jackson*
    *International Review for the Sociology of Sport*, 50(4/5) (2015): 490–495.
    Published by SAGE Publications Ltd. Reprinted with permission.

53. 'Unimagined China: Media, Technologies and the Fragmentation
    of National Olympic Audiences', *Kevin Latham*
    *The International Journal of the History of Sport*, 29(16), Special Issue: The
    Triple Asian Olympics: Asia Ascending – Media, Politics, Geopolitics (2012):
    2311–2325.
    © 2012 Taylor & Francis. Reprinted by permission of Taylor & Francis Ltd,
    http://www.tandfonline.com via Copyright Clearance Center's RightsLink
    service.

54. 'The Global Sport Mass Media Oligopoly: The Three Usual Suspects and More', *Alan Law, Jean Harvey and Stuart Kemp*
*International Review for the Sociology of Sport*, 37(3/4) (2002): 279–301.
Published by SAGE Publications Ltd. Reprinted with permission.

55. 'Public Relations and Sport in Promotional Culture', *Jacquie L'Etang*
*Public Relations Review*, 32(4) (2006): 386–394.
© 2006 Elsevier Inc. All rights reserved. Reprinted with permission from Elsevier via Copyright Clearance Center's RightsLink service.

56. 'Mass Media and the Experience of Sport', *Janet Lever and Stanton Wheeler*
*Communication Research*, 20(1) (1993): 125–143.
Published by SAGE Publications, Inc. Reprinted with permission.

57. 'Sports Page: A Case Study in the Manufacture of Sports News for the Daily Press', *Mark Douglas Lowes*
*Sociology of Sport Journal*, 14(2) (1997): 143–159.
© 1997 Human Kinetics Publishers, Inc. Reprinted with permission from Human Kinetics, Inc. via Copyright Clearance Center, Inc.

58. 'More Than a Sporting Touchdown: The Making of American Football in England 1982–1990', *Joe Maguire*
*Sociology of Sport Journal*, 7(3) (1990): 213–237.
Reprinted with permission from Human Kinetics, Inc. via Copyright Clearance Center, Inc.

59. 'The Global Media Sports Complex: Key Issues and Concerns',
*Joseph A. Maguire*
*Sport in Society: Cultures, Commerce, Media, Politics*, 14(7/8), Special Issue: Reflections on Process Sociology and Sport: 'Walking the Line' (2011): 965–977.
© 2011 Taylor & Francis. Reprinted by permission of Taylor & Francis Ltd, http://www.tandfonline.com via Copyright Clearance Center's RightsLink service.

60. 'The Marketing of the Women's National Basketball Association and the Making of Postfeminism', *Mary G. McDonald*
*International Review for the Sociology of Sport*, 35(1) (2000): 35–47.
Published by SAGE Publications Ltd. Reprinted with permission.

61. 'Sport as Kitsch: A Case Study of *The American Gladiators*', *Robert Rinehart*
*The Journal of Popular Culture*, 28(2) (1994): 25–35.
Reprinted with permission from John Wiley and Sons Ltd.

71. 'Twitter's Diffusion in Sports Journalism: Role Models, Laggards and Followers of the Social Media Innovation', *Peter English*
*New Media & Society* (2014).
DOI: 10.1177/1461444814544886
Published by SAGE Publications Ltd. Reprinted with permission.

72. 'Spain: Media Focus on the Geopolitical Issues of a Major Sporting Event',
*Emilio Fernández Peña and Miquel de Moragas*
*The International Journal of the History of Sport*, 27(9/10), Special Issue:
Encoding the Olympics – The Beijing Olympic Games and the Communication
Impact Worldwide (2010): 1501–1509.
© 2010 Taylor & Francis. Reprinted by permission of Taylor & Francis Ltd,
http://www.tandfonline.com via Copyright Clearance Center's RightsLink
service.

73. 'Women Reporting Sport: Still a Man's Game?', *Suzanne Franks
and Deirdre O'Neill*
*Journalism: Theory, Practice and Criticism* (2014).
DOI: 10.1177/1464884914561573
Published by SAGE Publications Ltd. Reprinted with permission.

74. 'Sports on Traditional and Newer Digital Media: Is There Really
a Fight for Fans?', *Walter Gantz and Nicky Lewis*
*Television & New Media*, 15(8) (2014): 760–768.
Published by SAGE Publications, Inc. Reprinted with permission.

75. 'From Broadcast Scarcity to Digital Plenitude: The Changing Dynamics
of the Media Sport Content Economy', *Brett Hutchins and David Rowe*
*Television & New Media*, 10(4) (2009): 354–370.
Published by SAGE Publications, Inc. Reprinted with permission.

76. 'Sport on the Move: The Unfolding Impact of Mobile Communications
on the Media Sport Content Economy', *Brett Hutchins*
*Journal of Sport & Social Issues*, 38(6) (2014): 509–527.
Published by SAGE Publications, Inc. Reprinted with permission.

77. 'Tales of the Digital Sublime: Tracing the Relationship between Big Data
and Professional Sport', *Brett Hutchins*
*Convergence: The International Journal of Research into New Media
Technologies* (2015).
DOI: 10.1177/1354856515587163
Published by SAGE Publications Ltd. Reprinted with permission.

78. 'Mediating the Olympics', *P David Marshall, Becky Walker and Nicholas Russo*
*Convergence: The International Journal of Research into New Media Technologies*, 16(3) (2010): 263–278.
Published by SAGE Publications Ltd. Reprinted with permission.

79. 'Football's Coming Home?: Digital Reterritorialization, Contradictions in the Transnational Coverage of Sport and the Sociology of Alternative Football Broadcasts', *Matthew David and Peter Millward*
*The British Journal of Sociology*, 63(2), Special Issue: Olympic and World Sport: making transnational Society? (2012): 349–369.
© London School of Economics and Political Science 2012. Reproduced with permission of Blackwell Publishing Ltd.

80. 'Sports Journalism: Still the "Toy Department" of the News Media?', *David Rowe*
*Journalism: Theory, Practice and Criticism*, 8(4) (2007): 385–405.
Published by SAGE Publications Ltd. Reprinted with permission.

81. 'Bill Simmons, Grantland.com, and ESPN's Corporate Reinvention of Literary Sports Writing Online', *Travis Vogan and David Dowling*
*Convergence: The International Journal of Research into New Media Technologies* (2014).
DOI: 10.1177/1354856514550637
Published by SAGE Publications Ltd. Reprinted with permission.

82. 'The Paradoxical Character of Live Television Sport in the Twenty-First Century', *Garry Whannel*
*Television & New Media*, 15(8) (2014): 769–776.
Published by SAGE Publications, Inc. Reprinted with permission.

83. 'Establishing a Typology of Social Media Uses in the Sport Industry: A Multidimensional Scaling Study', *Chad Witkemper, Matthew Blaszka and Jinwook Chung*
*Communication & Sport* (2014).
DOI: 10.1177/2167479514544951
Published by SAGE Publications, Inc. Reprinted with permission.

84. 'The EPL Drama – Paving the Way for More Illegal Streaming? Digital Piracy of Live Sports Broadcasts in Singapore', *Donna Wong*
*Leisure Studies* (2015).
DOI: 10.1080/02614367.2015.1035315
© 2015 Taylor & Francis. Reprinted by permission of Taylor & Francis Ltd, http://www.tandfonline.com via Copyright Clearance Center's RightsLink service.

# Editor's Introduction: Sport and Communication

*Raymond Boyle*

sport, is of course one of the very best things about television;
I would keep my set for it alone.
Raymond Williams, As We See Others, *The Listener*, 1 August, 1968.

The cultural and communications critic Raymond Williams was a fan of television sport. He discusses it in his first television review column for *The Listener*, a magazine that had been established by the BBC in 1929 to help promote intelligent discussion around initially radio, but later television. Despite the fact that Williams, one of the academic pioneers and father figures of Media and Communication Studies was interested in the relationship between sport and the media, the area itself remained substantially underresearched and largely absent from the growing literature around the media and popular culture until the late 1980s and early 1990s. To that end, it is fitting that an international journal now exists solely dedicated to this area of investigation, *Communication and Sport* appearing in 2013.

This volume pulls together a range of articles that offer a snapshot of academic engagements with sport and communication that have evolved and developed over the last number of decades. It is during this time that sport itself both symbolically and economically has become symbiotically linked with the media industries both at local and national level, but also as part of an international media culture. What these articles grouped together here to facilitate an ease of access highlight is both the sense of change in the sport media relationship, but also the strong element of continuity in a range of themes and issues. What is argued here is that by seeking to make sense of the place of sports in the wider cultural, economic and political environment that this also sheds light on the dynamics that surround the relationship between the media, popular culture and power relations within and across societies.

## The Volumes

As with any collection of articles a number of caveats regarding its construction are necessary. The research material gathered here comes from published journal articles. I have not included books chapters or sections of books, of which there are a growing number dedicated to investigating aspects of the media and sporting environment. By necessity there is a lot of excellent research material not included, and thus any selection is both personal in nature, and offers a snapshot (although hopefully an interesting and insightful one) of the material that exists in the sport and communication research area. Hence this is not an exhaustive or definitive list, and is certainly no attempt to create some type of canon of work within communication and media studies engagement with sports culture. Rather it offers a way into debates around the historical development of media sport, the political economy aspects of this relationship, as well as those around the symbolic, cultural and ideological aspects of mediated sporting discourse.

It also aims to capture that sense of continuity and change in what is a relatively young subject of study and while Volume IV focuses on the key role that digital is playing in re-shaping the sport and communication landscape, the other volumes serve to remind us that core debates around power relations and symbolic value are not exclusive concerns of the digital generation and that placing these in a broader historical context and trajectory can offer many insights, and perhaps avoid some ill though through conclusions.

Volume I, *History and Context: Heroes and Villains*, examines the historical origins of sports coverage across newspapers, radio and broadcasting. In so doing it highlights the key political, cultural and economic processes through which the contemporary sports–media relationship evolved. It also looks at some earlier academic engagements with the field of communication and sport. This section also traces the development of sports journalism practice and influence and also the evolving mediation of sports through radio and television coverage.

Volume II, *Sport, Media and Communicating Identities*, turns our attention to the key role that mediated sport plays in the field of representation. From international events such as the Olympics or the FIFA World Cup through to the reproduction of a range of identities from gender, race, ethnicity and national identity, we see how sports and their communication have come to play an important ideological role in society.

Volume III, *The Sports Communication Industries*, builds on these two volumes by examining how the communication industries have become intertwined with and helped facilitate the growth of sports industries and culture, and in so doing connected with associated communication aspects such as public relations and promotional culture. As the relationship between the media and sport has matured in the later part of the 20th century, the rise of sport as part of the entertainment industries has seen the sports media industries develop into an international business community.

Finally, Volume IV, *Sports and the Digital Age*, highlights how the communication industries in the digital age have continued to interact with sports and in particular examines how this has changed and reconstituted the relationship with spectators, fans and media consumers and citizens. Mediated sport has been at the forefront of changes in the converging media content industries ranging from issues of access to national events to the rise in value of specific sports content across new platforms forging new relationships with the mobile, always on audience for sports.

Defining the research parameters of the sport and communication field has never struck me as a particularly useful activity. By way of contrast, applying many of the same central concerns of media and communication studies around deepening our understanding of the relationship between cultural forms and commerce; mediation and identity formation and media and power are all areas that a study of communication and sport can help illuminate. It is hoped that these volumes make a contribution to that goal.

# Introduction: History and Context – Heroes and Villains

*Raymond Boyle*

## Introduction

This volume looks at the historical origins of sports coverage across newspapers, radio and broadcasting. In so doing it highlights the key political, cultural and economic processes through which the contemporary sports–media relationship evolved. It also looks at some earlier academic engagements with the field of communication and sport. This section also traces the development of sports journalism practice and influence and also the evolving mediation of sports through radio and television coverage.

The history of elite sport is inexorably bound up with the history of modern media developments. It is no accident that that latter part of the 19th century saw the establishment of sporting culture and organizations as integral parts of the wider fabric of industrial society, while this period also saw the significant growth of what we now recognize as the modern media industries. Initially through newspapers, then radio and television, sports increasingly became a key component of media content (in an age where such terminology would have been viewed as strange) and in so doing helped create what we understand as the central narratives of contemporary sports culture.

A number of pieces in this volume serve to remind us of the often forgotten or ignored central role that newspapers and radio in particular played in not simply relaying a pre-existing cultural form in some kind of neutral process. Rather these media were crucial intermediaries in reshaping and creating the meaning of sports in society and amplifying and elevating sports position within the social, economic and political development of modern nation-states.

## Before Television

The work of Roessner (2009) and Wiggins (1986) remind us of the central role played by the print media in constructing and reflecting key values and characteristics around iconic sports such as baseball in the United States that resonated with a wider cultural and political significance. The media through its representations of sport and the narratives around sports culture that they both constructed and publicized in turn helped create key symbolic aspects of national cultures around sporting identities. In so doing they helped to legitimize sports as an arena not only of conflict, but one infused with inherent acts of heroism and mythic figures and actors.

One might argue that while sporting heroism was embedded in sports discourse, it was journalisms ability to amplify and enhance this process and in so doing connect it with wider collective meaning that was so powerful. Journalism did not simply relay, it reshaped and reconstituted sport. The legacy created by the print media of viewing sport as a popular public form of activity that embedded and naturalized particular cultural values would prove to be a powerful one that would be amplified first by radio and then television. This research and the work here of Andrewes (2000), Boyle (1992), Huggins (2007) and Gilmore (1993) are attempts to make sense of the media's particular relationship with sport in the age before mass television and remind us the importance of placing the contemporary experience within a grounded historical context be that in the USA, Ireland, Australia or the UK.

For example Crosson and Dine (2011) remind us that even in countries such as Ireland, which did not conform to the classic economic industrial narrative that often is used to justify the particular sports–media relationship that emerges in society, rather other key drivers such as nationalism played a key role in shaping and infusing sports culture and how it is made sense of and amplified through its mediation by newspapers and national radio.

## Situating the Study of Sports

What this volume also reminds us is the relatively recent and still underdeveloped academic engagement with the relationship between the media and sport. Wenner's (2015) reflections are included here as they serve to remind us of the less then smooth evolution of the study of sport within media and communication studies. Academic boundaries were an important part in stunting the development of studies around sports media, where for many years the sociology of sport often treated the media as a footnote in studies, while media and communication studies did not deem it an area worthy of real focus and attention. Hall (1985) and Lüschen (1967) offer us a flavor of some of the attempts to rethink and reposition the role that sports culture plays in shaping modern society and highlighting the theoretical and methodological challenges involved in such a process and in setting out a broader agenda for research that recognized the growing importance not only of class, but of gender and identity politics. However, what is also striking about the latter 1967 piece is the absence of any recognition of the role that media may play in the process of reproducing sporting discourse or indeed the possibility that it might actually be reshaping it completely.

The legacy of this uneven research development means that our detailed historical understanding of the various relationships between sport and media organizations and mediated culture remains somewhat patchy. The work of Berkman (1998), Crawford (1992), Dahlén and Thomsen (2004), Haynes 1998; 2009; 2010) and Whannel (2005) in this volume all remind us of the potential richness of this area of study, and crucially, the importance for media and communication scholars (regardless if they are interested in sport!) of engaging with such studies.

Why does this matter? Well, because they serve to illuminate not just the media's relationship with the shifting values, politics and tastes in society, but also offer real original insight into the organizational development and internal cultures of media organizations such as the BBC. As Wenner astutely puts it reflecting on his introduction to this area in the 1980s:

> Not trained in sociology or sport per se, I thought the field of communication and media studies needed to discover sport. Later I came to think that the sociology of sport needed to discover communication and media studies (Wenner, 2015: 628).

The studies mentioned above in this volume offer a valuable snapshot of some of the key work that positions sports within the developing newspaper and radio industries. They should also remind us that much work around media history and sports relationship with media still remains to be done. It would of course be television and the study of television sport which would come to dominate much of the media sports research agenda.

## Television and Sport

The work of Birrell and Loy (1979) remains an important moment in legitimizing television sport as a subject deemed worthy of the scrutiny and attention given to other areas of the medium's output. It is important of course for younger media scholars to remember that in the UK for example, that it wasn't until the late 1970s, early 1980s that taking television seriously within the academy began to emerge. Although North American in focus the work of Birrell and Loy (1979) served not only to legitimize sport on television and media sport more generally as a legitimate area of study, but began to offer some possible methodological approaches to the study in this area. Here also the work of Bryant et al. (1977) was important in reminding us that visual media were often very much anchored in the spoken word and the power that mediated sports offered in terms of narrative development.

What we begin to see evolve is an approach to the study of television and media sport through a greater understanding of its codes and conventions and to some extent a recognition of the tensions between a more political economy approach to the subject and one focused on screen and textual analysis. Whannel's (1986) article was a cornerstone for a generation of communication scholars seeking to make sense of the media–sport relationship and keen to move beyond a purely textual analysis of the topic. It remains a classic analysis of the key moments that see the transformation of British sport between 1965 and 1985 and the role that television and commercial forces played in this process. It shows how that by understanding the political economy of television sport, it can deepen our broader understanding of the relationships between institutions, media and economic and political shifts in society. In so doing it raised the standard of communication and media studies research into sports culture and offered both a possible template for studying media sport and a conceptual framing that meant that studies of media sport began to be taken more seriously within the research community. Studies such as the USA-based examination of the promotional role of media in sports development (Satterlee, 2001) indirectly come out of the shifts that were taking place in the study of sports within the communication and media studies academy during the late 1980s.

## Conclusion

What emerges from the articles in this volume are a number of key themes that often shape the research agenda when sport is positioned with communication and media studies. We see the creation of something distinctive from sport, that of media sport; also the key role of journalism and newspapers in this process and the development of the codes and conventions of sports broadcasting and the role that sporting discourse can play in wider collective identity formations of class, gender and nation.

Crucial in this process is of course the issue of representations of sport and how they connect with, challenge or legitimize often deep-rooted assumptions and values in particular societies. Volume II looks in more detail at this area by identifying some key research studies around sports media and issues of representation.

# 'They Play in Your Home': Cricket, Media and Modernity in Pre-war Australia

*Frazer Andrewes*

## Tuning In

To say that cricket was an obsession for many Australians in the 1930s, and that every summer the mental world of Australia was structured and defined by the vicissitudes of national and international cricket, is probably not stretching the truth too far. For a sport that originally had been considered to be the most 'English of English Games', Australians rapidly championed it as their own and developed it into a national and distinctively Australian game.[1] For many fans, commentators and historians the early 1930s were the apotheosis of Australian cricket; the striding colossus of Don Bradman, the infamy of the 'bodyline' test series against the visiting Marylebone Cricket Club (MCC) team in 1932–33, and the subsequent retrieval of the Ashes when Australia toured England in 1934, all helped to prioritize this period in the mythology of Australian test cricket.[2] The national fascination with cricket, and the amount of feeling that both the playing of the game and the controversies it generated could stir up, were even patently evident to those who had not been embroiled in them since an early age. Egon Kisch, the radical Czech journalist whose attempts to enter Australia to speak at an anti-war congress in 1934 had been the cause of much comment in the Australian press, found the time between his leg-breaking, pier-head jump in Melbourne and his subsequent departure from Australia in 1935 to

**Source:** *The International Journal of the History of Sport,* 17(2/3), Special Issue: Sport in Australasian Society Past and Present (2000): 93–110.

fully appreciate the position of cricket (and bodyline) in the Australian psyche. 'Bodyline is connected with sport,' he wrote, 'but it also has a profound political significance. To write about Australia and to omit the bodyline affair would be like describing the Vatican without the Pope, or – but there is no end to such comparisons if we are to describe the significance of cricket for Australia.'[3]

What Kisch so observantly noted was that cricket in Australia assumed a cultural and political importance out of all proportion to its actual position as a sporting code; it is partly for this reason that I have chosen to focus this essay on the 1930s. I have also chosen this period because of its importance in the way the representation of cricket was technologized and commercialized. As other writers have noted, the radio broadcasting of cricket matches became a national event in the 1930s, at first for matches played locally only, but from 1934 for matches played abroad as well.[4] Richard Cashman has observed that cricket dominated the radio airwaves by the 1932–33 season, and in doing so capitalized on a rapidly growing radio audience.[5] It was particularly serendipitous for the Australian Broadcasting Corporation (ABC) that the first broadcast national ball-by-ball broadcasts coincided with the Bodyline tour, as it has been suggested that these broadcasts both enlarged the wireless audience, and whetted the appetites of those listening for live attendance of the matches.[6] What the introduction of match broadcasts did create, however, was a new focus for the commercialization of cricket, a commercialization, it must be said, which had put down solid roots long before the 1930s.[7] The advertisements and articles that swept in on the coat-tails of match broadcasting made it their business to sell modernity and in doing so lift Australia from the mire of the Depression on the strings of technological progress. As Rita Barnard has suggested, the 1930s were a decade of contradictions and sometimes jarring juxtapositions. 'They were certainly "hard times",' she writes, 'but as other histories suggest, the years of the Great Depression were also self-consciously "modern times" and modernity . . . was generally understood as having to do with the comfort, mobility, and pleasure promised by the "dime-store dream parade" of commodities.'[8] This study seeks to explore the promises of modernity and the way in which cricket provided a national vehicle for the dissemination of its messages. It will also explore the specifically gendered way in which this message was delivered, and comment on the effective marginalization of women from the cricket mainstream and, in effect, from the modernising process.

## 'Wireless Gave the Whole Country a Part in the Game'

The 1932–33 test series was a watershed in the broadcasting of cricket matches, and has been represented as the moment when the nation was brought together for the first time as a listening public. Bodyline, Ken Inglis states, enlarged the listening audience and gave the people the unprecedented feeling of being close to the action and involved in the controversy. 'When a ball from Larwood felled Woodfull on a Saturday afternoon in Adelaide and Jardine set a "bodyline" field for Larwood's next over against the injured Australian captain, listeners all over Australia could hear spectators hooting, share their outrage and ask their neighbours to listen.'⁹ In a country struggling to come to terms with the social and economic dislocations of the Depression, broadcasting enabled the people to come together and commune in a national obsession; isolated from the world, and in many cases from each other, the wireless annihilated distance.

At least that is what some perceived. Commenting on the test match played in Sydney in early December 1932, a Melbourne newspaper, the *Argus,* assured its readers that 'Broadcasting came into its own' in relaying the excitement to listeners so many miles from the action. 'The single voice which told the story of the day's play from the Sydney Cricket-ground poured a tale of woe and ecstasy into the ears of tens of thousands of adults and countless children in every State of the Commonwealth. Everybody interested in cricket – and everybody is now – envied the crowd which watched the struggle between Larwood and the Australian batsmen in Sydney; but wireless gave the whole country a part in the game.'¹⁰ According to the newspaper account, the city of Melbourne was festooned with 'a thousand scoreboards', outside shops and cafés and on bridges, which 'told the story of Australia's changing fortunes to a thousand separate crowds'.¹¹ The streets became congested with enthusiasts gathering under the scoreboards and the police, still wary of any mass gathering of the unemployed or indigent, had many of the boards removed.

The belief that the wireless had succeeded in bringing the nation together was infectious. Where many had blamed the ills of the modern world and its devices for the current period of want and uncertainty, technology seemed to provide them at last with the possibility of entertainment and relief, for a moment, from the stresses of daily life. A correspondent to the *Sydney Morning Herald* was most fulsome in his praise of the efforts of a cricket broadcaster, one who, indeed, deserved to 'receive the hearty commendation of his hundreds of thousands of listeners'. Unable to attend the match, the correspondent was still able to fully partake in and enjoy the unfolding spectacle. 'It was a delightful afternoon's pleasure to listen to his vivid description and witty comments. I can remember during my long experience of the game no more thrilling moments than those wherein he described the tense situation and seething excitement of the 70,000 people present while Bradman was pluckily struggling for his well-deserved century.'¹² Without knowing the context it could almost be assumed that he had witnessed these events in person. Another correspondent to the *Argus* neatly captured the air of excitement, tension and expectation that the wireless broadcasts brought to people all over the nation. 'What a wonderful thing is a Test match! Who cares, for the moment, if Britain pays America in gold? Who cares if Gandhi starves to death to gain his point? Who cares if a wool clip averages 6d. or if wheat brings less than 2/? All we want to know is "What's the score?" And yet our nerves are shattered by everlasting fears of the unknown. We tremble for the voice of the radio announcer, fearing the worst when he says, "A telegram from Sydney has just come –." We can do no work while the slow hands of the clock creep to the magic moment of the crossover.'[13]

Advertisers were quick to capitalize on the depth of such sentiment, and radio manufacturers sought not only to fill this gap, but even attempted to convince potential customers that listening to broadcast cricket would be just like, perhaps even better, than being at the real thing. Healing Golden-Voiced Radio purported to do just this. Their advertisement pictured a man literally on the edge of his seat, face intent and arm slightly raised while the spectral figures of cricketers in action hovered above him and his radio set. 'Unfortunately,' the copy declared, 'many people do not get the opportunity to actually see the games, but they do the next best thing, and that is to listen to them – faithfully reproduced on their Healing Golden-Voiced Radio. If you are not able to see a Test Match, you will not want to miss any of the thrills, so why not take a grandstand seat de luxe – in your own armchair and enjoy every moment of the game.'[14] The fruits of modernity offered the Australian people not only the chance to engage with their favourite sport anywhere in Australia, but also suggested that now anyone could also avail themselves of the best seat in the stands, an egalitarian dream at a time when the inequities of society were proving all too obvious.

It must be said, however, that not everyone embraced the introduction of cricket broadcasts or the way in which the rapid spread of news and controversy was facilitated, nor yet the increasing commercialism of the game and the desire for thrilling copy. The poet and humorist C.J. Dennis bemoaned in verse the evils the advent of cricket broadcasts had wrought on the farmer in the country.

> I reckon (said Dad) that the country's pests
> Is this here wireless an' these here Tests.
> Up to the house and around the door,
> Stretchin' their ears for to catch the score,
> Leavin' the horses down in the crop,
> Can you wonder a farmer goes off pop? . . .
> There's a standing crop an' the rain's not far,
> An' the price is rotten, but there you are:
> As soon as these cricketin' games begin
> The farm goes dilly on listening in.[15]

Other protests were not framed in such a humorous (or tongue-in-cheek) way as this. A common complaint was not that the matches were *broadcast* at all, but that what the ABC broadcast was insufficient. 'Fed-Up Listener', writing to the *Sydney Morning Herald*, railed at the 'niggardly' action of the ABC in only broadcasting short descriptions of the test matches, and refused to accept the ABC's explanation that during the day the Post Office could not spare trunk lines which were required for business. In an early example of consumer activism, 'Fed-Up Listener' urged all fellow listeners to work together for the reform of a system which took 'thousands of pounds . . . from listeners as licence fees' but which still held the consumers at 'the mercy of the commission'.[16] Still other authorities pondered whether the modern turn of cricket was really warranted at all, and didn't instead spoil the essential character of the game. At the height of the bodyline fiasco, the *Argus* editorialized on the current direction of the game and what appeared to be going wrong.

> The field of the spectator is now nation-wide. Passions are inflamed and partisanship is accentuated by publicity in its many modern forms; and when partisanship flies in at the door judgment leaves by the window. 'Stunting' has been indulged in to such an extent as could not eventually fail to produce bitterness upon some issue or other. Comment upon every phase of the game has been broadcast so continuously that the public mind has become obsessed by the controversy. From every point of view these developments are bad.[17]

The *Argus* and other newspapers were, however, not strangers to the lure of publicity and the commercial possibilities inherent in a popular and controversial story. Just two days before the publication of the editorial quoted above, the *Sydney Morning Herald* had published an article headed 'Opinions exchanged by wireless telephone', detailing an argument between several prominent players over the rights and wrongs of bodyline and its aftermath, which had previously been broadcast on radio in Sydney, Melbourne and Adelaide.[18] It was actions such as these, and the co-manager of the English team's comment early in the tour that 'too much publicity was the fault of modern cricket',[19] that led the *Argus* to point the finger at all the 'modern' problems of the game, including 'players, publicists and partisans'. 'All have assisted in distilling in the alembic of ultra-modernity an essence which has in it the rarefied elements of cricket, but it is not cricket as the world used to know it.'[20]

## Glimpses of Technological Marvels

The 1932–33 test series proved so popular with cricket-loving Australians for several obvious reasons. Firstly, the nature of the bodyline bowling and the ensuing furore focused unprecedented attention on the game and brought it centre-stage in the domestic politics and imperial relations of both Australia and the Great Britain. Secondly, the technological revelation of test match broadcasts captured the imagination of the populace and budding media entrepreneurs alike. The listening public quickly developed a taste for the ready access to scores, match reports and complete match relays anywhere in the country, regardless of where the game was played, the ABC realized the boost this could mean for radio licences, wireless manufacturers grasped what this could mean in terms of the sales of equipment, and other advertisers came to understand the growing nexus of cricket and cash. The *Argus* neatly summed up this attitude when commenting on the entrepreneurial spirit (excusing the pun) shown by those hoteliers who placed a radio and score-board in their establishments 'in the hope of stimulating trade by offering beer and cricket'. '"Give the public what it wants" is a good slogan; and every shrewd businessman gave it cricket news.'[21] The third factor, of course, was that everyone wanted to see, or hear, Don Bradman in action.[22] The 1934 return test series, in which Australia travelled to England, was, if anything even more eagerly anticipated than the bodyline series. Originally in doubt because of continuing wrangles between the MCC and the Australian Board of Control over bodyline, its eventual clearance was greeted with joy by the Australian public who saw in it a chance to avenge past grievances. The ABC, other broadcasters, and advertisers saw the possibility of furthering their revenue by exploiting a cricket- and technology-hungry population.

The main innovation of the 1934 test series, as most histories of the period have discussed, was the development of 'reconstructed', or what were later termed 'synthetic', broadcasts. Direct relays of the matches from England were, at this time, not able to be broadcast with any degree of reliability or quality. Instead, cables with the account of each over bowled were sent to Sydney from whence they were telephoned through to the ABC. At the studio these messages were turned into notes for the commentators. A scoreboard and chart with up-to-date field placings were also kept in the studio. Sound effects could be added to the commentaries from pre-recorded material, and from the commentator tapping one of three hemispherical pieces of wood to imitate the sound of bat on ball.[23] The fact that these broadcasts were immensely popular, and that the nation rapidly embraced wireless technology and the new techniques associated with it, can be deduced from the amount of air time the ABC was willing to spend on match commentaries. Inglis compared the coverage adopted by the BBC and the ABC during the test series, and found that while the BBC gave their listeners two ten-minute commentaries and an occasional half-hour description of particularly exciting play per day, the ABC offered continuous reporting through the night and into the small hours of the morning.[24] This 'fever' of test match excitement, as the *Argus* at one point chose to term it, was also manifested in both the sale of wireless sets and the number of licences issued. According to one report, the number of licences issued per month increased from 8,288 in April 1934 to 13,708 in May.[25] Wireless manufacturers also reported a 'remarkable increase' in their business and claimed that 'most manufacturers were working at high pressure to meet the demand'.[26] Neither the licencers nor the manufacturers had any doubt that the impending test series in England was the cause of the increase.[27]

The point that needs to be stressed is that such figures and descriptions not only attest to the keenness, bordering on fanaticism, which many Australian followed cricket, they also show that the populace was as caught up with the technology, the means of delivery, as with the game. Cricket was a game, as the newspaper editorials never tired of reiterating, bound up with tradition, empire, codes of conduct, honour and manliness, but it was also now, and again editorials grudgingly acknowledged this, a modern game and was increasingly subject to modern production and reception.[28] Australian society, by and large, embraced this with vigour. A report published to coincide with a large radio and electrical fair provided listeners with a tantalizing glimpse of the technological marvels due to be employed during the test broadcasts. Not only would the 'synthetic' broadcasts be heard, but

> Beam wireless and cable messages dealing in detail with every stroke played will be received during the earlier part of each day's play in the Tests. The radio-telephone will be employed at the luncheon and tea intervals and immediately after the drawing of stumps to enable [the commentators] to give [their] impressions of the play. Whenever it is possible to receive short-wave signals at sufficient strength, the actual running commentary which is to be transmitted from the British Broadcasting Company's Empire station will be broadcast.[29]

Such a growing passion for technology was seen to dovetail neatly into the already extant love of cricket. The *Sydney Morning Herald* editorialized that 'the drama, the colour, and the atmosphere of cricket, lend themselves far better to description than the movement and vicissitudes of most other sports, with the result that cricket has readers and listeners who far outnumber those who have opportunity to be spectators'.[30] Fortunately, then, cricket seemed to be well adapted to the demands of the modern fan.

## 'Not So Much Cricket as Drama'

As mentioned above, the main innovation of the 1934 test series was the use of 'synthetic' broadcasts, and it appears that these enthralled and puzzled listeners in equal amount. Those who were not alert to the methods employed in creating the ball-by-ball broadcasts seemed sure that the descriptions came directly from the ground; even some of those who did know of the procedure expressed doubt that what they had been told was true.[31] The broadcaster most credited with developing the technique, Charles Moses, even went to the length of exploiting another modern and rapidly expanding medium, the motion picture, by having a film made of the entire process of the commentary from receiving the cable to the announcer's reconstruction.[32] The Sydney-based broadcasting magazine *Wireless Weekly* also went to great pains in describing for its readers the process of the match broadcast, including publishing facsimile copies of the original cables, the messages as they were then transcribed, and even a photograph of one of the gramophone records which contained the recorded sound effects.[33] What makes this extensive article most interesting is the sense of delight it evinced in the construction of an entirely simulated environment. In some ways the fact that the broadcasts sought to present a version of an actual game of cricket was irrelevant. As the article revealingly states, 'what follows is not so much cricket as drama'.[34] While sport, in the best traditions of journalistic hyperbole, has often been described in the terms of a human drama, the representation of ball-by-ball broadcasts *was* shaped as fiction or drama and not as merely facsimile. Perhaps this is most adequately displayed in the semantic difference between the original term for the broadcasts, 'reconstruction', and its replacement, 'synthetic'. 'Reconstruction' implies an act of creation from the former constituent parts of an entity, whereas 'synthetic' suggests that which has been made to *imitate* a real event. In the 1930s 'synthetic' was also a very modern-sounding word, associated with man-made fibres and plastics, including, possibly, the Bakelite from which many of the listeners' radio sets were produced, and technological progress.

Perhaps it was no accident that cricket broadcasts were described in such a way. By 1934 radio dramas were a fast developing and increasingly popular form of entertainment for radio listeners, and their pattern and formula were no doubt familiar to radio habitués.[35] Indeed, it seems the drama genre had become so much a recognizable part of radio broadcasting that by 1935 the ABC were even not averse to providing dramatized re-creations of news items.[36] Describing the accoutrements of the recording studio, the *Wireless Weekly* termed them 'stage properties', used for creating a 'show'.[37] The magazine went as far as claiming that really what the listeners tuned in for at the dead of night was not the cricket *per se*, but rather the wonderful flights of invention the commentators brought forth. 'It is as a reconstruction that the broadcasts appeal to listeners. Very few listeners would be much the wiser if the cabled message were read out exactly as they were received; and such messages gain in interest as they are amplified.'[38] It was the imagination and the creation of a feeling of 'atmosphere' by the commentators and the assembled group of experts and technicians which was thought particularly worthy of mention and praise.

> It is worth while listening, just for the fine points of their descriptions, to hear how they simulate the shock of Bradman being out. Suppose he was out third ball of the over, they would see this from a glance at the message, yet they would have to describe two balls and the bowling of a third in a quiet way before they could say 'He's out. Bradman's out,' as though such a thing had not till that moment occurred to them. They must not seem too surprised. They must not work up to it in the manner of a playwright reaching up to his catharsis; it must all come suddenly, and take them by surprise, and it must sound quite natural.[39]

Finally, it asserted, 'If you listen to a description in a critical mood,' as no doubt a drama critic would, 'you cannot but be struck with the brilliance of the acting.'[40]

While the ABC seemed content to emphasize the dramatic qualities of their match descriptions, one commercial broadcaster fell back on another time-honoured tradition of popular entertainment to endear itself with its cricket audience. The Sydney station 2UW eschewed ball-to-ball descriptions, and instead offered a service that they assured listeners was an improvement on previous broadcasting techniques. What they instituted was 'not so much a cricket broadcast as a very entertaining vaudeville, with cricket scores and comments thrown in'.[41] While cricket was obviously still the main *raison d'être* of the broadcast, it appeared that as far as the broadcaster was concerned, providing a comedic and entertaining context was just as important.

> The chief vaudevillian is a Mr. Charlie Vaude, who romps around in the red-nosed comedian manner very effectively, and is assisted by Charlie Lawrence . . . and Renn Millar, and various other well-known Melbourne artists. They have what you might call a theme song: 'Who's afraid of the Big Bad Bear,' which they sing when an Australian bowls out an Englishman, and so on, and they make jokes on the state of the game, or on telegrams and 'phone calls received from listeners, and ask silly questions of the commentator, Mr. Vic Richardson.[42]

Maybe to leaven concerns about undue frivolity being associated with its broadcasts, 2UW emphasized that the distinguishing feature of its cricket service was that it announced the latest scores a few minutes before the other stations, and thus held the edge in actual cricket service if not in the dramatic description of play. What dramatic devices such as these sought to achieve was a sense of closeness and familiarity with a game which was being played 12,000 miles and (for eastern Australia) ten hours' time difference away. In an effort to maintain ratings and popular support, both networks and advertisers strove to present the immediacy and action of the game, at once bridging distance and bringing a sense of the visual where there was none.

## 'They Play in Your Home'

Lesley Johnson has written of the impact radio had in the 1930s in instituting structures and regimented notions of time through the use of time calls and the predictable occurrence of programmes.[43] She quotes a *Wireless Weekly* editorial of 1931 which declared that radio's development of time-consciousness was beginning to affect the population: 'The outcome is an observed quickening of our pace, better scheduling of all our movements and actions to a standard and accurate time.'[44] The broadcasting of the cricket matches from England in 1934 certainly seem to bear out this confident assertion. The *Wireless Weekly*, among others, prominently displayed the time of play, including lunch and tea intervals, in both English and eastern Australian time, and alerted listeners when to tune in to the broadcasts of all the different stations. It could be assumed, therefore, that thousands of Australians were doing exactly the same thing at exactly the same time through the mediation of their radio sets. As the *Argus* wrote, 'There are more than 1,000,000 wireless receivers licensed in Australia, and few are idle on Test match nights.'[45] But while the radio broadcasts encouraged temporal regimentation, they also suppressed distance and whittled time down to smaller and smaller increments. 'On Friday night, and all other Test Match nights, we in Australia, at a distance of 12,000 miles, will be in possession of minute details of the game . . . The time required for collecting the particulars of the occurrences relating to an individual ball, the passage of those particulars over the distance between England and Australia, and furnishing them to a listener in any part of any State, will occupy only a minute or two. Every effort is being made to keep the actual time down nearly as possible to one minute.'[46] Similarly, the same magazine's editorial pondered the speed at which the descriptions could be broadcast and the diminution of time and distance this entailed. 'One service claims that, after the first few nights . . . it will be putting a description on the air only three-quarters of a minute behind the game in progress in England; thus you will see the services considerably speeded up, and for those interested in the technique of broadcasting it will be interesting to observe whether the usual atmosphere of the cricket ground can be maintained at such a high speed.'[47] Like much else in the modern world, cricket was now also accelerating into the future.

To endeavour to create a feeling of presence and participation in the matches, wireless guides and advertisers, in collaboration with the broadcasters, provided listeners with scoring cards and field diagrams which they were supposed to consult and amend as the games advanced. It was suggested that those listeners not versed in the finer points of the game would benefit from keeping the *Wireless Weekly* score sheet beside them: 'To keep the score in detail imparts an added interest in the game, and this course alone provides the means for reflection, and settles the ever-present "post-mortem" during the regular adjournments of the game.'[48] One company developed a special 'radio cricket scoreboard' which, it claimed, had been adopted by the broadcasting stations for official use. The advertisement expressed the belief that not only was the 'Astor Radio Cricket Score Board' a novel and useful addition to broadcasting pleasure, but that it was a 'new thrill in Test Match Broadcasting', and the 'craze of 1934' which, by the time the matches started, very few homes would be without.[49] While avoiding the grand pretensions of the Astor scoreboard, *Wireless Weekly's* chart of fielding positions and list of the cricket terms the announcers would use, promised to provide an almost cinematic experience for the listening public. 'For those not well acquainted with the field positions, this Chart could be cut out and pasted on cardboard, and so placed conveniently when listening. You will soon pick the positions, and at once visualize the ball speeding away in its true direction.'[50]

Advertisements for wireless sets also offered the tantalizing fiction of attending all the matches and seeing the action. The Stromberg-Carlson

Receiver invited the listener to 'Imagine turning the dial and listening in direct to the lunch-time resumes by England's leading cricket authorities', and to envisage the even greater thrills of being able to pass from country to country and 'listen-in' to the world.[51] A Philips company advertisement was even more evocative of the rich possibilities of cricket broadcasts.

> They play in your home . . . A flick of the switch and the set merges into the background – surely this can be no radio receiver, but a pulsing, living thing. Let us close our eyes and listen – we have skipped twelve thousand miles, our cushioned armchair gives place to the grandstand. Who is that bowler? Ah! a voice at our elbow announces that the speed merchant is none other than Tim Wall. Again the bowler comes pounding down – a wicket falls – this is cricket.[52]

Such advertisements and scoring paraphernalia asked listeners to suspend belief for a while and immerse themselves in a world of cricket, one played many thousands of miles away but one which had been artificially re-created and disseminated for them through the radio. Distance and time became variables which could be schematized, diminished and controlled through the mechanism of the wireless, and cricket was modernized and repackaged for an increasing and hungry audience. It could be argued that radio had aided in democratizing cricket, and had turned what was an already strong passion into a truly mass-cultural event. Yet however democratic the appeal of cricket might have been, in terms of gender it was still packaged as being essentially a man's game.

### 'The Trouble with Men Is That They Take Their Cricket Too Seriously'

It is not to be doubted that many women listened in with as much eagerness as men to cricket broadcasts in the 1930s. As C.J. Dennis bemoaned in the poem previously cited, when the farm stopped working to listen in to the tests, it was 'Not only the boys and the harvester crew, But Mum and the girls gits dotty too.'[53] Issues of technological control and representation, however, could serve to render the position of women marginal. While women were specifically targeted as listeners and consumers of radio in the 1930s, it was presumed that real control of the technology would lie in the hands of men, whether those in the household or those who controlled the broadcasting. As cricket was taken to be a man's game (albeit with a significant female following), advertising, and newspaper and magazine copy, represented it as such.[54] Almost universally men were the only sex to appear in advertisements featuring the cricket tests as a marketing pitch. The Philips Radioplayer advertisement from 1934 featured the stylized figures of two men listening to the cricket on one of the company's products.[55] Ads for Diamond Batteries and ESM Radio both featured men, at ease in armchairs, soaking up the action from nearby radio receivers.[56] In one radio advertisement a man is depicted nonchalantly speaking into the telephone, 'The cricket? Yes, come right over – ours is a Raycophone.'[57] Men are the ones who figuratively controlled access to the cricket and the radio, reinforcing the male privileges in matters relating to both. In one of the few advertising images to include women, Ever Ready Batteries depicted a farming household engrossed in listening to a test match commentary. But here, too, men dominated. Those closest to the radio set are men, and the two women, mother and daughter, stand up against the wall while almost all the men sit or lounge around. The only figure more marginalized than the women is one at the very edge of the picture, an Aboriginal stock-hand who stands not only outside the door, but down a level from his white employers.[58]

Only too often were women pushed to the figurative margins in such ways. Women were clearly interested in cricket and were, in reality, just as likely to be consumers of the radio broadcasts. Richard Cashman makes the point that in the inter-war period women were as keen as men to exercise their right to leisure. He writes that while there are no accurate figures for the number of women attending test matches, some test players of the 1930s estimated that between 30 and 40 per cent of the crowds were women.[59] The English cricket journalist William Pollock, writing on the crowds during the 1936–37 English tour of Australia, asserted that tens of thousands of women would turn out to watch the test matches. In Adelaide, he wrote, 'They were on the ground hours before play began, and one morning a lady brought the domestic hearth to cricket: she arrived with the family green peas and conscientiously proceeded to shell them while she waited for the heroes.'[60] In Melbourne he was told that about 60 per cent of the huge crowds were women. 'To many of these women, Test cricketers are more thrilling than film stars . . . If they have the mind to, women can save cricket.'[61] Yet it was despite such evidence that suggested that women as much as men were passionately interested in the game that the dominant representations figured and appealed to men. Women were routinely the butt of jokes predicated on their supposed lack of knowledge about the game's finer points, and chided for their inability to take cricket matches for the serious business they were.[62] Even when their presence at the great communion of cricket was acknowledged they were still casually sidelined. During the 1934 test series the *Argus* commented on the deleterious effects the cricket broadcasts were having on everyday life. Not only was the 'march of science' increasing the lethargy of retail staff and helping the coffers of the electricity company, alcohol wholesalers and tobacconists, it was also to blame for an absence of shoppers, the majority of whom would have presumably been women.[63] The same article also hinted that women along with men stayed up into the small hours listening to the unfolding match on the radio, but found the time most useful in attending to domestic and feminine pastimes. 'The family man has not been left out. Long-sought buttons have been sewn on, pockets have been patched, and socks have been darned in quantity while the Australians were batting at Manchester.'[64] Yet women could and did see through the carefully constructed façade of male control. The captain of the English women's cricket team, touring Australia in late 1934, pointed out that while Australian crowds had a great sense of humour, by-and-large men's greatest failing was that they 'took their cricket too seriously'.[65] Cricket was, after all, only a game, but to men, it seemed, this was a truth that should not be expressed; cricket represented for them a mastery they were reluctant to relinquish.

## Fading Out

Cricket broadcasting in the 1930s opened new horizons for all associated with the sport, and its fusion with Bradman, bodyline and the Ashes served to consolidate it as the most popular sport in inter-war Australian society. Cricket could stand as the metaphor for many things: perhaps the strongest of these, at least amongst the more conservative and traditional, were the tie of Empire and the blood bonds of the Anglo-Saxon people. In 1934 the editor of the *Argus* wrote, 'It is a game which embodies many of the virtues which people of British stock cherish . . . It is a game which demands the surrender of individual glory to the common good; its vicissitudes cannot be resisted without good temper and self-control; and it is a game which requires moral and physical courage.'[66] Perhaps it was because of the perception that these intrinsic qualities bound the disparate Empire together that made the Bodyline debacle all the harder to take. But cricket also had appeal at a simpler, more personal level. In the dislocation of the early 1930s cricket was a comforting, comprehensible, supposedly unchangeable, link to happier times. Beneath a picture of young boys choosing sides before the start of a backyard cricket match, Exide wireless batteries placed this copy. 'Where is the man who can study this picture for a few minutes without experiencing a flood of happy recollections, carried back in memory to those carefree days when panics, depressions, strikes, or other national calamities meant nothing to our boyish minds.'[67] Cricket was safe, part of a lived experience. Yet cricket was also modernizing along with the rest of Australian society; that this advertisement was used to sell batteries for wireless sets used to listen to the broadcast matches asserts this.

Cricket became modern and helped disseminate modernity. No longer was it only the game of nostalgia and hoary imperial rhetoric. It had became a part of modern culture and new media. Radio drew cricket into its own web of progress and in doing so made the game just one of the many forms of mass entertainment which began to flourish in the 1920s and 1930s. Cricket also became part of a new formation of consumerism and commodification, and was 'sold' along with radios, razors, batteries, cigarettes and numerous other consumer goods. In this sense the game truly became a symbol of modern life in the 1930s. As one newspaper editor wrote, 'Cricket, like many other things in the British scheme of life, means far more than is apparent on the surface.'[68] It is unlikely that he meant this in the way this essay has suggested, but he, like Egon Kisch, realized that cricket could mean so much to Australian society. What match broadcasting and advertising in the 1930s did show, however, was how mutable this game could be to the demands of a nation intent on making their culture and society modern.

## Notes

1. R. Cashman, 'Australia', in B. Stoddart and K.A.P. Sandiford (eds.), *The Imperial Game: Cricket, Culture and Society* (Manchester, 1998), pp. 34, 47.
2. The literature, scholarly and popular, on both Bradman and bodyline is voluminous and varied. The latest works published on Bradman are C. Williams, *Bradman: An Australian Hero* (London, 1996), and Roland Perry, *The Don* (Sydney, 1995). Perhaps the most thorough treatment of the bodyline controversy can be found in R. Sissons and B. Stoddart, *Cricket and Empire: The 1932–33 Bodyline Tour of Australia* (Sydney, 1984).
3. E. Kisch, *Australian Landfall*, trans, by J. Fisher, I. Fitzgerald and K. Fitzgerald (Australasian Book Society, 1969 [1937]), p. 303. Kisch was famously refused entry to Australia because of supposed Communist affiliations. In defiance of this order he jumped from the ship onto the dock at Melbourne, breaking his leg in the process. The work from which this quote is taken is the description of his time in Australia and a commentary on Australian society as he perceived it.
4. B. Stoddart, *Saturday Afternoon Fever: Sport in the Australian Culture* (Sydney, 1986), pp. 92–3; R. Cashman, *'Ave a Go, Yer Mug! Australian Cricket Crowds from Larrikin to Ocker* (Sydney, 1984), pp. 92–4.
5. Cashman, *'Ave a Go, Yer Mug!*, p. 93.
6. Ibid., p. 94; K. Inglis, *This is the ABC: The Australian Broadcasting Commission 1933–1983* (Victoria, 1983), p. 36.
7. 'Commercialisation', in R. Cashman *et al.* (eds.), *The Oxford Companion to Australian Cricket* (Melbourne, 1996), pp. 115–17, provides a useful potted history of commercial involvement in Australian cricket.
8. R. Barnard, *The Great Depression and the Culture of Abundance: Kenneth Fearing, Nathanael West, and Mass Culture in the 1930s* (Cambridge, 1995), p. 21.
9. Inglis, *This is The ABC*, p. 36.
10. *Argus*, 3 Dec. 1932, 24.
11. Ibid.
12. *Sydney Morning Herald (SMH)*, 6 Jan. 1933, 4.
13. *Argus*, 5 Dec. 1932, 10.
14. *Bulletin*, 2 Nov. 1932, 5.
15. Quoted in *The ABC Cricket Book: The First 60 Years*, compiled by J. Maxwell (Sydney, 1994), p. 8.
16. *SMH*, 3 Jan. 1933, 5.
17. *Argus*, 21 Jan. 1933, 22.
18. *SMH*, 19 Jan. 1933, 9.
19. *SMH*, 17 Nov. 1932, 11. The co-manager, P.F. 'Plum' Warner, went further to state that 'Every feature of the private lives of the team was recorded on the journey of the Orient liner Orontes . . . That one player was adept at dancing, that another paraded the deck in short pants, or that another bathed in the morning or played deck tennis well had all been given prominence.' The *Argus* also reported Warner's speech, but seemed less inclined to heed his subtle hint. Under the article an advertisement advised

Warner would speak to the *Argus* luncheon club that day, and that his address would be simultaneously broadcast through station 3UZ in Melbourne. 17 Nov. 1932, 9.

20. *Argus*, 2 Jan. 1933, 6.
21. Ibid., 3 Dec. 1932, 24.
22. Sissons and Stoddart, *Cricket and Empire*, p. 111.
23. Inglis, *This is the ABC*, p. 37; Cashman, *'Ave a Go, Yer Mug!*, pp. 101–3.
24. Inglis, *This is the ABC*, pp. 36–7.
25. *Argus*, 25 May 1934, 12.
26. Ibid., 9 June 1934, 19.
27. Also see the *Wireless Weekly*, 8 June 1934, 32, which makes the same claim.
28. The editor of the *Sydney Morning Herald* tried to impart a sense of both the traditional and the modern in cricket in one of his editorials. 'The people who to-day rush to read cabled reports of the test matches in England before the news of the Disarmament Conference are of the same stock as the men who, when the Spanish Armada was approaching to attack them, insisted on finishing their game of bowls before getting ready for the defence.' 16 June 1934, 14.
29. *Argus*, 2 June 1934, 15.
30. *SMH*, 2 July 1934, 8.
31. Inglis writes that despite the fact that listeners were told before the start of play that the broadcasts were not actually coming from England, people would still lay bets as to whether it was. *This is the ABC*, p. 37.
32. Maxwell, *The ABC Cricket Book*, p. 11.
33. *Wireless Weekly*, 22 June 1934, 11–15.
34. Ibid., 12.
35. See R. Lane, *The Golden Age of Australian Radio Drama, 1923–1960: A History Through Biography* (Carlton South, 1994); also see Inglis, *This is the ABC*, ch.2.Cricket could also literally appear in radio drama. In an ongoing series, 'We Await Your Verdict', broadcast on the Sydney station 2BL, one of the hypothetical situations was a manslaughter charge brought against a bodyline bowler who struck a batsman in the head with a fast, rising leg-side ball. *Wireless Weekly*, 16 March 1934, 7.
36. L. Johnson, The *Unseen Voice: A Cultural Study of Early Australian Radio* (London, 1988), p. 166.
37. *Wireless Weekly*, 22 June 1934, 12.
38. Ibid., 13.
39. Ibid.
40. Ibid.
41. Ibid., 14.
42. Ibid.
43. Johnson, *The Unseen Voice*, pp. 107–110.
44. Ibid., p. 108.
45. *Argus*, 11 July 1934, 6.
46. *Wireless Weekly*, 8 June 1934, 17.
47. Ibid., p. 32.
48. Ibid., p. 18.
49. Ibid., 1 June 1934, 62.
50. Ibid., 8 June 1934, 20.
51. Ibid., 17 Aug. 1934, 18.
52. Ibid., 27 July 1934, 11.
53. Maxwell, *The ABC Cricket Book*, p. 8.
54. For a comprehensive survey of women's relationship with cricket in all its forms, see Richard Cashman and Amanda Weaver, *Wicket Women: Cricket and Women in Australia* (Sydney, 1991).
55. *Wireless Weekly*, 27 July 1934, 11.

56. Ibid., 17 Aug. 1934, 20; 18 May 1934, 40.
57. Ibid., 1 June 1934, 5.
58. Ibid., 27 July 1934, 46.
59. Cashman, *'Ave a Go, Yer Mug!*, pp. 69–70.
60. W. Pollock, *So This Is Australia* (London, 1937), p. 104.
61. Ibid., pp. 104–5.
62. The *Bulletin*, Australia's largest selling weekly in the 1930s, regularly featured in their sporting section the comic strip adventures of Bert and Gert. Throughout the bodyline series of 1932–33 readers could amuse themselves with Gert's constant cricketing gaffes and non sequiturs and Bert's continued bemusement at them.
63. *Argus*, 11 July 1934, 6.
64. Ibid.
65. *SMH*, 21 Dec. 1934, 11.
66. *Argus,* 9 June 1934, 20.
67. *Wireless Weekly*, 15 June 1934, 35.
68. *Argus*, 21 Jan. 1933, 22.

# 2

# Long Before Arledge . . . Sports & TV: The Earliest Years – 1937–1947 – as Seen by the Contemporary Press

*Dave Berkman*

The phenomenon of televised sports and how it is alleged to have re-shaped, dominated and even corrupted amateur and professional athletics – and a macho-prone American viewership which can't seem to get enough of it – has been the subject, in whole or in part, of a mini-library of sports literature the past 15 or 20 years.[1]

But what we are prone to ignore when we get caught up in what often becomes the 'over-analysis' of such phenomena, is that like most 'big things', their roots lie in rather humble beginnings. This is no less true of the almost immediate coming together of TV and sports – an inevitable relationship which began a half a century back at television's very inception. As Ron Powers has written in his "Supertube, the Rise of TV Sports" (an otherwise mindless paean to the grandiosity of the sports/TV relation; and especially to Roone Arledge, to whom he attributes the phenomenon[2]): earliest "[t]elevision needed something to eat, something live, something conspicuous and established as a field of human interest; something that could be transmitted from a relatively small, highly defined field of activity. [And so t]elevision sunk its teeth into sports."[3]

If we go back to the very beginnings of American, over-the-air, electronic TV[4] in 1937 (the year it emerged from the laboratory to begin experimental, over-the-air testing) through 1947[5] (the year before TV can be said to have

**Source:** *The Journal of Popular Culture*, 22(2) (1988): 49–62.

finally taken off in America[6]) and, through a search of what the periodical press had to say about sports and TV,[7] trace the roots of the relation between the two, what we find[8] is that sports dominated earliest American television.

It was all there in those years, much as we know it today: NFL telecasts on Sunday afternoon. Major league baseball. Stanley Cup playoffs. Horse racing. Boxing. Wrestling. Track meets. Basketball.[9] There was a good reason for this dominance: sports events in those pre-Arledge, dozen camera, super slo-mo, hyper-graphics days, did not have to be produced; they merely had to be televised. It was a lot cheaper to fill two hours by rolling a remote truck up to an Ebbets Field or a Madison Square Garden and pointing a couple of cameras at the action, than it was to produce two hours of studio-originated entertainment. The key words here are "cheaper" – a function of that lack of production; and "action" – that easily realized and televisable action which Powers described as live, human, and confined to a small, and well-defined physical area.

*   *   *

By 1937 similar, and compatible, systems of electronic television had been developed independently by the scientists Philo T. Farsnworth and Vladimir Zworykin. Their work, which was being refined in the laboratories of the Philco and RCA laboratories, respectively, had reached a point, as 1937 began, that a reasonable quality image – one consisting of 441-lines, compared to today's 525 – could now be transmitted over the air – and thus on-air tests of these two relatively perfected video systems began in the first months of 1937.

And, as the very first issue of the Sunday *Times* for 1937 made clear, it would be action on the playing field and in the arena, which many of those experimental telecasts would present. Tests utilizing what can be described as a 'medium resolution' picture during 1936, by the Philco Corporation's experimental station in Philadelphia, had "revealed how a prize fight might be televised."[10] And early TV *would* consistently focus its camera on both ring sports of boxing and wrestling – with the histrionics of the latter making wrestling perhaps the most popular fare in what might be termed the "pre-Uncle Miltie era" of television.

A story headed, "Radio 'Eye' Favors Baseball," in a May edition of the Sunday *Times*, reported that, at a session of an Institute of Radio Engineers conference, those who were working in television told their colleagues of plans "to televise outdoor scenes from parades to sporting events." Comparing football and baseball in terms of their 'televisability' – given the insensitivity of the iconoscope, which served as the pickup tube in the earliest TV cameras – the *Times* reported that it was baseball which was favored since (in those pre-nightball days) it was usually "played in the brightest months of the year and usually in fair weather," whereas "[p]ick-ups of football games were said to be less likely to be satisfactory, especially those extending into the late afternoon of the late season for this sport."[11]

While American TV at this time was limited to occasional, on-air, experimental telecasts, in England, a regular, British Broadcasting Corporation electronic TV service (utilizing the American technology developed by Zworykin at RCA) had been serving some 3,000 home receivers in the London area[12] since November of 1936. And even the staid BBC was offering a heavy sports diet to pioneer, British viewers.[13] The high school periodical *Scholastic*, in an article introducing its youthful readership to television in December 1937, began almost breathlessly in attempting to communicate the marvel of this new, electronic miracle, by its description of

> [a] group of tennis fans [who] sat in a room . . . in London last summer watching a tennis match that was being played 12 miles away on the famous court at Wimbeldon. It was *television* – perhaps the clearest and most successful public demonstration . . . to this time. . . . [As a] reporter . . . described it: "I saw it played on a screen, eight inches by ten. . . . It was a cloudy day, but the little miracle came off beautifully. [Don] Budge the size of your index finger, against [Frank] Parker, the size of your little finger, . . . hitting a speck of white. You could hear the impact of the racquets, . . . and barking of the linesman. . . ." [original emphasis][14]

Other than that it was the linesman, rather than John McEnroe, who was doing the barking, it was a Wimbeldon telecast, minus instant replays, no different from what we see today.

Alva Johnston, in the first of two lengthy articles he would write on TV for the *Saturday Evening Post* in May of 1939, to introduce that magazine's vast, 'middle-American' readership to TV coincident with the inauguration of regular, experimental service at the opening of the 1939 World's Fair, asserted that,

> nothing is so made to order for television as a world's championship prize fight. The bout takes place in a small, well-lighted arena and can be handled perfectly. The televiewer will see the fight on a screen of postcard or letter size, but he will see it; there will not be a thousand people standing on their seats in front of him to block his view.[15]

The very first telecast of a baseball game by the RCA/NBC New York station, which took place less than a month after the debut of regular TV service, occasioned an eight-column, banner headline, across the Sunday *Times* "Radio Page" of May 21st 1939: "Collegians Play Ball as Television Mirrors the Game." The *Times* radio editor, Orrin Dunlap, inspired by the doggerel of "Casey at the Bat" waxed:

> The sun was shining bright. . . . Flashing down the wavelengths the cry, "Play Ball!" rumbled in the mountaintops, it rattled in the dell, it struck upon the hills and rebounded on the flat. The players on Baker Field [the game was between Columbia and Princeton Universities] were seen stepping up to the plate on telescreens scattered throughout the metropolitan

area. . . . By television "high, fast and hard that spheroid flew; it sailed and sailed away.". . .

The problem, however, was that

[a] single camera anchored at one spot does not see the complete field; it leaves too much to the imagination. [It was also, like all cameras of that era, one equipped only with a single, fixed-focal length lens.] Baseball by television calls for three or four cameras, the views of which can be blended as the action calls for it. . . . [But] there is no doubt that the future will bring the complete picture. Then there'll be joys in Mudvilles of the air.[16]

Things improved considerably before that 1939 season was over when NBC, in September, telecast the first major league games – a Cincinnati-Brooklyn doubleheader from Ebbets Field. "Those who looked over the fence by radio," saw a much improved coverage. This time two cameras, including one equipped with a telephoto lens, were employed and the anonymous *Times* writer [Dunlap?] commented:

The idea that the electric "eyes" could never handle the scattered action of a baseball field faded at the Brooklyn diamond. [T]elecasting has improved 100% since the Princeton-Columbia game was viewed on the air through a single camera. . . . Now the ball can be seen; the players are no longer white dots on the screen.

But would the clubowners allow the cameras in the park on a regular basis? "Would there be 35,535 passing through the turnstyles if they all had tele-radios at home? And who would pay for it? That's the burning question. . . . The answer is generally the same – 'advertisers,' known in radio parlance as 'sponsors'."[17]

"Radio Takes Its Tele-Camera to See A Prize Fight," was another eight-column, banner head across a Sunday *Times* "Radio Page" occasioned by a televised sports event. "To see a prize fight telecast is 10,000 times more interesting than listening to a broadcast announcer," opined Dunlap. And, he concluded, "[t]here promises to be many thrilling moments of onlooking in the years to come if the telecasters can find a way to make it worth while [sic] to the promoters to permit the camera to spy on the ring."[18]

Football's turn was next – and its pioneering, New York telecast resulted, on October 15th, in a third, Sunday *Times* eight-column head about televised sports: "Television Forward Passes the Football to the Home."

Science has scored a touchdown at the kick-off of football by television. So sharp are the pictures and so discerning the telephoto lens as it peers into the line-up that the televiewer sits in his parlor wondering why he should leave the comforts of home to watch a gridiron battle in a sea of mud on a chilly autumnal afternoon.

While there were some problems according to Dunlap – e.g., where teams wearing different colored jerseys rendered by black-and-white TV as the same shade of grey – it was made clear to Sunday *Times* readers that televised football was a natural. Perhaps too much so – for, once again, the question was raised as to whether free viewing at home would discourage paid attendance: "[P]ermitting a telecaravan to camp within the gates [of a stadium] to toss scenes over the fence to a non-paying audience" is, according to college athletic officials, "not fair to those who buy tickets."[19]

In reprising the first half-year of regular TV service at the closing of the 1939 half of the '39–40 Fair, Dunlap reported that

> resistance is being encountered by [telecasters] when they attempt to pass turnstiles at baseball parks, . . . at the gridiron gates. . . . Why buy tickets and pay for transportation to a sports event . . . when one can sit effortless at home and see the same performance for nothing?

But, in the same article, and in one of the few instances where a writer in this period foresaw the possibility that television might someday not just be a supplicant, but actually come to dominate sports, Dunlap wrote,

> there are soothsayers who foresee the days when a world series, . . . and even football games and championship bouts will be staged chiefly for a tele-radio audience. . . . In much the same way as radio now controls entertainers through an artists' bureau, so television is foreseen managing athletes as well. . . . "[20]

At the end of the first year of regular, experimental service, the Sunday *Times* of April 28th, 1940 noted that, "[c]uriously enough the dramatics of professional wrestling have made it a popular favorite among televised sports."[21]

TV played a role, about this time, in a betting scam. According to Alva Johnston, the *Saturday Evening Post's* television specialist, bookies, unaware that races from New York City tracks were being televised, were accepting bets from viewers phoned immediately after a race had been run, but before their wire services reported the results.[22]

The New York City 'exurb' of Newburgh, as the result of a special, sales promotion campaign by RCA, was the one community in America where there was a high concentration of TV set owners. When Johnston visited there to check on how TV was affecting its set-owning families, he found that

> [o]utdoor sports usually received high ratings. [Brooklyn club president] Larry MacPhail allowed the opening of the Dodger[s' 1940 season] to be televised free of charge as a contribution to science. [Boxing promoter] Mike Jacobs has allowed several fight shows at Madison Square Garden to go on the air by television, because he foresees the day when big battles will all be television shows. His theory is that there will be a studio audience of 1000 at $100 a ticket at a championship bout, while . . . advertisers bid vast sums for the privilege of being a sponsor.[23]

Sports from the standpoint of participation, rather than that of the passive viewer, was the subject of an article by a parks recreation official in the August 1940 issue of *Recreation* magazine. "Television," Samuel L. Friedman wrote, "through the infinite possibilities of its combined visual and auditory expression, holds forth a magnificent promise towards recreation and education. . . ." Reporting on experiments his Los Angeles Recreation Department participated in over station W6XAO, he discussed how skills lessons in sports ranging from marble shooting to baseball, basketball and golf might be presented.[24]

Anticipating the "Wide World of Sports" kinds of minor and junk sports competitions which would come to dominate slow sports weekend afternoons, former NBC president Lenox Lohr predicted that, "[n]umerous feats of athletic prowess such as weight lifting, wrestling, tugs of war, calisthenics, body building and high diving might conveniently be brought into a television plant, . . ."[25]

In a Sunday article on the recently announced decision by the FCC to authorize commencement of full, commercial TV, beginning July 1st, 1941, the *Times*' T.R. Kennedy, Jr., reported that, on the basis of what had been seen during the two years of regular, experimental telecasting to then, one could expect a commercial TV service to give heavy emphasis to sports:

> During the past few months there has been ample opportunity to study the reaction of a limited New York audience to sports events, nearly 100 of which have been televised. As a result NBC program planners have placed outside pickups – the emphasis on sports – in the foreground of all televised "musts" of the future.[26]

The early World War II years would see literally nothing – at least as far as the general magazine press and the Sunday *Times* were concerned – about sports and TV. But from what we have seen was previously written about television in the pre-war years, it was clear that when the war-interrupted 'continuity' of TV's development began again, sports would play a major programming, and audience-attracting role.

One of the longest-running series – sports or otherwise – of post-war television, the Friday night Gilette-sponsored fight cards from Madison Square Garden, was, however, launched during the war. The *Times* of January 30th, 1944, reported that NBC and the razor company had signed an agreement to televise the matches[27] – an arrangement which would last through June of 1960.[28]

Jack Gould, in a December 1945 *Times* article about experimental, color TV demonstrations by both RCA and CBS, indicated what color might add to sports coverage, when he reported how the CBS demonstration, which showed the same football films first in black-and-white, clearly revealed the values added by the addition of color: "When a forward pass was thrown [in the black-and-white] version it was difficult to tell whether it had been completed or intercepted. In color . . . the outcome . . . was never in doubt . . . because of the distinguishing colors of the jerseys. . . ."[29]

The first event to focus widespread attention on television after the war, was the heavyweight title bout between Joe Louis and Billy Conn. (Conn had come closer to beating Louis in their first championship bout, than had any other challenger.) Johnston, in the first of what this time would be a three-part, consecutive week series on TV for the *Saturday Evening Post*, stated in the issue of March 9th, 1946, that it would be the Louis-Conn fight which "will give 'tele' a big lift and put it on the road toward becoming a billion dollar industry."[30] *Newsweek*, in its issue of June 24th, quoted "[n]etwork officials [who] called the June 19th broadcast [of the fight] 'the springboard for the greatest boom television has ever seen'."[31]

Kennedy, in a Sunday *Times* article following the fight telecast, analogized its significance for TV to that which the Dempsey-Carpentier match of 25 years earlier had had for the then infant medium of radio:

> Last week science not only repeated the event of 1921, but did it on a vastly higher and more complex electronic plane. Hundreds of owners of television sets in New York, Schenectady, Philadelphia and [via closed-circuit] in Washington DC [where there was no on-air television station] both heard and saw and missed little as the . . . main event passed quickly into history. . . . The video audience, according to those who staged the show, was the largest one to date, comprising more boxing fans by far than could have been packed into the stadium's seats and aisles.[32]

Johnston, in the second of those three, March 1946 *Saturday Evening Post* articles on TV, indicated his belief that whatever significance the Louis-Conn telecast may have had in launching post-war television, it could not be regarded as a precedent because it "is practically certain that . . . [it is] large chains of movie theaters [which] will present television pictures of events like world's champion fights, the World series, the Kentucky Derby, the football classics and other big outdoor shows."[33]

Bars, it turned out – not home settings or theaters – were where most of those in the few cities (which now also included Washington, Detroit and Milwaukee) which had an operating TV station during the earliest post-war years, first experienced television. And, given the predominantly masculine setting, it was sports which was the main attraction. At least five articles during 1947 – in *Time, Newsweek*, the Sunday *Times* and *Collier's* – focused on taverns, what were portrayed as their working-class patrons, and the sporting events their television receivers displayed.

*Time*, in its edition of March 24th, reported that while

> [t]elevision is not yet available in every Chicago home, . . . it is literally just around the corner. The city's only television station . . . reports that two-thirds of its audience takes in the show with lifted elbows at the 250 Chicago bars that own television sets.

Speaking in the "dese-dem-dose" style without which no bar owner would have credibility, one Chicago barkeep "analyzed the new drift:"

> "['B]out couple' monts ago business started gettin' stinkin'. We was losin' money, but fast. I gotta do somethin' to goose the place up. . . . I figure maybe dese guys is going to hockey games or fights an' I say, why not bring hockey or fights here. . . . So I buy dese gadgets. Slump in business stopped."[34]

It wasn't much different at "Gil's Bar on [Manhattan's] Eighth Avenue" – except that the previous week it "was almost deserted," *Newsweek* of June 16th reported. "Ed Abbott, bartender at Gil's knew why. 'Our television set is busted'," he explained. " 'So soon's we get a new one,' people'll drift back in again." *Newsweek* estimated 3,000 NYC bar-and-grills were TV equipped. "No longer a passing fad, television is fast becoming a magnet to attract bar patrons." What they were watching was baseball in the afternoons and boxing at night.[35]

Murray Schumach, a sports reporter for the *Times*, appeared on the June 22nd Sunday "Radio Page" with a story headed, "Television Attracts Bar Trade." Schumach had visited "Hussey's Bar and Grill over at Forty-seventh and Ninth. . . . It was sports . . . thanks to television." First a Dodger game, then a neighborhood club fight card.

> And so it goes. Good fights, bad fights; winning baseball, losing baseball – it's all the same at bars these nights with television. . . . Television is the best thing that's happened to the neighborhood bar since the free lunch.[36]

But there was a downside too, according to *Time* magazine of December 15th. " 'In watching the screen,' complained one bartender, 'people forget what is the prime purpose of a bar, which is to drink'." However, " 'you gotta have [TV] whether you want to or not . . . or you start holding hands with yourself'."[37]

As might be expected, a September 27th *Collier's* article, headed "Fifty Mile Bleachers," would mainly be about sports on television – which, in '47, meant sports as viewed on TV sets located in bars. Those with sets in the eight cities where TV stations were now operating, were experiencing 30 to 60% increases in business. "Bright signs pop up on open windows. 'See the Game tonight.'. . . 'Fights Here on Television Tonight.' A man in Elizabeth, . . . had to rip out fixtures and build wooden bleachers . . . to accommodate the crowds."[38] The significance?

> "Sports will be to television what music was to radio," is the prediction of General John Reed Kilpatrick, president of Madison Square Garden. . . . But what, in that event, will television do to sports? The question has ignited a major furor which most fans, busy with their beer and barside seats, have thus far overlooked.

Other sports executives also saw TV as boon more than bane – a vehicle to increase, rather than decrease, attendance at athletic events:

> [Fight promotor] Harry Markson . . . likes to tell the following stock but avowedly voracious story: "Friend of mine in Flatbush, a real-estate dealer, used to kid the pants off me, saying that fights were no good, that he'd never seen one in his life and never would. Then his old man bought a television set and this guy sees his first bout. Since then, he's been to the Garden five times this summer."[39]

*Time* of May 26th, 1947, carried a profile of early TV personality and sportscaster, NBC's Bob Stanton, the Giants' telecast announcer, who had been handling sports announcing since 1940. (He was also the announcer for the Louis-Conn fight.) Stanton, whom *Time* labelled, "Mr. Television,"[40] had to learn the rules of television sportscasting while on the air.

> There was no book of rules for television announcers. . . . Before many weeks he was supplying rules and statistics for bewildered sports fans, ignoring the obvious, calling an occasional play wrong to delight arm-chair experts, . . . keeping his commentary at a slow pace so that cameras could follow without jerky images. His friends helped out by bar-hopping and giving him reports of audience reaction. . . .[41]

Bill Slater (also a busy radio personality at the time – e.g., as host of Mutual Radio's nighttime quiz show, "20 Questions") was handling play-by-play for DuMont's Yankee telecasts – and was the subject of a similar piece in 'Mr. Harper's' "After Hours" column in the *Harper's* magazine of August. 'Mr. Harper' had spent a day with Slater at the Stadium. And he too saw sports as a TV mainstay: "Most telecasts are now sports events (baseball, wrestling, boxing, and tennis at this season) and other public events such as parades. . . ."[42]

*Nation's Business* judged "[t]elevision sports . . . as leav[ing] little to be desired. It gives you a better view than the coach has. 'You're like [Brooklyn Dodger president and general manager] Branch Rickey with three sets of field glasses [i.e. cameras],' says one sports follower."[43]

Not all TV sets where sports and other programming was being viewed were located in bars. Receivers were selling in sufficient volume, especially in New York, that by August, it was time for the *New Yorker* to take note of the video phenomenon. Writer Robert Rice spent a week with a Manhattan family (which had owned its set since before the war) to observe programming and its effect on family life: "On WNBT there were fights from St. Nicholas Arena [these replaced the Garden's regular Friday night bouts in the Summer] [and] on WABD there were wrestling matches from Jamaica Arena." The family and its guests chose wrestling. " 'Wrestling's more fun than fights'," the wife explained.[44] And on Saturday they viewed a Dodger telecast. The TV coverage was described (in typical *New Yorker* detail running four columns) but no summary judgement was rendered.[45]

There was still, however, the '47 World Series – the first to be covered by TV, and the Series some still feel is the most exciting ever played. Since it involved two New York teams, it became the occasion for major home receiver sales promotions. But the *Times'* R.W. Stewart was critical of the coverage: "[B]aseball's action continues to be more difficult to capture on the tele-screen [a situation made worse because Yankee] Stadium does not advantageously lend itself to television."

> At the same time, it was manifest that, through television, more individuals were seeing the annual classic simultaneously than ever before in its history and that, despite the limitations of the scene reproduced by the electric cameras, those in the tele-bleachers were getting a more intimate view of the game than those actually in the ball park.[46]

Nineteen-forty-eight would see television finally 'arrive.' And sports would remain dominant [see Note #8] – at least for another year or so. If the much more, entertainment-rich TV of today sees a smaller percentage of schedules devoted to sports, sports still remains a mainstay of television, and has, in the process, become dominated, as Leonard Shecter states [see Note #1], by the dollars bestowed on it by the tube. And so we see the addition of multi-billion dollar TV revenues resulting in 10-fold increases in athletes' salaries over the last 20 years; a 1986 World Series limited to teams located in the Northeast displacing the highest rated TV show for the first time in four months; a 24-hour sports cable network featuring NFL arm wrestling and Australian rugby, turning a profit; and a TV sports commentator becoming the most despised personality in America – while a 300+ pound mass of flesh is transformed into an instant celebrity. It is TV which took a joke of a football league – the very word "defense" was a no-no in the early AFL – possessing only one, better than average quarterback, *but* one with an image carefully tailored for television, and forced the NFL to accept it into membership as almost half of its operation, while two other leagues failed for lack of a network contract. To create and increase viewer interest across the country, television could necessitate such merger and expansion – so that we now see not only what was a 12-team NFL with 28 franchises, but baseball expanded from its once immutable and sacrosanct 16, to 26 teams. And it is a televised sports event which can command the highest price for a 30-second advertising spot in all of television, $600,000 – or *$20,000 per second*!

*   *   *

Sports and TV did come together almost at the moment of the latter's inception because, it needed that something which Powers described as live, human, and of manageable physical dimensions. And it proved a relation which, because of its obvious and inherent 'rightness', was seen by those writing about it, even at the medium's very beginnings, as natural and irrevocable.

## Notes

1. Among the very best of these was perhaps the very first, the late Leonard Shecter's "The Jocks." (New York: Paperback Library, 1970). As to the usurping, and corrupting nature of TV on sports, he wrote:

   > Television *buys* sports. Television *supports* sports. It moves in with its money and supports sports in a style to which they had to become accustomed and then, like a bought lady, sports become so used to luxurious living they cannot extricate themselves. So, slowly at first, but inevitably, television tells sports what to do. It *is* sports and it runs them the way it does most other things, more flamboyantly than honestly. [original emphases] [pg. 79.]

2. As this writer wrote in his review of the book for *Television Quarterly:*

   > In *Supertube,* Powers appears to be completely caught up in what he perceives as the overwhelming awesomeness of the lash-up between television and sports, and the synergistic outcomes of that combination. The result is a preoccupation with creating a rhetoric which itself matches the scope and magnificence he imagines in the phenomenon he is describing. Everything else – especially judgement – seems to suffer. [XX:111, 1985, pg. 96.]

3. (New York: Coward-McCann, 1985) pg. 46.
4. The electronic television which has been with us now for some 50 years, was not the first TV. During the '20s through the early '30s, a long-forgotten, mechanical system of television was actively promoted and experimented with. From 1931 to 1933 stations utilizing this extremely crude technology broadcast regular, daily programming in Chicago, Washington and New York City. The pictures produced, however, were virtually devoid of detail, and were displayed on receivers with screens which were limited to a practical maximum of 3" in size. For technical reasons not relevant here, nothing could be televised which did not take place immediately in front of the immobile cameras (or "televisors") which the system employed. Boxing, therefore, was the only sport it could carry – and that in a ring only a fraction of the standard size. A graphic illustration of the limitations of this doomed technology can be seen in a photograph from the Sunday *Times* of August 7, 1932: it showed a fighter knocked down by an opponent. His body was below the frame of the televisor. The picture's caption stated: "Letters from television observers applaud the prize fights of station W2XAB and continually ask for more action scenes on the air. One difficulty . . . is that when a contestant is knocked down he falls out of range of the radio 'eyes'." [Section 9, pg. 7.]
5. The 11 years covered here can be divided into five periods. The first, which lasted from 1937 through April 30th, 1939, involved occasional, over-the-air testing which could only be received on a limited number of sets – most in the homes of RCA/NBC and Philco engineers and executives. No home receivers were marketed during this period. The second began on April 30, 1939, at the opening of the 1939–40 New York World's Fair, when NBC, a wholly-owned subsidiary of RCA, inaugurated a regular, but officially still "experimental" broadcast television service in the New York City area. RCA, along with a number of other manufacturers, including Philco and DuMont, began manufacturing and selling home receivers. The third period, which lasted from July 1, 1941 through Pearl Harbor, was that of fully-commercial service – as in radio, time could now be paid for by advertisers. By the time of American entry into World War Two, there

were eight stations serving five cities: New York (3); Los Angeles (2); Chicago (1); Philadelphia (1); and Schenectady, NY (1). During the war, the fourth period, station construction, and production of home sets, was halted – and these eight stations served a total of under 10,000 receivers. [Figure from article by-lined, "Anonymous," "What's Happened to Television," *Saturday Review of Literature*, Vol. 25, No. 8, Feb. 21, 1942, pg. 16.] The fifth period, which might be termed "the final gearing up," lasted from the war's end in August 1945, through 1947.

6.   In nineteen-forty-eight, the number of receivers jumped from about 200,000 to around a million. According to the 1963 *Broadcasting Annual*, 250,000 receivers were produced in 1947 – and one million in 1948. Since not all sets made in a year were sold that year, the figures above can be considered a good approximation of sets in use. [Washington, DC: Broadcasting Publications, Inc.] pg. 7.)

7.   Read was everything published about TV in the general magazine press (as listed in *Reader's Guide to Periodical Literature*) and on the "Radio Pages" of the Sunday New York *Times* – some 140 magazine and 250 *Times* pieces in all.

8.   And also, what some of us can recall. The first telecasts this writer, at the time a Brooklyn, junior high school student, ever saw – on a Friday night at a friend's home, in the fall of 1947 – included an All-America Conference, Brooklyn Dodger-Miami Seahawks game from Ebbets Field, the Friday night Madison Square Garden boxing bouts, and wrestling from a local club – all of which ran against each other on the then three NYC stations. His family purchased its first set a month after the end of the period with which this study is concerned, in February of 1948. Madison Square Garden Knicks games and college basketball doubleheaders, Rangers hockey, nightly boxing and wrestling from local clubs as well as the Friday night Garden cards – and three months later the complete home schedules of the baseball Dodgers, Giants and Yankees – dominated the schedules of the three stations. The CBS-owned outlet, WCBS-TV, broadcast virtually nothing but sports.

9.   For example, the weekly TV log published in the Sunday New York *Times* for the week of March 17th, 1940 – a schedule picked at random – listed 16 programs of all types, totalling just under 16 hours. While only three were sports events, these three – an amateur boxing tournament, a professional fight, and a Stanley Cup playoff game – were scheduled to run two hours each, or almost 40% of that week's total telecasting. ["Telecasts This Week" included under "Notes on Television," Section 10, pg. 10.]

10.   Orrin E. Dunlap, Jr., "Signs of Progress," Jan. 3, Section 10, pg. 12.

11.   May 16, 1937, Section 10, pg. 12.

12.   L. Marsland-Gander, "Europe's Race to See by Radio Spurs Television," New York *Times* (Sunday) Aug. 22, 1937, Section 10, pg. 10.

13.   According to a 1938 *Time* magazine report, "In Britain, most popular television stunts have been telecasts of public events like tennis matches, boat races, fights,. . ." [Anon., "Television," Vol. 21, No. 21, May 23, pg. 25.]

14.   Bruce Rogers, "Television 'Just Around the Corner'?" Vol. 31, No. 11, December 4, pg. 6.

15.   "Television's Here," Vol. 211, No. 45, May 6, pg. 8.

16.   Section 10, pg. 10.

17.   "Watching a Televised Baseball Game," (Sunday) Sept. 3, Section 9, pg. 12.

18.   June 4, 1939, Section 9, pg. 10.

19.   Section 9, pg. 12.

20.   "Eyelids of Radio, Lifted at World's Fair, to Stay Open," New York *Times* (Sunday) Oct. 29, Section 9, pg. 12.

21.   "A Year of Television," Section 9, pg. 12.

22.   "Trouble in Television," Vol. 212, No. 13, Sept. 28, 1940, pg. 24.

23.   *Ibid.*, pg. 37.

24.   "Television as a New Aid to Recreation," Vol. 34, No. 5, pp. 305, 306.

25. "Programs for Television," [condensed from chapter in his book, *Television Broadcasting* (New York: Harper & Bros., 1942)] Vol. 8, No. 5, Nov. 1940, pp. 305, 306.
26. "Television to Be on a Commercial Basis by Mid-Year," May 11, 1941, Section 9, pg. 10.
27. Item from Jack Gould column, "One Thing and Another," (Sunday), Section 2, p g. 9.
28. Harry Castleman & Walter J. Podrazik, *Watching TV: Four Decades of American Television* (New York: McGraw-Hill, 1982), pg. 139.
29. "Video and Color," (Sunday) Dec. 23, Section 2, pg. 7.
30. "Television: Boom or Bubble?" Vol. 218, No. 36, pg. 9.
31. Anon., "Round-by-Round by Eye," Vol. 27, No. 25, pg. 65.
32. "Television Covers a Prize Fight," June 23, 1946, Section 2, pg. 7.
33. ". . . – Part II," Vol. 218, No. 37, March 16, 1946, pg. 22. (In fact, it has only been boxing matches featuring the few, recent ring superstars such as Muhammud Ali and Sugar Ray Leonard, which have proven theater telecast draws.)
34. Anon., "Barrooms with a View," Vol. 49, No. 13, March 24, 1947, pg. 63.
35. Anon., "Television in the Tavern," Vol. 29, No. 24, pg. 64.
36. "Television Attracts the Bar Trade," Section 2, pg. 9.
37. Anon., "'The Television Set'," Vol. 50, No. 24, pg. 50.
38. Edward P. Morgan, Jr., Vol. 120, (no issue no.) pg. 28.
39. *Ibid.*, pg. 32.
40. The awarding of this title by *Time* to a figure who, as television would burgeon, would remain relatively obscure – the Giants' radio announcers would soon be handling the TV mike duties as well – was a bit premature. Within two years, it would be Milton Berle who would be known as "Mr. Television."
41. Anon., "Mr. Television," Vol. 49, No. 21, pg. 77.
42. "A Complicated Business," [in "After Hours" section] Vol. 195, No. 1165, pg. 191.
43. Philip Gustafson, "Nickelodian Days of Television," Vol. 35, No. 7, July, 1947, pg. 74.
44. "Diary of a Viewer," [in "Onward and Upward With the Arts" section] Vol., 23, No. 28, Aug. 30, 1947, pg. 50.
45. *Ibid.*, pp. 52–55.
46. "Baseball on Video," Oct. 5, 1947, Section 2, pg. 11. (Continuity with the era under consideration here has been maintained in the person and talents of Harry Coyle, who directed that first Series telecast, and more than 30 since – up through the 1986 Mets-Red Sox matchup. For Coyle's views on how televised sports has changed over the past 40 years, see his: "'. . . the World Series with a Crew of Seven . . .'," in the NBC-published promotional book, *Connections: Reflections on Sixty Years of Broadcasting,* [New York, 1986] pp. 229–233.)

# 3

# Media Sport: Hot and Cool

*Susan Birrell and John W. Loy, Jr*

## McLuhan's View of Media in Society

McLuhan's celebrated statement, "the medium is the message", represents the essence of his thinking. McLuhan's basic thesis is that the real message of any medium is not the content but what the form of the medium itself reveals about the society. McLuhan discerns fundamental relationships between the historical development of a society and its media forms, and he divides human history into three eras: pre-literate, literate and post-literate. Each era is typified by the media found within it.

Pre-literate society is primarily on oral tradition society, rich in folklore and intimate communication forms. The invention of the printing press ushered in the literate era with its emphasis upon linear styles of communication. In recent years the invention of television, computers, and other electronic devices marked the beginning of the post-literate period and the development of the "global village".

Pre- and post-literate societies have much in common, particularly the sensory experience associated with their respective media. Both feature a diffused pattern of sensory stimulation, while the print-oriented experience of the literate phase of society features a linear, step-by-step progression.

McLuhan's term for media suited to literate societies is "hot" media, while post-literate media are classified as "cool". The basic criterion for McLuhan is the sensory participation demanded from the audience. Hot media – such as books, newspapers, and films – are media of "high definition", requiring low

**Source:** *International Review for the Sociology of Sport,* 14(1) (1979): 5–17.

participation from the audience. The "low definition" of cool media such as television, theatre, and cartoons calls for higher sensory participation. As McLuhan states:

> A hot medium is one that extends one single sense in "high definition". High definition is the state of being well filled with data . . . hot media do not leave so much to be filled in or completed by the audience. Hot media are, therefore, low in participation, and cool media are high in participation or completion by the audience. Naturally, therefore, a hot medium like radio has very different effects on the user from a cool medium like the telephone.[1]

For McLuhan, a medium is broadly conceived as any sensory extension of man. Among his interesting list of media (in addition to the expected examples – television, radio, movies, photographs, the printed word – he includes clothing, money, clocks, and the electric light bulb), McLuhan cites games, including sports, as "media of interpersonal communication".

McLuhan's conjectures about sport as medium and sport as content matter of other media are interesting and highly original. In general they can be dealt with as two separate issues and the implicit hypotheses made explicit for a more serious evaluation of the validity of McLuhan's ideas.

## Sport as Medium

Like many others, McLuhan contends that sport reflects the culture in which it is found: specifically, he argues that certain sports are "hotter" than others and thus best suited to the literate stage of societal growth. According to McLuhan, football has predictably overtaken baseball in popular appeal in America because baseball is a hot sport, developed in the literate society, while football is a cool sport, well-suited to the post-literate era. He observes:

> It is the inclusive mesh of the TV image, in particular, that spells for a while, at least, the doom of baseball. For baseball is a game of one-thing-at-a-time, fixed positions and visibly delegated specialist jobs such as belonged to the now passing mechanical age . . . When cultures change, so do games. Baseball, that had become the elegant abstract image of an industrial society living by split-second timing, has in the new TV decade lost its psychic amd social relevance for our new way of life. The ball game has been dislodged from the social center and been conveyed to the periphery of American life.
>
> In contrast, American football is nonpositional, and any or all of the players can switch to any role during play . . . It agrees very well with the new needs of decentralized team play in the electric age.[2]

Thus, one hypothesis about the relationships of sport and the media which McLuhan offers is that certain sport forms suit certain societal forms: cool sports are more popular than hot sports in post-literate society. That hypothesis might be testable if one could indeed classify sports according to "heat". McLuhan does not offer such a taxonomy but perhaps it is possible to refine his concept of "definition" to the point where it can be applied to sport.

McLuhan distinguishes media of high definition from media of low definition in terms of the participatory demands made on the consumer. Sports make the same demands upon spectators and audiences: the sport experience can be conceptualized as relatively more diffuse or more focused – diffusion being defined as a function of the demands put on the secondary participant in terms of sensory acuteness and sensory involvement. Thus diffusion can be understood as a sensory variety show: the spectator is bombarded by many aspects which demand his attention, but he must limit himself to only one. The more diffuse the choices, the more demanding is the involvement experience for the spectator.

The basic concept can be further clarified along two dimensions: locational diffusion and action diffusion. Locational diffusion is simply the amount of space required by the sport. Diving and boxing are low on this dimension; golf and football are high. Action diffusion is inversely related to the degree of linear progression of the game. Sport in which the ball moves freely between two teams, as in soccer and hockey, are the best examples of high action diffusion. Baseball, on the other hand, features a distinctively linear type action sequence.

To a degree, action diffusion is a function of the pace of the game action and the proportion of unexpected or unpredictable action. Generally, races are linear by nature and thus low in action diffusion. But auto racing is an exception because of the potential for action and accidents to occur anywhere on the track. For the fan intent on experiencing the sport event most fully, highly diffused action demands a great deal of attention and acuteness. A football fan, for instance, is called on to make some important decisions at each play in order to enjoy the game experience to its fullest.

Table 1 illustrates the diffusion dimensions of selected sports.

Those high in diffusion across both dimensions, like hockey and soccer, are most diffuse overall, while sports such as wrestling, diving and bowling are the most focused or linear.

**Table 1:** Diffusion ratings of selected sports

| | Diffusion dimensions | |
|---|---|---|
| Sports | Locational diffusion | Action diffusion |
| CLASS I auto-racing, basketball, football, hockey, lacrosse, roller derby, rugby, soccer | high | high |
| CLASS II baseball, golf, most races, tennis | high | low |
| CLASS III bowling, boxing, diving, fencing, field events, gymnastics, pool, wrestling | low | low |

According to the hypothesis inherent in McLuhan's statements on sport, the popularity of different sport forms should vary according to historical and cultural factors. There is only mild support for the historical thesis. For example, the late nineteenth century, the literate era for most of Western society, was a period of codification of sport. Specific rules were spelled out, and the approach to sport during this era was overshadowed by this very linear interpretation of sport. However, that thesis is less salient when applied to a more modern period.

The thesis would predict that Class III sports ought to have died out in American society or at least be suffering a severe loss of popularity because their forms are antithetical to the tenor of the times. However, this is decidedly not the case: witness the recent surge in popularity of tennis (Class II) and gymnastics (Class III), and the resurgence of baseball (Class II).[3]

Furthermore, if McLuhan hopes to convince his readers that the thesis has some validity from a cross-cultural perspective, he will have to furnish a more precise argument than this:

> Offhand, it might be supposed that the tight tribal unity of football would make it a game that the Russians would cultivate. Their devotion to ice hockey and soccer, two very individualist forms of game, would seem little suited to the psychic needs of a collectivist society. But Russia is still in the main an oral, tribal world that is undergoing detribalization and just now discovering individualism as a novelty. Soccer and ice hockey have for them, therefore, an exotic and Utopian quality of promise that they do not convey to the West. This is the quality that we tend to call '"snob value", and we might derive some similar "value" from owning race horses, polo ponies, or twelve-meter yachts.[4]

Actually, McLuhan's thesis might provide an interesting basis for a study of sport forms as they reflect the developmental stage of a society. Unfortunately, he has failed to provide a reasonable interpretation of football as opposed to hockey and soccer (are the latter really "very individualist forms of game"?), and falls back on a rather dogmatic explanation to justify his conclusions. A similar fault is evident in McLuhan's analysis of football as "nonpositional" and as a game in which "any and all players can switch to any role during play".[5] In fact, football has become even more structured and position oriented in the dozen years since McLuhan made his comments, a trend exactly opposite to what he would predict.

## Sport as Media Content

McLuhan claims that "the content of any medium is always another medium"[6] so it is not surprising to find sport as content matter for other forms of media, most notably television. By its very nature, sport should be successful as television content. McLuhan states, for example, that

. . . because the low definition of TV insures a high degree of audience involvement, the most effective programs are those that present situations which consist of some process to be completed.[7]

Indeed, the steady increases in the amount of sport on television in the past ten years, increasing network budgets for sport, and the success of such TV sport creations as Monday Night Football and Wide World of Sports attest to the general validity of McLuhan's argument.[8] Yet some sports are more popular television sports than others (see Table 2) and their popularity does not reflect their diffusion classification as might be expected. Indeed no discernible pattern emerges. Hypotheses derived from McLuhan have little power in explaining the data.

Another aspect of the problem is the notion of the translation of one medium into another. McLuhan is quite explicit in his belief that the translational powers of media can change the course of history. He states that certain politicians translate better into different media than do others. Compared to the cool Kennedy, he argues, Nixon was too hot for the television cameras, thus his poor showing in the Presidential debates of 1960.[9]

**Table 2:** Average U.S. audience per cent by sport type for three years[a]

| Year | 1970 | | 1973 | | 1975 | |
|---|---|---|---|---|---|---|
| Diffusion ratings | % | N | % | N | % | N |
| CLASS I | | | | | | |
| football[b] | 13.9 | 101 | 15.2 | 110 | 15.5 | 116 |
| basketball[b] | 8.0 | 47 | 7.4 | 72 | 8.0 | 71 |
| auto racing | 4.7 | 2 | 11.1 | 3 | 10.0 | 6 |
| ice hockey | 4.2 | 16 | 5.0 | 24 | 3.9 | 21 |
| soccer | | | | | 4.6 | 2 |
| class average | 11.2 | 166 | 11.3 | 209 | 11.7 | 216 |
| CLASS II | | | | | | |
| horse racing | 13.7 | 3 | 9.3 | 9 | 10.8 | 6 |
| baseball | 11.4 | 36 | 13.4 | 53 | 12.0 | 52 |
| golf | 5.6 | 69 | 5.5 | 81 | 6.8 | 58 |
| tennis | 4.2 | 5 | 5.1 | 321 | 4.1 | 64 |
| skiing | 5.8 | 16 | 5.2 | 1 | | |
| class average | 7.4 | 129 | 8.0 | 176 | 7.5 | 180 |
| CLASS III | | | | | | |
| bowling | 7.2 | 13 | 8.9 | 14 | 8.6 | 18 |
| boxing | | | 5.2 | 6 | 5.3 | 8 |
| fishing | 8.1 | 1 | | | | |
| class average | 7.3 | 14 | 7.8 | 20 | 7.6 | 26 |
| HYBRID TELECASTS | | | | | | |
| multi sport | 9.2 | 54 | 8.9 | 84 | 9.2 | 113 |
| track and field | 5.6 | 15 | | | 6.0 | 1 |
| Pan Am Games | | | | | 5.8 | 1 |
| World Games | | | 5.4 | 8 | | |
| class average | 8.4 | 69 | 8.6 | 92 | 9.1 | 115 |

Figures compiled from "Let's Look at Sports, 1975", "Let's Look at Sports: The 1973 Season", and "A Look of Sport: The 1969–1970 Season", Nielsen Television Index, Media Research Division, A. C. Nielsen Company.
[a]These figures include both regular season games and special events such as the Super Bowl, the World Series, the Stanley Cup. The Riggs-King tennis match is included in the 1974 figures and the Ali-Lyle heavyweight boxing championship is included in 1975.
[b]These figures include both professional and college games.

Even more dramatically, McLuhan contends that Hitler's hot personality was perfectly suited to the hot medium of radio. McLuhan declares:

> Had TV occurred on a large scale during Hitler's reign he would have vanished quickly. Had TV come first there would have been no Hitler at all.[10]

What are the effects, then, of translating the live sport event, generally a very cool medium into another, hotter medium? Specifically, what changes in the sport experience arise when the spectator follows sport through television rather than live attendance? In short, what does television do to the sport experience of the fan in terms of McLuhan's ideas?

The coolness or diffusion of television as a medium, relative to the medium of the event iitself, must therefore, be examined. The model in Figure 1 suggests that movement from the sport event as medium to television as medium should change the nature of the sport experience somewhat, through a focusing of diffuse action which is unavoidable due to limitations of broadcasting translation.

In the earlier days of television, effectiveness of sport coverage with only one camera varied from sport to sport. The singular focus was disastrous for sports such as baseball but had an almost negligible effect on a relatively more focused event such as boxing.[11] Increasing the number of cameras used to cover an event might appear to foster greater diffusion. But the action is still previewed by the producer who selects exactly which part of the total picture will be broadcast.

Other complex advances in technology have continued to limit the diffusion effect of television. Instant replay, isolated camera, stop action, slow motion, wide-angle lens, and split screen have all transformed the sport spectacle, disrupting the natural rhythm of the game and synthesizing the action through highlighting to enhance the excitement value.[12]

In general, television produces the following effects which are unavailable to the line event audience:

1. Changing the size of the image and permitting a greater range of vision (wide-angle lens, split screen).
2. Concentrating time diffuse events into a more manageable time span (highlights).
3. Manipulating time to dramatize action (instant replay, slow motion, stop action, highlights).
4. Focusing on one isolated action (isolated camera, instant replay).
5. Providing more statistical information.

| Time Dimension | Immediate | Simultaneous | | Delayed |
|---|---|---|---|---|
| Form of Sport Media | Event | TV | Radio | Newspaper |
| Degree of Coolness | Cool ———————————————➤ Hot | | | |
| Degree of Diffusion | Diffuse ⬅——————————— Focused | | | |

**Figure 1:** Relative "coolness" and diffusion of sport media

What television can not do is allow the spectator the freedom to choose the segment of action he wishes to follow. In addition, television does not provide the fan with the high degree of social integration with other fans and, more important, integration with the nature of the game experience itself.[13] As Orrin E. Dunlop, Jr., a writer for the New York Times, lamented in the early days of televised sport:

> (The fan) does not see the half of what is going on to make baseball the pleasure it has become *in* 100 years. The televiewer lacks freedom; seeing baseball by television is too confining, for the novelty would not hold up for more than an hour, if it were not for the commentator . . . What would old-timers think of such a turn of affairs – baseball from a sofa! Television is too safe. There is no ducking the foul ball.[14]

A more recent interpretation continues in the same vein:

> The networks with their zeppelins and zoom lenses, their dreamlike instant replays of color nad violence have changed football watching from a remote college pastime to something very much like voyeurism.
> . . . No matter how fine his TV reception, no beer and armachair quarterback can hope to see the true game. For all the paraphernalia, the tube rarely shows an overview; pass patterns and geometric variations are lost in a kaleidoscope of close-ups and crunches.[15]

Live sport spectation is a diffuse experience; media sport are focused events. How the spectator has resisted or adjusted to such shifts serves as a basis for speculation as to the future of media, sport, and the sport experience of the fan.

## The Future of Media Sport

With McLuhan as prophet, one might assume that the new electronic age with its diffuse and demanding nature drives people further and further from a linear interpretation of the world. Surely the media of the future will offer increasingly diffuse media experiences to the media sport consumer. But will super spectator ever abandon his television set? Will the media sport experience of the future be hot or cool? Speculative models for both positions exist; surprisingly some are beginning to creep into reality as well.

Through its technological breakthroughs, television is bringing a higher and higher degree of focus to a diffused sport world. In effect, television is providing the fan with a greater amount of information, both visually and through statistical recitations, and depriving him of the integrative aspects of the sport experience. Thus the close link with the game in its natural spectatorial form is broken in order to provide a higher informational picture of the game. Taken to an extreme, this will eventually lead to a homogenization effect on the media.

But contrary to McLuhan's theory, the new techniques of sport broadcasting seem to enhance the sport experience for the fan rather than diminish it. Although it removes him from the true context of the sport situation, the American spectator seems more than happy to accept the television sport experience.

If McLuhan's literate/post-literate society theory is correct, this first generation of television children to come of age – those in their early thirties, the first wave of the post-literates – should be expected to shun a hotter media experience for a cooler one. This does not seem to be the case. Instead, it is more likely the case that the first television generation has been brought upon the television sport experience, and that this has fostered a linear orientation to sport. Television has trained America to focus on particular bits of action and ignore, or perhaps never come into meaningful contact with, a live event experience. Perhaps this explains why many disgruntled fans leave a live game complaining that they could have seen it better on television.

Techniques such as isolated camera, instant replay, stop action, and split screen are designed to provide the spectator with knowledge, not an integrative sensory experience. Perhaps the American fan with his increasing mania for statistical information is being fed the diet of data he requests. Other revolutionary techniques or practices may go even further to satisfy him.

One innovation which has yet to make its actual debut is a method of telecasting sport events called "retarded live action television".[16] According to the news report of the invention, "at regular intervals, a frame of perhaps one second duration is discarded, and the blank space is filled by stretching out the others. The action can be slowed by 15 or 20 per cent without the viewer being conscious of any delay".[17]

Another potential change in sport due to television lies in the area of officiating. It has become obvious to the fan as well as the coaches that instant replay can not only recapture isolated action but rule violations as well. A replay can either confirm or contradict the judgement of the referee, and nowadays a referee is often more relentlessly monitored than the players. The camera can be used not only to confirm a ruled decision but to make one. During the 1974 NFL play-offs, the most memorable and spectacular play was the controversial last minute catch of a deflected pass by Pittsburgh Steeler Franco Harris. To be legal, the ball had to touch an opposing player between the initial contact with the intended Steeler receiver and Harris. The referee was not quite sure: he ran to the sidelines to confer with relay men in contact with the television production box. For the first time in media sport history, instant replay and slow motion techniques were used to confirm the officials' decision.

Despite agitation from many coaches, including Woody Hayes, to make regular use of instant replays for officiating purposes, the issue has not yet been seriously discussed.[18] In fact, arenas such as Capital Center in the

Washington, D.C. area which are equipped with telescreens for instant replay purposes generally refrain from replaying controversial calls by the referees.[19]

On the other hand, in 1973 the American Horse Shows Association introduced an experimental system for judging dressage championships. The system involved the video-taping of events at locations around the country and submitting them for review to a panel of judges. The measure is intended to allow riders to compete without the inconvenience and expense of transporting horses across country.[20]

Weibe[21] has attributed America's appetite for the media to the difficulty individuals find in trying to divest themselves of their fundamental egocentrism and acquire the concept of the "other". Their reluctance to deal with others is manifested in their susceptibility to the media. The media provides the illusion of interaction while actually removing the other and replacing it with "printed symbols of sounds or images, but never persons".[22] Perhaps this theory is personified by super spectator.

Followed to an extreme, this high information/low interaction orientation results in studio sport. Studio sport or scripted sport would eliminate all chance elements and all integrative aspects of sport contests. All that would remain would be the distillation of the contest, the result and the data. Sport, like the entertainment product it is, would become an athletic "Playhouse 90", with the Super Bowl featured as "Masterpiece Theatre". Plays would be repeated until the perfect take had been satisfactorily accomplished. Several examples can be cited which indicate that this orientation to sport is not as unrealistic as one might suppose.

To some extent, television already controls important game elements such as time outs. One special individual is designated to walk along the sidelines and signal the referee when the station needs time for a commercial.[23] Often these arbitrary interruptions can work to the detriment of a team. When Bill Russell was player-coach of the Celtics, he was once fined for refusing to call time out for the broadcasters because his team was enjoying the momentum of a catch-up victory and he realized that an interruption at that point could cost him the game.[24] The extreme of this sort of manipulation occurred during the 1967 Super Bowl when the half time kick and return were replayed because the audience had been detained by a commercial message.[25] Who knows how the live audience dealt with their bewilderment at the repetition.

Evidence to support a trend toward "process theatre" is examplified in the coverage of the USC-UCLA football game in 1974. During one running play, one instant replay camera followed USC back Anthony Davis to the line where the second camera smoothly picked up the coverage. The resulting spliced tape was highly effective and similar to techniques presently being used by sport movie producers.

In another instance, television producers restaged the start of a 500 meter swimming event they were taping because the cameras had missed the real thing. The staged start was then spliced in with the footage of the actual race.[26]

Another piece of evidence supporting a belief in the increasing focus of media sport is the increasing use made by fans of hotter media to supplement or replace their media sport experiences. The increased portability of electric media makes this more commonplace every day. Thus those in the stands often bring along a portable television so they can "see, the game better", while those who watch the game on television at home are apt to turn down the television audio and listen to the broadcast on the radio.

Clearly the fan who uses supplemental media is demanding more input. This could lead to a more diffused experience (in fact, that argument is propounded below). But in most cases, the fan uses a hotter, more focused medium to provide the information lacking in the cooler experience. Thus even in a situation in which the potential for diffusion is high, the media fan relies increasingly on hot, focused media.

In some situations, the fan's options are limited for him. An example can be drawn from the sky boxes in the Astrodome in Houston. Because the ridiculous distance from the live action all but prohibits the box owner from viewing the sporting event, box owners are virtually forced to watch the closed circuit broadcast of the live event in order to follow the game. Those who purchase skybox tickets are thus virtually forced to trade the cool media experience of watching the game itself for the hotter experience of television.

Moreover, a startling finding by Comisky et al[27] reveals that sport spectators are more attuned to the commentary of the announcers than to the visual portion of the game. In fact, in actual segments of a hockey broadcast devoid of exciting play, viewers were easily convinced by the announcer that they were watching a fiercely competitive game. In contrast, a more action-filled segment of the game was judged less exciting by the viewers because the announcers let the action speak for itself and offered little dramatic commentary. It would seem that when the information gained from one medium conflicts with that offered by another, the spectator relies more heavily upon the sense most attuned to hotter messages – the ear.

On the other hand, perhaps Americans are still captivated by sport on television only because a cooler medium has not yet presented itself. Future developments in television or in other media used to cover sport events might provide a more diffuse and demanding experience for the spectator.

Forty years ago, essayist E.B. White speculated about the Sport experience of the future. His concept of sport in the future was a totally diffuse one: "Not only did sport proliferate but the demands it made on the spectator became greater. Nobody was content to take in one event at a time, and thanks to the magic of radio and television nobody had to".[28] White illustrates the development of media sport through a super spectator who sits in the stands viewing the Yale-Cornell football game while simultaneously listening to the radio broadcast of the World Series from New York, monitoring the horse race presented on video sets located at either goal line, and glancing occasionally at the scores of other major or minor sporting contests being constantly revised by skywriters. "The effect of this vast cyclorama of sport was to divide the spectator's attention over-subtilize his appreciation, and deaden his passion'".[29]

Aldous Huxley's conception of the "feelies", his medium of the future, is in many ways similar. Apparently no senses are left unstimulated by the future total-experience medium. Society has progressed through an oral and a visual stage. Soon taste, feel and smell will also be incorporated, or as Huxley advertises: "Three Weeks in a Helicopter, an All-Super Singing, Synthetic-Talking, Coloured, Stereoscopic Feely. With Synchronized Scent-Organ Accompaniment".[30]

Amusing as their ideas must have seemed years ago. White and Huxley have proved to be accurate prophets. "Sensurround", the cinema technique used to enhance the viewers's experience of Earthquake and Midway, is the first step in the direction of Huxley's "feelies", and some practices and innovations can be cited as evidence of White's perceptiveness, e.g., the fan who buys two televisions so he can watch two sport programs at once. Charles Sopkin[31] experienced the ultimate in this regard. He closeted himself in a room with seven televisions, each tuned to a different network, and monitored all for "seven glorious days, seven fun-filled nights".

Wherever possible, the media keeps pace with demands for media variety. Telescreen, the huge replay screen in the Capital Center, makes it possible to fulfill White's predictions, for it is not limited to replaying action occurring on the floor below but might be used to broadcast another game altogether.

Similarly, because of a contract conflict during the 1973 season, CBS found itself in the unwitting position of presenting to its viewers their most diffuse sport experience to date. The lifting of the blackout required CBS to broadcast into the Oakland area both the Detroit – San Francisco and the Giants – Raiders games in the same time slot.

> The network does not plan to let momentum govern its coverage staying with long drives and periodic swingbacks. Instead it plans constant changing to show as much action as possible just as dial switchers of the past did before affluence led to two television set families and the piggyback concept.[32]

The best model of the super spectator of the future is the sport show producer. Anyone who has seen Two Minute Warning would have to be impressed by the cacophony and confusion of the sport producer's world. Seated in a control booth, he continually monitors the image from each camera being used while receiving a constant relay of information through an earphone. His function is to predigest sport for the viewer. He determines when to insert instant replay and which camera's image gives the most effective picture. It is he who sees the diffusion and makes the focus decision. He is perhaps the only person for whom the media sport experience matches the live event in terms of diffusion. Roone Arledge is the archtype of the media man of the future.

## Notes

1. Marshall McLuhan, Understanding Media (New York: New American Library, 1964), p. 36.
2. Ibid., pp. 211–212.
3. See Ron Fimrite, "Grand New Game", Sports Illustrated, August 11, 1975, pp. 10–13.
4. McLuhan, p. 212.
5. Ibid.
6. Ibid., p. 23.
7. Ibid., p. 278.
8. The prominence of sport on television probably requires little documentation. However, it might be noted that well over 1000 television broadcast hours per week are devoted to sport (Edvertising Age, October 22, 1973); that a record 76 million Americans tuned in the last game of the 1976 World Series (James P. Forkan, "Nets, Sponsors Ready to Play Ball", Advertising Age, March 15, 1976, p. 84); that the rights to broadcast the Olympic Games rose over 300 per cent, from $25 million in 1976 to $85 milion in 1980 (William Leggett, "Commercializing the Games", Sports Illustrated, August 9, 1976, p. 47; William Oscar Johnson, "A Contract with the Kremlin", Sports Illustrated, February 21, 1977, pp. 14–19); that television revenues for major team sports have risen 1000 per cent in the past twenty years (Ira Horowitz, "Sports Telecasts", Journal of Communication, Vol. 27, 1977, p. 160); that cost per minute for advertising during the Super Bowl in 1979 will be $350,000 (James P. Forkan, "Football Ad Prices Way Up", Advertising Age, January 16, 1978, p. 2); and that reliable sources estimate that the rights to telecast NFL contests during 1978–1981 will cost about $640 million (Forkan, 1978, p. 2).
9. McLuhan, p. 288.
10. Ibid., p. 261.
11. See William O. Johnson, Super Spectator and the Electric Lilliputans, (Boston: Little, Brown and Company, 1971).
12. See Brien R. Williams, "The Structure of Televised Football, Journal of Communication, Vol. 27, 1977, pp. 136–137, for a similar view.
13. Again Williams (Ibid.) reflects the same idea when he contrasts "stadium event" to the "medium event".
14. Orrin E. Dunlop, Jr., New York Times, May 21, 1939 as quoted in Johnson, Super Spectator, p. 39.
15. Stephen Kanfer, "Football: Show Business with a Kick", Time, October 8, 1973, pp. 54–55
16. "Retarded Live Television, New York Times, April 14, 1973, p. 43.
17. Ibid.
18. Sports Illustrated has argued for the use of TV cameras to make officiating decisions. See "Scorecard: Eye in the Storm", November 18, 1974, p. 26; "Scorecard: Delayed Relay", January 12, 1976, p. 6; and "Scorecard: Seeing is Believing", January 2, 1978, p. 7.
19. Peter Carry, "Big New E for Big New Eye", Sports Illustrated, March 11, 1974, p. 16.
20. "Video-Tape Helps Judges Pick Dressage Champion", New York Times, December 16, 1974, p. 73.

21. Gerhart D. Weibe, "Two Psychological Factors in Media Audience Behavior", in Alan Wells, Mass Media and Society (Palo Alto: National Press Book, 1972), pp. 208–217.
22. Ibid., p. 210.
23. William Leggett, "Stop the Game, I Want to Go On", Sport Illustrated, October 21, 1974, p. 73.
24. "TV Influences Sport", Newsweek, June 5, 1967, p. 66.
25. Johnson, Super Spectator, p. 59.
26. Leonard Shecter, The Jocks (New York: Paperback Library, 1969), p. 86.
27. Paul Comisky, Jennings Bryant, and Dolf Zillmann, "Commentary as a Substitute for Action", Journal of Communication, Vol. 27, 1977, pp. 150–153.
28. E.B. White, "The Decline of Sport", Second Tree from the Corner (New York: Harper and Row, 1954), p. 41.
29. Ibid., p. 42.
30. Aldous Huxley, Brave New World (New York: Bantam, 1932), p. 113.
31. Charles Sopkin, Seven Glorious Days, Seven Fun-Filled Nights (New York: Ace Publishing, 1968).
32. Jack Craig, "CBS Juggling Act", Boston Sunday Globe, November 4, 1973, p. 88.

# 4

# From Our Gaelic Fields: Radio, Sport and Nation in Post-Partition Ireland

*Raymond Boyle*

## Introduction

A nation is made from within itself; it is made first of all from its language, if it has one, by its music, songs, games and customs . . . we desire to especially emphasise what we have derived from our Gaelic ancestors – from one of the oldest civilisations in Europe . . . (Extract from the opening speech given on Irish radio [2RN] by Dr Douglas Hyde, January 1926, quoted in O ceallachain, 1988)

This article will examine the important role that media coverage of sport played in the legitimation of the post-1922 Irish Free State, and in particular the ability of radio to transform and construct sporting activity into symbolic national events which perform a wider political and ideological function. Sports coverage played a key role in the formative years of Irish broadcasting. The selective treatment given by radio to specific sporting events not only helped to amplify their importance, but actually played a central role in creating national events and organizations. The relationship between the broadcasters and the Gaelic Athletic Association (GAA) is examined with regard to the medium's role in promoting both this organization, and its specific view of what constituted 'legitimate' Irish cultural activity: activity that would find specific political connotations attached to it in a partitioned Ireland.

Sport supposedly has the ability to bring together people from different religious, ethnic and class backgrounds. In reality, sporting activity also has

**Source:** *Media, Culture & Society*, 14(4) (1992): 623–636.

the ability to reinforce, and even institutionalize, prejudices. It can act as a focal point in both asserting and creating a collective identity which inevitably excludes others. Though today television is the dominant medium for the presentation of sport, sixty or seventy years ago radio and the press played crucial roles in the development of sport both at national and international levels. I stress the important interrelationship that exists between radio and newspapers in helping to construct *national* pastimes. They transform sport from a simple rule-governed game into a tangible activity which can generate a degree of collective sensibility that in turn helps to legitimize more abstract political structures such as 'state' and 'nation'. This article places both the media and sporting activity (which have become increasingly interlinked), within a framework of reference that highlights the centrality of political and economic factors in the shaping of this relationship. It also opens up the more general debate which revolves around the relationship between the media, sport and national representations and identities.

## Broadcasting to the Gaelic Nation

Nation and state need each other: the nation needs the power of the state, the state needs the community of the nation. (Cronin, 1980: 3)

The role of broadcasting in Ireland can only be understood by examining the socio-political environment in which it was conceived. The formation of the 26-county Irish Free State in 1922 had not been uniformly accepted by all nationalists. The republican element was dismayed at the failure to secure and consolidate the unitary nation-state. The influence of cultural nationalism was such that it was broadly accepted that as the Gaelic nation had always existed, it was only the political state that remained to be forged. This perception of the antecedent nation would help shape the cultural policy of the new state, specifically with regard to broadcasting. The role of the state was to be one of protecting the 'nation' so that the indigenous cultural energies of the nation would be provided with channels through which they could freely flow. It was the state that required immediate attention. As Hutchinson notes: 'The aim of cultural nationalists is rather the moral regeneration of the historic community . . . Since a civilisation is a spontaneous social order, it cannot be constructed like a state from above but only resuscitated from the bottom up' (Hutchinson, 1987: 16). This resuscitation would also reflect the religious composition of the state, and the influence of the Catholic Church over the new political structures.

The prominence of official nationalism in post-partition Ireland was at the expense of the separatist tradition which had been responsible for the creation of the state itself. In part this process was legitimized by its connecting with the Gaelic literary tradition that had also influenced the separatist movement. Allied with this was the Church's rejection of English popular cultural activity which it viewed both as anti-Christian and as part of an insidious anglicization process.

The Church's reaction to what it saw as the undermining of the Gaelic nation (and thus its power base), coincided with the political needs of the new state to assert its independence, political strength and identity on an international stage. This expression of an insular, protectionist view of Irish culture found its clearest political articulation in the Fianna Fáil governments under Eamon de Valera during the 1932–47 period. He strove on a broad front to pursue the regeneration of the Irish nation through his domestic policies. A state-regulated system of broadcasting was in place by the 1930s whose organization and programme policies were in turn influenced by the nation-state assumptions discussed above, as well as the realization of the economic limitations of the Irish post-colonial economy.

The economy of the Irish Free State after 1922 was shaped by the structural weakness of native capital. When allied with the post-colonial dependent nature of economic development in Ireland, it becomes evident that these factors played a key role in determining the nature of the broadcasting structures that evolved. As has been noted: 'It was in the context of political difficulties experienced by the native bourgeoisie in securing the legitimacy of the newly independent post-partition state in the 1920s that a so called public service broadcasting system emerged' (Bell and Meehan, 1989: 92).

The need for the corporate state to intervene in the economy was consensually agreed upon and the new station was funded through a mixture of advertising revenue, licence fees and import duties on each radio receiver. However, in 1933, the then Minister of Finance Sean MacEntee redirected the import duties from wireless sales away from the broadcasters and to the exchequer. Two-thirds of the station's revenue was lost, and dependency on commercial advertising subsequently increased (Gorham, 1967; Gibbons, 1988).

At an ideological level, the institution of radio broadcasting was envisaged as a central instrument in both 'fostering' the native culture, as well as acting as an antidote to the 'harmful' characteristics of British popular culture. The term 'fostering' is crucial in understanding the role allocated to radio within the cultural domain of the state. Gibbons argues that 'the state derived its legitimacy from the existence of an antecedent nation, and thus the function of broadcasting was not to establish but to revitalise this nation, realising the cultural energies which, it was believed, had accumulated over centuries' (Gibbons, 1988: 222).

Thus while the legislation which brought 2RN into existence in 1926 emphasized the importance of its role in promoting 'national culture', the subsequent lack of funding by the state was to prove inconsistent with its intended aims. While public service broadcasting in Britain was initially funded by the licence fee to free it from the taint of commerce, the Irish State believed that, as the 'national culture' was organically embedded in the hearts and minds of the Irish people, there was no obvious reason why related radio output wouldn't be popular and thus capable of being funded by commercial (advertising) means. What you had in Ireland was a state-controlled public service broadcasting infrastructure (Irish broadcasting was in fact an extension of the civil service, specifically the Department of Post and Telegraphs) which, through lack of state funding, found itself dependent on commercial advertising.

It is against this backdrop that we examine the relationship between the media and sport in post-partition Ireland. The economic protectionist policies of the Fianna Fáil governments during the 1930s and 1940s were part of a wider project to regenerate a Gaelic civilization that wished to sever its cultural links with Britain. In this process the Catholic Church would play a central role in defining the cultural parameters of the nation. This intertwining of Catholicism and cultural nationalism was such that 'cultural life in the new state was dominated by a vision of Ireland, inherited from the period of the Literary Revival, as a rural gaelic civilisation that retained an ancient pastoral distinctiveness' (Brown, 1981: 98).

Gaelic games were one such cultural site on which Irish ethnic distinctiveness could be expressed. The Gaelic Athletic Association (GAA), created in 1884, was one manifestation of the 'new nationalism' of the latter part of the nineteenth century (Foster, 1988; Mandle, 1987). It took elements of games long forgotten, codified them and placed them within an organizational and institutional structure which forbade the playing or watching of 'foreign games'. By the 1920s and 1930s it had become one of the cultural vehicles used to express popular nationalist sentiment. It was one of the things that made Ireland *different* from Britain.

The GAA's stronghold was in the rural heartland. In part through radio coverage it was *rural* aspects of cultural activity (such as Gaelic games), that became the dominant internal as well as external image of the country, despite the inconsistencies inherent in such a discourse (like the fact that a sizeable section of the population lived in urban areas such as Cork and Dublin). Sport became an arena in which 'Irishness' could be asserted. Gaelic games were projected as the antithesis of the urban industrial sports of the British, particularly soccer. They were Irish, rural and celebrated the moral worth of the peasant but, as in other areas of cultural activity, the legacy of British rule could be seen even in such a quintessentially nationalist organization. Gaelic games promoted manliness, athletic prowess and the importance of rule-governed activity, just as Victorian sporting organizations did in Britain. As Mandle comments, 'popular culture everywhere made strikingly similar demands of its games, and elicited strikingly similar responses that had particular national variations but an unchanging core' (Mandle, 1983: 115). Radio played a central role in the process of building Gaelic games into national events.

## Radio, Sport and Nation

In post-colonial Ireland, radio's cultural role was shaped by the continual need of the state to assert its political independence and acquire a legitimate power base. Radio sport became an important area in the development of national activities that the state seemingly presided over. The specific characteristics of radio broadcasting, its immediacy and 'actuality' quality, when allied with the nature of live spectator sport, proved to be a popular substitute with listeners unable to attend the live event. The siting of the receiver within the domestic environment also connected with that family and home-centred pattern of cultural activity encouraged by the Catholic Church.

Irish radio took elements from both the public service and the commercial models of broadcasting. Sport was popular and allowed the station to fulfil its wider cultural remit. The fostering of national cohesion was not, however, the sole prerogative of the radio. The developments in mass schooling, the national press and the expanding transport system were all crucial in this process. When radio's immediacy, 'actuality' quality and ability to eradicate distance was combined with its domestic location it found itself playing a particularly central role in the process of nation-building.

A crucial point is the mediating role played by radio. Radio is not a neutral agency that simply relays the event to the listening audience. It is an active process that alters the relationship between spectator and event. The listener doesn't see the game (naturally), but is given a verbal image of the sport. In other words a feeling of what the game is, its significance and substance, is transmitted via the medium. Unlike the printed medium, radio is immediate and 'real': sport as it happens. Spatial distance from the event is eroded, and the listener is transported in imagination to another part of the country, as part of a wider imagined community (Anderson, 1983). In Ireland, such was the scarcity of receivers, especially in rural areas, that communal gatherings in 'wireless' households or even in town centres for specific broadcasts were a frequent occurrence. The All-Ireland hurling final between Kerry and Kildare in 1926 was one of the very first sporting events in Europe to be given live coverage on radio. In Tralee, Co. Kerry, a crowd of about a thousand people gathered in the main street to listen to the match:

> At half time and with things looking blue for Kerry, every man, woman and child in the crowd marched on to St John's church nearby and said the rosary for a good result. They weren't let down and the perception that football is a para-religious ideology in Kerry is backed by a long tradition. (O ceallachain, 1988: 209–10)

The creation through this communal experience, allied with the nationwide audience construction of the actual sporting commentary, helped to provide a lived, shared experience. As Hall comments:

> This is the first of the great cultural functions of the modern media: the provision and the selective construction of *social knowledge,* of social imagery, through which we perceive the 'worlds', the 'lived realities' of others, and imaginarily reconstruct their lives and ours into some intelligible 'world-of-the-whole', some 'lived totality'. (Hall, 1977: 340–1)

Radio did not simply relay the games to the audience, but played a key role in helping to *construct* and *amplify* them to a central position within what seemingly constituted a national culture. In so doing radio helped *make* the GAA a truly symbolic national organization in the minds of its listeners. This was achieved not just through the intrinsic qualities of the games them-selves, but by the building and fostering (through the mediating process of radio) of identities and social groupings based around the parish, the county and ultimately the country.

This process involved the developing of a common national memory. Great games and players became ingrained in the national psyche. In Ireland the coverage of what were presented as being the 'native games' of the coun-try was increasingly mediated by the voice of one individual: Micheal O'Hehir. Tim Pat Coogan, in discussing his disappointment at finding out what it was like to attend an All-Ireland final 'live', as opposed to listening to it on the radio, noted that 'Micheal O'Hehir had made it all seem much more patriotic, large-scale, significant somehow' (Coogan, 1976: 52). This is a typical reac-tion of people whose sole access to the sporting event was through the medium of radio. The role of O'Hehir in transforming the games into events was important, and his voice became synonymous with Gaelic games as he helped popularize the radio broadcasts.

Coverage of Gaelic games was seen to be of paramount importance to the GAA who, as custodians of Ireland's 'native games', expected a new Irish medium to devote substantial time to these activities. Indeed such was the powerful position of the organization that it also wanted to tell 2RN who could and could not commentate on its matches. Between 1933 and 1937, the two organizations remained at loggerheads over the situation, which resulted in a number of matches not being covered. By 1938, with the arrival of Micheal O'Hehir, the situation calmed and radio projected Gaelic games to a new national audience.

In 1930 the launch of a Sunday night sports programme provided the GAA with a national platform for its activities and from this moment GAA results were carried on the radio. But tension between the GAA and the broadcasters again came to the fore when soccer results were carried alongside those of the organization. This seemed particularly provocative to the GAA which banned its members from playing or even watching 'foreign games'. The GAA felt that it was not receiving the coverage from radio that it deserved. In fact the initial Director of 2RN was a Gaelic reviv-alist, Seamus Clandillon, who encouraged coverage of Irish music as well as sport. However broadcasting continued to find itself involved in battles with an organization that had difficulty in appreciating the key role that radio played in its growth.[1]

In 1954 Radio Eireann (formerly 2RN) had planned to broadcast two major sports events on St Patrick's Day. One was the GAA Railway Cup Finals (Irish football and hurling), the other was a soccer international between

Ireland and Scotland. Both were being played in Dublin. To carry them, Radio Eireann was carrying the Gaelic games on its stronger Athlone wavelength, while the soccer match was to be relayed via Dublin and Cork (this emphasized the rural/urban split in the popularity of the sports). However, events were complicated by the fact that the hurling match, which was being broadcast in English, would also be relayed to an audience in Africa via Radio Brazzaville.[2]

With a 15-minute interval due in the hurling match it was proposed that this valuable broadcasting time could be utilized by relaying a quarter of an hour of the soccer match. When the GAA heard of what was to happen they reacted sharply. Its President, Mr M.V. O'Donoghue

> was reported as saying that this was an insult to the nation, a mockery of the GAA, an abrogation of nationality, and another winning attempt to give an imperialistic game a national complexion. Apparently it was considered undesirable to have it known outside Ireland that soccer was played in Dublin on St. Patrick's Day. (Gorham, 1967: 244)

As a result the GAA refused Radio Eireann the right to broadcast the hurling final, if soccer was to be carried in the same programme. The Director of Broadcasting decided not to cover the match.

## Our Daily Sport: Newspaper Coverage of Gaelic Games

Radio, of course, was not the only medium covering Gaelic sports in this period. The three national newspapers – the *Irish Independent, Irish Times* and *Irish Press* – also played a role in their promotion, though it was the *Press* that took the lead in these developments.

The *Irish (Daily) Independent* was a descendant of the Irish *Freeman's Journal* which had been broadly supportive of the old Irish parliamentary party. It was broadly conservative in editorial outlook, attracting a predominantly urban lower-middle-class readership. The political orientation of the Independent Newspapers Organization, which is supportive today of Fine Gael, could in the early years of the state be identified as pro-treaty and anti-republican in stance. The *Irish Times* was the voice of the protestant community in Ireland, thus finding its readership among the urban middle and upper classes, especially within the professional sector. The *Irish Press* was founded in 1931 by the leader of the Fianna Fáil party, Eamonn de Valera. The aim of the paper was to provide a platform for the views of the Fianna Fáil party, and particularly to articulate their brand of Irish republicanism. Much time had been spent in examining the techniques used in the newspaper industry abroad, with the American industry providing many of the ideas for the new paper. It was more populist in both layout and content than the other national dailies of the time, securing and helping to create a rural readership which to a large extent had been bypassed by the urban orientation of the *Times* and *Independent*. Both the political and class loyalties of these reading publics would be reflected in the nature of the coverage given to sport.

In quantitative terms, the *Irish Press* devoted more space to sport than any other Irish newspaper (see Table 1). It is important to note that in Britain during the 1930s sports coverage in the popular press played a vital role in attracting and helping to secure a readership in the newspaper circulation war. In Ireland, the popularity of the *Irish Press* was in part a result of its political affiliations, but also of its catering for an increasing public interest in sport, especially indigenous activity. It has been widely perceived that the *Irish Press* 'is credited with having given the first decent coverage in an Irish newspaper to Gaelic games' (Oram, 1983: 173).

There is no doubt that the *Press* did devote a large amount of space within its sports section to coverage of Gaelic games, with the paper providing more coverage of Irish sport than any other Irish national daily newspaper.[3] However, to view this in isolation gives a misleading picture. During the soccer season, the 'Irish Free State League' was extensively covered as were a host of other sports including horse racing, rugby, athletics and boxing. Thus while the *Irish Press* did improve the coverage given to Gaelic games, this was just a segment of their sports coverage and, as Gaelic games became more popular, partly due to press and particularly radio exposure, so the amount of space devoted to them in newspapers other than the *Irish Press* increased. While the press and radio initially saw themselves in competition with each other, it soon became obvious that interaction between them could be mutually beneficial. Newspapers increasingly provided the background information to sporting events that would be listened to on the radio.

It would be wrong to view the *Irish Press* as simply a Gaelic games sports paper. It gave better coverage to soccer and rugby than both the *Irish Independent* and the *Irish Times*. As the *Press* devoted proportionally more newspaper space to sport, it may be argued that regardless of the connotations associated with the sports covered, the editor realized that extensive sports coverage played an important part in selling newspapers. When attention is turned to the *Press's* treatment of Gaelic games, the process of nation-building becomes evident. What we see is an effort to construct, through language, a symbolic political and cultural entity: the Irish nation-state. The 'native

**Table 1:** Percentage of total newspaper space given to sports coverage during the period 1932–62

|  | *1932* | *1942* | *1952* | *1962* |
|---|---|---|---|---|
| *Irish Press* | 16–19% | 10–12% | 18–23% | 24–32% |
| *Irish Independent* | 12–16% | 5–8% | 12–16% | 14–18% |
| *Irish Times* | 10–12% | 5–8% | 12–15% | 16–18% |

games' of the country are portrayed as having always existed in their present form and of being part of a traditional culture. This regeneration of tradition, and the grafting of Gaelic games to this wider ideological construction of a Gaelic civilization, was one of the key mediating roles played by the press and radio during the 1930s and 1940s. Here was a youthful state, the cultural parameters of which were inexorably linked to an unbroken thread of customs and beliefs that stretched back into the past, and seemingly pointed the way to the future.

Tradition, as Hall argues, 'is a vital element in culture, but it has little to do with the mere persistence of old forms. It has much more to do with the way elements have been linked together or articulated. These arrangements in a national-popular culture have no fixed or inscribed position, and certainly no meaning that is carried along, so to speak, in the stream of historical tradition, unchanged' (Hall, 1981: 236). He also notes how these 'traditional elements' can be rearranged, even reinvented, 'so that they articulate with different practices and positions, and take on a new meaning and relevance' (Hall, 1981: 236). It can be argued that this was the case with the 'traditional sports'. Both the press and radio helped to establish and map out a tradition for Gaelic games, while at the same time being *active agencies* themselves in a process that was creating, reconstituting and perpetuating the mythological connotations associated with these activities. The interlinking of the press and radio in their coverage of sport was vital.

## The Press and Radio

The effects of radio and newspaper coverage of sport were twofold. They elevated awareness of sport while also contributing to the building of the country's national passion for sport. In the Irish Free State this role was given a cutting edge by the political and cultural overtones of a country going through the initial stages of transformation from a colony to post-colonial state. During the state-building years of the Fianna Fáil governments of the 1930s, and the associated economic problems that this entailed, sport was an important arena in which a collective-popular identity could be expressed. This nation-building, the cultivating of the individual sporting hero and the continual reconstruction of 'traditional' identities of parish and county, are just some of the dominant discourses that can be discerned in media coverage of Irish sport.

Radio and newspaper coverage of the 1932 Tailteann Games, for example, provided an opportunity to integrate domestic Irish sport with that of other nations through an international Gaelic cultural festival. The following extract from the *Press* gives a flavour of the emphasis that it placed on the international nature of Gaelic sport and culture. When Ireland played an American select team at Gaelic football it was headlined as 'America's Football Challenge', and the paper went on to declare that

> The football challenge which this third Tailteann Games has brought
> to the worth of native football at Croke Park tomorrow has aroused the
> interest and attention of all Ireland . . . We are confident in the freshness
> and fitness of Ireland's selection to maintain our supremacy against the
> world. (9 July 1932)

Such was the 'unity' of the Gaelic world, that the paper could extend a warm
welcome to a touring South African hurling team as 'Our Gaelic Friends from
South Africa' (22 July 1932). In reality Gaelic games are not international
sports, unlike the colonially planted games of soccer and rugby, but an event
such as the Tailteann Games created the illusion that Ireland's Gaelic influence knew no geopolitical boundaries.

In partitioned Ireland, the question of cultural and political boundaries
was particularly pertinent. In the Northern Ireland state, the 'foreign' nationalism of the south was refracted in part through the Unionist newspapers,
and the reporting of sporting issues was one area through which this process
took place. The removal, in 1938, of President Douglas Hyde from the list of
GAA patrons by that organization on the grounds that he had attended a soccer match between Ireland and Poland gave *The Northern Whig* (21 December
1938) the opportunity to emphasize to its readers the extent to which 'the
Gaelic Athletic Association was

> symptomatic of the spirit of primitive tribalism that passes currently for
> enlightened nationalism in Southern Ireland. It is a travesty of patriotism
> and of culture; it engenders sectional hatreds, restricts and distorts the
> outlook of thousands and makes its advocates the laughing stock of more
> advanced and progressive nations. (Kennedy, 1988: 229)

## The 'Golden Age' of Gaelic Sport

The period from the 1930s through to the 1960s has fuelled a retrospective
proliferation of books, television programmes, newspaper articles and the
like that have all charted, and in their own uncritical way, propagated the
nostalgic recreation of a 'golden past': an era of great games and great individual players etched in the collective memory of the nation. The media of
the period played a central role in this process. They also helped develop the
cult of the sporting hero, as well as defining regional identities and characteristics. On radio, Micheal O'Hehir became synonymous with Gaelic games
and Irish sport.

As radio listening gained in popularity its sporting output increased and
diversified. In 1949 *Sports Stadium* was launched, providing a weekly roundup of views and reports that became a regular feature of the Radio Eireann
programmes (Gorham, 1967: 185). The relationship between radio and the
press also became increasingly interactive during this period. The 1947
All-Ireland final was held in the Polo Grounds, New York, with Radio Eireann

relaying the match live in Ireland. The game has become ingrained in the national-popular sporting memory of the country. It emphasized the symbolic links between Ireland and America, and the important role that Gaelic games played in the culture of the expatriate Irish: a little bit of Ireland in a foreign land. Micheal O'Hehir, reporting from New York, had promised the listeners that 'It will be a great day for the Irish over here and I trust the radio will make it so for the folks back at home' (*Radio Review*, 13–19 September 1947). The first radiowave photograph that was sent across the Atlantic was of the 1947 match. The action photograph appeared the following morning in the *Irish Press*. According to the *Radio Review* (20–26 September 1947), it gave 'a home touch to the historic game taking place so far away'. It was a match that helped to deepen the sense of national belonging for all Irish people, wherever they resided, as they 'took part' in the event via radio and the press.

## Conclusion

The mediation of sport by radio and the press was part of a wider consensus-building project which helped facilitate and consolidate the socially conservative strand of nationalism which the state embodied up to the 1960s. Through both the press and radio, a self-image of the country was held up that emphasized that Irish culture was not only rich in regional variation but that, through its sporting traditions, Ireland was a nation bound together by a common sense of collective identity.

The language used to describe sport, be it on radio or in the press, was the language of totalities. 'We', 'our' and so on all encouraged the individual listener or reader to identify with the event as one member of a wider national community. Media sport was an uncritical projection of what Irish culture supposedly was and what it was not. It was a process of cultural *exclusion* as much as *inclusion*. Gaelic games were one of the things that made the Irish different. To view this complex process as solely media imposed is of course too simplistic. Communal identities are lived out in language and actual social relations and not simply dumped upon the recipients by the ubiquitous media.

Radio, through its mediation of Gaelic sport, helped to give shape to the character of the rural community. The emphasis on parish and county, and the identification of individual star players from particular parishes was important.[4] There was also a clear gender division in the media coverage of sport. Sport was a male-dominated cultural activity in Ireland. Women were not encouraged to participate, and the media coverage given to camogie was scant in comparison to the resources devoted to male sports. Connotations of manliness were inscribed both in the written and spoken coverage of sport. This reflected the prevailing social attitudes towards the role of women in society, which were heavily shaped by the Catholic Church. Indeed, sport played an important role in the process of reproducing and naturalizing the gender divisions that existed in society, a usage of sport not unique to Ireland. It helped to perpetuate the view that a woman's role in society was essentially passive, and certainly not one that allowed her to express herself on the sports field.

The links between the political elite and sport has a long history that is not of direct concern here. What is of interest is the way that radio has taken aspects of sporting competition and reconstituted them into a wider cultural and ideological construction of national stability. The pinnacle of the Gaelic games season is the All-Ireland Hurling and Football finals that take place in Croke Park during September which has been, and continues to be, an occasion that radio portrays as the coming together of the Irish nation to participate in its national games. In the absence of royal patronage, as in the English Cup Final, there is the presence of an array of dignitaries including the President, the Taoiseach, leading members of the Catholic Church and members of the main political parties. The pageantry of the pre-match band and the playing of the national anthem all help to create a concrete image of a national community.

As I have argued, the press and particularly radio mediate, legitimize and amplify aspects of this complex process that symbolically unites the rural and urban community, as well as pulling together the cultural nation around a focus of national stability. Through mediatized sporting rituals a feeling of history and unbroken tradition is invoked: a national way of life. As Chaney notes: 'Rituals are a representation of the collectivity, a collective performance in which certain significant aspects of social relationships are given symbolic form and force' (Chaney, 1986: 122).

In the Republic of Ireland radio coverage of national sporting events provided an arena through which nationalistic feelings could be vented in an unproblematic manner. Sport seemed to provide an essentially 'safe' channel of national self-expression: 'safe' in terms of political stability because it tended to mask the political and structural changes that needed to occur within the whole of Ireland if subordinate groups were to exercise more power over their own lives. While not advocating a 'bread and circuses' scenario, it is important to understand the role the media played in constructing sport as part of a national psyche that ultimately reinforced the dominant political system.

The historic role of radio and the press in transforming specific sporting events into national and political ritual is, of course, not unique to Ireland. What I have argued here is that the media played a key role not simply in relaying a popular cultural activity but, as active agencies, shaped and restructured for readers and listeners their understanding of the character of sporting events. In Ireland this process was influenced by the specific prevailing political and economic forces. Almost seventy years after the foundation of the state, and within different political and economic parameters, the media, through its interaction with both domestic and international sport, is still playing a key role in the ongoing process of national identity formation.

## Notes

1. An example of this can be seen in a recent GAA history which gives radio barely a passing reference (de Burca, 1980).
2. This station was based in the French Congo, and Radio Eireann material was relayed thanks to an arrangement with the French national broadcasting service RTF. This situation had come about partly through the lobbying by Irish missionaries in Africa who wished to be kept in touch with what was happening in Ireland.
3. Ironically neither the paper's sports editor nor deputy editor were Irish. Joe Sherwood was English and Herbert Moxley was Welsh, both having a proven track record in knowing what was needed in sports coverage to sell newspapers.
4. The role of the provincial press was particularly important in this respect. Again little critical work has been done in this area of sports journalism and its function at a community level in helping to focus attention on the local Gaelic football and hurling teams.

## Bibliography

Anderson, B. (1983) *Imagined Communities: Reflections on the Origins and Spread of Nationalism.* London: Verso.

Bell, D. and N. Meehan (1989) 'Cable, Satellite and the Emergence of Private TV in Ireland: From Public Service to Managed Monopoly', *Media, Culture and Society*, 11(1): 89–114.

Brecht, B. (1979/80) 'Radio as a Means of Communication: A Talk on the Function of Radio', *Screen*, 20(3–4).

Brown, T. (1981) *Ireland: A Social and Cultural History 1922–1979.* Glasgow: Fontana.

Cardiff, D. and P. Scannell (1987) 'Broadcasting and National Unity', in J. Curran et al. (eds), *Impact and Influences: Essays on Media Power in the Twentieth Century.* London: Methuen.

Chaney, D. (1986) 'The Symbolic Form of Ritual in Mass Communication', in P. Golding et al. (eds), *Communicating Politics.* Leicester: Leicester University Press.

Coogan, T.P. (1976) 'An Old Lady and Her Pupils', in L. McRedmond (ed.), *Written on the Wind.* Dublin: RTE/Gill and Macmillan.

Cronin, S. (1980) *Irish Nationalism: A History of its Roots and Ideology.* Dublin: Academy Press.

de Burca, M. (1980) *The GAA. A History.* Dublin: Cumann Luthchleas Gael.

Fisher, D. (1978) *Broadcasting in Ireland.* London: Routledge & Kegan Paul.

Foster, R.F. (1988) *Modern Ireland, 1600–1972.* London: Allen Lane.

Gibbons, L. (1988) 'From Megalith to Megastore: Broadcasting and Irish Culture', in T. Bartlett, C. Curtin et al. (eds), *Irish Studies.* Dublin: Gill and Macmillan.

Goldlust, J. (1987) *Playing For Keeps. Sport, the Media and Society.* Melbourne: Longman Cheshire.

Gorham, M. (1967) *Forty Years of Irish Broadcasting.* Dublin: Talbot Press.

Hall, S. (1977) 'Culture, the Media and the Ideological Effect', in J. Curran et al. (eds), *Mass Communication and Society.* London: Edward Arnold.

Hall, S. (1981) 'Notes on Deconstructing the Popular', in R. Samuel (ed.), *People's History and Socialist Theory.* London: Routledge & Kegan Paul.

Hall, S. (1986) 'Popular Culture and the State', in T. Bennett et al. (eds), *Popular Culture and Social Relations.* Milton Keynes: Open University Press.

Hutchinson, J. (1987) *The Dynamics of Cultural Nationalism: The Gaelic Revival and the Creation of the Irish Nation-State.* London: Allen & Unwin.

Kennedy, D. (1988) *The Widening Gulf: Northern Attitudes to the Independent Irish State.* Belfast: Blackstaff.

Mandle, W.F. (1983) 'The Gaelic Athletic Association and Popular Culture, 1884–1924', in O. McDonagh, W.F. Mandle and P. Travers (eds), *Irish Culture and Nationalism, 1750–1950*. London: Macmillan.

Mandle, W.F. (1987) *The Gaelic Athletic Association and Irish Nationalist Politics 1884–1924*. Dublin: Gill and Macmillan.

Meehan, N. and Bell, D. (1986) 'Public Service versus the Market. A False Polarity? The Case of Irish Broadcasting', Paper presented to the International Television Studies Conference, British Film Institute, London.

O ceallachain, S. (1988) *Sean Og: His Own Story*. Dublin: Brophy Books.

Oram, H. (1983) *The Newspaper Book: A History of Newspaper in Ireland*. Dublin: Mo Books.

Thomas, A. (1980) *Broadcast and be Damned*. Melbourne: Melbourne University Press.

Tierney, M. (1984) 'The Public and Private Image of the GAA – A Centenary Appraisal', *The Crane Bag, Media and Popular Culture*, 8(2).

# 5

# Drama in Sports Commentary

## Jennings Bryant, Paul Comisky and Dolf Zillmann

*A content analysis of sportscasters' description
of football action reveals that a sizable portion
is devoted to a dramatic embellishment of the game.*

As the prominence of television in the lives of Americans has steadily increased since its introduction a little more than a quarter century ago, so has the place of sports on television. For example, total sports telecasts by the three major networks increased by almost fifty percent from 1971 to 1975, resulting in a total of 505 sportscasts for 1082 hours of television time during the 1975 season (4). These numerous hours of sports spectaculars hardly go untended. Out of A. C. Nielsen's total audience estimates for all-time favorite television programs through mid-1976, 6 of the top 10, and 15 of the top 25 attractions (60 percent) were sports contests (4). This huge following for televised sports has led one sports analyst, using the vernacular of the medium itself, to label the mass audience for electronic athletics "Super Spectator" (3).

Whereas Super Jock has received considerable attention from professional students of human nature (e.g., 1, 2), Super Spectator has rather successfully eluded the eye of social and behavioral scientists. Moreover, very little serious attention has been given to some rather important features of the electronic diet on which he thrives. For example, although it would initially seem that the fan in the stadium would become more thoroughly engrossed in the athletic competition than the fan at home because of the heightened emotional reactivity that may result from crowd involvement

**Source:** *Journal of Communication*, 27(3) (1977): 140–149.

through social facilitation processes (6), it may be that dramatic embellishments from professional television commentators may more than substitute for the "human drama of athletic competition" that the television spectator misses by not being in the sports arena. Indeed, initial investigations suggest that dramatic commentary can have a substantial effect on the perception and appreciation of a broadcast game.

*The present investigation was designed to determine*
*what dramatic features are used by professional sportscasters*
*to enlighten the television sports fan*
*and add excitement to the weekly sports viewing fare.*

Since professional football typically receives more coverage (80 network telecasts in 1975) than any other single sports event and tends to attract a larger audience than other sportscasts (an average audience of 16.3 percent of U.S. television households in 1975) (4), this research examines coverage of professional football exclusively.

A systematic content analysis was conducted on six professional football games telecast over a three week period during the 1976 season. Two games from each major network were analyzed. The games were: San Francisco Forty-Niners vs. Los Angeles Rams (ABC), New England Patriots vs. New York Jets (ABC), Dallas Cowboys vs. Chicago Bears (CBS), Philadelphia Eagles vs. Minnesota Vikings (CBS), Miami Dolphins v. Baltimore Colts (NBC), and Dallas Cowboys vs. New York Giants (NBC).

The analysis assessed the proportion of commentary devoted to description of play versus dramatic or humorous enrichments. The dramatic commentary was further examined to determine the extent to which the announcers relied on derogation or praise to accomplish their goals. Another interest included assessment of the forces depicted as being in conflict. More specifically, it was determined whether the announcers relied on team, interpersonal, or intrapersonal conflict in their dramatic commentary. And finally, the dramatic references were categorized according to the dramatic motif involved.

In each of these analyses, the commentary of all of the six games combined was initially examined to give a more general, comprehensive picture of network coverage of professional football. Second, comparisons of coverage between networks were made to examine similarities and differences in the narrative presentations of the announcers employed by ABC, CBS, and NBC. Of course, such comparisons between networks barely assess the relationships in the manifest content of the commentary of a small number of sportscasters and are not necessarily representative of explicit sportscasting policies of the various networks. However, since each network employs only a few "star" announcers who are utilized over and over, it is probably safe to assume that, to the average fan, the voice of the "sports announcing team" represents the image of that network in sports.

In order to evaluate the telecasts in adequate detail, the six professional football games were recorded off the air onto video-cassettes. The unit of analysis for the content analysis was a single sentence of commentary spoken by a professional announcer; that is, each sentence of the audio portion of the telecast spoken by an announcer was analyzed separately. Two coders (one male, one female) classified each sentence, while a third coder (male) operated the playback equipment and acted as an additional coder for sentences in which the two coders disagreed. The two coders arrived at greater than 90 percent initial agreement on the categorization of sentences. The third coder agreed with one of the two primary coders in every instance of initial disagreement, thus providing for total agreement on the coding of all sentences for two of the three coders.

*The sentences were classified as descriptive, dramatic, or humorous.*

A sentence was deemed to be *descriptive* if it appeared to recount the action of the game or clarify facts of play that had occurred off-camera that were essential to the action. A *dramatic* sentence was one which seemed to have been intended to create the impression of conflict, intensify a struggle or emphasize something that was essentially superfluous to an account of the play as such, but which could further the spectator's interest in the game. A *humorous* sentence was one that seemed to have been intended to be funny. Many humorous sentences also had dramatic elements (e.g., a humorous anecdote which described an old rivalry in which one player had gotten the better of his competitor). Other humorous sentences were merely "throwaway" lines apparently serving to make the sportscasting team appear more "personable." Both dramatic and humorous sentences were divided into derogatory, neutral, or complimentary categories, depending on whether it appeared that the announcer intended to bestow praise or criticism. If the sentence seemed to malign or put down the person or thing involved it was classified as *derogatory;* if it appeared to enhance the status of the object of the statement it was categorized as *complimentary;* and if there appeared to be no enhancement or diminution of stature intended the sentence was classified as *neutral.*

To distinguish between the various forces in the dramatic "struggles" presented in the sentences, four categories were formed: team, interpersonal, intrapersonal, and other. *Team* drama consisted of encounters which involved major units of the team or the entire team. Examples include sentences describing a team struggling to overcome a series of injuries or simply trying to defeat another team. *Interpersonal* drama involved situations pitting one person against another. Examples include two halfbacks of the same team competing for one position or opposing quarterbacks trying to better each other's passing records. A sentence was coded as *intrapersonal* drama if it focused on a player trying to overcome personal attributes or limitations, such as a "jinx" or lack of speed. The *other* category was included to accommodate a variety of non-human elements, such as a race against time, or the weather, or other environmental elements. Further distinctions were made between sentences that were *performance-related* (e.g., concerned with speed, ability, or physical prowess), *career-related* (e.g., concerned with professional advancement or financial gains), or *other.*

A final and major categorization concerns the nature of the *dramatic motif.* Fifteen general dramatic motifs commonly employed in sportscasting were identified and established as discrete categories.

1. The *competition* motif included orientations toward retaliation or revenge, direct challenges, struggle for the same job or position, contests between rookies and veterans, and conflicts between age and youth.
2. The *glory* motif incorporated elements of fame, recognition, reputation, and achievement of records.
3. Sentences coded under the *gamesmanship* motif were involved with questions of strategy, management ability, leadership, and ability to implement innovations.
4. The *human interest* motif included items relating to personality, family, school or regional affiliation.
5. Sentences dealing with strength, physical prowess, size, speed, or stamina were classified as fitting the *physical competence* motif.
6. The *history* motif included items related to nostalgia, tradition, or general statistics.
7. The *performance competence* motif included elements of ability, proficiency, versatility, consistency, opportunism, and precision.
8. Sentences relating to professionalism or draft or trade status were defined by the *personnel* motif.
9. The *spirit* motif circumscribed orientations toward desire, determination, enthusiasm, unity, or momentum.
10. The *pity* motif involved sentences relating to loss of advantage, underdog status, or injury.
11. Dramatic elements such as compensation for prior shortcomings, comeback, rebuilding, general improvement, overcoming adversity, exceeding or falling short of expectation, or expressions of intense emotions related to achievement were collected under the category of the *old-college-try* motif.
12. The *comparison* motif included comparisons with one's own prior achievements, with others, and with established norms and standards.
13. The *urgency* motif encompassed notions of importance of winning, implications of a win or loss, importance to the team, pressure, a "must" situation, and necessity of holding onto the lead.
14. Items focusing onto "still having a chance" of winning or losing comprised the *miracle* motif.

15. The external forces motif was reserved for sentences relating to the effects of the environment, time, officiating, fan support, and luck.

Each sentence was assigned to the most appropriate of these motif categories.

*Chi-square analyses were performed on the frequencies*
*of sentences in all defined categories, both*
*by network and for the three networks combined.*

From the 6 games analyzed, a total of 5728 sentences were coded, or an average of about 955 sentences per game. Of these, an average of 690 per game, or about 72 percent were classified as descriptive. For the remaining commentary, approximately 27 percent, or an average of 251 sentences per game, were recorded as serious dramatic sentences, while the remaining 1 percent, or 14 sentences per game, were classified as humorous. As can be seen from Table 1, the frequency of descriptive sentences significantly exceeded the frequency of dramatic sentences [$\chi^2(1) = 265.7$, $p < .001$] and the frequency of humorous sentences [$\chi^2(1) = 1072.8$, $p < .001$]. However, the finding that more than one-fourth of the commentary in televised professional football is "dramatic" would appear to be rather significant. This certainly supports the contention that the role of the contemporary sportscaster involves more than reporting the action. He has the additional duty of complementing the drama on the field and, presumably, of generating involvement and excitement for the television spectator.

There were also several significant network differences in type of commentary selected, with NBC employing more descriptive sentences than CBS [$\chi^2(1) = 15.9$, $p < .001$], and with CBS, in turn, employing a significantly greater number of descriptive sentences than ABC [$\chi^2(1) = 9.4$, $p < .01$]. Exactly the reverse relationship occurred with dramatic sentences, with ABC using more dramatic embellishments than CBS or NBC. However, the only statistically significant differences occurred between the most frequent (ABC) and least frequent (NBC) employers of such embellishments

**Table 1:** Frequencies of descriptive, dramatic, and humorous sentences by network

| Network | Type of sentence | | |
|---|---|---|---|
| | Descriptive | Dramatic | Humorous |
| ABC | 602[c,A] | 263[b,B] | 23[a,C] |
| CBS | 680[c,B] | 260[b,AB] | 4[a,A] |
| NBC | 788[c,C] | 231[b,A] | 14[a,B] |
| Networks combined | 2069[c] | 754[b] | 41[a] |

*Note:* The reported frequencies represent the mean scores derived from the analysis of two games. The chi-square analyses were performed on the actual frequencies of the two games combined. Differences between frequencies were analyzed within networks (horizontal comparisons, lower-case superscripts) and across networks (vertical comparisons, upper-case superscripts). Frequencies having no letter in their superscripts in common differ significantly at $p < .05$ by chi-square tests.

$[\chi^2(1) = 4.1, p < .05]$. ABC proved to be the network of humor as well as drama, employing significantly more humor than its nearest competitor in that category, NBC $[\chi^2(1) = 4.4, p < .05]$, which, in turn, used more humor than CBS $[\chi^2(1) = 11.1, p < .001]$. These findings demonstrate that ABC implements its policy of presenting "the human drama of athletic competition," but they intersperse in their dramatic framework more humor than either CBS or NBC.

Although there were many more descriptive sentences than dramatic and humorous sentences combined, the latter two types of sentences are still well-represented. And when the dramatic and humorous sentences are examined independent of the descriptive ones, some interesting patterns occur. For example, as can be seen in Table 2, when networks are combined, and when the manner in which the announcers use drama to build up or tear down a player is considered, we find that there are significantly more complimentary dramatic sentences than neutral ones $[\chi^2(1) = 33.8, p < .001]$, and more neutral than derogatory dramatic sentences $[\chi^2(1) = 239.0, p < .001]$. Evidently sports announcers do not think that disparaging a player or team is appropriate behavior (cf. 3) or else they do not find it effective in creating excitement.

When humorous sentences are examined independently, it appears that only the ABC sportscasters employ more than a token amount of derogatory humor, and even ABC uses only about 9 such sentences per game. This may be surprising, especially when these findings are compared with findings from content analyses of the humor of prime-time television entertainment fare, where more than two-thirds of all humorous incidents involve hostile or disparagement humor, and where CBS, which employed only about one such incident per game in sportscasting, is by far the most frequent employer of disparagement humor (5). Evidently the norms for

**Table 2:** Frequencies of dramatic and humorous sentences by network and valuation

| Network | Dramatic sentence | | |
| --- | --- | --- | --- |
| | Derogatory | Neutral | Complimentary |
| ABC | 30[a,A] | 98[b,A] | 136[c,B] |
| CBS | 23[a,A] | 92[b,A] | 146[c,B] |
| NBC | 26[a,A] | 96[b,A] | 111[b,A] |
| Networks combined | 77[a] | 285[b] | 392[c] |

| Network | Humorous sentence | | |
| --- | --- | --- | --- |
| | Derogatory | Neutral | Complimentary |
| ABC | 9[b,B] | 12[b,B] | 3[a,A] |
| CBS | 1[a,A] | 3[a,A] | 1[a,A] |
| NBC | 2[a,A] | 10[b,B] | 3[a,A] |
| Networks combined | 12[a] | 24[b] | 6[a] |

Note: The reported frequencies represent the mean scores derived from the analysis of two games. The chi-square analyses were performed on the actual frequencies of the two games combined. Differences between frequencies were analyzed within networks (horizontal comparisons, lower-case superscripts) and across networks (vertical comparisons, upper-case superscripts). Frequencies having no letter in their superscripts in common differ significantly at p < .05 by chi-square tests.

televised sports entertainment and other types of television entertainment differ greatly when it comes to the use of derogation and praise.

*In the networks combined, the sports announcers*
*relied most heavily on intrapersonal conflict*
*to create the "drama of sports."*

As shown in Table 3, intrapersonal conflict is relied upon more extensively than team conflict [$\chi^2(1) = 21.2$, p < .001], which is used more frequently than interpersonal confrontation [$\chi^2(1) = 129.9$, p < .001], which is employed more often than dramatic exchanges with all other remaining forces [$\chi^2(1) = 182.2$, p < .001], When comparisons are made across networks, it is apparent that ABC is fonder of interpersonal conflict than either CBS [$\chi^2(1) = 24.3$, p < .001] or NBC [$\chi^2(1) = 3.9$, p < .05]; and ABC uses significantly more sentences relating to team struggle than NBC [$\chi^2(1) = 4.4$, p < .05], and a nonsignificantly greater number than CBS [$\chi^2(1) = .5$, p > .10]. On the other hand, CBS tends to be oriented more towards intrapersonal drama than either NBC [$\chi^2(1) = 5.0$, p < .05] or ABC [$\chi^2(1) = .6$, p > .10]. When the mainstay of drama on prime-time television is considered – action-adventure or crime drama – which employs interpersonal conflict between protagonists most extensively, it is surprising that the sports dramatists make so little use of interpersonal conflict. This is especially unexpected when examined in light of recent findings which demonstrate that intense dislike between protagonists is a major contributor to appreciation in some kinds of sports events (7).

When dramatic sentences are divided into categories of performance-related, career-related, or other, and when network differences are collapsed, it becomes apparent that most dramatic sports commentary is oriented towards the performance dimension [$\chi^2(2) = 1959.7$, p < .001; with 1361, 77 and 152 such sentences, respectively]. When examined across networks, performance themes are presented almost equally often, with sentence frequencies of 462 for ABC, 447 for CBS, and 452 for ABC [$\chi^2(2) = .3$, p > .10]. When career-oriented dramatic statements are considered, however, ABC (44) is once again the deviate, presenting such sentences more frequently than CBS (12) [$\chi^2(1) = 19.8$, p < .001] or NBC (22) [$\chi^2(1) = 3.7$,

**Table 3:** Frequencies of sentences by network and forces in conflict

| Network | Forces in conflict | | | |
|---|---|---|---|---|
| | Team | Interpersonal | Intrapersonal | Other |
| ABC | 105[c,B] | 57[b,C] | 121[c,AB] | 4[a,A] |
| CBS | 98[c,AB] | 25[b,A] | 138[d,B] | 4[a,A] |
| NBC | 85[c,A] | 43[b,B] | 113[d,A] | 6[a,A] |
| Networks combined | 288[c] | 124[b] | 371[d] | 13[a] |

Note: The reported frequencies represent the mean scores derived from the analysis of two games. The chi-square analyses were performed on the actual frequencies of the two games combined. Differences between frequencies were analyzed within networks (horizontal comparisons, lower-case superscripts) and across networks (vertical comparisons, upper-case superscripts). Frequencies having no letter in their superscripts in common differ significantly at p < .05 by chi-square tests.

p < .10]. In general, given the interest demonstrated by sports periodicals and the news-media in the career of the sports "star," it would appear that dramatic comments related to careers might be underrepresented for maximal entertainment value. It is even more noteworthy that in the six professional football games examined, not a single mention was made of personal finances, a human interest feature that Super Spectator appears to enjoy a great deal.

> *A major consideration was with the dramatic*
> *motifs commonly employed by sports announcers.*

The mean frequencies per game of the various dramatic motifs are presented in Table 4, where they are broken down by network and by dramatic motif across networks. If the frequencies of the employment of dramatic motifs by network combined are examined, it is noteworthy that, taken together, the four most frequently employed dramatic motif categories (general ability, old-college-try, gamesmanship, and comparison) account for more than half of all dramatic sentences. When one compares these motifs with those commonly associated with classical drama (e.g., glory, spirit, urgency, miracle, pity, external forces) or with those which seem to be employed rather often on prime-time television popular dramatic fare (e.g., urgency, competition, physical competence, human interest), it becomes rather clear that television's professional football commentators have a very different style of dramatic presentation. Whether sports commentators on television have found a better way to entertain, or whether they have not yet found the best way to generate excitement for the sports event, has yet to be determined, but it is clear that

**Table 4:** Frequencies of sentences by dramatic motif and network

| Dramatic motif | ABC | CBS | NBC | Networks combined |
|---|---|---|---|---|
| General ability | 62[b] | 51[ab] | 44[a] | 157[G] |
| Old-college-try | 41[b] | 27[a] | 30[ab] | 98[F] |
| Gamesmanship | 22[a] | 31[a] | 30[a] | 83[EF] |
| Comparison | 28[a] | 23[a] | 25[a] | 76[E] |
| Physical competence | 11[a] | 19[b] | 21[b] | 51[D] |
| Spirit | 15[a] | 16[a] | 15[a] | 46[CD] |
| Competition | 19[b] | 9[a] | 17[b] | 45[CD] |
| History | 16[a] | 14[a] | 12[a] | 42[CD] |
| Human interest | 22[b] | 13[a] | 7[a] | 42[CD] |
| Urgency | 12[ab] | 19[b] | 9[a] | 40[BCD] |
| Glory | 13[a] | 11[a] | 13[a] | 37[BC] |
| External forces | 8[a] | 13[a] | 9[a] | 30[B] |
| Pity | 9[a] | 12[a] | 8[a] | 29[B] |
| Personnel | 8[b] | 6[ab] | 3[a] | 17[A] |
| Miracle | 4[a] | 4[a] | 5[a] | 13[A] |

*Note:* The reported frequencies represent the mean scores derived from the analysis of two games. The chi-square analyses were performed on the actual frequencies of the two games combined. Differences between frequencies were analyzed within dramatic motif (horizontal comparisons, lower-case superscripts) and within networks combined (vertical comparisons, upper-case superscripts). Frequencies having no letter in their superscripts in common differ significantly at p < .05 by chi-square tests.

there are definite preferences for dramatic motifs in professional football telecasting.

Comparisons of frequencies of the employment of the dramatic motifs broken down by networks are also revealing. In many categories, the three networks are very similar in terms of their frequency of use of types of drama. For examples, in eight of the fifteen different dramatic motifs (glory, gamesmanship, history, spirit, pity, comparison, miracle, and external forces) no significant differences in mean frequency by networks occur (all chi-square values associated with $p > .05$). Of the remaining seven categories, the variance is relatively equally distributed across networks in three motifs: general ability, urgency, and personnel. In one motif category, competition, CBS is clearly the deviate network, employing significantly fewer statements relating to competition than NBC [$\chi^2(1) = 5.7$, $p < .02$] or ABC [$\chi^2(1) = 7.24$, $p < .01$]. Regarding the remaining three areas, ABC is significantly different from the other two networks, carrying nearly twice as much human interest material as CBS [$\chi^2(1) = 4.7$, $p < .05$] and three times that of NBC [$\chi^2(1) = 14.7$, $p < .001$]; relying more heavily on the old-college-try motif than either CBS [$\chi^2(1) = 5.8$, $p < .02$] or NBC [$\chi^2(1) = 3.4$, $p < .10$]; and utilizing themes relating to physical competence much less than CBS [$\chi^2(1) = 4.9$, $p < .05$] or NBC [$\chi^2(1) = 7.0$, $p < .01$]. These general trends tend to document that ABC is a maverick where it apparently tries most earnestly to be: in bringing sports "up close and personal."

In summary, systematic analysis of the commentary from six professional football telecasts reveals that a sizable portion of the audio track of television coverage of professional football is devoted to dramatic embellishments of the game. It would seem that the sportscaster serves not only to fill in the knowledge gaps left by the limitations of the visual dimensions of television, but to add histrionics to the "human drama of athletic competition." It would also appear that the sports announcer's dramaturgy is already rather stylized, with a great deal of reliance on a relatively small number of dramatic motifs. There is, however, some variation within networks which appears to be rather consistent. It remains to be seen whether increasing diversification in sportscasting will develop, or whether existing patterns in presenting dramatic features of televised sports commentary will stabilize. Perhaps more importantly, we have yet to discover the impact these electronic histrionics have on Super Spectator and on the nature of his games.

## References

1.  Fisher, A. C. *Psychology of Sport.* Palo Alto, Calif.: Mayfield, 1976.
2.  Goldstein, J. H. (Ed.) *Sports, Games and Play.* Hillsdale, N. J.: Lawrence Erlbaum, in press.
3.  Johnson, W. O., Jr. *Super Spectator and the Electric Lilliputians.* Boston: Little, Brown and Co., 1971.

4. "Let's Look at Sports." Chicago, Ill.: A. C. Nielsen, 1976.
5. Stocking, S. H., B. S. Sapolsky, and D. Zillmann. "Is There Sex Discrimination in Humor on Prime-Time Television?" *Journal of Broadcasting*, in press.
6. Zajonc, R. B. "Social Facilitation." *Science* 149, 1965, pp. 269–274.
7. Zillmann, D., J. Bryant, and B. S. Sapolsky. "The Enjoyment of Watching Sports Contests." In J. H. Goldstein (Ed.) *Sports, Games and Play*. Hillsdale, N.J.: Lawrence Erlbaum, in press.

# 6

# Sport and the Media in Ireland: An Introduction

*Seán Crosson and Philip Dine*

The symbiotic relationship that has existed since the mid-nineteenth century between sport and the media – from the popular press, through newsreels and radio, to television, and beyond – is so well established as hardly to require comment. However, the very familiarity of this long and successful marriage should not blind us to its abiding, and abidingly remarkable, affective power, both for individuals and for communities, real and 'imagined', of all kinds. We may thus legitimately pause to reflect on the key role played by the media in establishing the local, national and international significance of what are inherently ephemeral and objectively trivial corporeal practices. Whether it be through the national football cultures of England and Scotland, or the national cycling cultures articulated through Spain's *Vuelta*, Italy's *Giro* and, especially, the *Tour de France*, sport annually continues to mobilise millions of spectators, whether physically present or, especially, by means of the mass media. This is even more obviously true of such major international competitions as the World Cup, European Championship and European Champions League competitions in association football. To pursue a little further the example of the *Tour de France* – an event launched in 1903 by the specialist sports newspaper *L'Auto*, as part of a combined commercial and political circulation war with its rival *Le Vélo* in the wake of the Dreyfus Affair – we might even argue that France's 'great bike race' is actually and annually brought into existence by the media. As Jacques Marchand, one of the event's most seasoned reporters, once remarked: 'cycle road racing does

**Source:** *Media History*, 17(2), Special Issue: Sport and the Media in Ireland (2011): 109–116.

not really have spectators, it has readers above all' (Marchand 11). For Marchand, the fleeting vision of the race itself meant little to the crowds massed on the roadside. Indeed, they became conscious of its significance – as lived experience, rendered comprehensible and thus comprehended – only when the event had been variously reconstituted, and thus effectively translated, by its only permanent spectators, that is the accompanying journalists.

This special number of *Media History* is conceived as a contribution to the ongoing scholarly analysis of sport's social significance, as a set of mass-mediated practices and spectacles giving rise to a complex network of images, symbols and discourses. Its specific aim is to examine the distinctive contribution of various sports – as communicated by a range of mass media – to the creation of modern Irish identities. For sport inhabits a central place in Irish life, more possibly than in any other country in Europe. Indeed, sport provides a defining element in many Irish people's sense of themselves and their country. One might even suggest that given the loss of an indigenous language to most Irish people and the increasing secularisation of the country, sport is as important as a distinct marker of identity now in Ireland as at any point in the country's history. And this in a country in which the emergence and consolidation of Irish nationalism and the building of the Irish state were inextricably linked with sport, in particular the Gaelic Athletic Association (GAA), still the largest sporting organisation on the island. Indeed, uniquely again in international sport, Gaelic games (essentially amateur in ideology and practice) continue to be the most popular sports followed and practised in Ireland, despite the significant and growing popularity of non-indigenous sports such as soccer and rugby. Given the recent celebrations in 2009 to mark the 125th anniversary of the GAA's founding, it is thus particularly appropriate that we should focus on a parish-based institution that is present in all 32 counties of the island of Ireland, and thus north and south of the still-contested international border.

Yet while sport has occupied a central position in Irish life, one cannot underestimate the role of the media in popularising and affirming this position. A recurring subject of the contributions that follow is the impossibility of appreciating the position of sport in Irish life, particularly since the mid-nineteenth century, without considering the role of the media. The movement of sport's representation, as in other countries, has encompassed the print, radio, cinematic, televisual and virtual (via the internet) media, and this progression is charted here in our contributions, particularly as it relates to the first three of these media. However, in Ireland, the relationship between sport and the media has been complicated by the fact that much of this media emerged, and continues to emanate, from non-indigenous sources, particularly Britain and America, and there is an intriguing encounter apparent here, as Crosson and McAnallen note in their contribution to this special number, with indigenous sport. Indeed, in his 1884 letter of acceptance to Michael Cusack to become the first patron of the GAA, Archbishop Thomas Croke of

Cashel indicated his awareness of the popularity of British media in Ireland when he remarked on what he called the 'vicious literature' which 'we are daily importing from England' and the need for 'our national journals . . . to give suitable notices of those Irish sports and pastimes which your society means to patronise and promote' (Croke).

Sport already had a number of publications dedicated to it in Ireland prior to the foundation of the GAA in 1884, namely the sporting papers the *Irish Sportsman and Farmer* and *Sport*, though neither gave coverage to Gaelic games but focused rather on sports such as hunting and horse-related activities, rugby, tennis and cricket (Rouse 54). Within a few short years of the foundation of the association, there were two more, *Celtic Times,* initiated by the GAA's founder Michael Cusack, and *The Gael,* both, though short-lived, a testament to the growing popularity of Gaelic games in this period (Duncan 106–7).

In post-partition southern Ireland, the state's control of the media played a significant role in affirming and promoting a particular, and quite insular, version of Irishness. In this context, Gaelic games played a pivotal role as a marker of Irish culture – particularly as distinct from that of Britain, evident in the frequent broadcasting of Gaelic games from the founding of 2RN, the first radio station in the Irish Free State, in 1926, and the exclusion of perceived non-Irish games such as soccer and rugby. In the north of Ireland, the BBC began transmitting from 1924, though its efforts to advance distinctive local cultural practices, such as sport, were hampered 'by intense political and public hostility to anything suggestive of an "Irish" identity' (Connolly 471). Although the contributions to this volume are focused primarily on the relationship between the media and sport in the south of the island, the challenges that partition brought for sport and the media are also aspects of the contributions, including Conor McCabe's analysis of the tensions surrounding the administration of association football in Ireland post-partition.

While radio in the south of Ireland was quick to exploit sport as a means of attracting audiences, Irish newspapers were slower to realise its importance. However, with the launch of the *Irish Press* in 1931 and its growing popularity, significantly contributed to by its extensive coverage of sporting events, particularly Gaelic games, both the *Irish Independent* and *Irish Times* increased their coverage of sport in Ireland substantially (Oram 173). The *Press,* in particular, played an important role not just in affirming the antiquity and centrality of Gaelic games in Irish life, but also the position of sport in general in Ireland as an important marker of identity. As Raymond Boyle has noted: 'The effects of radio and newspaper coverage of sport were twofold. They elevated awareness of sport while also contributing to the building of the country's national passion for sport' (Boyle 631–2).

With the launch of Ireland's first dedicated national broadcaster, Telefís Éireann – now Raidio Teilifís Éireann (RTE) – on 31 December 1961, home-produced television arrived in Ireland, and would play a central role in continuing the popularisation of sport, in particular Gaelic games. The first live television broadcast of an All-Ireland final was in September 1962, and as television became an increasingly important part of people's lives, so too did its coverage of sport. While soccer and rugby have enjoyed considerable coverage and popularity on Irish television, with horse racing, athletics and boxing also receiving significant exposure, Gaelic games still typically attract the biggest audiences each year for sporting events. This coverage focused primarily on the semi-final and All-Ireland stages for the first 30 years or so of RTÉ's existence, but the arrival of Sky television and the increased broadcasting of live soccer games have encouraged the expansion of coverage of Gaelic games in Ireland. This has also been added to by the advent of two more national television channels over the past 15 years, TG4 and TV3, and one Irish-based cable sports channel, Setanta Sports, all of which have given considerable coverage to sport, including Gaelic games. In Northern Ireland, BBC Northern Ireland and Ulster Television (UTV) were slower to broadcast Gaelic games, focusing primarily where local sporting events were concerned on soccer, in particular the domestic Irish league. However, the success of teams from Northern Ireland in the All-Ireland Football championship since the early 1990s, and indeed the development of the peace process, has seen increasing coverage given to Gaelic football, particularly on BBC Northern Ireland.

Despite the popularity of sport on television, radio coverage of sporting events has continued to have a huge following among Irish listeners. While Micheál Ó Muircheartaigh earned a reputation until his retirement in 2010 as one of the finest commentators on live sport in any country for his Gaelic games commentaries on RTÉ Radio 1, the centrality of Gaelic games coverage on local radio, and particularly of soccer on national radio stations Today FM and Newstalk – both established in the past 10 years – all testify to the continuing importance of this medium in Ireland for sporting enthusiasts (Cronin, Duncan, and Rouse 177–207).

The relationship between sport and the media has been an area of increasing international research, with scholars such as Goldlust (*Playing for Keeps*), Whannel (*Fields in Vision, Media Sport Stars*), Wenner (*MediaSport*), Rowe (*Sport, Culture and the Media*) and Blain and Bernstein (*Sport, Media, Culture*) all underlining the central role that the media plays in 'producing, reproducing and amplifying many of the discourses associated with sport in the modern world' (Boyle and Haynes 8). When we speak of the media's role in broadcasting or communicating sport, it is a function that goes beyond merely relaying sporting events to an audience; radio and other media have a crucial role in influencing how such sports will be received by the manner in which they mediate the sports they broadcast. This is a recurring concern of the contributors here. Radio in particular affirmed the popular communal engagement with Gaelic games as they grew in popularity in Ireland, with the Kilkenny versus Galway All-Ireland senior hurling semi-final one of the first live broadcasts of a sporting event in Europe, when transmitted by 2RN on 29 August 1926 (Cronin, Duncan, and Rouse 179–80). The prominent images of families gathered around a radio in the first indigenous cinematic coverage of an All-Ireland final by the National Film Institute, in 1948, reflected both an awareness of the importance of radio to people's engagement with sport and also the fact that many people in the audience would probably have listened to the match live on the radio in the first instance.[1] The hiring of Michael O'Hehir to provide the commentary for this footage – famous across Ireland for his sporting commentary on radio since 1938 – further affirmed this connection.[2] With the arrival of live television coverage in 1962, O'Hehir would continue to play a crucial role in the commentary on Gaelic games until his retirement in 1986 (Cronin, Duncan, and Rouse 179–80).

In the Irish context, the relationship between sport and the media remains significantly under-researched, although the 125th anniversary of the GAA in 2009 has encouraged much needed and important reflection on this relationship, at least as it applies to Gaelic games. Where work has been done in this area, including by Marcus De Búrca (The *G.A.A.*), Raymond Boyle (*From Our Gaelic Fields*), W.F. Mandle (The *GAA and Irish Nationalist Politics*), Luke Gibbons ('From Megalith to Megastore'), Mark Duncan ('The Early Photography of the GAA'), Mike Cronin (*Sport and Nationalism in Ireland; The GAA*), and our contributor Paul Rouse (*The GAA*; 'Michael Cusack'), it has emphasised the crucial relationship between sport and media, particularly in terms of the popularisation of sport in Irish life. Boyle, in his pioneering study of the relationship between Irish radio and Gaelic games post-partition, noted how:

> sports coverage played a key role in the formative years of Irish broadcasting. The selective treatment given by radio to specific sporting events not only helped to amplify their importance, but actually played a central role in creating national events and organisations. (Boyle 623)

The chief beneficiary here was the GAA, and the sports the association promoted, particularly Gaelic football and hurling. As Gibbons has also observed: 'both radio and the press contributed substantially to creating a *nationwide* audience for Gaelic games, thus establishing the Gaelic Athletic Association as a truly national organisation' (Gibbons 73). Boyle was also keen in his study to stress the 'important interrelationship that exists between radio and newspapers in helping to construct *national* pastimes. They transform sport from a simple rule-governed game into a tangible activity which can generate a degree of collective sensibility that in turn helps to legitimise more abstract political structures such as "state" and "nation"' (Boyle 624). Thus, political and economic factors are crucial to understanding the development of the relationship between sport and the media in Ireland. This is also a concern of our contributors, who note the important role that the media played in both popularising and legitimating the GAA as the promoters of *the* Irish sports. In contrast, Conor McCabe notes how a publication such as

*Football Sports Weekly* argued strongly for the recognition of the preferred sport of its publishers, association football, as equally entitled to be regarded as a hugely important part of Irish people's identity.

These issues indicate how sport in Ireland, as elsewhere, has had an importance beyond that of a mere recreational activity for some time, and the focus of several essays in this issue is sport's political relevance in the formative period of Irish team sports. While the position of Gaelic games as being among the most popular sporting pursuits in Ireland today is undeniable, this was, of course, not always the case. Jeff Dann's study here charts the popularity of British sports in Ireland in the later nineteenth century through an examination of magazines published in elite Irish schools of the period. He finds, as others have noted as regards the emergence of sport in the same period in Britain, that there was a close relationship between sport and theories of personal development, clearly articulated within an imperial context. Playing British sports, particularly rugby and cricket, for those who contributed to these magazines, did not conflict with people's sense of patriotism and Irishness, though this was an Irishness that was clearly imagined, unlike that favoured by those who promoted Gaelic games in the same period and subsequently, within an imperial context. Dann's analysis of the mediation of these sports in these publications indicates the complexities of evolving identities in this period.

The GAA was founded at a point when Gaelic games were in considerable decline, with the distinct possibility that they would not survive beyond the turn of the twentieth century. Indeed, the ban on members or players of the association attending or participating in 'foreign' games was at least partly a response to the growing popularity of sports perceived as 'British', such as cricket, in Ireland throughout the nineteenth century, a matter also remarked upon in Croke's acceptance letter to Cusack quoted above. A crucial ingredient in Gaelic games' development was the role of popular media, particularly newspapers and sporting publications of the 1880s and 1890s, and the fortune that the association had in attracting journalists of the highest calibre to write on its games. Indeed, as Paul Rouse observes in his contribution, at least three of the seven (though as Rouse notes there may have been up to 14) people, including its first secretary Michael Cusack, at the celebrated founding meeting of the association in Hayes Commercial Hotel in Thurles on Saturday 1 November 1884, were journalists. Their contributions, particularly those of Cusack, were crucial in spreading the word regarding, and thus popularising, Gaelic games in Irish life. Rouse's article also highlights the fascinating and tumultuous period in which the association was founded, and the many challenges it faced, including that of a media initially largely hostile towards the association and its aims.

While Rouse provides an insight into the role that the print media played in the emergence and popularisation of Gaelic games, Crosson and McAnallen explore the important information provided by surviving newsreels, in particular those produced by the Pathé company, on these evolving sports and Irish society in the early twentieth century. With a strong focus on the British market in particular, these films offer a fascinating insight into the encounter between colonial representation and indigenous Irish culture. Drawing inspiration from Mike Huggins' work on the role that newsreels played in the promotion of association football, Crosson and McAnallen argue for these fascinating, if short and sometimes misleading (particularly with regard to the heavily accented English commentary), depictions in terms of the explanations that they offer today of the changing aesthetic of the sports depicted, their role in promoting and maintaining the status quo and the reaction of the GAA to the contemporary media and its representation of its games.

While an analysis of the media offers unparalleled insights into the development of a range of sports in Ireland in this period, the various means of communication themselves played a crucial role in the popularisation of sport in the country, and indeed, in the case of soccer particularly – as Conor McCabe observes – effectively affirmed the division of the island politically. Crowd problems reported at soccer matches in the 1920s suggest that sectarian tensions were also in evidence at sporting occasions, while abuse of referees would appear to be far from a new development in the game of soccer. McCabe's analysis of the weekly sports newspaper *Football Sports Weekly* between 1925 and 1928, reveals the tumultuous and challenging circumstances that surrounded the emergence of association football in Ireland. Condemned as 'imperial' and 'un-Irish' by nationalists, and particularly many leaders and supporters of Gaelic games in Ireland, *Football Sports Weekly* played a crucial role in defending soccer and asserting its relevance to Irish identity. As McCabe indicates, soccer in this period did grow rapidly across Ireland, though unlike rugby, and Gaelic games, it arguably articulated the political tensions and divisions on the island more than any other sport, as rival associations emerged north and south of the border to administer the sport. In this context, the media played a crucial role in both documenting and affirming the emerging sporting – and to some extent political – identities across the island.

While the popularity of association football in Ireland is aided significantly by the huge following among Irish people for soccer clubs in England and, to a lesser extent, Scotland, rugby football, particularly through the success of Ulster, Munster and Leinster in the Heineken-sponsored European Rugby Cup, would appear to have adopted and incorporated some of the central, and most clearly defining, aspects of Gaelic games, particularly the relationship between place, community and team. Having, since 1995, adapted successfully to a system of professionalised provinces – which itself parallels the time-honoured province-based structures of the GAA and draws affective strength from popular investment in the island's 'Four Green Fields'[3] – Irish rugby has attracted both mass spectatorship and media enthusiasm through its skilfully marketed show of locally rooted authenticity. However, as

Liam O'Callaghan outlines in his essay, the 'tradition' of Munster rugby is very much a media creation of the past 10 years, and one that is not supported by the historical practice of rugby in the province. Indeed, as O'Callaghan argues, for much of the preceding century, the province was characterised by bitter rivalries between the main heartlands of Cork and Limerick, both at club and regional administrative levels, where the club game was of far greater importance, with provincial ties poorly attended and attracting often negative comment in the press. Yet it is the press itself, particularly following the advent of professionalism in 1995, and the successes of Munster in the Heineken cup from 2000 onwards, that played a crucial role in popularising the myth of the proud and ancient tradition of Munster rugby and its attendant qualities, as much moral as material.

The articles that follow together explore the historically symbiotic relationship of sport and the media, elucidating the mechanics of that mutual support against the backdrop of the very specific cultural politics of Ireland. In the Irish context, the central importance of the GAA in the development of cultural and political nationalism – and in the subsequent establishment and consolidation of a distinctively Irish state – can hardly be overstated. As a particularly clear exemplar, the case of the GAA underlines the broader value of the academic study of the history and sociology of modern sports, and particularly of its specific contribution to the imaginative life, and thus the identity politics, of European (and other) nation-states. The combined associative and affective functions of sport over the past century and a half are unimaginable without the simultaneous emergence of the mass media, in Ireland as elsewhere. The present case studies thus seek to contribute to the ongoing elucidation of that still essential structural and perceptual linkage.

## Notes

1. Footage of this game between Cavan and Mayo is held in the Irish Film Institute.
2. The intimate linkage between the media and the very profitable state encouragement of gambling on horse racing – on which O'Hehir also became a regular commentator, as did his son Tony – is also illustrated by the establishment in 1930 of the Irish Free State Hospitals' Sweepstake, which ran in various guises until 1986.
3. A celebrated folk song by the Irish musician Tommy Makem, *The Four Green Fields* (1967), celebrates the island's land and people, while lamenting the British colonial presence in the north-eastern province of Ulster (specifically in six of its historic nine counties).

## References

Blain, NeiL and Alina Bernstein. *Sport, Media, Culture: Local and Global Dimensions.* London: Routledge, 2003.

Boyle, Raymond. 'From Our Gaelic Fields: Radio, Sport and Nation in Post-partition Ireland'. *Media, Culture and Society* 14.4 (1992): 623–36.

Boyle, Raymond, and Richard Haynes. *Power Play: Sport, the Media and Popular Culture.* Harlow: Pearson Education, 2000.

Connolly, S.J., ed. *The Oxford Companion to Irish History.* Oxford: Oxford UP, 1999.

Croke, T.W. *To Mr Michael Cusack, Honorary Secretary of the Gaelic Athletic Association. The Palace, Thurles, 18 December 1884.* 15 Sept. 2008. <http://multitext.ucc.ie/d/Archbishop_Croke_the_GAA_November_1884>.

Cronin, Mike. *Sport and Nationalism in Ireland: Gaelic Games, Soccer and Irish Identity since 1884.* Dublin: Four Courts Press, 1999.

Cronin, Mike, Mark Duncan, and Paul Rouse. 'Media'. *The GAA: A People's History.* Cork: The Collins Press, 2009. 177–207.

De Búrca, Marcus. *The G.A.A.: A History.* Dublin: Cumann Lúthchleas Gael, 1980.

Duncan, Mark. 'The Early Photography of the GAA, 1884–1914'. *The Gaelic Athletic Association, 1884–2009.* Ed. Mike Cronin, William Murphy, and Paul Rouse. Dublin: Irish Academic P, 2009. 93–110.

Gibbons, Luke. 'From Megalith to Megastore: Broadcasting and Irish Culture'. *Transformations in Irish Culture.* Cork: Cork UP in association with Field Day, 1996.

Goldlust, John. *Playing for Keeps: Sport, the Media and Society.* Melbourne: Longman, 1987.

Mandle, W.F. *The GAA and Irish Nationalist Politics.* Dublin: Gill and Macmillan, 1987.

Marchand, Jacques. *Le Cyclisme.* Paris: La Table Ronde, 1963.

Oram, H. *The Newspaper Book: A History of Newspapers in Ireland, 1649–1983.* Dublin: Mo Books, 1983.

Rouse, Paul. 'Michael Cusack: Sportsman and Journalist'. *The Gaelic Athletic Association, 1884–2009.* Ed. Mike Cronin, William Murphy, and Paul Rouse. Dublin: Irish Academic Press, 2009. 47–59.

Rowe, David. *Sport, Culture and the Media: The Unholy Trinity.* Buckingham: Open UP, 1999.

Wenner, Lawrence A. *Media Sport.* London: Routledge, 1998.

Whannel, Garry. *Fields in Vision: Television Sport and Cultural Transformation.* London: Routledge, 1992.

———. *Media Sport Stars: Masculinities and Moralities.* London: Routledge, 2002.

# 7

# A Speculative Paradigm on the Birth of the Modern Sport Spectacular: The Real Madrid and Eintracht Frankfurt European Cup Final of 1960

*Scott A.G.M. Crawford*

Allen Guttmann's model on the nature of modern sports[1] stands, despite some bruising challenges, as a productive starting-point in any analysis of the nature and function of modern sport. Thus Guttmann's concepts of sacred/secular, equality, specialization, rationalization, bureaucratization, quantification and records are all very apparent in the emergence and evolution of what was a post-World War II phenomenon, a European soccer championship. However, by the 1950s there was what this writer chooses to call the emergence of the 'sport spectacular'.[2]

The choice of the 1960 European Cup Final as the first modern sport spectacular is open to debate. Why not select the inaugural European Cup Final of 1956 played in Paris? What of the 1948 London Olympics and notions of international sport providing revival, rebirth and conflict resolution following the end of the Second World War? In terms of international super-powers flexing their athletic muscles at the height of the Cold War, a case could be made for selecting the 1952 Helsinki Olympics. There the heady successes enjoyed by the hammer and sickle of the Soviet Union marked the arrival of a new influential force in global sport. In 1956 the Olympics relocated to a new continent, Australia, and European and American audiences

**Source:** *The International Journal of the History of Sport,* 9(3) (1992): 433–438.

read about, listened to and watched cinema highlights of Australian athletes achieving stunning success, especially in the swimming pool.

At the 1960 Rome Olympics, relayed television links with many other countries around the world helped in a cultural refocussing of sport. Instead of world audiences watching Olympic highlights on news film at the cinema, a growing audience of international television viewers were fed programmes spotlighting what were, in many respects, the unofficial world championships in a variety of sports.

The notion of communicating the athletic event to a wider social group seems of critical importance. Certainly, by the 1970s the charisma and folk-hero status of an athlete like Muhammad Ali meant that his celebrated fights – the 'Rumble in the Jungle' and the 'Thriller in Manila' – stand as examples of an already established vehicle that is described here as the modern sport spectacular.

It was in the 1950s that television established itself as the major cultural conduit in both Europe and North America. When the BBC decided to televise an evening athletics meeting live from London's White City Stadium in October 1954 it could scarcely have realized the impact of its decision. A Russian group of athletes (the first-ever visit by a Soviet team to Britain) representing Moscow, took on a London team. The race of the evening was a titanic contest between Vladimir Kuts and Christopher Chataway over 5000 metres. The final lap is a classic of filmed sports competition which Chataway won by one tenth of a second in front of two exhilarated audiences: a packed stadium of 40,000 people and a television audience at home of several millions.

## Guttmann's 'Ritual to Record' Model

While Allen Guttmann accepts that the passions, rituals and myths of modern sports, and in our case professional soccer, may be seen as a secular religion he argues that the bond between the secular and the sacred is gone. 'Modern sports are activities partly pursued for their own sake, partly for other ends which are equally secular.'[3]

Guttmann's second distinguishing characteristic of modern sports is that there is a dual sense of equality. Everyone has an opportunity to compete and playing conditions for all are similar.[4] In 1960 when Real Madrid and Eintracht Frankfurt played their preliminary games, stadia and crowd location may have been hugely different, but the dimensions of their playing areas and the timed duration of the contest had to fit into a universally agreed norm.

As with virtually all modern professional sports, specialization has been seen to be critical for success. By 1960 European soccer had established clearly defined roles for defenders, link players, mid-field players, strikers and wing men. Guttmann emphasizes how that with medieval mob football 'there was room for everyone and a sharply defined role for no-one'.[5] Gento, the sensational Real Madrid winger, played so wonderfully well in the European Cup Final because he had honed unusual specialist skills. He trained by running the 100-yard dash in 10 seconds with the ball at his feet. In other words, he had practised to become a specialist. He was the fastest winger in world soccer. Puskas, on the other hand, the 33-year-old Real Madrid striker, was portly rather than lean. Although he had useful acceleration he was no sprinter. His nickname was the 'Galloping Major'. He did not travel up and down the pitch to collect and then distribute the ball. However, he was the doyen of all strikers. He moved quickly to the open space, he possessed good reflexes, he had a high level of dribbling flair and a cannon-like shot off either foot. In the second half of the Final, he scored three goals in 15 minutes.

Guttmann's fourth concept is rationalization and of course by 1960, and indeed much much earlier, world soccer observed 'organized, rule-bound play'.[6] Moreover players, at least at the level of European Cup matches were virtually year-round players who practised and trained at what was a job. 'There was a whole way of life concentrated on the single goal of athletic excellence.'[7]

Bureaucratization in soccer was especially well developed and refined. It is noteworthy that track and field and rugby world championships were not established until relatively recently. In Europe, long before the notion of European political/economic solidarity was launched, there was the establishment of a soccer alliance. On 21 May 1904 seven European countries agreed to form the Fédération Internationale de Football Association (FIFA). The first World Cup competition took place in 1930 and in June 1954 the Union of European Football Associations (UEFA) was founded. One year later in 1955, under the authority of UEFA, the inaugural Champions Cup final took place in Paris between Real Madrid and Reims.[8]

Guttmann's final components in his modern sports model are those of quantification and records. 'The statistics of the game are part and parcel of the statistics of modern society.'[9] It was winning results that helped shape the legend and mystique of the Real Madrid team that came to Hampden Park in May 1960. They won the 1956 championship 4–3 (against Reims); 1957: Real Madrid 2 – Fiorentina 0; 1958: Real Madrid 3 – Milan 2; 1959: Real Madrid 2 – Reims 0.[10] Their 1960 victory, then, was a fifth consecutive European Cup triumph, and confirmed them as the greatest team of the era. No team since has established a record sequence of five championships.

In his *Sports Spectators* Allen Guttmann has a section entitled 'Modern Spectators' where he looks at what he calls the 'people's game'.[11] Guttmann, as well as noting the sheer numbers who watch soccer world-wide, then asks the leading question: 'Why then do people watch?'[12]

For this analysis of the 1960 European Cup Final the answer seems critical and should reveal much. There was something intriguing going on when nearly 130,000 Scottish spectators filled a Glasgow stadium on a Wednesday night to watch two teams, neither of which had one British, still less a Scottish, player. Indeed the only national representative in this sports drama was one J. D. Mowat of Glasgow – the referee!

Historically there had always been large numbers of spectators at Hampden Park. In 1933, at the height of the depression, there were 134,710 spectators. In 1937, also when Scotland played the old rival England, 150,000 tickets were sold.[13] However, in 1960, there was the conundrum of 130,000 spectators coming out to watch a group of foreigners play a game that had once been Britain's national forte and pastime.

Arguably Guttmann's most useful concept is his notion of 'representational sport'. By this Guttmann means a fusion or coming together of 'individual identification with the athletes and collective membership in the community'.[14]

Two additional writers and thinkers have commented on this general area and they, together with Guttmann, give a sense of the merging of community and celebration that characterized Hampden Park on the evening of Wednesday 18 May 1960. C.L.R. James, the West Indian social historian and cricket commentator-philosopher, articulates, in his *Beyond a Boundary*, a view of society in which culture is an interweave of a complex tapestry. In this mosaic all the parts are critically important to the functioning of the whole. As James noted, 'What do they know of cricket who only cricket know?'[15] Put differently, James is advocating a view where sport, traditionally seen as something on the periphery, is central to, and significant for, everyday living.

Sports historian Alan Metcalfe, in a 1991 conference presentation, examined North of England sport in the mining communities of East Northumberland from 1800 to 1914.[16] For him, a key ingredient in unravelling the puzzle of why working-class people took part in and supported local sport was the feeling of 'community'.

Unquestionably Guttmann, James and Metcalfe in their concepts of 'representation', 'centrality' and 'community' help to explain the social forces and the dynamics of the Hampden Park crowd.

> A thunderous roar went up as the final whistle sounded. It was Glasgow' – and Scotland's – salute to the wizards from Spain. The famed 'Hampden Roar' went up again as the victors ran around the field holding the cup aloft.[17]

Richard Holt makes the point that 'In a land of "No Gods and precious few heroes" [Scotland] football has come nearest to filling a cultural void.'[18] It should be noted also that on the night of the Real Madrid–Eintracht Frankfurt game there was neither distraction nor alternative. No soccer games were going on at nearby Parkhead and Ibrox, the home stadia for Celtic and Rangers respectively. 'Glasgow can claim to have been the first and most fanatical footballing city in Britain.'[19]

A final concept is the transmission or cultural exchange of the game as a communal drama with not just a British but a European radio and television audience. Although the numbers of television sets per family unit in

North America were significantly higher than in Great Britain, there was a universal reshaping of audience offerings.

> By 1960 television was firmly part of the sporting scene . . . It allowed farm kids in Nebraska to watch Unitas march his team toward that final score. It permitted Oklahoma ranchhands to watch their native son Mickey Mantle bat for the Yankees.[20]

The events on the evening of 18 May 1960 went out on 'Eurovision' and by 1968 30 European television authorities had signed up to broadcast the European Cup Final.[21]

## Conclusion

The model outlined in this essay has many weaknesses. For example, the 1960 European Cup Final was not televised to the USA. It did not get a write-up in *Sports Illustrated*. For a North American audience the game was virtually a non-event. Lest it be thought that *Sports Illustrated* confined itself to the North American scene, the issue of 23 May 1960 did have a considerable international flavour. The death of Aly Khan, the famous playboy and race horse owner, was covered, a photographic essay showed the leisure goods on sale at the Hermès store in Paris, and an in-depth piece described sport and athletic heroes in Australia.[22]

The *New York Times* of 19 May 1960, while it briefly reported on the game, had columns upon columns on the forthcoming heavyweight boxing championship bout between Ingemar Johansson (Sweden) and Floyd Patterson (USA).[23] Even *The Times* devoted much more space to Ted Dexter of Surrey scoring 104 runs. Indeed, nearly as many column inches were used for the England-Poland under-23 soccer games played in Warsaw as were used for the European Cup Final.[24] In certain respects then, the game did not have global significance and impact. Nevertheless, it electrified Europe and today, 32 years later, it is held up as an exemplar of soccer at its best.

For an entertainment occasion to be labelled as a 'spectacular' certain social and cultural ingredients must be present. There must be the element of uniqueness – a 'one of a kind' situation. There has to be a level of performance that is transcendent. There has to be a rare chemistry between actor(s) and audience. The 'happening' is so special that a whole series of legends spring up around it. The event rapidly evolves into a celebration etched in historical consciousness but coloured by individual anecdotes and collective reminscences. Such was the case with Woodstock, the extravaganza of popular rock music at the end of the 1960s. In a similar fashion there is the aura and mystique of 'The Great Match'. The game came to be seen as symbolic of an age of innocent challenge and camaraderie. The tenor of the game was friendly. Brutal tackling and defensive 'bottling up' was all in the future.

The *New York Times* wrote: 'The night truly belonged to Puskas'.[25] *The Times* saw Puskas (Hungary), Gento (Spain) and Di Stefano (Argentina) as international magicians who captivated and then energized a vast Scottish audience.

> . . . the quality of their forward play and ball control was of such finely drawn skills, of such accuracy, imagination, and indeed, impudence, as to bring thundering down around them vast waves of delighted appreciation from Hampden's mighty crowd.[26]

What of the Scottish press? The *Daily Record* put soccer on its front page, reducing Mr Krushchev, the then Soviet premier, to half a column and a belligerent photograph. The dominating headline ('Esta Madrid') opened thus:

> Roar upon roar surged down on the excited jubilant men of Madrid as they trotted round Hampden Stadium last night . . . European Cup held aloft. This was the salute of 127,000 fans for one of the most dazzling displays of soccer wizardry ever seen in Scotland. This was the thunderous climax to 90 minutes of football extraordinary.
> Glasgow was gay, glorious and hectic for this, the first-ever European Cup Final to be staged in Scotland. In sparkling sunshine thousands mingled on the Hampden trek. Accents from all over the globe mixed with the Glasgow burr as the good humoured crowd spilled across the city.[27]

This article has set out to draw up a preliminary model of the birth of the modern sport spectacular. The Real Madrid-Eintracht Frankfurt soccer match at Hampden Park, Glasgow, on 18 May 1960 was selected for a number of reasons. It satisfactorily illustrated Guttmann's seven-stage 'ritual to record' model of modern sport. In terms of three further concepts – representation, centrality and community – the game, the setting and the cultural environment symbolized something above and beyond a good game of soccer. An eleventh concept concerned the European rather than national communication reaches of the event. The final concept explored the necessary dimensions of an event if it is to be classified as 'spectacular'. Gento, the dashing Real Madrid winger recalls:

> We were aware that the day was something special, even for us. I don't think any of us wanted the referee to end the match, and I think that was true of the crowd. Also I think it was our best display. . . .[28]

Clifford Geertz in a chapter of *Local Knowledge* writes about the social history of the imagination and makes the point that groups of individuals make sense out of what happens to them by the construction and deconstruction of symbolic systems.[29] Richard Holt, discussing British urban soccer fans, put it this way, 'Football was like a mirror that reflected back the image the crowd wanted to see'.[30] On the night of 18 May 1960 that reflection must have buoyed up the spirits and bolstered the identities of not just the 127,261 Hampden Park spectators but the legion of radio and television fans in a network of other European countries.

A Spaniard recalls the cultural magic of that occasion:

> I remember the ambience that the team [Real Madrid] would create in the whole country, especially when it played against another European team . . . every time that RM played and won, the whole country (especially the male population) would take pride in the RM victory as if it had been their own . . . During the game the whole country was paralysed. Businesses were closed, the streets were deserted and the attention of all focussed on the game. For those ninety minutes soccer transcended the daily problems of Spain and the country was mesmerized by the 'meringues' as the media portrayed them . . . RM made Spaniards a happy people.[31]

## Notes

1. A. Guttmann, *From Ritual to Record* (New York, 1978).
2. The 1936 Olympics has been excluded from this discussion because of the political clout of the Nazi state and the ideological barnstorming that went on under the umbrella of 'sport'.
3. Guttmann, op. cit., p. 26.
4. Ibid., p. 26.
5. Ibid., p.37.
6. Ibid., p.40.
7. Ibid., p.44.
8. J. Arlott (ed.), *The Oxford Companion to Sports and Games* (London, 1975), pp. 344–54.
9. Guttmann, op. cit., p. 48.
10. Results, *World Soccer*, June 1980, p. 22.
11. A. Guttmann, *Sports Spectators* (New York, 1986), p. 104.
12. Ibid., p. 176.
13. Arlott, op. cit., p.356.
14. Guttmann, *Sports Spectators*, p. 182.
15. C. L. R. James, *Beyond a Boundary* (New York, 1983), preface.
16. A. Metcalfe, 'Sport and Community: The Mining Communities of East Northumberland, 1800–1914', a paper presented at the North American Society for Sport History meeting, Chicago, 26 May 1991.
17. *New York Times*, 19 May 1960, p. 52.
18. R. Holt, *Sport and the British – A Modern History* (Oxford, 1990), p. 260.
19. Ibid., p. 170.
20. R. Roberts and J. Olson, *Winning Is the Only Thing* (Baltimore, 1989), p. 111.
21. Arlott, op. cit., p. 354.
22. Various articles, *Sports Illustrated*, 23 May 1960.
23. New *York Times*, 19 May 1960, p. 52.
24. *The Times*, 19 May 1960, p. 21.

25. *New York Times*, 19 May 1960, p. 52.
26. *The Times*, 19 May 1960, p. 21.
27. *Scottish Daily Record*, 19 May 1960, p. 1.
28. An undated report – no author included – headlined 'The European Cup 1955–1980' received from the Mitchell Library, Glasgow, 28 April 1992.
29. C. Geertz, *Local Knowledge: Further Essays in Interpretive Anthropology* (New York, 1983), Ch. 2.
30. Holt, op. cit., p. 173.
31. J.-M. Fernandez-Balboa: personal communication dated 6 May 1992.

**8**

# Sport on Commercial Norwegian Radio 1988 to 2003

*Peter Dahlén and Ragnhild Thomsen*

## 1. Introduction: Research on Radio Sport

Although a neglected area of study, some academic studies of radio sport have recently emerged against the background of an ever-developing market. In the United States, where more than 400 million radios receive signals from over 10,000 radio stations sports broadcasting has become a major genre: "Over $2.3 billion is spent on sports radio advertising annually. It is a promotional stable." (Schaaf, 2004, pp. 147–148)

In his study on the history of Notre Dame football broadcasting, *The Fighting Irish on the Air*, Gullifor (2001) presented a key map of the development of radio (and TV) sport in the United States. Gullifor showed how investment increased from the 1980s onwards. In 1982, Notre Dame collected $75,000 in radio revenue, and in 1983 earned its first ever six digit figure from selling radio rights when it secured $550,000 in a 5-year contract with Mutual (Mutual was bought in the mid-1980s and became Westwood One). At the beginning of the 21st century, Mutual/Westwood One pays more than $1 m dollars for the exclusive network radio rights to Notre Dame football, more than double what it paid in the mid-1980s (Gullifor, 2001, pp. 68–73, 160).

In an equally groundbreaking and well-documented work, on the play-by-play history of *Sports on New York Radio*, Halberstam (1999) described how sports talk radio was born in New York in 1964 when "the encyclopedic-minded Bill Mazer arrived in New York and introduced the market to its first-ever

**Source:** *Trends in Communication*, 12(2/3) (2004): 117–130.

telephone sports talk show" (pp. 319–320). In the 1970s the play-by-play announcers still enjoyed great prestige in New York, but talk shows were starting to carve a niche. On July 1, 1987, Emmis Communications turned their country formatted WHN into WFAN, the nation's first all-sports station, and, in the words of Halberstam, "the sports radio landscape was forever changed" (pp. 321–322, 378; see Stavitsky, 1995, pp. 88–89). In 1992, WFAN was sold to Infinity Broadcasting, and by 1997, 10 years after it went on air, WFAN was said to reach 1.3 million people a week, with morning host Imus turning over 50% of the audience to the rest of the radio station: "By its 10th anniversary, the all-sports trail blazer was the envy of America's station operators," and since 1987 "more than 50 [radio stations with an all-sports format] have sprouted all over America" – most of them trying to emulate WFAN (Halberstam, 1999, pp. 327–328).

According to Halberstam (1999), in the late 1990s sports talk radio was well established with all-sports radio stations housing different personalities, "some brasher and some softer, some funnier and some more opinionated" (pp. 346–347). An important part of this development occurred when ESPN Radio (run by Disney-owned ABC) was formed in 1992 and broadcast over WFAN on weekends (Halberstam, 1999, pp. 187, 378–379). Catsis (1996) made another major contribution towards mapping the activities and businesses of radio (and TV) sport in the United States. In the United Kingdom, extensive live coverage on football is available both on television and on radio through stations such as BBC Radio 5 Live and BBC Radio Scotland. In addition,

> a substantial quantity of talk-based football content is now available on television and radio. These programs include discussion-based programs like *Any Sporting Questions* on Radio 5 Live, phone-in programs like Radio 5 Live's *606* or Reel Radio's *Reel Football Phone In* as well as comedy-based programs like Radio Scotland's *Off the Ball*. These talk-based programs are also found in many other European countries, most extensively in Italy. (Morrow, 2003, pp. 166–167)

In Scotland, O'Donnell (2003) published a study of another football-based program *Saturday Super Scoreboard*, launched in 1978 on the commercial station Radio Clyde. As one of the most listened-to radio programs in the western part of Scotland, it regularly draws audiences of over 300,000 – 14% of the population aged four and over in that area. This "reflects an audience pull many television programmes would be envious of." According to O'Donnell, this situation "is by no means restricted to Scotland. So great is radio sports coverage in certain parts of Catalonia, for example, that radio sport there has been termed a 'macrogenre'" (pp. 211–212).

Other studies on radio sport in the United Kingdom include Boyle's (1992) analysis of the link between sport on the radio and broader nation-building processes in Ireland, while Haynes (1999) investigated the origins of the relationship between the Football Association and the BBC in the formative years of 1927 to 1939. A book by the senior football commentator Green (2000), *The Green Line*, on his 25 years in the BBC (on Radio 2 and Radio 5 Live) is also worth mentioning.

In Germany, Gödeke (1976) wrote about the importance of radio sport there during the postwar period. In Sweden, Dahlén (1999) published his dissertation on the Swedish Broadcasting Corporation's radio sports coverage seen in a historical perspective, 1925 to 1995. Dahlén also published on several aspects of early radio sport for youth (2000e), sport in children's educational radio (2001), the popular events around the nationalistic "Vasaloppet" Ski Race in 1952 (2000b), and various other elements of the history of Swedish radio sport (2000a, 2000c, 2000d).

## 2. Norwegian Broadcasting – A Short History

The first radio service in Norway started in 1924, and in the following years a number of small, privately owned companies were established in different regions (Syvertsen, 1991, pp. 332–333). In 1933, the public service institution, the Norwegian Broadcasting Corporation (NRK) was established and during the next 60 years, NRK built up a roster of main sport events, some of them inherited from its predecessor the Broadcasting Company (Kringkastingselskapet; cf. Whannel, 1992), and including ski jumping, skiing, and football.

Until television was inaugurated in 1960, NRK had only one radio station. The NRK broadcasting monopoly partly came to an end in 1981 with the deregulation of broadcasting and the advent of local radio, initially on an experimental basis. Advertising was prohibited, by regulation, for all broadcast media in Norway. The local broadcasters therefore had to come up with different solutions to finance their activity, and bingo, lottery, and "voluntary license fee" were among the sources of income. However it was difficult to draw a clear line between legal and illegal financing, as some types of sponsoring and announcements were allowed despite the advertising ban (Halse & Østby, 2003, p. 197). The development of local radio after the 1981 broadcasting deregulations was rapid, and within a few years numbered 300 stations (Fossum, 1997, pp. 59–60). NRK, moved to address this new competition from local radio and transnational commercial satellite stations. In 1985, NRK opened its second national radio station, P2 (with the original station labeled P1).

The period from 1982 to 1993 was a golden age for sport on NRK Radio, according to former Sports Head Arne Porsum (personal communication, March 19, 2004). With the establishment of a second nationwide station, the sports department got considerable elbowroom to broadcast a greater number of events. The management also understood that sports content was important to attract listeners to other programs in addition to the sports broadcasts themselves.

In 1988, new legislation allowed for permanent local broadcasting and introduced advertising as a source of income. This development was motivated by the emergence of chains of local radio stations, both through illegal trade where stations were bought and sold, usually camouflaged as mergers, and through sophisticated networking arrangements bartering local advertising for national news notwithstanding regulations prescribing local production and ownership.

Through such arrangements the owners of the news source could offer their advertisers de facto near-national coverage. The Legislature was forced to act: "In line with the prevailing liberal ideology, the solution was simply to move the limit and allow a national commercial radio channel." (Fossum, 1997, p. 61) The first private commercial radio channel with national coverage, P4, commenced broadcasting in September 1993. The 10-year license for P4 was allotted to Radio Whole of Norway (Radio Hele Norge, RHN), a company dominated by Swedish-owned Kinnevik.[1] As a political compromise, and in line with the tradition of broadcasting in Norway, public service obligations were imposed. The license terms were vague. The only demands stated explicitly were that P4 had to establish their own news department. However, P4 undertook to build on the fundamentals of public service in the widest sense, emphasizing news, debate, service radio, interaction with the listeners (i.e. phone-ins), "experience radio," and sport (Fossum, 1997, p. 62).

Just 2 weeks after the launch of P4, on October 2, 1993, NRK relaunched its radio services, with three profiled and well-defined stations. The existing channels, the "mainstream" channel (P1), and the "cultural" channel (P2), were supplemented by a third, the "youth" channel Petre (as P3 is pronounced in Norwegian, an acronym for "Program" and "Three"). Petre was launched to recapture the young listeners' segment that had been lost to local radio stations during the 1980s and early 1990s (Skogerbø, 1997, p. 115).

This relaunch was a deliberate response (Fossum, 1997, p. 59). NRK intended to continue being the leading public service broadcaster in Norway. To ensure its hegemony and to meet the mounting challenge from an increasing number of competitors, radical changes were necessary to discard old political regulations and to modernize the institution and its output. The new three-channel division of NRK radio was not without problems, most pressing were the questions of where to place sport and programs in the Sami minority language. A new management relegated sport to the youth channel P3, which only had a coverage area of 90%. Accordingly, in the graduation to three stations and extensive formatting, sport suffered in NRK for some years. In 1996, the sports broadcasts were relocated to P1, the main station, and the conditions improved: "sport had to be on the most popular channel, which is P1" (Fossum, 1997, p. 64). Since then sports coverage has increased.

With the establishment of a nationwide, commercial radio station and a third NRK station in 1993, Norwegian radio stations started formatting their output. Hence, formatting and programming are two central instruments to consider when studying the significance of sport on Norwegian radio stations. Formatting is a phenomenon dating from the 1950s, when the American radio station KOWH-AM found that it could recruit more listeners by restricting the music played to a limited number of popular songs. Since then formatting has been a means to attract a chosen audience segment by use of specialized music profiles. Formatting was an unknown phenomenon in Norway until 1993, since then most radio stations in Norway have been clearly formatted and well-defined.

## 3. Nationwide Radio Stations

We now show how, and why, sport has been given high priority on some commercial Norwegian radio stations. The Norwegian radio landscape can be divided into three distinct levels. The highest level is the nationwide stations, and until 2003 this consisted of two: Norsk Rikskringkasting (NRK), which provides several public service stations and is financed by a licence fee, and P4, a commercial, privately owned station. The second level is comprised of chains of local radio stations that together cover large parts of the country.[2] We will compare two key chains, Radio 1 and Jærradiogruppen, and see how these are moving in different directions in terms of sport.[3] At the third level of the Norwegian radio landscape there are around 250 independent, local stations. We will explore a couple of these and show how they use sport in their activities. We stress that the most popular local radio station in Norway, Radio 102 Haugesund, is an independent, commercial station that gives sport high priority.

P4 was established in 1993 as the first nationwide radio station in addition to NRK, as well as the first nationwide, commercial station in Norway. P4 adopted the approved format Adult Contemporary (AC), which has a soft music profile addressed to adults between 25 and 49 years of age, especially women, as its main target group. Radio hosts with easily recognizable personal styles characterize AC-stations, and the audience knows what to expect when tuning in. The program schedule is intended to be inclusive, that is, everybody can listen to it, and the least objectionable music for the target group plays a leading role in nearly all the programs (70% of the broadcast time).

Sport was a priority area in P4's activities from the very beginning, both as part of the editorial content and as a means of branding. From its establishment the station has competed and cooperated with NRK in terms of sport, a dual posture worth noting. P4 and NRK cooperate in securing the rights to broadcast sports events operating the European Broadcasting Union (EBU) policy of open radio access to such events. As a member of EBU, NRK has the rights to major international events, and gives P4 some access. Conversely, P4 owns the radio rights to some important events, such as national and international handball that it shares with NRK. In this respect P4 and NRK are complementary rather than competitor stations. Sports Head Morten Scott Janssen (personal communication, March 23, 2003) for P4 said that his station "always have had a very good dialogue with NRK, and the main reason is that we provide so different products that we don't compete with each other, but we are substitutes. . . . We feel that we complement each other."

Thus, P4 and NRK view one another as complementary stations due to different formats and programs. Commercial radio stations such as P4 use formatted program techniques to include and satisfy a wide range of listeners, and the sports broadcasts therefore contain a mix of music, small talk, and short features from the arenas while NRK transmits entire sports events whole. P4 is well defined and clearly formatted. Its rules require that talk is interrupted every 3 minutes by music. This reflects research estimating the audience attention-span at a couple of minutes, and because the station wants to attract all types of listeners particularly women (Morten Janssen, personal communication, March 23, 2003). P4 has worked hard to build credibility regarding the sports coverage. NRK with its long track record was a more trusted sports broadcaster, and the audience distrusted the blended formats. P4 therefore had to change the audiences' listening habits, and persuade them to prefer mixed programs consisting of music and short sports features. Janssen claimed that the audience "has got new habits because they actually don't need to listen to every single kick. They *can* be friends with their wife without missing something. To give them that confidence has been important to us during all these years." Janssen stressed that "our format is holy. We cannot mess with it; it is our most important competitive advantage" (personal communication, March 23, 2003).

Nonetheless P4 and NRK *are* in fact competitors because they both cover most major national and international sports events. Sports Head Grethe Gynild Johnsen (personal communication, February 17, 2004) in NRK commented

> we give one another access to each others' events because we are in principle of the opinion that radio rights should be free for everyone, but we compete in giving these events content. . . . We have to compete regarding which station fills the broadcast with the best content. Then the listeners have to decide which is the best.

Producing sports broadcasts is expensive; so why does P4 give priority to this kind of content? As a commercial enterprise P4 finds sports coverage profitable. According to Janssen, P4 broadcasts sport because it is a natural theme for a public service broadcaster. In addition, sport is profitable because the audience wants it: "We make radio based on what the listeners really want to hear, and the listeners unquestionably want to listen to sport." Janssen also stressed that "sport is something one can make money on" (personal communication, September 23, 2003). P4 generates some income on advertisements around sports broadcasts, but branding is the primary benefit. In addition to the editorial content, P4 also uses sport through sponsoring Norwegian teams and players. This investment indicates that the station "has sport and uses sport and that you get sport here" (Janssen, personal communication, September 23, 2003). This sponsorship allows P4 to project its brand.

The establishment of P4 in 1993 marginalized the local radio stations, threatening to take both their advertisers and listeners (Halse & Østbye, 2003, p. 245). This has, however, not been the case with sport, and because of relatively different products, P4 has modestly influenced the sports programs in local stations. P4 focuses on nationwide sport, while the local broadcasters offer partisan coverage of local teams. Employees in both P4 and local radio stations tend to regard each other as supplementary, not competitive. Below we show how Norwegian local radio stations have used sport content.

## 4. Chains of Local Radio Stations

*Radio 1* has for many years been the leading chain of local radio stations in Norway. Today it consists of stations in the country's four biggest cities. Radio 1 has a centralized management in Oslo that determines schedules and directions for the entire chain. The stations have, over the years, become clearly formatted and well-defined. They are streamlined and sound more or less the same in Bergen, Oslo, Trondheim, or Stavanger. The radio chain deploys the format Contemporary Hit Radio (CHR) to maximize audience.[4] CHR-stations target the 12 to 34 age group. Content is characterized by a fast-pace, high share of music, small amount of talk, and energetic radio hosts. Contests and branding are important; news has secondary significance. Radio 1 also uses elements from a variant to the AC format, and focuses on women as an important target group.

Sport had been central to the editorial content in at least two of the Radio 1 stations. Coverage has now been minimized with formatting focusing on target groups, marked demands, and profitability. Thus commercialization influenced editorial content. This was particularly evident in Bergen and Trondheim where the local soccer teams in the premier division ("Brann" in Bergen and "Rosenborg" in Trondheim) have a large following. The Radio 1 stations have traditionally covered their away matches; a unique level of coverage. Until 2003, the stations transmitted games in their entirety to a loyal and substantial fan base. A former employee in Radio 1 in Trondheim, Roy Arne Salater (personal communication, January 26, 2004), recalled that almost the entire city listened to Radio 1 coverage. He recalled the priority given to sport: Besides a comprehensive coverage of Rosenborg; the station broadcasted handball, ice hockey, and sports news every morning and evening. It even sent reporters to Brussels to attend the draw of Rosenborg's opponents in the Champions League. The chairman and players of the club were among the audience at home. Advertising for the sports broadcasts sold well, and the soccer reporter achieved celebrity status in the city, a unique achievement in Norwegian radio.

However, the central management decided to cut the sports coverage, reducing the sports broadcasts to a formatted mixture of small talk, music, and short sports features. Some listeners objected to this adjustment; one listener expressed this opinion at Rosenborg's web page:[5]

> Last year Radio 1 gave excellent live-coverage of all of Rosenborg's matches. . . . This year however, they have completely changed strategies. . . . Now there is a lot of empty small talk and summaries throughout the match interrupted by seemingly endless bits of music.

A year later (2004) a new owner, the international media corporation SBS Broadcasting, removed the remaining sports content. After a gradual reduction, Radio 1 in Bergen is not transmitting sport at all and Radio 1 in Trondheim has terminated its focus on Rosenborg after 13 years of coverage. The competing radio station RadioAdressa has now bought exclusive rights to the club's activities.[6] Interviews with former/present employees of the Radio 1 chain suggest that they do not endorse the management's decision on this.

In management's view sport is a poor fit in well-defined, formatted stations such as Radio 1. Since 1996, in the formats deployed, sport was a nonpreferred area. Although of interest, it did not command resources within the CHR-format (Pål Thore Krosby, personal communication, January 26, 2004[7]). This format is directed to young, urban, and up-to-date people with considerable purchasing power, and a typical listener is a highly educated woman who enjoys movies, cafés, and shopping. The sports audience did not correspond to this profile principally because they had no loyalty to Radio 1 beyond sport. The removal of sport can therefore be explained as being a fear of losing regular listeners and the recognition that sport does not sufficiently appeal to the target audience. Sportscasting also imports costs of production and rights that greatly exceed those of the single DJ operating from the studio.

Former and current staff in the local Radio 1 stations however disagree with management, stressing the importance of sport in local identification, observing that the chain has dropped one of the more important service, local journalism because of cost. They argue that it does not matter if sport is incompatible with the wishes of the main target group; as long as the sports broadcasts occur outside prime time, that is, evenings and weekends, they will probably attract more listeners than what the radio stations normally could expect at such times. Kim Rud Pettersen (personal communication, January 23, 2004), football reporter at Radio 1 in Trondheim from 1988 to 2001, commented on the decline of sports coverage:

> a majority of the strategies are designed centrally and for the person sitting in Oslo it is hard to see why the people living in Trondheim support Rosenborg. . . . And they then conceive a collective strategy that is usually

made up of music and various humorous features and other content, often at the expense of sporting activities because they envision a nation-wide focus, rather than a local focus.

Roy Arne Salater (personal communication, January 26, 2004), a former employee in Radio 1 in Trondheim underlined that:

> it really surprises me that Radio 1 cancelled the sports coverage. Some of the sales staff that worked in Radio 1 were selling advertising like hotcakes to the football matches, so it was very surprising when they suddenly cut that off. . . . What Radio 1 has done, is moving away from one of the things I think is the most important of all, that is local journalism. The local broadcasts are a local station's strongest point. I am almost embarrassed on behalf of Radio 1, that has ruled out Rosenborg. They can't even call themselves a local radio station anymore, but perhaps they don't want to do that either. It is easy solutions that can bring in as much money as possible.

Despite dropping sports coverage, Radio 1 still regards sport as valuable in branding terms. As a commercial enterprise Radio 1 postures only towards profit, a policy that is clear in its treatment of sport. Through sponsorship sport remains a means to maintain a local identity. In Bergen, Radio 1 sponsored and supported local indoor soccer tournaments. In return for free advertising, the name Radio 1 is now attached to the tournament's name, Radio 1 Løkkecup,[8] and its logo is exposed on tournament posters all over Bergen several times a year. Radio 1 in Oslo, is a commercial station that does not transmit sports coverage at all, but nevertheless uses sport in its activities. The station sponsors one of the local premier division soccer teams, and in return gets its logo projected on the players' and coaches' sweaters.

To summarize, Radio 1 is a commercial radio chain that has removed sport as editorial content due to increased formatting and focus on younger target groups. The chain, however, still uses sport as a means of branding. Below we present a commercial chain that moves in the opposite direction in terms of sports broadcasts.

*Jærradiogruppen* is a chain of 17 local radio stations privately owned by Herman Skretting and A-pressen, a media corporation with business activities within newspapers, printing, TV, and electronic media. The chain emerged in 1997 when Skretting expanded from owning only Jærradioen, a successful local radio station on the West coast of Norway, to become the owner of several stations around the country. In contrast to the Radio 1 chain, the stations belonging to Jærradiogruppen all have a unique identity and can barely be regarded as a unit. This is changing, however. The owners try to streamline the stations and make them sound more similar to compete with P4 for advertisers at the national level.

The stations have already adopted the same target group (13 to 40 year olds), music profile, and style for the radio hosts. Furthermore, the national strategy implies transferring successful programming formats, including sports formats, from one station to the others. A model station in this respect is Jærradioen, the key station in the group, which boasts a very popular sports program concept. Now, we will examine how the station transmits sport and emphasize how it differs from the methods applied by the Radio 1 chain.

Jærradioen is faithful to its sports traditions despite formatting and commercialization. The station still transmits a significant number of sports events, and it uses the format of sports broadcasts that it did in the 1980s. While Radio 1 replaced entire transmissions of events with a mixture of music, small talk, and short features from the arena, Jærradioen still broadcasts entire matches (except for a 2 minute commercial break every quarter of an hour). Sports editor Åge Fjermestad (personal communication, January 23, 2004) in Jærradioen said that "We have held on to a concept since we started in 1987, we haven't changed a thing in the concept. It functions very well. It is dangerous to keep thinking that one should think new. We have a concept that is so secure that we wouldn't change it". Fjermestad emphasized that Jærradioen tries to provide good entertainment by being positive, representing local interest, and it does not have to be "sour, critical and negative like a journalistic angle would be."

Jærradioen values the large audience for sports broadcasts that does not necessarily fit into the target group or return to the frequency the next day. Still they are valued at Jærradioen because they are loyal to the station's sports broadcasts and attract advertisers. Some of the sports listeners also stay tuned to Jærradioen out of loyalty. The sports broadcasts are not profitable in themselves, but enhance the station's profile.

These two chains illustrate how local conditions can determine the emphasis on sports coverage for local radio stations. In the absence of a high profile local team sports coverage has very limited appeal for radio stations. Conversely where there are two or more competing high profile teams overt support for one over the other risks alienating listeners. Where there is a single dominant team, with widespread local support, sports coverage provides strong local identification.

We have shown how two commercial radio chains regard sport differently. Now, we focus on independent local radio stations and see how sport can be worthwhile to them in different ways.

## 5. Independent Local Radio Stations

The most popular local radio station in Norway (that with highest number of listeners in its own area) is an independent, commercial station that gives sport high priority. Each news bulletin contains sport, and the station transmits soccer or handball matches every weekend. It might be expected that a station as popular as *Radio 102* Haugesund[9] would adopt the same policy as the Radio 1 chain and offer sports programs as a mix of music, sports features, and small talk to satisfy a wide range of listeners. This is not the case. Radio 102 transmits entire games as Jærradioen does. The station tries to keep a share of 50% music and 50% sport in sports broadcasts, and never interrupts a game with music. Manager and editor Per Helgesen (personal communication, February 12, 2004) said that Radio 102 stakes a lot of money and resources on sport to keep its position in the local media market. The station competes with another radio station as well as with television and newspapers, and regards sport as a competitive advantage aiming to provide better coverage than its competitors.

Their reason for giving priority to sport is that it engages people. Still, Radio 102 is conscious that sport has a limited place in the schedule if it is to avoid alienating listeners who do not take an interest in this type of content. Another reason for broadcasting sports events is that they actually recruit more listeners than what the station could otherwise expect at certain times. Most games and events take place during the weekends, which generally are a poor time for radio. Helgesen (personal communication, February 12, 2004) pointed out that "Radio is a strong medium Monday to Friday, and there are some [listeners] on Saturdays but very few on Sundays. So it [sports broadcasting] is actually about recruiting more listeners than we normally would have on Sundays." It is interesting to note that although Radio 102 evidently is a formatted station, with a music share of 60%, competitions and other types of interactivity with the listeners as well as a high degree of awareness of what the audience wants, the sports broadcasts are not consistent with the rest of the program offering. As already mentioned, this is due to the perception that sport increases the ratings at certain times.

Sports clubs have been among the owners of Radio 102 since its establishment in 1985. A characteristic of Norwegian radio stations is that the local stations were originally established by interest groups spreading ideological and religious information. Due to the advertising ban the owners originally had no commercial motives. The sports clubs and Christian organizations that owned Radio 102 used the radio to inform people about their activities. Gradually, however, Radio 102 became a joint-stock company and the founders sold their shares, chiefly to the local newspaper *Haugesunds Avis* that today has a share of 76%. There are still some ideological organizations among the owners, but Radio 102 today regards itself as a commercial enterprise. The goal is to generate income, and their activities started yielding good profits in recent years. To achieve profitability to shareholders, messages were limited and relegated to nonpeak time (Per Helgesen, personal communication, February 12, 2004). As radio has become increasingly professional and commercial, the sports clubs have withdrawn from ownership and from providing editorial content.

Some of the local radio stations continue to be run by religious or ideological organizations that regard broadcasting as a means of spreading a particular message. To recruit listeners, some of them offer a general schedule where sport is among the program genres employed to attract listeners to inform them about a certain viewpoint. *Radio Øst* (Radio East) is one of the stations that regard sport as a way of getting in touch with a wide range of people. Manager Nils Gunnar Haraldseid (personal communication, February 4, 2004) explained that "We were not interested in making a radio just for the Christians. We wanted to make a radio for the public. And of course make them become interested in what Christians stand for."

Radio Øst considers itself as a sort of public service radio, although according to the licensing authorities it is a commercial radio station because it provides paid employment For this reason we have included ideological stations in an article about trends in sports coverage on Norwegian commercial radio. Profit is not a goal for Radio Øst, and none of its shareholders make money from it. Although other commercial stations cover sport due to their financial motives, Radio Øst has, therefore, purely ideological reasons for the use of sport. The sports coverage is limited to updates of results and achievements, and the extent of coverage is comparable to other current affairs topics (Nils Gunnar Haraldseid, personal communication, February 4, 2004). Up until 1992, however, the station did have a more ambitious sports policy. This included transmissions of entire ice hockey matches with two full-time employees merely covering sport. This commitment was reduced because many of the listeners found the sports coverage to be too extensive.

## 6. Radio Sport Broadcasting Rights

In the time of broadcasting monopoly (pre-1981) NRK would negotiate with the various sports associations to transmit their activities. In the absence of competition the rates were relatively modest, and because the radio and television negotiated jointly, radio rights were cheap. The question of radio rights received new significance when the Norwegian Parliament inaugurated local radio stations in 1981 ending the broadcasting monopoly. Some of the new stations sought to offer sports coverage but met resistance. For example the Norwegian Football Association (NFF), which controlled rights to the most popular events, feared losing attendance at the arenas if games were transmitted on the radio.

Gradually, the NFF softened its attitude, allowing local radio stations to broadcast sport by granting the individual soccer clubs power to enter into agreements with their local radio stations. NFF only requested to be informed about agreements to prevent local radio stations reselling their rights to other stations. The clubs themselves decided whether the radio stations would pay for the rights in cash or by advertising barter. Some clubs have charged considerable sums, and Jærradioen has since 1990 paid in total more than 118,700 to Viking and Bryne, two top division soccer teams, while Radio 1 in Trondheim paid approximately 11,900 a year to Rosenborg in addition to buying exclusive seats at the arena and promoting the team on the air.

The establishment of P4 in 1993 raised further questions regarding radio rights. NRK held the rights to transmit most major sports events, and P4 therefore had to negotiate with its competitor to get access to these events. As a friendly gesture, NRK allowed the newcomer to participate in their rights. During the 1994 Winter Olympics at Lillehammer, NRK also gave assistance with administrative challenges, studio facilities, and by permitting P4 to transmit parts of NRK's broadcast on its own frequency (Arne Porsum, personal communication, March 19, 2004; Morten Scott Janssen, personal communication, September 23, 2003).

The balance between the nationwide radio stations changed, however, in 1995. As a member of the European Broadcasting Union (EBU), NRK owns the rights to most major international sports events. P4 is not an EBU member, but it gets access to these events through agreements with NRK. This type of resale is a practical arrangement that can be found in many countries, and is approved by the EBU (Grethe Gynild Johnsen, personal communication, February 17, 2004). In 1995, P4 secured some rights, securing exclusive rights to the handball World Championship for women. NRK obtained P4's cooperation to transmit those matches. Women's handball is extremely popular in Norway due to the national team's international success. From this year on, NRK and P4 have alternately exchanged radio rights.

NRK and P4 cooperate first of all because both institutions support EBU's position that radio rights should be available for everyone. This view has an ideological basis of free news communication as well as a practical recognition that technological equipment renders it possible to broadcast secretly (Grethe Gynild Johnsen, personal communication, February 17, 2004). Therefore, the stations do not compete on events, but on offering the best content from the activities. The second reason why NRK and P4 work together is that they do not particularly regard each other as competitors due to the difference in products. Despite the negotiations about access and conditions, P4 and NRK have a stable relationship regarding radio rights. The present agreement lasts until some time in the year 2005, but the stable situation will most likely continue beyond that date.

## 7. Recent Developments

By the beginning of 2004, a second nationwide commercial radio station, Kanal 24,[10] was established and the expansion of the radio field once again raised questions concerning radio sports rights. The issue was whether the newcomer would have access to Norwegian soccer. Some years ago, P4 secured exclusive rights to the commercial broadcast of soccer, intending to keep future competitors at a distance. Kanal 24 is, however, partly owned by TV2, a privately owned commercial TV station established in 1992 and the television equivalent of P4. This fact was to challenge P4's contract on soccer rights. The media agreement between TV2 and the Norwegian Football Association stipulated that TV2 would also own radio rights if it obtained control of a commercial radio station. The NFF thus had to reconsider the exclusivity given to P4. These circumstances resulted in an ongoing dispute between P4 and NFF that has not yet been resolved.

This dispute about soccer rights illustrates how radio has become an integrated part of television agreements. This threatens P4 because both Kanal 24 and NRK Radio have a close relationship to significant television players, TV2 and NRK TV respectively. P4's future position in one sport is now unclear as TV2 has secured the rights to broadcast handball next year (Morten Scott Janssen, personal communication, September 23, 2003). However even P4 benefits from the rise of all-inclusive media agreements. The station is partly owned by the Swedish media corporation Modern Times Group (MTG) that also owns the television station TV3, distributed via cable and satellite and received by around 65% of the Norwegian population.[11] The TV station owns the broadcasting rights to the Champions League, and as an associate station P4 is able to share in these rights in exchange for advertisements for TV3 (Morten Scott Janssen, personal communication, March 23, 2003).

Because of its short time in operation, the significance of sport on Kanal 24 remains to be seen. Today, the station offers a 4-hr weekly sports magazine every Sunday afternoon; it invests in children's sport by awarding scholarships and it distributes aid to individuals and associations in need of new equipment.

## 8. Conclusions

In this article, we have discussed the outcome of the deregulation of Norwegian radio during the 1980s and 1990s, by focusing on sports matters. Alongside the NRK, a public service institution, we have located players at three main levels. For P4, the first private commercial radio station with national coverage, sport is a priority area, while the leading chains of local radio stations at the second level, Radio 1 and Jærradiogruppen, have moved in different directions. Due to formatting policies, Radio 1 has gradually reduced their sports coverage, while Jærradiogruppen continues to give priority to sport, as do, for different reasons, the third level in our study, the independent local radio stations Radio 102, Haugesund, and Radio Øst.

## Notes

1. Today Modern Times Group (MTG) dominates (http://www.eierskapstilsynet.no/database/dbprogs/).
2. The chains are to some extent profiled as nationwide to advertisers.
3. *jærradiogruppen* is the jær radio group. Jær is short form of Jæren, a region on the West coast of Norway.
4. See http://engberg.com/formater.hrm

5. Rosenborg's Web page is http://www.rbkweb.com/skrivut/1809. The expression quote was posted February 25, 2003.
6. http://www.propaganda-as.no/php/art.php?id-100785.
7. Pål Thore Krosby was a managing director and editor of Radio 1 from 1996 to 2001.
8. *Løkkecup* is a cup at a local playing field.
9. Haugesund is located on the West coast of Norway.
10. *Kanal* 24 means channel 24.
11. http://www.tv3.no/index.phtml?pagetype=document&document=178&nav=171

# References

Boyle, R. (1992). From our Gaelic fields: Radio, sport and nation in post-partition Ireland. *Media, Culture and Society, 14*, 623–636.

Catsis, J. R. (1996). *Sports broadcasting.* Chicago: Nelson-Hail.

Dahlén, P. (1999). *Från Vasaloppet till Sportextra. Radiosportens etablering och förgrening 1925–1995.* [From the "Vasaloppet" Ski Race to *Sportextra.* The Establishment and Expansion of Radio Sports *1925–1995*], Stockholm, Sweden: Stiftelsen Etermedierna i Sverige.

Dahlén, P. (2000a). Att skriva mediehistoria. Den svenska radiosporten ur ett period iseringsperspektiv. [Writing media history. The Swedish radio sports in a period perspective]. *Nordicom Information* nr 1.

Dahlén, P. (2000b). Karusellmannens underbara öden och äventyr. Radion och Vasaloppet 1952. [The wonderful adventures of the carousel man. Radio and the "Vasaloppet" Ski Race in 1952]. In Bo G. Nilsson (Ed.): *Idrottens själ.* Fataburen 2000, Stockholm, Sweden; Nordiska museet.

Dahlén, P. (2000c). Radiosporten laddar om. [Changing gears at the radio sports desk]. *JMG Granskaren* nr 1, Göteborgs universitet.

Dahlén, P. (2000d). Ska medierna bevaka lokal eller nationell sport? [Should the media cover local or national sports?]. *JMG Granskaren* nr 1. Göteborgs universitet.

Dahlén, P. (2000e). Ungdom, sport och medier. Om populär idrottspropaganda. [Youth, sport and media. On popular sports propaganda]. *Aktuell beteendevetenskaplig idrottsforskning. SVEBIs årsbok 2000*, Lund.

Dahlén, P. (2001). Hälsolära, gymnastik och idrott. Kroppskulturen i skolradion 1930–1939. [Health education, gymnastics and sports. The body culture in educational radio 1930–1939]. *Aktuell beteendevetenskaplig idrottsforskning. SVEBIs årsbok 2001*, Lund.

Fossum, H. (1997). The Norwegian radio reform. In U. Carlsson (Ed.): *Radio research in Denmark, Finland, Norway and Sweden* (vol. 1, pp. 59–69). Gothenburg, Sweden: Nordicom Review.

Green, A. (2000). *The green line. Views from sport's most outspoken commentator.* London: Headline.

Gullifor, P. F. (2001). *The fighting Irish on the air. The history of Notre Dame football broadcasting.* South Bend, IN: Diamond Communications.

Gödeke, P. (1976). *Der Stellenwert des Sports im Hörfunkprogramm: dargestallt an der Entwicklung des Sportfunks bei drei Rundfunkanstalten seit 1945 unter besonderer Berücksichtigung des NWDR (NDR/WDR)* [The validation of sports in radio programming: Exemplified presentation of the development of radio sports on three channels since 1945, with special reference to NWDR]. Münster, Germany: Vlg Regensberg.

Halberstam, D. J. (1999). *Sports on New York radio. A play-by-play history.* Lincolnwood, IL: Masters.

Halse, K. J., & Østbye, H. (2003). *Norsk Kringkastingshistorie* [The history of broadcasting in Norway]. Oslo, Norway: Samlaget.

Haynes, R. (1999). There's many a slip twixt the eye and the lip: An exploratory history of football broadcasts and running commentaries 1927–1939. *International Review of the Sociology/of Sports, 32*, 143–156.

Morrow, S. (2003). *The people's game? Football, finance and society.* Hampshire, England: Palgrave Macmillan.

O'Donnell, H. (2002). Fitba crazy? *Saturday super scoreboard* and the dialectics of political debate. In A. Bernstein & N. Blain (Eds.), *Sport, media, culture* (pp. 211–226). London: Cass.

Schaaf, P. (2004). *Sports, Inc. 100 years of sports business.* Amherst, NY: Prometheus.

Skogerbø, E. (1997). Radio for the few or for the many? Experiences from the political history of local radio in Norway. In U. Carlsson (Ed.), *Radio research in Denmark, Finland, Norway and Sweden* (pp. 107–121). Gothenburg, Sweden: Nordicom Review.

Stavitsky, A. (1995). Ear on America. In E. C. Pease & E. E. Dennis (Eds.), *Radio: The forgotten medium.* New Brunswick, NJ: Transaction.

Syvertsen, T. (1991). "Culture" vs. "business:" Structural changes in Norwegian broadcasting. In H. Rønning & K. Lundby (Eds.), *Media and communication* (pp. 331–344). Oslo: Norwegian University Press.

Whannel, G. (1992). *Fields in vision. Television sport and cultural transformation.* London: Routledge.

# 9

# Local Radio Sport from the Producer's Point of View

*Peter Gilmore*

I must say at the outset that I hope to convert the BSSH into a society for the preservation of sport on radio, because there is no doubt that radio coverage of sport, particularly local radio coverage, is in serious decline and is under increasing threat.

A wide range of audience research shows consistently that radio coverage of sport is a turn off for a large part of the potential audience, particularly that part of it that is female. There are strong commercial pressures to reduce the amount of sport coverage and to replace it with more music. As a result, the amount of airtime is being reduced, and the quality of sports coverage is also suffering. In the last five years the number of stations regularly offering live football commentary on a Saturday afternoon has fallen by 75%; only five or six commercial local stations still offer this on a Saturday, let alone at mid-week. The others will take an occasional match if their local team is involved in an important cup tie, but not otherwise.

There are, in my view, serious flaws in the research on which this is based. It is purely quantitive and can be used by the managers of radio stations to justify the reduction of "chat" to the absolute minimum, with such slogans as 'if it can't be said in ten seconds, it can't be said'. To the extent that such ideas are taken seriously, they impose terrible limitations on the potential of radio. I'm sure that if we took a straw poll here today we would find that our favourite radio presenters are those who have a definable character and

**Source:** *Sport in History* (formerly *The Sports Historian*), 13(1) (1993): 26–30.

who we wish to listen to for their own sake as well as for the information they convey.

As a producer, my task is in some ways like that of an artist facing a blank canvas. On a Saturday afternoon I have four hours to fill and most of it will depend on what actually happens while we are on the air. I can have a fair idea of what the main elements in the programme will be, as I know which matches local teams are involved in and what other local and national events I want to cover, but the most unpredictable element is whether or not the lines from the remote locations will be available at exactly the time I need them. BT telephone links are notoriously unreliable and I must try put the programme together in such a way as to get round technical failures without disruptions. In a sense, I am like a wicket keeper who has to ensure that any wides bowled by the bowlers do not go for four byes. I try to be prepared and to anticipate potential problems, at the same time as I am building a balanced programme.

The costs are surprisingly large. A full commentary on a match will cost £700 for a four hour line, which used to be only £300 not so long ago, plus a fee to the home club of up to £300. By the time the costs of a reporter and engineer have been added in, it is difficult to provide a live commentary from an away game for less than £1200. Home matches come a good deal cheaper, because we use our own permanent land lines from the local ground, but with a significant number of away matches and other coverage during the week, you are looking at £50,000 a year to give a proper level of football coverage. If your local team gets to the Cup Final, the size of the radio team is bigger and the amount of line time you need is greater and the cost will be in the region of £4000 for the afternoon's coverage.

So sport comes expensive and would not be possible without commercial sponsorship. Originally local commercial stations were not allowed to accept programme sponsorship, but this was relaxed by the Independent Broadcasting Authority (IBA) in the 1980s. Radio Trent was the first to arrange sponsorship of its sports coverage. Initially, John Smith's Breweries paid £25,000 a year, for which they received an agreed number of brand mentions in the programme and commercials inserted into the advertising breaks. Currently, such sponsorships run at about £75,000, close to half our total budget for sport. They have been the saviour of sport on local radio and though originally seen as a way of financing additional coverage, they are now essential to the funding of our mainstream programming.

Another important source of funds has been through match sponsorship. Commercial organisations are offered a package by the PR company that organises such deals between sports authorities and sponsors. This package can include, as well as the match itself, a professional quality radio coverage, with brand mentions. This is offered, free, to independent radio stations and plays an important part in filling out their sports coverage with events from all over the country and the world. This source of sports input has grown in the last eight years or so, to the extent that about half the sports coverage is provided in this way and there is now virtually no 'old fashioned' free lance input to the independent radio network. Such a system has great organisational advantages, for instance in getting accreditation to cover the Formula One GP in Britain, which is immensely complicated and barely worth the hassle for a single local station. On the other hand the PR organisation can easily feed suitably tailored reports and interviews to Radio Broadland, which has a local interest in the fortunes of the Lotus team and its drivers.

The live broadcast on Saturday is the highlight of the week for me, as I have to live on my wits and feed information to the commentators, including all the background statistics to fill out their commentary. This is not to say that I am the oracle on all sorts of information on sports, but I do have a wide range of sources from which I hope to be able to find what I need and quickly.

Sunday football is a nightmare for radio sport and Monday night is even worse; sports reporting is a job that requires a seven day a week commitment, including Bank Holidays. There are compensations, such as the coverage of the Monaco GP, mounted at the behest of a sponsor, who was also involved in the sponsorship of one of the drivers, and who asked that the whole operation be mounted from the yacht in the harbour which he had chartered. There were great problems in getting the necessary lines connected up to the yacht, and I was in a state of constant concern that the broadcast would come to an abrupt end as the lines were carried away by a passing speedboat.

In my view the reporter's relationship with his subject should be objective, or at worst, very mildly partisan. This is not a view shared by all in the business. I recall a report by a London local station on a match in which West Ham were defeated 5-1; this was reported as a totally inexplicable act of God. If the local team is playing badly, this must be reported; in five years at Nottingham I have employed any number of professional reporters, but of these, only one was able to be critical of the local teams.

Radio Trent is blessed, if that is the word, with the presence of Brian Clough, the peoples' England manager, and the greatest manipulator of the media now operating. I cannot over emphasise the influence and authority of Clough. He is probably the only club manager who can inspire awe and fear in his chairman. To a sports reporter he is, of course an extremely interesting individual, but it has to be said that dealing with him on a day to day basis can induce a nervous breakdown. I have seen a succession of reporters arrive in Nottingham with the intention of cracking Clough. Nine out of ten end up being manipulated by him. His contempt for the representatives of the media is matched only by his skill in managing them. On one famous occasion, there was a story running that he had been approached to become manager of the Welsh national team. This was milked for all it was worth until Clough, who had no intention of taking the job, instructed the club board to refuse him their consent. He told them they would have to stand only a single day's flak from the press, but was able himself to milk the story even further in the aftermath of the board's decision.

Minority sports present a challenge to local radio, and one which I have in the past tried to meet. Perhaps the most bizarre was the national championship for Artistic Roller Skating, which took place in Leicester, on our patch. The reporter, not surprisingly, knew nothing about the sport, but as is often the case with minority sports he was given a great deal of help. The national coach took him on to the rink to give him a feel of what was involved and taught him a few simple moves; his performance was marked by the judges assembled for the championship. But those days are gone unless there is sponsored coverage available. In the past we have covered canoeing, white water rafting and angling. As you can perhaps imagine, reporting on angling is a severe trial of a radio reporter. Often very little appears to be happening and it takes a very expert commentary to maker it interesting. It usually seems that angling matches take place in pouring rain, with equipment dripping with water and likely to short out at any moment. Now we can't afford either the cash or the time to cover minority sports to any extent. Swimming in Nottingham is. quite a major activity, with a number of good quality local performers and Speedo, the costume manufacturers, have a factory in the town but we don't give any coverage. On the other hand Rugby League, which is a very small minority sport in our area, was reported a couple of weeks ago by us and practically every other station when the local team, Nottingham Outlaws won their first match in some three years.

The squeezing out of minority sport is not confined to independent stations, the BBC local stations have equally been forced to cut back. The system of funding is such that BBC stations are bidding on a central cash pool of unknown size for their week by week expenditure. If they collectively spend heavily in the early part of the season, a particular station may find that there are no funds to cover the local team's games in an exciting end of season run at promotion.

There is of course a lot of behind the scenes work to do to set up the arrangements for major programmes. Taking a local station to a Cup Final is a major performance and something of a nightmare, particularly if you adhere to the arrangements laid on by the Football Association, which limit the size of the crew to four and offer only the most limited facilities for ancillary interviews and other material to support the actual match commentary. It has been my practice for several years to cultivate a close relationship with the Wembley Stadium press office; this has enable Radio Trent to have a crew of ten, its own outside broadcast vehicle on site and facilities for direct line interviews both from within the stadium and from the approach areas outside. This has been well worth the several good lunches it has cost, though we have not yet found a way of coping with the requirements of the local authority. Brent Council have a curious relationship with Wembley and insist on vetting and approving in advance the arrangements for each major event, often requiring what appear to be petty and most inconvenient rearrangements at the last minute.

The relationship between the News desk and the sports side of the station is not easy. The news people are glad to have us as a means of filling their bulletins on a slow news day, but appear to have no feel for the news values of sports stories, either in selecting which sports items to use as fillers or in recognising the occasions when a sports story ought to be on the main news in its own right. A classic example was the reporting by Radio Trent of England's last match in the 1990 World Cup. The sports desk had prepared a full report and interview with the team manager, but none of it was used on the main news bulletin, because the News editor 'hadn't noticed' the item, or had failed to recognise its significance. More work needs to be done to improve the mutual understanding of the two sides.

# 10

# How Should We Theorize Sport in a Capitalist Patriarchy?

*M. Ann Hall*

The major assumption in this brief comment is that sport, no matter how broadly or narrowly it is defined, is a cultural practice that sustains structured relationships of domination and subordination. I think it is also possible to make the same assumptions about play and games. All three, therefore, can be conceptualized and theorized as *real social practices*. They are neither idealist abstractions as liberals/positivists would have us believe, nor are they simple products of material conditions as some neo-marxists* insist. They are, as Gruneau (1983:50) puts it, ". . . constitutive social practices whose meanings, metaphoric qualities, and regulatory structures are indissolubly connected to the making and remaking of ourselves as agents (individual and collective) in society." Play, games and sports, then, are forms of cultural production and as such they are creations of human agency. They can be transformed.

As cultural forms they are tied to modes of domination such as those between social classes and between the sexes.[1] This does not mean that play, games and sports have been created in some determinate way by those who have more resources due either to their "superior" class position (ruling class) or sex (males). What must be specified is exactly *how* these cultural representations come to embody capitalist class relations and patriarchal gender relations in the first place. Finally, even though sport is dependent upon and reflective of the material conditions in the society in which it exists, it also opposes those conditions. In other words, in a cultural sense it is

**Source:** *International Review for the Sociology of Sport*, 20(1/2) (1985): 109–115.

viewed as largely inconsequential, disconnected and somewhat autonomous from the dominant economic and political structures which govern social necessity. Therein lies the fascinating paradox of sport.

A major emphasis in North American and British sociology of sport has been directed at the extent to which play, games and sport reproduce class relations and inequality in western, capitalist societies. However, perhaps this states the focus a little too simplistically, because there are a number of variants. David Whitson (1984) has carefully examined some of the issues and debates which emanate from the domination/subordination and reproduction/transformation literature in the sociology of sport. His primary exemplars are Richard Gruneau, Rob Beamish, and Alan Ingham.

Gruneau (1983), for example, has argued that through sport we can experience transcendence and a sense of agency, but it is limited to an individual as opposed to collective experience. He suggests further that, as a cultural form, sport can and does play a role in dramatizing resistance to a specifically capitalist social order and therefore helps sustain subordinate group identifications and aspirations. Beamish (1982), on the other hand, argues that the character of sport (what he is discussing is North American sport) is determined by the societal mode of production, in this case capitalism. His prime concern is the valorization of athletic labour as capital expands to create surplus value. His is a sophisticated, comprehensive analysis of the rationalization and commodification of North American, male, professional sport. A final example is a recent paper by Ingham and Hardy (1984) whose problematic, as Weberians, is the reproduction of relations of domination and subordination. They also introduce the notion of "contested terrain" – recreational sport being one such terrain – and show how cultural hegemony is maintained and reinforces the control of dominant social groups.

These are just examples but, taken together, they represent a critique which focusses on developing an alternative to the abstracted empiricism, functionalism, and positivism which has characterized so much of American and Canadian sociology of sport. Their commonality is that sport is viewed culturally and historically as something which is socially constituted and not as an abstract "object". It is a cultural form or social "practice".

What all this work has recognized is that we, as North Americans, live in an advanced capitalist society. What it has failed to acknowledge, beyond the superficial, is that we (both women and men) live in a highly patriarchal society as well. Certainly, those writing from a neo-marxist or materialist perspective recognize that taking account of gender means far more than describing sex differences or documenting male dominance; at the very least it means an incorporation of feminist theory and critique into the analysis. Gary Whannel (1983), for instance, in his useful little book, *Blowing the Whistle*, which is about the place of sport in socialism, makes some very meaningful observations concerning the role of feminism in sport. He comments also that there is surprisingly little discussion of sport in feminism and he is correct on all counts. Whitson (1984) argues that it has been disabling to conceive of domination in traditional class terms alone. He suggests that the sex/gender system as it is reproduced in sport is one site where patriarchal cultural hegemony is being challenged and that it is important to address its theoretical significance. Beamish (1984) explains how a materialist analysis would further our understanding of "gender-related issues" in sport and physical education. I will return to his discussion presently. Willis (1982) brilliantly discusses the role of sport in the reinforcement of common-sense ideologies which assert the superiority of men, and how women actually collude in these ideological definitions. Finally, my colleague Bruce Kidd has consistently recognized the importance of gender and feminism in his work on the political economy of Canadian sport. There are probably others, but this is just to mention some of the existing material with which I am familiar. I want to both recognize and commend all this work because it is vitally important. However, I wish also to offer a critique and suggest an alternative.

## The Critique: Production-Biased Materialism

The essence of my critique is that all this work, useful as it is, still sees the class struggle as the motor of history and, to quote the Australian sociologist Bo Connell (1983:61), its transmission, gears, steering, and stereo system as well.[2] It relies on a pre-feminist historical materialism whereby the sphere of production is given analytic primacy, with the result that a structuralist model of capitalist production relations is used as the context within which gender relations are examined (Connell, 1983). This is precisely what Beamish (1984) does when he attempts to explain the materialist "problematic" and show how it could "encompass" issues related to gender. He defines the materialist problematic in the following way:

> "The materialist problematic puts labor and the objective dimensions of class at the center of its tableau for basically three reasons. First, the primary alienation of humankind from nature creates production (or labor) as the negative ontology of social history. Second, the separation of labor into the private and social, abstract and concrete, is the substance of class-divided or civil society. Finally, the eventual practical objective of the materialist problematic is the transcendence of the unbalanced, exploitative distribution of productive responsibility and rewards (material and cultural) that are inherent to the social relations of civil society." (p. 65)

He then goes on to show that Marx's obvious silence on the question of gender is neither a total nor necessary omission because Marx's "oeuvre" does not and cannot represent a finished system. If I have understood Beamish's argument correctly, it goes something like this: Gender is a component of the materialist problematic, but only at the level of concrete historical events and not within the formal sphere of abstraction. History (the concrete) cannot be subordinated to logic (the abstract). Socially organized reproduction and its linkage with socially organized production can only be understood at the level of the concrete and not the abstract. So far so good, although nowhere does Beamish clearly indicate what he means by the social organization of reproduction, except to allude to kinship structures, clan structures, and families. Sexuality is noticeably absent from his discussion. However, there is more. He introduces the idea of the Hegelian "dialectic" (logical contradiction) and argues that, in grasping the dialectic of reality concerning class, the materialist is compelled to encompass gender-related issues (for example, domestic labour, gender segregation in the workplace, etc.) in the exploration of social labour. Beamish does not indicate what "compels" the materialist to do so, except perhaps a guilty conscience. He then utilizes several concrete examples of the Canadian sport experience to illustrate how the materialist position can illucidate elements central to gender and opportunities for participation in sport.

The problem with the Beamish analysis, in my opinion, is not what he has done but what he leaves mysteriously unsaid and unfinished. All he seems to have argued is that there is a patriarchal (my term, not his) structuring of production within the sports world. Admittedly, this is an improvement over many analyses of the relation between gender and class which relegate patriarchy to the family, sexual and ideological activities, and capitalism to the workplace, production and the state. However, what he ignores totally is that there is also a class structuring and class differentiation of sexuality, one of the principle gender categories. In short, Beamish, like all production-biased materialists, fails to see that an analysis of the patriarchy/capitalism relationship goes far beyond merely encompassing gender issues within a fundamentally unchanged materialism. What I am saying is that feminism, specifically marxist and socialist, has mounted a fundamental challenge to the way socialists/materialists go about analyzing society. In short, my colleagues in North America have paid lip service to this challenge but have not really taken it very seriously. I want now to be less critical and more constructive in suggesting an alternative.

## An Alternative: Theorizing the Capitalism/Patriarchy Relationship

There has now developed a very extensive literature which focusses explicitly on the interaction of class and gender as bases of inequality and sources of oppression. In North America and Britain this is commonly referred to as "leftist" feminist scholarship but, unfortunately, it is often difficult to sort out the differences and commonalities between traditional marxist, radical, and socialist feminist schools of thought (cf., Jaggar, 1983). Adding to the confusion is the broad range of issues discussed within the rubric "patriarchy" and the fact that there is not, as yet, a tightly knit and logical system which represents a theory of patriarchy (Connell, 1983).[4]

At the level of abstraction, there are primarily two schools of thought regarding the intersection of capitalism and patriarchy, class and gender. One (variously referred to as "socialist", yet sometimes "radical" feminism) accords capitalism and patriarchy roughly equal weight as sources of women's oppression and exploitation. This "dual-systems" or "parallel-structures" approach sees patriarchy as equally complete and fully analogous to class structure, and seeks to analyze the interconnections and overall relationship of each to the other. This theory is not, as many point out, without its difficulties, not the least of which is the problem of integrating issues of sexuality and personal formation (except via some kind of functionalism) because its organizing principle is the social division of labour (Connell, 1983). More serious perhaps is the problem of explaining power relations *within* a given sex (e.g., the oppression of lesbians) because social power has been derived from the biological differentiation of male versus female. The second principal theoretical framework (usually described as "marxist feminism") does not claim patriarchy as analogous to class structure at all, but sees the family (or sexuality and gender relations at large) as the site of the reproduction of relations of production. This too has been criticized, primarily along the lines that reproduction theory itself is both ahistorical and functionalist (cf., Connell, 1983:55–56).

The point I am trying to make here is that there is now a comprehensive, sophisticated body of scholarship which addresses directly the many problems inherent in understanding the relation between gender and class, patriarchy and capitalism. Granted there are not many solutions, but I think the following points seem fairly clear: (1) class cannot be understood except in connection with gender and vice versa; (2) "class and gender categories have to be treated as emergent social practices by which groups are constituted and by which they constitute themselves" (Connell, 1983:37); (3) gender relations (like class relations) are in essence power relations whereby men, as a social group, have more power over women than women have over them; (4) the two sets of relations, whether they are called patriarchy and capitalism, relations of production and relations of reproduction, or class and gender, are somehow hinged together, but the problem of their articulation gets stuck in functionalism unless the structures themselves are reformulated in terms of the social *practices* (e.g., sport) that compose them (Connell, 1983:64–65)[5]; and, (5) in the final analysis, the way out of this jungle of abstraction towards an understanding of the capitalism/patriarchy relationship is through a focus on historical change (Connell, 1983). historical "problems" (Buechler, 1984), or the historical concrete (Beamish, 1984).

## Concluding Statement

What I have presented here is extremely schematic and sketchy. There are a myriad of issues not addressed, such as the actual categories defined and produced by patriarchy, how these categories are constructed and reconstructed in the interaction of class and gender, the relation of biology to history (particularly crucial for any explanation of gender oppression in sport), marxist structuralism and the debates about patriarchy/capitalism, to name just a few. Nor have I shown explicitly the relevance of all this to the social analysis of sport, except to point out the futility of a production-biased materialism which currently characterizes the sociology of sport literature. What I do suggest, as I have done in different contexts (Hall, 1984, 1985), is that, until we can sort out these issues and others, there will be little true understanding of sport as an ideological institution with enormous symbolic significance which contributes to and perpetuates cultural hegemony oppressive to those, both women and men alike, on the bottom rungs of power.

## Notes

1. There is no particular reason for choosing these particular relations of domination except that it seems the most practical. However, there is still no logical justification to stop at two when it could be argued that race, ethnicity, age and so forth are equally as important. The only response is that class and gender appear to be the most general and the most powerful and that understanding their particular articulation gives us "the deepest insight into the way the world works and the best chance of changing it" (Connell, 1983:78).
2. I am quite indebted to Bob Connell for some of the ideas which follow here. I happened, fortuitously, to be reading his *Which Way Is Up? Essays on Sex, Class and Culture* (1983), while I was writing this paper. I highly recommend his essays since it is very evident that he is familiar with a good deal of the marxist and socialist feminist literature.
3. The reader will no doubt have noticed that there has been no mention of the work of my female colleagues within the sociology of sport. The problem is that there are hardly any who write from within a socialist/marxist feminist framework. Nonetheless, the work of Theberge (1984), Bray (1984), Boutilier and San Giovanni (1983), and Hargreaves (1982) is fairly representative of what is available.
4. See Beechey (1979) and Barrett (1980) for highly useful discussions. Connell (1983: 50–51) suggests that the following represent patriarchy's scope and subject matter: origins of the subordination of women; the cultural practices that sustain it; the sexual divison of labour; formation of character and motive; the politics of sexual object choice; the role of the body in social relations; the strategies of resistance movements; the conditions for the overthrow of male dominance.
5. Richard Gruneau (1983) has made these same points regarding our theoretical conceptions of class and sport.

## References

Barrett, Michele (1980): *Women's Oppression Today*. London: Verso Editions.
Beamish, Rob (1982): "Sport and the Logic of Capitalism" In: R. Gruneau and H. Cantelon (eds.): *Sport, Culture and the Modern State*. Toronto: University of Toronto Press.
Beamish, Rob (1984): "Materialism and the Comprehension of Gender-Related Issues in Sport". In: N. Theberge and P. Donnelly (eds.): *Sport and the Sociological Imagination*. Fort Worth: Texas Christian Unversity Press, pp. 60–81.
Beechey, Veronica (1979): "On Patriarchy". In: *Feminist Review* 3, pp. 66–82.

Boutilier, Mary A., San Giovanni, Lucinda (1983): *The Sporting Woman*. Champaign, IL: Human Kinetics Publishers.

Bray, Cathy (1984): "Gender and the Political Economy of Canadian Sport". In: N. Theberge and P. Donnelly (eds.): *Sport and the Sociological Imagination*. Fort Worth: Texas Christian University Press.

Buechler, Steve (1984): "Sex and Class: A Critical Overview of Some Recent Theoretical Work and Some Modest Proposals". In: *Insurgent Sociologist* 12 (3), pp. 19–32.

Connell, R. W. (1983): *Which Way Is Up? Essays on Class, Sex and Culture*. Sydney: George Allen & Unwin.

Gruneau, Richard (1983): *Class, Sports and Social Development*. Amherst: The University of Massachusetts Press.

Hall, M. Ann (1984): "Towards a Feminist Analysis of Gender Inequality in Sport". In: N. Theberge and P. Donnelly (eds.): *Sport and the Sociological Imagination*. Fort Worth: Texas Christian University Press, pp. 82–103.

Hall, M. Ann (1985): "Knowledge and Gender: Epistemological Questions in the Social Analysis of Sport". In: *Sociology of Sport Journal* 2 (1), 25–42.

Hargreaves, Jennifer (ed.) (1982): *Sport, Culture and Ideology*. London: Routledge and Kegan Paul.

Ingham, A., Hardy, S. (1984): "Sport, Structuration. Subjugation and Hegemony". In: *Theory, Culture and Society* 2 (2) pp. 85–103.

Jaggar, Alison M. (1983): *Feminist Politics and Human Nature*. Totowa, NJ: Rowman & Allanheld.

Theberge, Nancy (1984): "Joining Social Theory to Social Action: Some Marxist Principles". In: *Arena Review* 8 (2), pp. 11–19.

Whannel, Gary (1983): *Blowing the Whistle*. London: Pluto Press.

Whitson, David (1984): "Structure, Agency and the Sociology of Sport Debates". In: *Theory, Culture and Society* (forthcoming).

Willis, Paul (1982): "Women in Sport in Ideology". In: J. Hargreaves (ed.): *Sport, Culture and Ideology*. London: Routledge & Kegan Paul.

# 11

# A Pageant of Sound and Vision: Football's Relationship with Television, 1936–60[1]

*Richard Haynes*

It is widely acknowledged that television has transformed, and is constantly transforming, professional football in the way in which it is organized, played and spectated. New deals are continually struck for astronomical fees as television companies, multinational sponsors and governing bodies seek to exploit the world game commercially. In Britain, the relationship between football and television has not, however, always been sanguine and throughout their historical association the struggles over the representation of the sport through the lens of the camera and the microphone, who this mediation is for, and when or how it is delivered, have often proved volatile. The main causes of these disruptions and altercations have been a set of conflicting agendas which reflect the historical infrastructure of football as a professional sport and the unique political economy of British broadcasting formed by an uneasy marriage between public service broadcasting and commercial (otherwise labelled 'independent') television. How the discourses of these cultural industries combine or conflict, and ultimately construct televised football as a popular cultural form is a central focus of this article.

## BBC Television and Football: Early Developments

BBC Television officially began broadcasting to a select few in November 1936. As with radio, the BBC had set about experimenting with television outside broadcasts, pushing the available technology to the limit. After the

**Source:** *The International Journal of the History of Sport,* 15(1) (1998): 211–226.

inaugural television outside broadcast (outside broadcast) of the Coronation ceremony for King George VI in May 1937, Gerald Cock, the BBC's first Director of Television, pursued his personal enthusiasm for sport by providing a meagre London-based audience of 2,000 with the first sight of a televised football match with the Home International between England and Scotland from Wembley in April 1938. This was one of the many 'firsts' in the BBC's coverage of sport, and as the *Radio Times* had promised in its last issue of 1937: 'Make no mistake about it – there will be big moments to make a big year in the television outside broadcasts of 1938.'[2]

Negotiations for televising the sport came up against the same arguments and opposition that radio had endured ten years earlier.[3] The threat to attendances of other matches was perceived as being too great by the FA Council which was not amenable to the idea of televised football, despite the more positive attitude to broadcasting from the Secretary of the FA, the former referee Stanley Rous.[4] Cock had initially approached Rous in December 1937 and due to the intransigence of the Council wrote to him again in February 1938 saying: 'Television is on trial. Here is the beginning of a great industry, the progress of which depends to a great extent on the co-operation of institutions such as the FA.'[5] Under the then pioneering spirit of Rous the FA Council finally conceded to the BBC, allowing it to televise both the international between England and Scotland (9 April) and the 1938 FA Cup Final between Preston North End and Huddersfield Town (22 April). A measure of how important these outside broadcasts were to the BBC's fledgling television service can be gauged from the following excerpt which appeared within a new review column of the *Radio Times* written by a group of contributors under the single pseudonym of 'The Scanner' and addressed to the select audience for television. In the issue falling between the two 'live' television broadcasts 'The Scanner' promised:

> almost the biggest television broadcast of the year – the Cup Final. A fortnight ago the mobile unit operated in the stadium to televise the England v Scotland international match. To me and, I expect, to you, the transmission seemed perfect. But those concerned at Alexandra Palace mutter knowingly, 'You wait for the Cup'. So keen are they to improve on the perfect that experiments on the best positions for cameras will be carried on until the last moment.[6]

The above excerpt also hints at television's expectant cultural role – asking us to 'wait for the Cup' – and within this context the earliest signs of televised football's formal properties (the experimentation with camera positions) and institutional development.

The possibility of (re)producing 'live' visual transmissions from football stadia clearly introduced a new popular cultural spectacle. The direct transmission of football into the home proved to be more than a technological necessity during the formative years of television, the 'immediacy effect' as Caughie[7] suggests was both an 'essential characteristic and an aesthetic virtue of the new medium'. Of course by 1938 football supporters were already accustomed to seeing visual reproductions of their sporting heroes within cinema newsreels, albeit several days, even weeks after the event had taken place. As one observer from 1938 wrote of early television coverage of sport in *The Times:* 'To see these events as they take place is something different in kind from a news-reel after the event; it has a particular thrill and would alone make the possession of a set worth while.'[8]

The overtly delayed screening of newsreels and their brief film highlights bear no comparison to the effect of television's immediacy, and while the newsreel certainly used football as part of its own rationale of information and entertainment, the footage from football – consisting of as many shots of the crowd as the play itself – was not the motivating force for attendance at the cinema for the millions who flocked there during the inter-war years. Conversely, the contention of the present article is that football, and more generally the whole field of television outside broadcasts from sporting events, were crucial to the manner in which the BBC sought to define what television actually was, and that within the initial throes of developing a television service there are some residual discourses which continue to pervade contemporary debates regarding televised football.

Although early television broadcasts had the capacity to transmit pre-recorded film, delayed recorded highlights of football matches were not introduced at any significant level until the mid-1950s. Therefore, the majority of televised games were 'live' and as a consequence could potentially distract football followers from attending, or participating in, another match being played on the same afternoon, amateur or professional. It was the possible effect live broadcasts could have on attendances which accounted for the intransigent mood of the football authorities who were unsure of the new technology and its social consequences.

At first, television would not appear to be a threat of any significance; after all when the television service closed with the outbreak of War in September 1939, only an estimated 20,000 viewers were able to watch the couple of hours' programming from Alexander Palace each day.[9] Moreover, despite the advertising rhetoric – 'Television is Here – You Can't Shut Your Eyes to It' – the new medium played second fiddle to radio, which by the late 1930s had firmly established itself in millions of households across the country. It had not been until the Television Advisory Committee established single standard for television in February 1937, approving the Marconi-EMI system rather than the one pioneered by John Logie Baird, that the perception of television rose above that of a gimmick. As one feature which reviewed the first year of television in *The Times* suggested: 'Up to that point lack of space and time had severely hampered the efforts to transform television for the private viewer from an ingenious toy into a serious entertainment.'[10] It is perhaps due to the uncertainty pertaining to the new medium and the fact that radio commentaries had gained a degree of respectability amongst the football authorities that they initially allowed television cameras access to the game on a purely experimental footing. Arsenal FC, not averse to self-publicity under the management of George Allison,[11] featured strongly in several of the earliest television broadcasts. Indeed, the BBC had used two Arsenal teams (presumably the first team and the reserves) while conducting private experiments in televising outside broadcasts in 1937, several months before they broadcast publicly from Wembley in April 1938. Two games were also broadcast from Highbury Stadium later in the year, the BBC transmitting second half action from both the FA Charity Shield between Arsenal and Preston North End (26 September 1938) and England's 3-0 victory over the Rest of Europe (26 October 1938) which gave BBC viewers an early experience of two young rising stars of the English game, Stanley Matthews (aged 23) and Tommy Lawton (aged 19).When the Second World War broke in September 1939, the Football League suspended all football except for that played by the Armed Forces, and the BBC, changing tack to support the 'national interest', also withdrew from its urge to innovate with outside broadcasts and suspended its infant television service.

## Post-war Developments

In the immediate post-war years the BBC sought to consolidate its television service after its resumption in June 1946 in the shadow of radio. As Corner has highlighted in his retrospective cultural analysis of broadcasting, the BBC emerged from war as a national institution, where a radio could be heard from every household.[12] However, the BBC had maintained its bureaucratic cultural character, coupled with the Reithian rhetoric which saw the broadcaster as an 'embassy of the national culture' with specific constitutional obligations. The coverage of the FA Cup Final had already established itself as part of the broadcasting calendar, and the FA reaffirmed its willingness to continue its association with the BBC by permitting a radio commentary on the last 30 minutes of any one cup-tie plus the Cup Final in full.

By 1946 professional football in England and Scotland had also resumed full League programmes for the first time since 1939. In the shadow of War the desire for mass entertainments created a fillip to football attendances which peaked between 1947 and 1949 with aggregate attendances at English League games exceeding 40 million per season, representing an income of £4 million at the turnstiles. Football's dominant position within British popular culture (among both men and women) had never appeared so secure, and it is therefore no surprise to see the BBC once again turning towards the sport as a mechanism for capturing a broader audience, this time for television.

In an unprecedented move during a period of continued rationing for scarce resources the BBC gained permission from the Government to broadcast the 1947 Cup Final during hours when the domestic use of electricity was otherwise prohibited (the programme was broadcast between 2.45 and 5.00 p.m.). As a public service broadcaster the BBC was clearly doing its duty in presenting an event considered to be of national significance. However, as with radio, there were ideological battles which needed to be fought regarding television's role within society, even for a comparatively restricted audience – only 30,000 joint radio and television licences at a cost of £2 had been issued to London viewers by the end of 1947.[13] The BBC steered between the competing discourses which stressed the need to either inform and educate or, as with the coverage of football, and sport in general, to entertain. The Labour government's exceptional decision to permit the broadcasting of the Cup Final during restricted hours of domestic electricity use prompted a number of complaints, of which the following excerpt from the *Radio Times* letters page is representative:

> It would be interesting to know who withheld permission for church services during similar hours to be broadcast on Easter Day so that many invalids, mothers of young children, and those with ageing and helpless parents might join in the observance of the most solemn day of the Christian year by the Established Church of this country. Mrs. A. Imrie Swainston. London N6.[14]

Although similar arguments regarding the disabled, the aged and the immobile have equally been used to justify television's coverage of major sporting events, it is clear that the BBC had difficult ideological decisions to make regarding the information entertainment nexus and its conception of the popular. At a period when generic codes and conventions of television were still embryonic, and the flow of a television schedule had still to be developed – for instance, audiences were advised to take a selective approach to viewing from the three to four hours of programming – sport challenged vigorously for its place within an *ad hoc* approach to television broadcasting.

It is probably this ideological dilemma which led the BBC to inscribe the Cup Final with specific cultural importance, which detracted from its entertainment value. By emphasizing the cultural and national importance of the Cup Final the BBC was also able to deflect the principal economic argument put forward by the football authorities that live broadcasts would affect the income of League clubs playing on the same day as people stayed at home either to listen to commentaries or to watch a match in the comfort of their own home.

In a period when aggregate weekly attendances at League matches continued to soar, the Football League maintained its reluctance to allow its member clubs and players to appear on television with the exception of the Cup Final and international matches. The ban emphasized the fears held by the League President, C.W. Cuff, that television as a visual form of communication was a far greater threat to attendances than the coded accounts delivered over the radio. Although radio commentaries of League matches had become a staple of post-war Saturday afternoon broadcasting, the League forced the BBC to withhold the identity of the match concerned and even then only provide coverage of the second half. These measures were clearly designed to persuade those with an interest in football to attend the home fixtures of their local club.

The Football League was not alone in its attempt to maintain control over television exposure in order to keep spectatorship an exclusive experience for those who went through the turnstiles. Other sporting bodies, most notably the Jockey Club and the Boxing Board of Control, were equally suspicious of television in the immediate post-war period, the latter specifically envious of the money changing hands between boxing promoters and television companies in the United States.[15]

In November 1944 many of Britain's sporting organizations, including the Football Association and the Football League, led by the Greyhound Racing Association, had banded together to form the Association for the Protection of Copyright in Sport (APCS) in anticipation of the resumption of live telecasts from sport. Apart from the immediate fear that television would diminish gate receipts, the APCS was fearful of the 're-diffusion' of sporting events in public places. As the conflict between the BBC and the sports promoters came to a head, F.S. Gentle, vice-chairman of the APCS, drew the attention of all concerned to one surreptitious event of 1951, where before the televising of a fight from Birmingham 'people went round the streets looking for aerials, and paid 2s.6d. to go into private houses to view it'.[16]

Such anecdotes about the early days of television viewing habits are commonplace, although the majority do not involve such exploitative behaviour on the part of those fortunate enough to posses a television set. The imaginary prospect of thousands of young men prowling the streets in search of a television aerial in order to watch their sporting heroes on the small screen clearly had wider social and political consequences. After a noticeable drop in attendance's at Football League matches on the day of the 1950 Cup Final between Arsenal and Liverpool, the Post-Master General established a Sports Television Advisory Committee to monitor fluctuations in attendances at sports events during selected sports transmissions on BBC television. Their report a year later showed a significant drop in League attendances across the country as Newcastle United overcame Blackpool in the 1951 Cup Final. It had been suggested at an earlier FA Council meeting to defer the Final by one week thereby avoiding a clash with the final day of the League programme. However, this was rejected in favour of restricting the BBC's coverage exclusively to the second half. Luckily for those viewing the match at home, Jackie Milburn scored his two winning goals after the half-time interval!

In a further written report from the Post-master General's office, the Assistant PMG, Mr Grammans, believed it was necessary to monitor the effect of television ownership on attendances over a prolonged period before making any final conclusions about the relationship. However, he did draw attention to what he viewed as the harmful consequences of televising the Cup Final:

> At this stage the only point on which we can be reasonably certain is that the televising of certain major events, such as the Football Cup Final, results in reduced attendances at other sporting events held on the same day, and that this effect is more marked at minor sporting events.[17]

But before the PMG report was even published, the Football League had placed significant pressure on the FA – the guardian of the game at all levels – to ban live transmission of the 1952 Cup Final.

However, fears of an emergent social dimension to early television spectatorship bore no comparison to the threat held by re-diffusion within cinemas. Despite football's growth in appeal in the immediate post-war years, audience figures for the cinema far outstripped attendance at any other popular form of entertainment during the Great British weekend. Hence, with the possibility of cinemas re-diffusing television pictures the APCS attempted to enforce a form of copyright, to be held by the sporting authority concerned for the broadcasting of individual sporting events. The concept of copyright diverged from previous arrangements between broadcasters and British sporting organizations. For instance, the BBC had always considered any payment to the FA as a 'facility fee' for access to football premises and/or compensation for any lost revenue through loss of seats caused by camera positions, sound technicians or commentators. The 'facility fee' rarely topped 25 guineas because the BBC held the view that their broadcasts rather than hinder attendance at football actually aided the promotion of the game and, as outlined above, the corollary of broadcasting sporting events was its beneficial function towards a thriving, common national culture, an ideology shared by both the BBC and all the sporting organizations concerned.

However, the APCS were now claiming that television as a visual medium was exploiting the performance of sportsmen and women who played their sport under the rules and auspices of the sporting organizations. Ironically, radio commentary was now considered to be more akin to press reportage as it provided a second-hand coded narrative or description of play and unlike television it did not convey the sports performance in actuality. The main thrust of the APCS argument is illustrated once again from the following quote by F.S. Gentle, the organization's vice-chairman, when he claimed 'that a promoter of a sporting or spectacular event should be placed in the same legal position regarding the televising of his production as the author, composer or playwright'.[18] Within this statement can be read a series of contradictory yet interrelated issues which pervade the contemporary sports/media nexus but which at that specific moment in the history of British sport were not completely configured, and would not be until the introduction of the intermediary concerns of sponsors and agents in the late-1960s to early 1970s.

Perhaps the most pertinent question to ask is: where within a team sport such as professional football does the copyright on performance actually lie? Gentle's statement emphasizes the complicity of sports performers (both amateur and professional) in relation to the sporting and social codes and conventions of 'playing the game' overseen by the governing bodies and institutions of sport.

Within football, players were tied to the retain and transfer system. This highly subservient position of the professional footballer would eventually be challenged and overcome during the 1960s, and within the malaise of the post-war negotiations between sport and television the portents of these power struggles were beginning to emerge.

## Copyright, Floodlight and Competition

Three specific forces were to have far-reaching consequences for the relationships not only between football and television, but also within the professional game between players, clubs and the football authorities. They were: pressures to change the copyright law; the introduction of floodlit football; and the introduction of competition from commercial ('independent') television.

### Whose Copyright?

One of the five main aims of the 1950 Beveridge Committee's report into broadcasting, which adhered to the Labour government's view of maintaining a television monopoly, recommended that the BBC develop television 'as part of the work of the corporation, but with due regard to its problems'.[19] This specifically included the dilemma over the copyright of sporting events on which the Committee, in typical British style, advocated a compromise whereby the BBC would gain a right to televise subject, to terms to be settled by agreement or arbitration. However, within a climate of uncertainty caused by the threat of cinema re-diffusion, the FA, after withholding permission to screen the 1952 Cup Final, established a joint committee with the Football League to discuss the question of financial terms for football broadcasts by the BBC.

Television boycotts from within football and other 'national' sports (most notably The Grand National) prompted questions to be asked in Parliament. The debate centred upon a way of reconciling private interests with those of the public at large, the prospect of which was made all the more complex by the newly appointed Tory government's proposals to break the BBC television monopoly by introducing a commercial station.[20]

Earl Jowitt, an opponent to commercial television due to his experiences in the United States, proposed that there should be a copyright, not in the performance itself but in the television image of a sporting spectacle and the interests concerned – the BBC, the cinemas and the sports promoters – should get together to see how the copyright should be 'parcelled out'.[21] Throughout

1952 and 1953 as the wider debates on broadcasting worked their way through Parliament, numerous pleas from the House of Lords argued for a statement from the Government to break the deadlock on televised sport. Lord Brabazon stated that it was 'a question of arranging hard business facts between promoters of sports and televisors';[22] and the Government was criticized by Lord Lucas for being 'dilatory' in dragging its heels over the publication of the Copyright Committee report which was also addressing the issue of televised sport after being appointed in April 1951.

In the event, the report, published in October 1952, followed a similar line to that advocated by Earl Jowitt in order to break the deadlock between promoters and the BBC. The report recommended that the sole performing right should be vested in the BBC (or any other broadcasting authority). It was felt that such an arrangement would enable the broadcaster to control re-diffusion of an event, and from the fees so earned recompense the sports promoters for any loss of gate receipts thus incurred. It was felt 'that if a similar right were accorded to sports promoters it could not be restricted to them, but would have to be granted more widely'.[23] In order to ensure a fair fee for the public performance of copyright material, the committee proposed that a tribunal system be established to settle disputes. The notion of arranging fees therefore overturned the Beveridge Reports' earlier suggestion that gave the broadcasting authority legal right to televise events irrespective of the promoters wishes. In its leader comment *The Times* argued:

> The broadcasters will have to account with the promoters, to whom they will be able to pay a fair share from the proceeds of fees which their new right will enable them to charge. The promoters, for their part, cannot be compelled to admit the television cameras to their grounds; but if they do they must be satisfied with a fair payment and in case of dispute the amount must be settled by a tribunal appointed for the purpose. This is a working solution of an obstinate problem. Only experience can test its value. Common sense will approve its enunciation.[24]

The report appeared to thaw the cool relations between the sports promoters and the BBC, whose temporary estrangement ended the following week as the parties concerned engaged in 'exploratory' talks. Indeed, the FA had already overturned its policy of banning live coverage of the Cup Final by July 1952 and suggested that League clubs should bring their games forward to avoid clashing with the 1953 final. They had also agreed to second-half coverage of two England internationals during November 1952 against Wales and Belgium subject to ticket sales at Wembley. However, it was not until February 1953 that a financial package was decided upon, the BBC agreeing to pay a £1,000 fee for the Cup Final in May of that year.

By the end of 1952 the demand for television sets was beginning to outstrip their production, and 'live' coverage of the major sporting occasions, along with the prospect of watching the forthcoming Coronation of the Queen in

1953, proved the most seductive televisual events and reason to invest in the new medium. Lord Lucas attempted to capture the publics desire for these major outside broadcasts with the following statement in January 1953:

> The public wanted the televising of public events, and had a right to expect it. They had invested large sums in television sets and would not be confined for long in watching the antics of *Muffin the Mule*. By far the best programmes were the outside television broadcasts, and unless the matter was resolved there would be diminution in public interest in television, which would affect not only the BBC but also, the industry.[25]

Such rhetoric concurred with Lord Reith's notion of the BBC's position in public life, and the construction of national identity through the broadcasting of civic events, within which sport played a significant role. Moreover, the concern for the coverage of national events was part of a wider discourse which held that if television was to capture the imagination of the British people, as a powerful, educational form of communication, the BBC must maintain its status as a broadcasting monopoly. This was diametrically opposed to the policy ideas laid down in the Conservative government's 1952 White Paper on broadcasting, and its proposed introduction of sponsored television. The fear of Lord Lucas and his supporters was that a commercially driven television service would outbid the BBC for the major public events and would ultimately lead to the end of the Corporation, the degradation of programme quality (a conception based on an unfavourable value-judgement of American television), and ultimately the end of television itself!

As discussed below, commercial television struggled to make inroads into the BBC's monopoly of the coverage of sport in its formative years, placed at a distinct disadvantage by the BBC's relative experience within the genre and its excellent contacts with sporting organizations.

## Floodlit Football

There had been experiments with the floodlighting of football as early as 1878 when an estimated 20,000 spectators watched two select teams at Brammal Lane, Sheffield. Powered by two Siemans generators, two lamps were positioned in opposing corners and erected upon wooden towers, 30 feet high.[26] Further experiments in floodlighting continued during the 1930s, although they were against the will of the FA. In August 1930 the FA had passed a resolution prohibiting any of its member clubs from taking part in such games. This ruling was not rescinded until December 1950 with the provision that no competitive game could be played under artificial light without prior permission of the FA.

The introduction of floodlighting enabled clubs to play mid-week matches on dark winter evenings, opening up a further opportunity for thousands of football supporters to see their heroes for a second time within a week.

Moreover, because the floodlit matches were non-competitive and not subject to the Football League's ban on televised coverage, the BBC took its opportunity to approach the clubs involved directly to gain access for its cameras. This was a great boost to the BBC's attempt to improve the profile of its football broadcasts. Due to the League ban the BBC had filled several Saturday afternoon schedules with matches from either amateur football (the Amateur Cup and the Senior London Cup were to feature several times from 1948 to 1954) or from fixtures involving the armed forces. These matches were a poor substitute to the appeal of watching the household names from the professional ranks. Floodlit football provided a form of access previously denied.

One League club, in particular, helped to pioneer the introduction of televised floodlit matches in Britain. Wolverhampton Wanderers, an original member of the Football League, were one of the most successful English clubs throughout the 1950s, and spearheaded the use of floodlighting in the British game. Under the stewardship of Secretary-Manager, Major Frank Buckley, and tactically coached by manager Stan Cullis, they were League Champions in 1954, 1958 and 1959; runners-up in 1950 and 1955; and FA Cup Winners in 1949. Wolves were also amongst a group of League clubs which began to test their style of play (based on the long ball) against clubs from overseas, and it was the mixture of floodlit football and television which provided British audiences with their first glimpse of football from the 'Continent'.

In December 1954, Wolves, West Ham and Chelsea played a memorable series of matches against 'Continental' opposition including AC Milan and two teams from Hungary, Voros Lobogo and the army sponsored club Honved. The English public had been made aware of the Hungarian talent for football in dramatic style one year earlier when their national side humiliated England by inflicting a 6-3 defeat, the first time England had lost to an overseas side at home. The defeat was given extra significance because it had been televised by the BBC. To many, the Hungarian style of football based upon quick short passing and movement off the ball was a revelation. The power of television's immediacy upon the ever-growing audiences of the mid-1950s was realized as Puskas and Hidegkuti tore the English defence apart. Television's promise of the exotic was thrillingly realized by its coverage of such rare football events.

Similarly, Wolves' game with Honved in December 1954 holds an equally powerful place within the formative years of television broadcasts of European football. At first sight, a football match played on a muddy, waterlogged pitch one wet Monday night in the West Midlands would not appear to have held much appeal. However, the game had an element of revenge about it as six of the Honved players had been involved in the crushing defeat of England. Television, perhaps for the first time, focused the attention of the wider viewing public to the significance of club football to the health and status of the nations most popular sport. With their 3-2 victory over Honved, Wolves were heralded as the unofficial European Champions by the English press.

The BBC had positioned its audience as witnesses to the salubrious event, the health of the national sport riding on the back of a single clubs' fortunes. Here, television's ideological work was emphatically realized with the substitution of club for country. The coverage of the Wolves' victory under the murky lights of Molineux and its subsequent plaudits proved to be a portent of televisions' future love affair with mid-week European football, where gauging the quality of both the English and Scottish style of play against that of the 'Continentals' has been a perennial motif. Recalling the many televised, floodlit, games which Wolves played during the 1950s, Billy Wright commented:

> To bring over, as Wolves and other clubs have, great teams from Russia, Hungary, Brazil, Argentina, Austria, Germany and France, to mention but a few countries, is to my mind, a wonderful investment. Yes, I mean to use the word *investment*, because it really does apply in this case, for in addition to the thrill of seeing these colourful characters on parade, I think it has proved a wonderful source of value to the millions of youngsters I know look in to see such as Ferenc Puskas do his tricks.[27]

Domestically, the advent of mid-week friendlies under floodlight also enabled English and Scottish clubs to compete against each other in front of the cameras. Unfortunately for the clubs concerned, the football authorities north and south of the border did not look on such fixtures quite as favourably as the fans who were eager to witness the outcome of such culture clashes.[28]

By the summer of 1953 the England national team had played its first competitive match under floodlight at the Yankee Stadium, New York, during a prolonged tour of North and South America.[29] Moreover, by 1955 the FA recognized the benefits of midweek evening kick-offs for Cup replays, and in 1956 the Football League sanctioned the use of floodlights for those games rescheduled because of postponement.

Yet the official recognition of floodlighting raised another query for the football authorities to address: the payment of players. The maximum wage was based on a weekly rate and, therefore, players could not expect to receive extra payment for midweek fixtures. Throughout 1954 and 1955 officials from Sunderland FC approached the FA with the proposal that League clubs should be permitted to pay their players an extra £5 for appearing in floodlit matches. Sunderland's idea was not accepted. However, with the increasing level of televised matches, due in part to the rise of floodlit games, the Players Union, under the Chairmanship of Jimmy Guthrie, approached other unions operating in the entertainment field, such as the Variety Artists Federation, with the intention of gaining some form of remuneration from television for its members. According to Guthrie, footballers as public performers ranked for consideration in the matter of fees as in any other form of entertainment.

In January 1956 Guthrie discussed the contention that players should receive a fee when football matches were televised with the director of administration of the BBC, Sir Norman Bottomley. Guthrie approached the so-called 'informal exchange of views' with the idea that if a fee was negotiated, half would go to the players and half would go into a players accident fund.[30] However, the BBC contended that fees for televised games was an issue to be settled between the players and their employers. One week later Guthrie was in discussion with the FA and the Football League which deflected his demands once more by reiterating the regulations which forbid payment and left him with the suggestion that the only way to change this situation was for the clubs to alter the regulations themselves.

The negative responses from both the broadcasters and the football authorities fuelled Guthrie's indignation and led the Union, in March 1956, to place a ban on their members appearing in floodlit matches before television cameras unless a fee was paid. Guthrie approached Wolves players who pledged their support to the Union in the campaign for additional payment for televised or floodlit matches. Wolves were due to play the Spanish side Atletico Bilbao the following week and their backing of the Union's stance prompted the League Management Committee to discuss the matter on the Saturday prior to the game. In a reply to the Union's demand, the League was prepared to negotiate with the players over fees on the condition that the proposed ban be removed immediately, the principle of the maximum wage recognized, and the transfer system retained. At the eleventh hour the Union rescinded its ban and stated that they had 'agreed a mutual basis for joint consultation between the League and the Players Union for the resolving of outstanding problems'.[31] The football authorities, who were soon to move into extensive negotiations with both the BBC and the newly formed ITV for television rights, had maintained their hegemonic position within the governance of the game and its finances, a position they would continue to hold until another player revolt inevitably emerged in the 1960s. The above events are another reminder of how television began to transform not only the wider perceptions of viewing football, but also the upheaval it brought to the institutional fabric of the sport itself.

## Competition: BBC and ITV

The struggles over television copyright and the introduction of floodlighting (which had effectively increased the volume of football and, therefore, its potential audience) were signposts to a new pattern of commercialized sport, which was reflected by broader shifts away from the immediate post-war years of austerity to an emergent, conspicuous, consumer culture. Although football's association with the processes of consumer culture were not fully realized until the mid-1960s, apotheosized by the exploitation of George Best, the arrival of a commercial television service in 1955 generated a new, competitive approach to the coverage of the sport by the BBC. As Garry Whannel has documented, with competition bearing down on the activities of the Outside Broadcast department, the chief negotiator for contracts,

Peter Dimmock, had initiated changes within the BBC's sports programming, while producers within other television genres were far more complacent.[32] In 1954 BBC Television introduced a new sports omnibus programme, *Sportsview*. Broadcast on a Wednesday evening, at first a fortnightly, and then a weekly programme, *Sportsview* adopted a magazine format which combined filmed material with studio presentation and interviews. There was much emphasis placed on sporting 'personalities', with the imperative of winning support from a 'family audience' uppermost in the minds of the programme's producers.[33] Football was to feature strongly throughout the programme's history, as it has within its successor *Sportsnight*, but arrangements with the Football League in 1954 were far from resolved.

The aggregate level of attendances at League games for 1954–55 had fallen by over two million from the previous year, and Arthur Drewry, the President of the League, announced in May 1955 that the ban on any extensive coverage of football on television would be continued. With the knowledge that ITV would soon be up and running, the League for the first time in its association with broadcasting had some leverage with regard to reaching a level of remuneration it felt would forgo the loss of revenue from falling gate receipts. However, the League management committee remained divided over the subject. The main concern was financial, but a sub text for much of the indecision was a fear of the unknown.

The management committee was clearly making decisions based on the wider debates raging at the time regarding the appropriate role of television in the lives of British people. From its initial squabbles with broadcasting after the introduction of radio in the inter-war years, the football authorities had been willing to accept the Reithian precept that commentaries on sport had an important place in the nation's affection. But, by the mid-1950s the tenets of Reithianism were eroding, being dismissed as culturally outdated and outmoded at a time of significant social and economic change. The Conservative Party had swept to power in 1951 behind images of the affluent worker. A television set was the defining symbolic object' of a 'New England'[34] and, the introduction of a commercial service was considered an appropriate means of expanding the rapidly growing field of the broadcasting service. However, the prospect of commercial television, with advertising jingles and quiz shows, led to derogatory criticism from both the Left (who gave a moral warning about the debasement of working-class culture) and the Conservative cultural elites (who railed against the processes of Americanization). League Football, which had standardized and rationalized the 'folk' game into a mass spectator sport, paradoxically clung to its patriarchal, working-class roots by checking the level of commercial progress and restricting the social and economic transgression of its labour force (the players) through the mechanisms of the retain and transfer system and the maximum wage. However, the expansion of television, and the wider cultural transformations associated with it, would ultimately lead the sport towards a less incongruous circumstance in the sports-media complex, and yet, in 1954 opinion was clearly divided as to how football should proceed.

The development of relations between the television broadcasters and football invariably fell on the shoulders of key individuals within the respective institutions. As competition in television beckoned, it was left to the younger executives within both the League and the FA, who had a clearer grasp of the economic, social and political climate, to produce the dynamic impetus needed to develop the televised game. Alan Hardaker, in 1954 the Football League's assistant secretary to Fred Howarth, was delegated the job of nego-tiating with the BBC. As Hardaker noted later in his autobiography: 'Fred Howarth knew little about the medium, and cared little about it, and passed what responsibility he had in this connection on to me. It was the first time he had given me any sort of job, and I was delighted to take it on.'[35]

The representation of impending changes in League opinion on television are plain to see within this account, if the old guardians of football 'cared little' as to the future of the sports relationship with television, then such ambivalence was not shared by Hardaker who, as events transpired, became increasingly aware that television was of vital importance, not only to the growth of the new medium, but also to the game itself. This was made no more apparent, than when Dimmock suggested to Hardaker that the BBC was willing to pay a staggering quarter-of-a-million pounds for an undisclosed level of televised coverage of League matches.[36] However, no sooner had the unofficial offer been made than it was rescinded, due to the plain fact that the BBC could not afford to spend such a sum on live outside broadcasts. But the episode clearly fuelled the economic appetite of the League's assistant secretary, as the potential riches of television were bared for the first time.

By March 1955 both the BBC and the ITA had submitted proposals to televise filmed excerpts of League matches, with the promise that no prior knowledge of the games covered would be given to the audience. Meanwhile, as the League pondered its possible future with television, the FA continued its contract with the BBC for broadcasting the Cup Final, as terms were agreed in August 1955 for a further three years coverage (1956–59). It was a symbolic gesture of loyalty by the FA, whose growing recognition of the BBC's capacity to transform the event into a shared national ritual was duly being repaid. Moreover, allied to these institutional ties was the technical ability of the BBC, which even by 1955 had grown immensely. For instance, the corporation had in 1954 televised several football matches from overseas via its 'Eurovision' links with mainland Europe. By comparison, the ITV network was unknown, both in terms of its staff, and its ability within the field of outside broadcasting. With *Sportsview* the BBC had developed a full-time sports production unit. ITV, organized within a federal, regional system and hampered by its lack of any centralized sports co-ordination or production, was placed at a distinct disadvantage towards the coverage of sport before it even began broadcasting in the Autumn of 1955.[37]

Within this context, the League ultimately turned to the BBC. In an almost arrogant show of victory, the BBC announced its contract with the League on Thursday 22 September 1955, the very day commercial television was launched in Britain. The agreement, for one season, was for the telerecording of 75 matches, with the stipulation that each recording was neither to exceed five minutes (unless there was only one game available, in which case ten minutes were allowed) nor could they be televised before 10 p.m. A circular was sent to League clubs to provide 'every facility' to the BBC, and those concerned in the recordings would receive a five guinea facility fee.[38]

The acquisition of the rights to League football was a fillip to the BBC's growing sports portfolio. Two weeks before the deal was announced Dimmock had introduced a brand new programme scheduled for Saturday evenings. *Sports Special* was a sister programme to the mid-week magazine *Sportsview*, placing emphasis on the day's sporting action rather than interviews and filmed reports which were an essential ingredient of the latter programme. The expansion in sports programming had been due to the success of *Sportsview* in attracting what Dimmock described as 'a large and growing audience for sports programmes'.[39] In the context of ITV competition, the BBC had not only made a decisive breakthrough in persuading League football to be televised, but had also created the ideal vehicle within which the filmed highlights could be broadcast to the armchair sports fan. Indeed, *Sports Special* was part of the BBC's general increase in programming within this period. Between the beginning and end of September 1955, the BBC had boosted its aggregate weekly hours of programmes from 41 to 49 hours per week, just one hour below the Postmaster General's ceiling for permitted hours of television. This was part of BBC Television's effort to stave off the arrival of ITV. Sir George Barnes, the Director of Television Broadcasting, addressing the issue in the *Radio Times* pronounced:

> Although with powerful competitors bent upon exclusive contracts, we shall not have the same choice of events and performers that we have hitherto enjoyed, the BBC will continue to give the most varied and diverse television programmes to suit all tastes of a nationwide audience – an audience which is increasing through the addition of one million new licences a year. This service is paid for by those viewers; it owes no allegiance to anyone else.[40]

Barnes was cocking a snook at ITV, suggesting that the new television service would have little allegiance to its viewers, and would restrict its range of programming to cater for the tastes of its sponsors, the advertisers. However, sport, and specifically League football, could potentially match the ITV companies' and the advertisers' needs by providing mass, popular entertainment. Although the League management committee had given the BBC permission to televise filmed highlights – for a sum it would not divulge – the possibility of negotiating a contract with commercial television had not been ruled out.

In May 1955 the ITV's weekend companies, Associated Television (ATV) and Associated Broadcasting Company (ABC), had made initial approaches to the League. According to *The Times* an offer of £1,000 per match had been offered to screen live games in London, but at that time the League management committee were still adamantly against such an arrangement.[41] A considerable breakthrough did appear to surface as the rights came under negotiation in the summer of 1956, after the BBC's first year of filmed highlights. ATV proposed that in return for a fee in the region of £50,000 it could televise the second half of up to 35 League matches per season, with a delayed kick-off at 6.15 p.m. Furthermore, ATV promised to compensate clubs for any lost revenue caused by televising the game (which was estimated by *The Times* to be in the region of £60,000)[42] and to recompense travelling clubs for having to remain away from home overnight because of the late kick-off. As a further inducement, ATV also offered to make a special film to advertise the League across the ITV network. This package, devised to usurp the dominance of the BBC in the coverage of football, was the first proposal for live football with any substance and persuasion. Still fearful of television, the management committee decided to refer the offer, and wait for a report to a special meeting, two months later. But, as Hardaker remembered, 'the offer was so good it almost made one believe in fairies at the bottom of the garden'.[43] At the special meeting in Blackpool the management committee initially voted to accept the offer from ATV, the first time the League had formally agreed to live televised football. However, a large contingent of clubs who were strongly against live coverage were absent from the ballot. Therefore, a second special meeting was arranged in Manchester, where by 38 votes to 10, representatives of the League clubs rejected ATV's terms, and deferred indefinitely the prospect of covering League matches live. Negotiations for Saturday evening matches resurfaced briefly during the 1960/61 season when ABC offered the League £142,000 (£92,000 for exclusive rights and £50,000 to advertise the game) for the second half of 26 games, selected from all four divisions. The idea, according to Hardaker, was to use the Saturday evening schedule as a public relations exercise 'to present football and the League in the best possible light and give the public, including millions of women who watch television on Saturday nights a taste of the excitement and spectacle of first-class football'.[44] Similarly, the management committee stated that: 'It is difficult to envisage a more favourable business deal for any form of professional sport.'[45] Dissenting voices from within and outside the game raised the awareness of the League's management committee once more to the affect on wider popular entertainments. Specifically, Mr R.B. Jones, secretary of the Arsenal Supporters Club, feared that many would 'stay at home on a bad afternoon in anticipation of getting his football by the fireside in the evening'.[46] Moreover,

Sir Tom O'Brian, general secretary of the National Association of Theatre and Kine Employees and president of the Federation of Film and Theatre Unions, called a meeting between the parties concerned from television and football, and argued that the proposed deal would jeopardize the livelihood of 100,000 people. In the event, one game between Blackpool and Bolton Wanderers was shown 'live' as a means test; according to Hardaker it was a rather dull affair, and with that disappeared ITV's chances of clinching the deal.

During the period in question, this was the nearest ITV came to wrestling the exclusive rights to League football away from the BBC. With the breakdown in negotiations between the ITV companies and the Football League, the BBC stepped in with a modest offer of £20,000 for Saturday evening filmed highlights for the 1956–57 season, which was renewed for another year (1957–58) and then three more years (1958–61). For the remainder of the 1950s and most of the 1960s ITV continually lost out in the battle to obtain rights to football. All that remained were the odd scraps from mid-week FA Cup replays or attempts to organise alternative football competitions, like ABC's five-a-side football on Sundays.[47] Because of the reasons stated above, and the institutional power of the BBC, the ITV companies found it incredibly difficult to break the hegemony of its now established adversary. The ITV companies were to remain in the shadow of the BBC until 1966 when a more centralized sports production unit was established to provide economies of scale, and a more coherent style for its audience.

## Conclusion

The evidence within the above narratives illustrates the fluctuating speed with which television and football accommodated the needs and requirements of each other. The political wranglings and hegemonic struggles during the formative decades of televised football between the broadcasters, the administrators and the players are complex and contradictory. The resonance between the BBC's statutory commitment to public service and the ritual symbolism of the Cup Final (north and south of the border) both served to knit together a shared national culture, and at the same stroke, move the professional game beyond its straightforward origins of payment for play in front of spectators towards a set of complex relations whereby the sport supports and is supported by television, which increasingly has acted not as a secondary, ancillary industry, but an integral, constituent part of it, economically and culturally dependent. The residual shadow of the early negotiations for televised sport remain at the forefront of football's economic and cultural success. Therefore, we need to understand the complexities of contemporary relations between broadcasters, football governing bodies, clubs, players and spectators within the context of these uneasy beginnings to fully appreciate televised football as a pageant of sound and vision.

## Notes

1. A. Briggs. *The History of Broadcasting in the UK. Volume 3: The War of Words* (Oxford: Oxford University Press, 1970), p. 129.
2. *Radio Times*, 31 Dec. 1937.
3. BBC Radio began broadcasting from football in January 1927 and came up against stern opposition from both the press and the Football League.
4. S. Rous, *Football World: A Lifetime in Sport* (London: Faber and Faber, 1978).
5. S. Barnett, *Games and Sets: The Changing Face of Sport* (London: BFI, 1990).
6. *Radio Times,* 22 April 1938.
7. J. Caughie. 'Before the Golden Age: Early Television Drama' in J. Corner (ed.), *Popular Television in Britain – Studies in Cultural History* (London: BFI, 1991), p. 23.
8. The *Times,* 23 Dec. 1938.
9. *BBC Handbook* 1940.
10. *The Times,* 7 Jan. 1938.
11. Arsenal had featured in the film *The Arsenal Stadium Mystery* (1938) as part of its public relations campaign during this period.
12. Comer, *Popular Television.*
13. *BBC Handbook* 1949.
14. *Radio Times*, 28 April 1947.
15. G. Whannel, *Fields In Vision: Television, Sport and Cultural Transformation* (London: Routledge, 1992), p. 23.
16. *The Times*, 26 Sept. 1951.
17. *The Times*, 13 March 1952.
18. *The Times*, 26 Sept. 1951.
19. *The Times*, 18 Jan. 1951.
20. White Paper, *Broadcasting: Memorandum on the Report of the Broadcasting Committee 1949* (Cmnd. 8550. London: HMSO, 1952)
21. *The Times*, 3 May 1952.
22. *The Times*, 26 June 1952.
23. *The Times*, 14 Oct. 1952.
24. Ibid.
25. *The Times*, 22 Jan. 1953.
26. M. Golesworthy, *The Encyclopaedia of Association Football* (London: Sportsmans Book Cub, 1957).
27. B. Wright, *Football Is My Passion* (London: Sportsmans Book Club, 1959), p. 82.
28. After much wrangling among the Scottish FA a televised floodlit game between Falkirk and Newcastle United was well received by the Scottish press who thought attempts to ban such games represented, 'a fear which many feel is exceeding the bounds of common sense' *Glasgow Herald,* 30 Sept. 1953.
29. B. Wright, *The World's My Football Pitch* (Tiptree: Arrow, 1956).
30. *The Times*, 4 Jan. 1956.
31. *The Times*, 12 March 1956.
32. G. Whannel. *Fields in Vision.*
33. G. Whannel. '"Grandstand", the sports fan and the family audience', in J. Comer (ed.), *Popular Television in Britain.*
34. S. Laing, *Representations of Working-Class Life 1957–1964* (London: Macmillan, 1986), p. 29.
35. A. Hardaker, *Hardaker of the League* (London: Pelham Books, 1977), p. 222.
36. Ibid.
37. B. Sendall, *Independent Television in Britain. Volume 1:1946–62* (London: Macmillan, 1982).
38. *The Times*, 22 Sept. 1955.

39.  *Radio Times*, 2 Sept. 1955.
40.  *Radio Times*, 16 Sept. 1955.
41.  *The Times*, 18 May 1955.
42.  *The Times*, 21 July 1956.
43.  A. Hardaker, *Hardaker of the League* (London: Pelham Books).
44.  *Manchester Guardian,* 17 Aug. 1960.
45.  Ibid.
46.  Ibid.
47.  Whannel, *Fields in Vision,* p. 48.

# 12

# 'Lobby' and the Formative Years of Radio Sports Commentary, 1935–1952

*Richard Haynes*

Commentaries cannot in fact be turned out to a set pattern of excellence like shells or razor blades. There is no single measure of speed to suit every listener, no perfect pitch or cadence, no standard blend of scene setting and associative idea. There are nevertheless certain principles that underlie good commentary, and these principles have reached a stage of development that justifies their statement and analysis.[1]

## Introduction

Seymour Joly de Lotbinière was the British Broadcasting Corporation's Director of Outside Broadcasts from 1935 to 1939, and then again encompassing radio and television from 1946 to 1952, before concentrating on television outside broadcasts (OB) from 1952 to 1955. Affectionately known within the BBC as (and from herein called) 'Lobby', he came from upper-class roots but used his acute sense of the listeners' needs and his 'common touch' to innovate, develop and refine the modern techniques of sports commentary that connected the emerging national audience to the major sporting events of the time. His legacy was the evolution of the generic codes and conventions of sports broadcasting that augured a new era of sporting vernacular, a new language of sport and society. This paper aims to address just how important Lobby was to the formative years of sports broadcasting in the UK and analyse his specific contribution to the institutional principles of running commentary as they emerged in the BBC.

**Source:** *Sport in History*, 29(1) (2009): 25–48.

In analysing Lobby's influence at the BBC, of central concern was how do commentators learn to commentate? This is not easy to discern. The autobiographies of numerous British sports commentators quite often reveal a highly individualistic approach to commentary.[2] More often than not commentators had to find their own way in the bewildering world of broadcasting. They learnt their craft from instinct as much as technique. But Lobby argued there were guiding principles to the technique and spent several years leaning his analytical ear towards the spoken word and gently persuading the main exponents on how they might improve their 'art'. This article draws on papers held at the BBC's Written Archives Centre, some of which have also been used in other popular histories of sports broadcasting, most notably by Christopher Martin-Jenkins on cricket and more recently Dick Booth's history of radio commentary.[3] However, where these studies principally focus on the emerging style of particular commentators and Lobby's influence on their development, this article is preoccupied with his contribution to the occupation of radio commentary more broadly.

It is widely acknowledged in the broad discipline of history that biography can offer a way in to understanding and interpreting the past but that placing too much emphasis on the deeds of 'great men' quite often masks wider processes and confuses individual intentions with wider consequences. Thus in focusing on Lobby there are potential limitations to the version of history this produces. Nevertheless, in concentrating on his professional life and the constraining factors and contingencies that impinged on his work – institutional, economic, social, cultural and political – it is possible to understand why and how certain decisions were made with regard to broadcasting from sport at any given time and place.

Lobby's professional biography, therefore, stands as a way in to understanding how commentary technique evolved, was institutionalized and was later taken forward by a whole host of household names in British radio coverage of sport.

## 'Lobby': A Career in Broadcasting

Aside from having one of the most pompous-sounding names in the BBC's history, Seymour Joly de Lotbinière was undoubtedly one of the most important figures in developing the exposition and craft of sports commentary. He was one of the few broadcasting pioneers who, with a frame of 6 feet 8 inches, looked down on the BBC's first director-general, Lord Reith. But it is the standing of Lobby in the esteem of his peers and contemporaries that makes him an outstanding figure in the history of British broadcasting.

As Chris Wrigley has noted, in the first half of the twentieth century it was 'not uncommon to have grandparents, parent, uncles and aunts and brothers and sisters who had all been employed in one part of the empire or other'.[4] In this context, Lobby had prodigious ancestry. His father was Brigadier-General

Henri Gustave Joly de Lotbinière (1868–1960) of the Royal Engineers and his grandfather, Sir Henri-Gustave Joly de Lotbinière (1829–1908), had been a senior politician in Quebec, Canada, and was lieutenant governor of British Columbia between 1900 and 1906. Lobby was born in Buckinghamshire in 1905 and was educated at Eton College and Trinity College, Cambridge, where he studied economics and law.[5] His upper-class upbringing was firmly rooted in the obstinately rigid class culture of the Edwardian era. Crucially, as Ross McKibbin has argued, wealth was not necessarily the key indicator of 'being upper-class'.[6] Rather, status and wider cultural symbolism were equally if not more important and Lobby enjoyed a clear social and cultural authority from attending both Eton and Cambridge. The cult of 'athleticism' promoted in the English public-school system played its part in this respect.[7] In sport, and due to his tall frame, Lobby became a competent rower in a halcyon period of the sport at Cambridge and was part of the Third Trinity Boat Club. Again this aspect of Lobby's social life reflected the elitist culture of university sport. 'The Third' was open only to Old Etonians and Old Westminsters, another marker of exclusivity in an already privileged environment. As Tony Mangan has noted regarding the place of rowing in student life at Cambridge, 'there were men of reading, rowing men and men who attempted both'.[8] Judging from his academic and rowing records, Lobby fitted into the latter category; neither excelling in his studies or sport, but engaged with both aspects of Cambridge student life.[9] Such experiences bolstered the view that the varsity fixtures between Oxford and Cambridge – the boat race in particular – were important features in the sporting calendar. Varsity fixtures featured strongly in the BBC's formative coverage of sport, eventually bestowing the boat race with national importance well beyond its popularity as a sport.

In January 1927, aged 21, Lobby was admitted to Lincoln's Inn and was called to the Chancery bar in 1930 where he practised law from his chambers at New Court. According to Pimlott-Baker, it was Lobby's 'concern for people' that led him to turn his back on a lucrative career as a barrister and instead take up a new opportunity at the fledgling BBC in 1932.[10] Radio in Britain was only a decade old when Lobby joined the Talks Department amid a group of 'high flying' producers and administrators who would, before long, be influencing the future of the BBC.[11] In August 1935, after three years in Talks, in a young organization that enabled a fast-track trajectory into management, Lobby succeeded Gerald Cock into the role as Director of Outside Broadcasts. Cock had overseen the BBC's earliest forays into the coverage of sport from 1927 and was to become the BBC's first Director of Television in 1935. Along with producer Lance Sieveking, he had paved the way for coverage of sport and established important relations with the governing bodies of British sport.[12] Lobby had clearly impressed senior management at the BBC from an early stage of his broadcasting career and was moving into a role of high responsibility for someone just turned thirty. He had not been in the role long when, in November 1936, he was thrown into one of the seminal moments in the BBC's early history. Lobby was returning late from an outside broadcast when he passed the raging flames engulfing the Crystal Palace in South London. Lobby found himself delivering a running commentary of events as they unfolded. The commentary proved a portent of the immediacy of broadcast news, delivered after the evening papers had ended their runs and before the morning papers could deliver the previous day's news.

Reviewing the various memos, correspondence and papers written by Lobby, one is struck by the assuredness of his knowledge and instruction on the process of commentary and in the organization of the Outside Broadcast department more generally. It is clear that Lobby had a calm analytical approach to broadcasting that enabled him to make judgements as to what sounded good and what sounded bad; how to ensure the experience of the listener was always of prime concern. To his credit, Lobby wrote some extensive guidelines, not simply on the general technique of commentary but also on how to handle individual sports. He had an intuitive understanding of what made sense to the listener and viewer. Some of his critical analysis of commentary and advice were viewed in some quarters with a sense of resentment. His perfunctory interjections may – given his Etonian background – have been viewed as stern, abrupt and even sanctimonious. Even revered commentators such as cricket commentator John Arlott did not escape Lobby's critical analysis of their work. Some time later, in an interview for the BBC, Arlott recalled:

> Old Lobby said 'now listen, I think you have a very vulgar voice. I can't understand why people want to listen to it. But you've got a very interesting mind and I think you better continue.' He was pretty good Lobby really. He was a harsh critic but his criticisms were invariably right. And of course, mine was, and is, a vulgar voice.[13]

In reviewing autobiographical and interview accounts by leading British commentators who began their careers under Lobby's charge, it is clear he was viewed with both reverence and affection. Rugby and cricket commentator Peter West characterized him as a man 'endowed with a most genial nature and a clear, incisive, cultured mind'.[14] Racing commentator Peter O'Sullevan remarked that Lobby 'had managed to survive Eton without emerging totally convinced of his superiority to less favoured mortals';[15] while all-round outside broadcaster Wynford Vaughan-Thomas noted that Lobby was the 'unlikely Lenin of the commentary revolution' who was 'unfailingly courteous and considerate, with a cool analytical mind which he may have inherited from his remarkable father'.[16] Most tellingly with regard to the evolution of what might be called the modern commentary technique, Robert Hudson, who later succeeded Lobby as Head of OBs noted, 'He had legal training and a penetrating mind. To him we owe the original conceptual thinking about radio and TV commentary. Prior to his arrival, people just talked and hoped for the best.'[17]

What follows is an exposition of Lobby's 'conceptual thinking' about commentary and how it influenced the practice of the select group of individuals who emerged as household names as radio commentators of sport during the 1950s and 1960s.

## The Demise of 'Square One'

One of the key interventions Lobby oversaw was the end of 'the grid system', whereby a plan of the sports arena was published in the *Radio Times* as a visual aid to listeners.[18] In taking control of the BBC's OB department in 1935 Lobby had inherited a disparate team of commentators. Most were freelance. Many had been recruited for their expertise in sport rather than broadcasting and had learnt the technique of commentary almost 'off the cuff'. The BBC's earliest commentators included characters such as Captain H.B.T. ('Teddy') Wakelam, who covered rugby union; George Allison, a director and manager of Arsenal Football Club, who commentated on football; R.C. Lyle, who handled horse racing; and Sir Pelham 'Plum' Warner, who had been the MCC's Chairman of the Board of Selectors, and broadcast reports from cricket. These pioneers of commentary were thrown in at the deep end. Many of the early contributors to sports broadcasting were upper-middle-class, public-school-educated-either Old Etonians or Old Harrovians – and, as John Arlott later recounted, they were 'innovators with impeccable accents'.[19] The plan in the *Radio Times* had become an essential feature of BBC broadcasts from sport. They acted as spatial guides to the listener but also required a secondary voice to announce and explain exactly where on the plan the action was taking place. Thus began the institutionalized practice of using a secondary commentator or 'number two', more commonly known as a 'Dr Watson'. The device of using a plan and a secondary commentator was originated by one of the first producers of OBs, Lance Sieveking. Sieveking had witnessed the graphical interpretation of baseball in Times Square, New York, an innovative electronic scoreboard, twelve feet high and thirty feet long, having been introduced to the public in 1914.[20] With information remotely relayed from the stadium by telegraph to a controller lodged in the Times building, the bright lights of the scoreboard mapped out the location of a batsman's strike on the plan of a baseball park. For radio broadcasts, the number two helped provide background information to the listener. His interjections either set the scene of the event, with comments on the weather or playing conditions, or pinpointed action on the field of play with reference to the plan in the *Radio Times*. John Snagge, another early BBC OB producer who would go on to be a leading BBC announcer and commentator in his own right, recalled the role of the number two in the autobiography of Wakelam:

> The job itself is not so easy as many people believe. A good No. 2 must be able to work with all and every commentator, and each commentator has entirely different methods. It should not be the job of No. 1 to make openings for No. 2, rather it is the job of No. 2 to find the moments and to be prepared to fill in when and if No. 1 wants to take a rest during an interval. He must have a good knowledge of the game, but not so much that he interrupts or corrects No. 1. Two people talking at once into a microphone produces chaos in the loudspeaker.[21]

Not all 'Dr Watsons' were as knowledgeable and professional as Snagge and, in a 1943 radio talk, Wakelam reflected on his career as a commentator and recalled a letter he received from a listener from Leeds in 1933. The correspondent railed 'Dear Sir, You must be a man of considerable restraint, else how could you have kept your hands off the blithering idiot you had alongside you last Saturday? My advice to you is strangle him'.[22] After the Second World War, Wakelam did no further commentaries; his style was too monotonous and stilted for the ears of the post-war audience.[23] The demise of his style and the annoyance to some listeners of the 'number two' signalled a change in the technique of commentary. Indeed Snagge, whose resonant voice according to another commentator, Max Robertson, 'was perfect for any pomp and circumstance' and gave 'immense significance to his utterances', represented an emergent group of BBC staff who operated under Lobby's direction and whose role switched between OB manager, producer and commentator.[24] In 1935 Snagge became second in command to Lobby in the OB department. In 1931 he had become 'the voice' of the Boat Race, a role he remarkably maintained until his retirement in 1980.

Perhaps because of his vast experience as a number two, it was Snagge who entered into prolonged discussion with Lobby regarding the merits of the rather mechanical technique and its stultifying shortcomings for the listener. In 1937 the issue of the number two commentator appears to come to a head. Crucially, the device of using a number two and the use of terms like 'back to square one' became tired and something of a cliché. In a memorandum to all regional directors of outside broadcasts Snagge reports on lengthy discussions in the OB department regarding the value of squares in football coverage. Although a decision had been made to continue with the use of a number two, with 'some modifications', it remained clear to both Lobby and Snagge that there were certain drawbacks to the technique which required remedy. In December 1937 Snagge reported:

The use of the word 'square' is, we think, redundant. For several reasons:

1. That it has become a Music-Hall joke.
2. That its constant repetition is irritating.

3. That very often the time for slipping in the squares is so short that the addition of the single word 'square' is all that is heard by listeners, and the number which follows is very often drowned by the commentator re-starting.[25]

The use of an eight-square grid for both rugby and football clearly had its detractors towards the end of the 1930s. Listeners wrote in to the BBC with suggestions of ways to enhance the technique (for example, by increasing the number of squares to twelve). In spite of suggestions from the public and regional directors to keep the grid system, prolonging its use to the outbreak of war in 1939, the days of its use were themselves numbered. After the war the technique disappeared completely.

New, more competent and confident voices of sport were beginning to emerge in the late 1930s. They were a set of broadcasters who would set the benchmark for outside broadcasting both during the war and the immediate post-war era. Again Lobby appeared to have his finger on the pulse of this change, although politically it threw up sensitive issues regarding the management of those who had already done the pioneering work, becoming household names in the process.

A good example came with an experimental rugby commentary where instead of one lead commentator it was decided to have two lead commentators sharing the microphone (a practice continued to this day). Wakelam and Howard Marshall were employed to share commentary on rugby and were listened to carefully by Lobby and another senior manager, Lindsay Wellington, then Director of Programming. In a memo to Lobby, Wellington noted:

> I thought the comparison most unfavourable to Wakelam. By Marshall's standards he seemed to have scarcely more than a single attribute, and that a doubtful one: his machine-gun rapidity of style was certainly a remarkable trick of the tongue, but it is so sustained, so unvaried, so monotonous, as to convey little of excitement. What struck me most was that Marshall, not only conveyed a delightful personality, but an extraordinary varied and picturesque scene. One became identified through him with the game and the crowd. His description, always leisurely, yet kept pace with the game, was varied in mood and built up admirably to crescendos and diminuendos of excitement. His vocabulary is much richer and, to me, pleasantly odd. Wakelam's monotone is by comparison dull.[26]

From this analysis Marshall's lyrical style was the future and depended far less on the mechanics of a printed plan and secondary commentator due to his ability to paint a picture and give the listener a 'pair of eyes' through varied description and a narrative of light and shade. Ultimately Lobby realized the strength of this argument and had therefore employed Marshall as his first and principal commentator for ball-by-ball cricket from 1934 – a sport Wakelam felt was not suited to radio commentary after his own attempt at covering the sport in the late 1920s.[27] However, in 1937 Lobby moved with caution; Wakelam was one of the BBC's stars of commentary and in his response to Wellington the personal politics of replacing him with Marshall were clearly of concern:

> I do not think we shall be able to drop Wakelam for Howard Marshall where international matches are concerned since Marshall would not be willing to replace him. This is perhaps just as well as we use Marshall a fair amount. Anyhow, Saturday's experiment has shown us that we shall always be safe in falling back on Marshall for rugger.[28]

Lobby's defence of Wakelam – at least his unease in sacking him – reflected Wakelam's status as the first sports commentator the BBC had ever used. Perhaps sentiment and Oxbridge loyalty played their part. But the need to find more skilful broadcasters cast in the mould of Marshall was now his imperative and from the late 1930s through to the immediate post-war years the BBC OB department went on a sustained recruitment drive to find more talented commentators. More crucially, the comparison also confirmed there were new techniques emerging that pointed towards underlying principles of 'good commentary'.

## The Art and Techniques of Commentary

> The commentator's first duty is to make listeners feel that they have left their own fireside for the scene of action – that they really are looking on at something actually in progress.[29]

In radio sports commentary the character and characteristics of the commentator play an enormous role in the listener's understanding and imagining of what is taking place. As Crissell points out, 'for all the commentator's objectivity there is a sense in which we become almost as conscious of him as of the events themselves'.[30] From internal memoranda and correspondence it is plain Lobby knew and understood this premise of commentary and its impact on the audience to a remarkable degree. It had been his drive to progress commentary to new levels of sophistication that saw an end to the perfunctory 'square one' technique. His analysis of what commentators did, how they behaved, how they delivered a line and conveyed a scene has become folklore among the team of commentators Lobby recruited and nurtured. The OB department became a tightly run affair and under Lobby's management would continually strive to do a better job. A significant aspect of this process was the weekly review of programmes. Raymond Baxter, who joined the department in 1950, recalled the routine of a departmental meeting every Monday and its impact on commentary practice:

> There would come the moment when Lobby, turning over the pages of the OB diary, which was a very impressive large book, would say 'programmes

since we last met'. And he would then analyse every single programme in which the department had been involved. And in the presence of everyone say exactly what he thought of it. And that was great discipline.[31]

How the OB department constructed its audience reflected the educated upper-middle-class background of its staff.[32] There survives a range of publications, some publicly available, others within the BBC archive, that hint at Lobby's deep and firmly held beliefs about the technique of commentary and how it should be done. In June 1937 he wrote a two-page article for the *Radio Times* under the title 'Would You Like to be a Commentator?' in which he characteristically upholds the unique skills of the commentator and suggests an ability to cope with two or more things at once is a prerequisite. As he makes clear,

> A commentator must be able to describe one impression in neat smooth-running sentences, and at the same time he must be registering his next impression. He must be watching the broadcast as a whole to see that it is not losing shape, and he must be noticing what effects are likely to be reaching listeners so that he can explain them and yet not talk through them.[33]

The notion that a commentary has 'shape' was essentially about delivering a coherent narrative that 'helps materially in creating a picture in the listener's mind'.[34] Being conscious of the audience has always been key to commentary, which is why in his first ever commentary Teddy Wakelam was provided with a 'stooge' – a blind man recruited from the charity St Dunstan's – to whom he delivered his commentary.[35]

If this kind of discipline proved lacking, Lobby would unceremoniously unpick a commentator's performance and suggest areas for improvement. Lobby spent some considerable time reviewing commentaries. Commentators were advised time and again to listen to their own commentaries. The volume of discussions on the topic ultimately led Lobby to set some of the core principles of commentary down on paper. In a memorandum from December 1942, Lobby was confident that the OB department team had reached 'some sort of framework on which better performances can be built'.[36] A good commentary was a bespoke compound of ingredients: setting the scene; description of action; giving the score or results, regularly and succinctly; 'effects' from the stadium, to be explained but not interrupted; associative material – sometimes known as 'homework' – such as historic facts and figures or personal information; and assessment of the significance of the occasion and key moments – who is likely to win, what it means, and so on. Lobby's insistence on having 'a good stock of associative ideas' would become standard practice throughout the BBC's coverage of any outside broadcast event, exemplified by broadcasters such as Richard Dimbleby.[37] Lobby suggested the principle was 'easier to exemplify than to analyse' as it depended on the event, its history, the spectator's point of view and the commentator's own personal experiences. But all these 'associations' could be used since 'the commentator must take all knowledge for his province and select his associative ideas from the widest possible field'.[38]

The reflective analysis was a form of 'stocktaking', as Lobby saw it, 'so that future experiment wastes the least possible time on what has already been tried and found wanting'.[39] The general principles, given meticulous exposition by Lobby in a 48-page pamphlet from 1942, included the following:

1. The listener must be persuaded that he is in a 'ring side seat'.
2. The listener's attention must be held while he is in his 'ring side seat'.
3. Different types of broadcast demand different treatment of commentary.[40]

Each of these broad statements was given more detailed treatment in the document. The first hints at the journalistic ideology of commentary, which included references to 'no faking'. Included here would be what every listener wanted to hear: the score, to be given 'without delay of any sort'. The second suggests the importance of capturing and maintaining an audience that placed more emphasis on entertainment – 'telling the "story" attractively and with competence'. Both would prove to be enduring principles of BBC sports coverage. There was emphasis on the commentator being 'natural and friendly', 'making a striking start and neat finish', building 'suspense interest' in order to 'work to a climax', 'show assurance' and 'maintain speed', blending material into a 'well shaped story' and never showing 'partiality' that 'may effect the accuracy of his commentary'. All these traits had to become second nature to the commentator, but most importantly had to be learnt. Commentators also had other contingent matters to deal with – when timings went wrong or technology failed, which in the 1930s and 40s was very commonplace. There were also some clear don'ts, such as the 'judicious use of "wise cracks"' and avoidance of 'irritating the listener'.[41]

Throughout the late 1930s and the 1940s major sports were analysed in detail for their own traits in coverage and commentary. Each sport presented its own set of problems for live radio: athletics was considered too drawn-out to hold the listener's attention for any length of time; billiards similarly extended over a prolonged period which made it 'almost impossible to pick a moment when the event is reaching its climax'; boxing required two commentators, one to describe the fight, the other to analyse the match and the technical performance of the contestants; cricket was slow and meant 'the commentator cannot rely on factual description to fill more than about half his time'; football and rugby presented 'a complicated sequence for the listener to assimilate'; horse racing needed to be broken down into the preliminaries, the start and the race itself, the latter presenting acute problems of identification due to the speed of the horses and the varying proximity of the race to the commentator; tennis was considered 'almost impossible to prescribe any treatment that is wholly satisfactory' as play was fast and 'the sameness of the strokes makes for monotony'; and finally rowing demanded a considerable amount of associative material due to the length of races or lack of visibility of the race itself.[42] Nevertheless, each diagnosis of the difficulties in covering individual sports found their remedy. In his conclusion, Lobby reiterates the commentator's role is an 'extremely complicated one'. 'But', he emphasizes, 'it must be remembered that natural "facility" at the microphone is half the battle and that technique cannot be acquired all at once.'[43] The recruitment of individuals with talent and confidence at the microphone proved one of the core tasks for Lobby and the OB Department from the mid 1930s to the early 1950s as the BBC expanded its coverage of sport.

## The Recruitment and Management of Commentators

> I think on the whole, though, that where possible it is far wiser to stick to the games which you really know, and to the fields upon which you yourself are known. And it is my firm opinion that anyone is a mug just to take a thing in haphazard fashion for the cash side.[44]

Lobby spent much of his time and energies on recruiting and developing commentators. The early career path of a sports commentator is both opaque and invariably circumstantial. Many of the household names of BBC sports commentary owed their start in broadcasting to a chance meeting or phone call from an old acquaintance, being in the right place at the right time. However, there were established avenues to the microphone emerging as early as the 1920s. The 'old boy' network of public school, Oxbridge education or time spent in the armed forces was usually the key to getting on in the brave new world of broadcasting.

From 1936, as the OB department sought to expand its range of activities and find new voices, there was a constant stream of commentary tests on new hopefuls. As broadcasting became a viable career opportunity, so the BBC was flooded with 'wannabe' announcers and commentators. They had heard Allison, Wakelam and Snagge and, much like Rex Alston, who joined in 1941, saw an opportunity to visit some of Britain's finest sporting events. Whatever the motivation, many interviewees soon realized there was much more to the 'art of commentary' than just talking a 'good game'. Commentary demanded a range of skills that needed to be mastered.

The producer who Lobby asked to oversee most of the BBC's tests before the Second World War was Michael Standing. Standing, who would go on to be a war correspondent on the Western Front and ultimately become the Head of Variety for many years after the war, famously penning the BBC's 'Green Book' – the *Variety Programming Policy Guide* – had joined the BBC in 1935. In the late 1930s, after joining the BBC, he was soon doing OBs around the country, including *Standing on the Corner*, Test cricket and other public events, and was cast in the mould of Lobby's new team of commentator/ producers. As far as recruitment went, his duty was to make arrangements for auditions – including short-listing interviewees, agreeing access to venues and, once the tests were completed, writing short reports on each and every individual regarding their suitability. The reports focused on voice tone, mellifluousness, colour of narrative and the ability to keep up with the action. Also included in the reports were short recommendations for future action – 'showing potential', 'possible potential' and 'absolute no's'.

One of the main challenges of the process was finding a suitable venue and adequate content for the applicants to comment on. Where possible arrangements were made with the owners of sporting venues in the London area. But all too often this was either impractical or simply too costly. On some occasions, therefore, the OB team had to be more inventive and it was not too long before interviewees were asked to make their way to the seventh floor that provided access to the top of Broadcasting House to provide a running commentary on the bustling West End streets below. In the edict that OB commentators should be able to describe any scene before them there lay a portent of the meandering cricket commentaries of Brian Johnston and Henry Blofeld of *Test Match Special* fame. In their commentaries, setting the scene with a comment on a passing red London bus was given nearly as much import as action on the field of play. On one occasion interviewees were asked to commentate on a table-tennis match between BBC employees in the canteen of the BBC Staff Training College. No event was too mundane for the test.

No matter where the tests were held, the point of the exercise was to ascertain whether or not the person could convey the scene before them in a clear, interesting voice. The comments on the reports were candid and often circumspect – 'poor voice', 'slight Cockney accent', 'blew up through nerves', 'a precious voice' but 'inclined to be facetious' and simply 'bad – bad'.[45] One unsuspecting applicant suggested the BBC producers attend the Vaudeville Theatre in London's Strand to listen to his nightly prologue. Standing's remark on the suggestion was unequivocal: 'I have judged him without going to the theatre.'[46]

Some of the BBC's leading commentators of the period were not immune from this high-minded, highly critical tone of their assessors, including one of the BBC's first commentators on ice hockey, Canadian-born Stewart MacPherson. In autumn 1936 Lobby had been eager to find someone to commentate on ice hockey. In the late 1930s the sport had gained a new popularity as a spectator sport and Britain was home to eleven teams.[47] In 1936 also the British national team was crowned Olympic, World and European champions. Although British by birth, most of the national team had played at one time or another in Canada and the club sides were increasingly importing talent from North America to bolster their squads. Serendipity smiled on MacPherson when, after pestering the assistant head of OBs John Snagge, he was rewarded with an audition with five other hopefuls.[48] In his autobiography MacPherson recalled his luck in the audition when he realized it was to be held at Wembley Arena on a match between Harringay and Wembley – a venue and teams he knew 'like the back of my right hand'.[49] Most of the players had played in Winipeg, Canada. He also had the good fortune to listen to all four other applicants before he came to the microphone. As he explains: 'Kismet dealt me a wonderful hand that evening for I was last to do my stuff. I was in a position to see where the others made mistakes and to try to avoid the pitfalls when my turn came.'[50] Others had been stilted in their commentaries – some, according to MacPherson, overwhelmed by the speed of the play, others burdened by too much prescripted material. MacPherson simply drew on his knowledge of the game and prior experience of broadcasting in Canada:

> When I was given the nod to take over the mike, I grasped it firmly and rattled off everything I could see going on in front of me. Names came to me easily and it was natural that I should be able to talk glibly about a game I had known since childhood. I had no notes but felt the best plan was to talk plainly and quickly, describing points that I reasoned might seem strange to a new Hockey fan.[51]

MacPherson's reflections on his own performance, particularly his speed of tongue, were certainly given credit at the time, but he may have been surprised at the more critical comments his performance received: 'Fluent; very Canadian; very dramatic, perfect knowledge of the game, but, having no humour like Bob Bowman, his rather overpowering American voice, all on one note, bores into one's head with the persistence of a pneumatic drill. *Efficient, but very newspapery.*'[52] MacPherson would go on to be one of the BBC's prominent voices during the war and immediate postwar years, renown for commentaries on boxing and one of Lobby's favourite commentators. His assessment hints at a prevailing prejudice in the BBC for anything too 'American', too sensationalistic ('very news-papery') and too vulgar and far removed from 'standard English' for British audiences to bear ('overpowering').

Lobby's method for testing new commentators continued in the immediate post-war years, another period of expansion in the OB department. During the war new commentators had come to prominence, including Richard Dimbleby and Wynford Vaughan-Thomas, both cutting their teeth on sports OBs before venturing wider to cover life from 'the Front' and state occasions. Others such as Raymond Glendenning and Rex Alston became the BBC's most prominent voices on sport, first during the reduced hours of coverage of sport in the war years, then subsequently on the wide array of sports broadcasts that grew from 1946. Between them Glendenning and Alston covered football, rugby union, golf, greyhound racing, motor racing, cricket, boxing, horse racing, tennis and athletics. In October 1945 there was already a feeling that Glendenning was being overstretched and over-used across his main sports of football, boxing and horse racing. With the prospect of covering the 1948 Olympic Games in London new commentators were at a premium.

New talent did come from an emerging crop of post-war sports journal-ists, many using connections from time spent in the armed forces to get their foot in the door. Commentators such as Kenneth Wolstenholme, Peter West, Max Robertson, Brian Johnston, Peter Dimmock, Harry Carpenter, Murray Walker and Raymond Baxter (who joined from the British Forces Network) all began their careers with the BBC between 1946 and 1950, having served in the armed forces, and would go on to have long and distinguished careers in the BBC in both radio and television. It was a period of great expansion in the OB department, which fostered a particular kind of 'chumminess' at its headquarters in Broadcasting House. As Raymond Baxter later recalled:

> In the office of the outside broadcast department there were assembled a bunch of highly professional maniacs. For instance, we played cricket in the corridor, this was Brian Johnston's idea of course. We didn't call him 'Johnners' in those days, we used to call him 'BJ'. I shared an office with Rex Alston and we got on very well although you could scarcely have two more disparate people. . . . It was a remarkable period, because there was a col-lection of people of quite extraordinary personalities and capability, all under the control, and I use the word advisedly, of the great Seymour de Lotbiniere, who was Head of Outside Broadcasts and literally invented the technique of outside broadcasting which hasn't really changed today.[53]

OB staff worked as a team; according to Glendenning they often frequented known OB pubs, the Mason's Arms or the Dover Castle, and were generally a highly motivated and committed group of individuals operating under the tutelage of Lobby.[54] What emerged in the late 1930s, through the war and the immediate post-war years, was a team of exceptionally talented broad-casters. In contradistinction to Wakelam's claim of employing an 'expert' in the sport, the established vogue during this period was to recruit and foster multi-skilled broadcasters who could turn their skills to any given sport or outside broadcast.

## Managing Talent

Managing commentating 'talent' became an increasing burden for Lobby and introduced some acute issues for the BBC more generally. From the earliest days the BBC had been insistent on its policy that announcers remained anonymous in name and accent. This conservative philosophy dictated that news broadcasts were impartial, delivered by 'the BBC' in 'standard English' and not by credited individuals. However, the work of the OB department and the roster of freelance commentators worked to a different set of principles.

From the early 1930s it was not unknown for commentators to be introduced by name and, somewhat contentiously, be announced as working for or having an association with particular newspapers. In an OB meeting on sport in 1937 Snagge recalled an occasion before R.C. Lyle's broadcast from the 1934 Grand National when he received a phone call from Gladstone Murray, the editor of the *Times*, instructing him to announce the commentator as having an affiliation with his newspaper. Each year this practice continued by verbal agreement although, Snagge suggests, with 'no justification under our licence for mentioning the *Times*'.[55] Once the precedent had been set all freelancers with careers in journalism would make a similar claim to be introduced in association with their newspaper. In 1937 the situation became so overt that Lobby requested a list of commentators who were also journalists to be compiled. The results, below, revealed nearly all the pioneers of early sports commentary to have press associations.

> Howard Marshall – *Daily Telegraph*
> Harold Abrahams – *Sunday Times*
> B. Darwin – *Times*
> W.J. Howcroft – *Morning Post*
> C. B. Fry – *Evening Standard*
> H.B.T. Wakelam – *Morning Post*
> George Allison – *Daily Express*
> Marjorie Pollard – *Morning Post*
> Ivan Sharpe – *Allied Newspapers*
> Charles Eade – *Daily Sketch*
> H.E. Symons – *Sunday Times*
> J.E. Holdsworth – *Cycling Correspondent*
> Beril Rudd – *Daily Telegraph*
> Evelyn Montague – *Manchester Guardian*

The announcements were viewed as a form of advertising, an anathema to the BBC's Reithian ideals. In June 1938 Lobby made a final decision 'that a commentator should not be taken on if a condition of his use is that such acknowledgment must be made' and that mention of journalistic ties was appropriate in programme notes but not in the final billing.[56] Sports commentary had been one area where announcers were known, in contrast to the anonymity of other 'BBC voices'. But self-publicity and commercial advertising was strictly taboo.

## New Voices from the Regions

Lobby not only managed the BBC's network coverage of sport but also helped coordinate the coverage of sport in the nations and regions through directors of outside broadcasting in the BBC's main centres of Glasgow, Manchester, Birmingham, Belfast, Cardiff and Bristol. Not all BBC commentators lived in the metropolitan area and this brought with it issues of power and authority. Many new commentators were recruited by regional directors, were employed on a strictly freelance basis and got their start in sports commentary on opt-out programmes originally on the Home Service, and after the war, in the Light Programme. Glendenning (Northern Ireland), Wolstenholme (North West) and Vaughan-Thomas (Wales) had all made the grade through their initial experiences in the nations and regions and Lobby was constantly urging new talent to come through the BBC's UK network. Regional directors of OBs were left to their own devices but there was an edict to maintain contact with London HQ as to the suitability of commentators and guidelines on good commentary technique were forwarded when deemed necessary. However, when a big sporting event arrived the 'star' commentators from London were sent out to cover the occasion. This hierarchy of command, from London to the regions, was reason for resentment and dispute. Arguments were invariably raised regarding the blooding of new talent and analysis of their merits and, somewhat contentiously for London, the competence of their 'star' men when they operated outside the capital. For instance, there are several traces of arguments and animosity between Lobby and the North Regional Director of OBs Victor Smythe. Smythe had been with the BBC from its earliest period as a company in the 1920s and clearly felt he knew the operations of radio inside out. The sensitive nature of this relationship often reached its peak during the largest OB taken from the North region, the Grand National. The National caused all manner of problems as a broadcast event. Negotiations for access never ran smooth with Aintree's owner Mirabel Topham and the difficult logistics of transmitting the event effectively led to vexed messages of how things should be done. In 1938 Lobby was eager to reduce the build-up to the event and concentrate on the race commentary itself. 'I am all for cutting down racing preliminaries to essentials and no more',[57] Lobby wrote to Smythe, who replied: 'I have heard a good deal of adverse comment on our curtailment. . . . My own feeling is that to cut a race down to a mere rapid recital of runners and straight into the race provides a bald effect.' Pointedly he continued: 'This clashing of opinion makes me wish more and more that London was a little closer to Manchester, and that you could occasionally spend a few days coming round and meeting the type of listener who appreciates his broadcasting but seldom, if ever, writes about it.'[58]

Similar tensions grew in other BBC centres, where local knowledge of particular sporting events and the audience for them could cause friction for Lobby and senior management at Broadcasting House if not handled with care. The cultural significance of rugby union in Wales was a case in point. In autumn 1947 Lobby wanted to continue with an idea he hatched the previous year in the coverage of rugby union from Cardiff Arms Park. The match involving Wales and Australia was to be covered by two commentators, each rotating in a twenty-minute cycle in order to give respite from continuous commentary. Lobby had in mind an up-and-coming Welsh commentator, G.V. Wynne-Jones, who would work alongside the 'staff' rugby commentator Rex Alston. The pair had first worked together the previous season in Paris, when the experiment of dual commentary was first launched. In his autobiography Alston recalls his surprise at the 'self-confidence' of the 'novice': 'Prospective commentators outside the BBC usually require several matches in which to pick up the technique, but Wynne-Jones sailed into his task without a trace of nerves. The fact that someone was present who could take over, should my voice fail completely, was of great psychological value to me.'[59] Although the sentiment is complimentary to the Welsh 'novice', the underlying tone of Alston's analysis was slightly sanctimonious. In his own memoir, Wynne-Jones reflects that he was terribly nervous of his first major commentary with Alston, whom he gave due deference when it came to the 'staff' man's professionalism and abilities to organize the commentary.[60]

Regarding coverage of the Welsh game against Australia, the Welsh Programme Director A. Watkins Jones agreed in principle with Lobby's suggestion of using Alston alongside 'their man' but warned: 'Our audience in Wales expect to hear Wynne-Jones throughout the game on this occasion, because with his regular coverage of club games at present in the Welsh Home service he is establishing himself as their own popular commentator.'[61] Rugby commentaries were hugely popular in Wales and per capita drew some of the BBC's largest audiences for any form of programming. Technically the split commentary went well and continues to be used in football to this day. Unfortunately, the contrasting styles of commentary – the Welsh tones of 'Geevers' (Wynne-Jones) and the 'schoolmasterly' approach of Alston – did not. In a private and personal letter to Lobby, Watkins Jones suggested 'Alston put his foot in it badly on two occasions'. First, he had suggested the Welsh crowd were 'preparing to boo' an Australian penalty kick; and secondly, when Wales won a penalty Alston remarked 'You can tell that from the shout of the crowd. They'd boo if it was the other way round.[62] Innocuous as these comments may seem to contemporary audiences, in 1947 they would have been deemed an affront to Welsh sensibilities, with the suggestion the crowd were being 'unsporting' and even cheating. Welsh criticism was not confined to listeners. Word had reached Captain Walter Reid, secretary of the Welsh Rugby Union. The WRU threatened to halt future broadcasts in Wales if Alston were allowed to do any further commentaries. This led Watkins Jones to conclude: 'It looks, therefore, as if your scheme was doomed from the start and in the circumstances had best be abandoned.[63] The impasse on Alston led to a compromise in coverage: BBC Wales decided to cover only the second half of Welsh games for the remainder of the season, enabling Wynne-Jones to work alone. Lobby conceded that perhaps critical comments about the Welsh crowd – or any other home nation for that matter – were better coming from one of their own. But, unbowed, he also argued that 'Reading between the lines it seems clear that you are sacrificing a first half broadcast for Welsh listeners in order not to raise the Alston issue'.[64]

It was suggested Alston might be reintroduced to the Welsh environment in order to 'redeem himself through the more neutral fixture between the Barbarians and Australia – the view being the BBC should persevere with its staff commentators rather than cave in to the demands of local audiences. The issue of English sports commentators operating in Scotland, Wales or Northern Ireland has endured throughout the BBC's history, causing internal strife when London forces the hand of regional directors, and external consternation from national audiences who rail against the metropolitan point of view.[65]

## Conclusion

Lobby had entered into the world of broadcasting at a critical moment in its history. The early pioneering spirit of technicians and the first producers of radio outside broadcasts, particularly Gerald Cock and Lance Sieveking, had revealed what was possible and whetted the appetite for live coverage of sport among the BBC's emerging national audience. By the mid-1930s some commentators, most notably Wakelam and Allison, had gained national recognition and were synonymous with the coverage of certain sports. The frequently didactic approach of the BBC under Reith, which sought to improve the cultural taste of its listeners, had started to soften by the late-1930s and sport as entertainment was considered a vital ingredient of the programming mix.[66] The policy of using sport to capture an audience and reveal the BBC's sensitivity to popular taste would gain greater momentum after the Second World War under the stewardship of the BBC's third director-general, William Haley. Television, too, would present new challenges and opportunities to cover sport, although its influence on the management of the outside broadcast department and its team of commentators did not take hold until the 1950s, when its pull on resources increased to match the burgeoning audience for television.[67] The period 1935–1952 proved an influential time in the formation of new bonds with sport, both at individual and institutional levels. Lobby and his team of commentator/producers forged strong ties with governing bodies of sport, clubs, venues and sportsmen and women. Some of these ties were fraught with problems, not least with the Football League, who remained suspicious of the impact of broadcasting on attendances for more than half a century.[68] However, the power of broadcasting to place the listener in the 'front row' helped foster within the BBC a sense of delivering a national service of import and occasion. Through the voice of the commentator, radio drew upon the ready-made interests of disparate individual listeners and constructed a national audience with common values and an understanding of the place of sport in society. As Crisell has argued, it invariably did this in its own image,[69] which in much of its output produced an elitist and conservative culture born of the upper-class and upper-middle-class background of its producers and presenters. Many commentators of this period shared the same social background. In some instances this brought a recognizable authority to their voices due to their educated 'Home Counties' backgrounds. On other occasions, as we have seen above, it alienated certain listeners because of its south-east metropolitan overtones. During and immediately after the Second World War, the recruitment drive for commentators broadened the range of accents from sport. Most notable examples were Arlott, Wynne-Jones, Vaughan-Thomas and the Canadian MacPherson. Sport also brought a different aspect of public life to broadcasting and ultimately into the home. In order to capture the imagination of the listener and convey the varied sporting events the BBC attempted to cover, Lobby built a team of expert broadcasters who grew to understand the grammar of the medium in which they worked that was inimitably mixed with a passion for sport itself. In listening to and overseeing their work Lobby instituted the principles of radio commentary. Lobby's work in the outside broadcasting department carries a significant influence and wider historical legacy to sports broadcasting in Britain. Most crucially, it was his attention to detail and the ability to introduce and apply a coherent set of principles that enabled him and others to analyse the quality of sports commentary, a process that endured into the television era.

## Notes

[1] S.J. de Lotbiniere, 'Some notes on commentary', 1942, BBC Written Archives Centre (hereafter WAC), R30/428/1.

[2] H.B.T. Wakelam, *Half-time: The mike and me* (London, 1938); George Allison, *Allison calling* (London, 1948); Rex Alston, *Taking the air* (London, 1951); Raymond Glendenning, *Just a word in your ear* (London, 1953); Max Robertson, *Stop talking and give the score* (London, 1987); Gareth V. Wynne-Jones, *Sports commentary* (London, 1951).

[3] Christopher Martin-Jenkins, *Ball by ball: The inside story of cricket broadcasting* (London, 1990); Dick Booth, *Talking of sport: The story of radio commentary* (Cheltenham, 2008).

[4] Christopher Wrigley, 'The impact of the First World War', in C. Wrigley, ed, *A companion to early twentieth century Britain* (Oxford, 2003).

[5] Anne Pimlott Baker, 'Joly de Lotbinière, Seymour (1905–1984)', in *Oxford Dictionary of National Biography*, 2004, available online at http://www.oxforddnb.com/view/article/51249, accessed 15 Feb. 2008.

[6] Ross McKibbin, *Classes and cultures: England 1918–1951* (Oxford, 1998), pp. 1–2.

[7] J.A. Mangan, *Athleticism in the Victorian and Edwardian public school: The emergence and consolidation of an educational ideology* (London, 2000).

[8] J.A. Mangan, '"Oars and the man": Pleasure and purpose in Victorian and Edwardian Cambridge', in J.A. Mangan, ed., *A sport-loving society: Victorian and Edwardian middle-class England at play* (London, 2006), p. 96.

[9] Private correspondence with First and Third Trinity Boat Club, Feb. 2008.

[10] Pimlott Baker, 'Joly de Lotbinière'.

[11] Asa Briggs, *The history of broadcasting in the UK, vol. 2: The golden age of wireless.* (Oxford, 1965); John Snagge and Michael Barsley, *Those vintage years of radio* (London, 1972).

[12] Richard Haynes, '"There's many a slip' twixt the eye and the lip": An exploratory history of football broadcasts and running commentaries on BBC radio, 1927–1939', *International Review for the Sociology of Sport*, 34 (2) (1999), pp. 143–56; Mike Huggins, 'BBC radio and sport 1922–39', *Contemporary British History*, 21 (4) (2007), pp. 491–515.

[13] *I'll eat my hat*, BBC Radio Five Live, 25 Dec. 1995.

[14] Peter West, *Flannelled fool and muddied oaf: The autobiography of Peter West* (London, 1987), p. 122.

[15] Peter O'Sullevan, *Calling the horses* (London, 1994), p. 105.

[16] Wynford Vaughan-Thomas, *Trust to talk* (London, 1980), pp. 129–30.

[17] Robert Hudson, *Inside outside broadcasts* (Newmarket, 1993), p. 11.

[18] Haynes, '"There's many a slip"'.

[19] John Arlott, 'A new way', in Bryon Butler, ed., *Sports Report: 40 Years of the best* (London, 1987), p. 21.

[20] *New York Times*, 9 Oct. 1914.

[21] Wakelam, *Half-time*, p. 261.

[22] Draft script for talk by Teddy Wakelam, BBC Services Network, 8 Aug. 1943, BBC WAC, H.B.T. Wakelam Talks.

[23] Booth, *Talking of sport.*

[24] Robertson, *Stop talking*, pp. 45–8.

[25] J. Snagge to regional directors, 3 Dec. 1937, BBC WAC, R30/428/1.

[26] L. Wellington to S.J. de Lotbiniere, 23 Nov. 1937, BBC WAC, R30/428/1.

[27] Martin-Jenkins, *Ball by ball.*

[28] S.J. de Lotbiniere to L. Wellington, 25 Nov. 1937, BBC WAC, R30/428/1.

[29] De Lotbiniere, 'Some notes on commentary'.

[30] Andrew Crisell, *Understanding radio* (London, 1994), p. 44.

[31] *I'll eat my hat*, BBC Radio Five Live, 25 Dec. 1995.

[32] Crisell, *Understanding radio*, p. 132.

[33] *Radio Times*, 4 June 1937, p. 12.

[34] S.J. de Lotbiniere to Assistant Controller of Programmes, 29 Dec. 1938, BBC WAC R30/428/1.

[35] Wakelam, *Half-time.*

[36] De Lotbiniere, 'Some notes on commentary'.

[37] Jonathan Dimbleby, *Richard Dimbleby: A biography* (London, 1975).

[38] De Lotbiniere, 'Some notes on commentary'.

[39] Ibid.

[40] Ibid.

[41] Ibid.

[42] All quotes from de Lotbiniere, 'Some notes on commentary'.

[43] Ibid.

[44] Wakelam, *Half-time*, pp. 331–2.

[45] Selected commentator test reports, Aug. 1936–Oct. 1936, BBC WAC, R30/428/1.

[46] Commentators report, 27 Oct. 1936, BBC WAC, R30/428/1.

[47] Phil Drackett, Flashing blades: The story of British ice hockey (Ramsbury, Wiltshire, 1987).

[48] Stewart MacPherson, *The mike and I* (London, 1948).

[49] Ibid., p. 36.

[50] Ibid., p. 37.

[51] Ibid., p. 38.

[52] Commentators report, 27 Oct. 1936, BBC WAC, R30/428/1.

[53] *I'll eat my hat.*

[54] Glendenning, *Just a word in your ear.*

[55]  J. Snagge cited in memorandum, Assistant Controller to S.J. de Lotbiniere, 16 March 1937, BBC WAC, R30/428/1.

[56]  S.J. de Lotbiniere to MRD, 7 June 1938. BBC WAC, R30/428/1.

[57]  De Lotbiniere to Smythe, 20 Jan. 1938, BBC WAC, R30/428/1.

[58]  V. Smythe to S.J. de Lotbiniere, 28 Jan. 1938, BBC WAC, R30/428/1.

[59]  Alston, *Taking the air*, p. 89.

[60]  Wynne-Jones, *Sports commentary*.

[61]  A. Watkins Jones to S.J. de Lotbiniere, 20 Oct. 1947, BBC WAC, R30/428/3.

[62]  A. Watkins Jones to S.J. de Lotbiniere, 22 Dec. 1947, BBC WAC, R30/428/3.

[63]  A. Watkins Jones to S.J. de Lotbiniere, 2 Jan. 1948, BBC WAC, R30/428/3.

[64]  S.J. de Lotbiniere to A. Watkins Jones, 6 Jan. 1948, BBC WAC, R30/428/3.

[65]  Richard Haynes and Raymond Boyle, 'Media sport, in Neil Blain and David Hutchinson, eds, *The media in Scotland* (Edinburgh, 2008), pp. 253–70.

[66]  Asa Briggs, The BBC: *The first fifty years* (Oxford, 1985).

[67]  Garry Whannel, *Fields in vision: Television sport and cultural transformation* (London, 1992).

[68]  Richard Haynes, 'A pageant of sound and vision: Football's relationship with television, 1936–60', *The International Journal of the History of Sport,* 15 (1) (1998), pp. 211–26.

[69]  Crisell, *Understanding radio.*

# 13

# The BBC, Austerity and Broadcasting the 1948 Olympic Games

*Richard Haynes*

We believe that the Games will end being a very big 'story' and that a sufficiency of broadcasting facilities efficiently administered will be important to British prestige throughout the world.[1]

## Introduction

The quotation above is taken from an internal memo from the BBC's then Director of Outside Broadcasts, Seymour Joly de Lotbiniere, to the Senior Controller of Programmes. It emphasized the importance to the BBC of its preparations to broadcast from the 1948 London Olympic Games. De Lotbiniere, commonly known as 'Lobby', was the BBC's Director of Outside Broadcasts from 1935 to 1940 and once again after the war from 1946 to 1955. 'Lobby' was an incredibly influential character in the history of sports broadcasting and was the BBC's general manager for its coverage of the 1948 games. From 1935 he had devised a set of guiding principles for the BBC's coverage of sport on both radio and television that arguably endure today. The 1948 games produced a landmark phase in his career and British sports broadcasting more generally. It signalled the emergence of a new relationship between the BBC and the governing bodies of sport. It produced a new scale of broadcasting operation in terms of the logistical and strategic planning required in the coverage of a major sporting event such as the Olympics. Finally, it also proved a key period in rekindling interest in

**Source:** *The International Journal of the History of Sport*, 27(6), Special Issue: Europe and the London Olympic Games 1948 (2010): 1029–1046.

the BBC's fledgling television service, suspended at the outbreak of war in 1939 and reintroduced in 1946. Understanding why coverage of the London games proved to be such an important aspect of the BBC's programming in 1948 and how the managers and producers of the Outside Broadcasting Department coped with the constraints of economic and political austerity is the focus of this article.

## In the Shadow of War

The wider social, economic and political context of the BBC's coverage of the games was all-important. As recent histories of the immediate post-war period in Britain have acknowledged,[2] there were long and strong shadows cast by the severity of war: there was the loss of US economic support crippling the UK economy still paying for the war effort; the constraining austerity policies of the new Labour Government and the continuation of rationing; and the drive towards nationalization of many utilities underpinned by Keynesian demand management. All these processes had an influence on the BBC. In spite of some detractors, it maintained its position as a broadcasting monopoly and its news output was no longer under direct influence of the Ministry of Information. The BBC's Director General, Sir William Haley, was determined to assert the BBC's independence from the state after the war and at times during the immediate post-war period relations with the Attlee government were strained.[3] The BBC had gained respect for its informative role during the war. 'Like the nation', recalled Welsh broadcaster Wynford Vaughan-Thomas, it had 'stood up to the ordeal with courage and skill'.[4] Its programming had changed through the war, less about 'improvement' and more geared towards informing and entertaining in a stratified 'cultural pyramid'. During the war the BBC had increasingly responded to popular taste to 'provide the listener with an element of choice without sacrificing the old Reithian seriousness of purpose'.[5] Under a new sense of freedom, pro-grammes such as *It's That Man Again* (*ITMA*) and *The Brains Trust* flourished and regularly drew 14 million listeners.

Sport had been marginalized during the war, dependent on 'significant degrees of initiative and improvisation' to keep it going between 1939 and 1945.[6] There had been an initial moratorium on sports broadcasts in the early phase of the war; Post Office line restrictions and petrol rationing severely restricted the Outside Broadcasting Department and 'much of the glamour had gone out of such national sporting events'.[7] In spite of being 'heavily pruned' the BBC had reintroduced running commentaries on sport wherever possible. According to Asa Briggs, the expansion was warranted on four grounds: it added greatly to the variety of broadcast material; it gave the pub-lic a 'reassuring impression of normality'; there was much 'virtue in actuality'; and outside broadcasts dealing with topicality gave an impression of the BBC's resourcefulness and vitality.[8] The commentator Raymond Glendenning did much to convince the sporting authorities that sports broadcasting helped the morale of the forces and the British public.[9] Sports coverage did much in assisting the move from the 'cultural elitism' of pre-war programming so favoured by the BBC's first Director General, John Reith.[10] More broadly, the BBC Outside Broadcasts Department advanced its reputation enormously during the war with live broadcasts from across Europe as reporters such as Vaughan-Thomas, Richard Dimbleby and Stewart MacPherson joined the Allied advance on Nazi Germany. In 1943, as the new Director of Empire Programmes, de Lotbiniere had been integral to the establishment and planning of the War Reporting Unit and the international transmissions from foreign fields, and many of the reporters would return in peacetime to commentate on sport. Arriving back in London fearing doom and gloom among general austerity, Vaughan-Thomas commented: 'I found an Outside Broadcasts department which had been charged with a new dynamism by its war experience, and soon new colleagues came to join us, who each brought a new approach to the business of running commentary.'[11] These new recruits would include John Arlott, Brian Johnston, Rex Alston and Max Robertson. Many of them had served in the armed forces. All would play their part in the coverage of the 1948 Olympic Games and go on to become the household names of broadcast sport in the 1950s and beyond.

Outside broadcasting, then, had been important for transporting the listener to the front line of the war and had innovated new ways of binding the audience to a common national cause. As Scannell and Cardiff note, radio 'gave the individual an unprecedented sense of himself as part of the larger community'.[12] In peacetime, broadcasts from sport and state occasions would prove the most immediate connection from the home to communal public life. The 1948 Olympic Games would prove no exception, but it required immense planning on the part of the BBC to ensure that both the nation and an international audience could share what was initially viewed as a most unlikely pageant of sport so soon after global war.

## Legacy and Lessons of Berlin, Helsinki and St Moritz

Even before the war was over Lord Aberdare, IOC member and chairman of the National Association of Boys' Clubs had indicated that the Olympic Games would return in 1948.[13] In a move to promote the ideals of the games, he approached the BBC through his friend Harold Abrahams with an idea for a talk on the Olympic movement and in January 1945 a script was written for the programme *Sporting Record*, then produced by Raymond Glendenning for the Forces Programme. The script dismissed the notion that 'the Olympic spirit is dead' and claimed that the 'true spirit of sportsmanship' would return, 'avoiding the nationalistic twist which the Nazi Government gave to the 1936 festival'. However, the programme was never made, Michael Standing, the acting Director of Outside Broadcasts before Lobby's return, concluding that 'the subject could hardly be discussed without reference to the participation of our enemies in the next Games and we feel that that perhaps is not a matter best raised just at the moment'.[14]

In February 1946 Lobby, now returned as Director of Outside Broadcasts, wrote to senior management in the BBC to announce: 'I have heard on a side wind that it is likely that before the month is out there will be an official announcement that the Olympic Games are to be held in this country in 1948'.[15] According to Lobby, Lord Burghley, chairman of the Olympic Organizing Committee, would 'blow the gaff' at a press party held at six o'clock – just in time for the morning newspapers – and the BBC, eager to get a scoop, approached Burghley to make an announcement after the seven o'clock news that night.

With the games confirmed, the BBC set about planning its coverage. Internal economic pressures on the BBC were immense but the mood remained positive. If there was one overbearing external pressure it was to showcase the technological skills and organization of the BBC to international visitors. There was a perception that the efforts of Lobby and his team would be judged in the context of the Nazis' efficient and technologically advanced media centre of 1936 that had introduced closed-circuit television. In the shadow of war, in an age of severe economic hardship, it was considered important for Britain to host the games successfully. For the BBC, the games were a point of prestige, but also an opportunity to showcase how it thought outside broadcasting should be done.

In many ways the BBC had nothing to prove; its broadcasts during the war had been the main source of information to people in occupied nations across Europe. But in 1936 the Reich Broadcasting Company had accommodated an array of international broadcasters showcasing a limited television service.

In a rush to impress their visitors in 1936, the Nazi Party had been keen to innovate television coverage by transmitting several hours of each days events to selected venues. There was coverage from the main stadium and the swimming arena.[16] There were fewer than 1,000 sets in the entire country, almost all situated in public halls.[17] One venue included the Joy Village, located near Funkturn, where large-screen television was part of wider entertainment that showcased German athleticism and culture.[18]

The Nazis' introduction of closed-circuit television had been judged an outright failure in some quarters. For one correspondent from *The Times*, the 'picture resembled a very faint, highly underexposed photographic film, and were so much worse than ordinary transmissions from a studio that many turned away in disappointment'.[19] An American journalist likened the images to 'humans floating in a milk bath'.[20] The different camera systems had not been synchronized and were prone to blackouts and were often too cumbersome to capture the fast-moving action.

The BBC's athletics commentator at the 1936 games, Harold Abrahams, gave briefings to other commentators based on the official film *Olympia* directed by Leni Riefenstahl. Distribution and exhibition of the film had been very restricted across Europe, but the British Olympic Association had purchased a print and invited Lobby and other members of the BBC's Outside Broadcast department to its screenings. *Olympia* was used to train the BBC's new crop of commentators in order to practise their commentaries on some of the more obscure events – to British eyes at least – and also for the television producers to consider ideal camera positions.

Other intelligence had also been gathered to assist the planning of the BBC's coverage. Some of the information came from unlikely sources. Lobby and the BBC engineers obtained plans for the 1936 broadcasts, as well as a blueprint for broadcasting the aborted Helsinki games of 1940. They were acquired from former BBC staff member Henry Riddell, one of the many British civil servants sent out to Berlin during the Allied occupation of the German capital immediately after the war. However, in the post-war devastation and with political division in Berlin, access to German documentation in the city was not easy. Although the Olympic Stadium was in the British quarter of the city, the Russians had removed most of the Olympic library and documentation had been consigned to the Commission for Physical Culture in Moscow.[21] The Berlin Broadcasting House was in the heart of the Russian quarter and Riddell confessed: 'To enter Broadcasting House here is not easy for the British but I got my spies out and they did find one item in the library of Broadcasting House'.[22] It was the *Radio Guide Book*, much cherished by Lobby. Riddell also included a pamphlet issued by the organizing committee of the 1940 Helsinki games entitled *Olympic News Service*, providing much-needed details of commentary positions, cabling, recording equipment and other technical requirements. The information was indicative of what would be needed for the coverage from Wembley.[23] Lobby wrote to thank Riddell for his detective work and hinted at the austerity in Britain in contrast to the devastation, subterfuge and political turmoil of Berlin at this time, remarking: 'I can imagine that you are having a pretty tough time in Germany. Things seem gloomy enough here but what it must be like there is, I expect, beyond the imagination of anyone who has not been over to see for themselves'.[24]

## Our Man in St. Moritz

As well as information from Berlin and Helsinki, the BBC also had first-hand experience of broadcasting arrangements for the 1948 Winter Olympic Games in St Moritz, Switzerland. Staff commentator Max Robertson had covered the skiing, bobsleigh and the Cresta run for the BBC and clearly enjoyed his time in the Swiss Alps, recalling in his autobiography that 'everything was new and shining' and the occasion took him 'away from the dreary rationing and petty restrictions of post-war Britain'.[25] However, his general impression of the event and its organization was altogether more glowing than that of his producer Konrad Syrop. His report suggested the Swiss organization was 'inefficient and unbusinesslike'. The facilities for broadcasters were far from what had been promised: 'The equipment, while supplied in considerable quantity, was untested, kept breaking down and was of a type unsuitable for the purpose.' All in all, the impression of the Swiss hosts was that 'their organization combined inefficiency with red tape and created chaos'.[26] The Swiss had clearly found the games a burden and in the immediate run-in to the London games the Secretariat General of the Societe Suisse de Rediffusion, Mr de Reading, wrote to Lobby to send his best wishes, but sarcastically concluded 'you have all my sympathy'.[27]

## Negotiation and Planning

The 1948 London games proved a test of the BBC's Outside Broadcasts Department's collective knowledge and strategic planning. It was without doubt the largest broadcast event the BBC had ever undertaken by that time and would arguably prove to be an invaluable experience in the planning of the Coronation in 1953, recognized by broadcast historians as a landmark event in the social history of British television that popularized the new medium.[28]

The 1948 games came at a crucial time in the development of outside broadcasting as sport producers aligned their coverage with the wider light entertainments policy emerging at the BBC. From 1946 sport was to form a central aspect of the new entertainment policy, given added impetus by Haley. Conscious that broadcasting was entering a new phase of development and that the BBC's monopoly was under the spotlight from government and the wider public (the licence fee had doubled to £1 after being static for 24 years), Haley believed that raising the standards of the BBC would never be successful unless its broad contract with the listener included entertainment. Sport entered into the lexicon of light entertainment and was predominantly broadcast on the BBC's Light Programme. As negotiations for the 1948 games would show, the value of sport to the BBC would soon begin to pull harder on resources. Sport was key in attracting and maintaining listeners and the BBC would be neglecting its duty of entertaining its audience 'if it disregards that part of its triple function'.[29]

### Finance and Rights Fees

Financing the coverage of the games was of grave concern. As the drive to expand the scale of entertainment and outside broadcasts moved ahead, it was to be achieved in a stricken economy. Haley had reeled in expenditure across the BBC and at the height of the fuel crisis in February 1947 the BBC's television service was pulled off the air in order to save money before resuming its modest service in April of the same year. As one of the BBC's chief engineers, Robert Wood recalled, 'The 14th Olympic Games put a huge strain on our resources. Everything was still being done on a shoe-string, but now – used to all that radio could do – people expected more and more of us, unaware of the technical shortages we faced'.[30]

Initially, as early as October 1946, Haley and the Acting Controller of the BBC, R.J.F. Howgill had agreed that Lobby and the OB department move ahead with plans for the BBC to undertake the entire broadcasting arrangements of the games themselves, shouldering the whole cost with a request that estimated costs be provided in due course.[31] Moreover, the Director General had also opened negotiations with the newly formed Society for the Protection of Copyright in Sport – acting as a trade body on behalf of the governing bodies of sport in negotiations over broadcasting coverage – and it was agreed that the London games fell outside the ordinary run of sporting events and additional fees would be paid. These were facility fees and not intellectual property rights or 'broadcasting rights', but it is worthwhile noting that payment to cover the games was being established as a matter of course.

By the end of 1946 Lobby had set about opening up lines of communication with the organizing committee and had begun the thorny task of providing a financial estimate upon which a final budget could be arrived. Lobby favoured more reticence regarding the BBC's commitment. Facilitating the entire broadcasting arrangements for the BBC and all visiting broadcasters was a daunting undertaking. His concern was well founded. The BBC had never been involved in such a large-scale outside broadcast with multiple venues, simultaneously serviced to multiple international broadcasters. In December 1946 he wrote:

> I see one difficulty ahead in that we should not finally commit ourselves
> to financing all the broadcasting facilities until we know what the bill will
> be, and it will be a good while before that can be worked out. I should not
> be at all surprised to find the bill would be of the order of £50,000 or
> more – to judge from Engineering division's £12,000 estimate for the
> South African tour.[32]

Indeed, BBC engineers did not provide a full estimate until spring 1947 revealing the true nature of the resources required.

According to the engineers' first list of 'approximations of likely expenditure', the entire cost of the building works, purchasing of equipment and labour would be near £130,000.[33] The engineering division also requested that the BBC retain all of the 104 members of staff in post, enforcing the stoppage of any divisional leave throughout the duration of the games and reducing the BBC's commitment to all other outside broadcasts by at least 50 per cent.[34] The escalating costs were initially met with horror by Haley, who instructed Lobby to reduce the estimate by 25 per cent occasioned by reducing the level of service (reducing the number of microphone positions, for example) and renewing negotiations with the organizing committee regarding sharing the burden of providing a radio centre to host international broadcasters. Haley was himself called upon to privately negotiate the cost of access to Wembley and other venues, meeting Lord Portal, the chairman of the Olympic Organizing Committee in April 1947, where it was agreed that the BBC would provide remuneration for the loss of income in ticket sales. The BBC's plan was to have 15 commentary booths, 17 open microphone positions and a further 100 seats for visiting broadcasters, taking up a total 330 of the best seats in the stadium. The estimated price was £12,000 and Holt, the director of operations for the games agreed that the 100 seats could be given free (worth an estimated £3,150).

Although Lobby had conducted site visits and had begun, somewhat tentatively, to estimate the cost of the operation, with little over 12 months to go very little building work had yet taken place. A large part of the building works for the games fell to Sir Arthur Elvin, owner of Wembley Stadium. The BBC emphasized the need for sufficient accommodation near the stadium in a building that could house a range of technical, operational and informational needs. Perhaps realizing the scale of operations and the reticence of the BBC to stretch its escalating budget still further, Elvin agreed to lease the Palace of Arts, built as part of the 1924 Empire Exhibition, as the venue for the Radio Centre. The BBC would have to pay for the renovation of the building and in July 1947 a revised budget was presented that skirted close to £200,000. Haley, now resigned to the prospect of paying facility fees, a substantial investment in technology and the capital expenditure of building works demanded one final attempt at sharing the costs of building the Radio Centre. For, as a memo from the Senior Controller Nicolls to Lobby suggested, he was 'doubtful as to whether we can get away with not paying for the seats at Wembley' but doing so might act as a 'bargaining factor in relation to their paying for the building work'.[35]

From the archival evidence, the prospect of passing on the cost of the building work to visiting broadcasters who stood to benefit from their construction does not appear to have been raised. The point is important when we reflect on the overtly commodified spaces of television and sport in the contemporary Olympic regime: the inflated rights fees and the technological and operational costs.

Unfortunately for the BBC, by autumn 1947 it was clear that the organizing committee, severely starved of resources itself (the cost of hosting the games was close to £700,00 and Wembley itself ran at a loss of £200,000), would not relent. In a stinging memo to Haley, Nicolls, wrote: 'We had vague assurances from them in the early part of the negotiations that they would build the Radio Centre for us, on which they have now ratted!'[36]

While Nicolls's rage may have been well-founded, the responsibility and cost of hosting the broadcast facilities for the games squarely fell in the lap of the BBC. Arguably, in 1948 we saw the first instance of broadcasters carrying some of the burden of the games as a global media event.

## Hosting the Olympic Broadcasts

The 15-day sports extravaganza would consist of 136 events in 30 locations, with competitors from 58 nations. In a draft script for a broadcasting handbook for visiting media, Lobby highlighted the challenge these figures presented: 'Take another look at those few statistics and then try to imagine how they affect the BBC which not only has to provide its own coverage of the Games in more than 40 languages, but which has to supply for all-comers the necessary outside broadcasting facilities'.[37]

In the event, the BBC catered for 250 broadcasters from 60 different radio stations and, apart from initial chaos on the opening day, the coordination of the technological services and hospitality of the BBC was well received. In planning the use of the facilities the great unknown was precisely how many of these broadcasters would want to cover any given event, whether it would be 'live' or recorded, what language they would be transmitting in and whether or not broadcasters would want to link commentators from different venues. As Lobby wrote in August 1948, in his first official report of the broadcasting organization at the Radio Centre:

> [The Centre was] a consulting ground where producers could take advice from the engineers on the best way of overcoming problems of lines of communications and where the technical staff could make use of the linguistic knowledge of the BBC producers who were pulling together the story of the Games for all the countries of the world.[38]

This sense of camaraderie between hosts and visitors is probably no coincidence so soon after the sacrifices of war. It echoed a wider sense of comradeship across the games in the face of economic hardship and austerity. As Brian Glanville later reflected:

> Looking back from this vantage point in time at an event, which excited one as a schoolboy, one can see that there was, about these 1948 Games, a certain, almost primeval, innocence. The very improvisation of it all, the very limitation of events and athletes, the very absence of the ultra-organized, deeply professionalized, Iron curtain teams, gave the Games a dewy allure.[39]

The notion of getting along, adapting to situations and working things out characterized both the games and the efforts of the broadcasters. Lobby had also been keen to mirror the services enjoyed by the press corps and requested a bar to be installed in the Radio Centre. After much protracted negotiation over a licence, a bar was installed to provide an area for relaxation and socializing for host and visiting broadcasters alike.

## Black Friday

The games opened amid chaos for BBC managers and was soon labelled 'Black Friday'. The Radio Centre found itself handling heavy bookings from Wembley and as the timetabling of events got progressively worse with the afternoon session starting 35 minutes late, the 100m heats taking one hour instead of 30 minutes and the high jump running over by an hour, the changes caused enormous problems. Visiting broadcasters had pre-booked allotted slots on one of the 36 channels emanating from the mixing desks housed in the Palace of Arts and found their slots were no longer congruent with the action on the track. Peter Dimmock, then a young television producer, recalled the reason for the delays:

> I was looking after the television and Lobby was masterminding the radio. Radio was a real headache for the Olympic Games and he was master-minding that. They discovered, right at the very beginning, that they hadn't measured the track right. So they had to stop everything and re-measure it, and adjust it. That threw all the overseas transmission times out of kilter. And Lobby had to sort that lot out.[40]

Planned bookings were rescheduled and the management of multiple broadcasters with different languages and different needs became too much to handle. Lobby later reflected: 'We had not realized how many technical operations would be affected by the changes . . . one or two broadcasts became casualties'.[41] The inauspicious start to broadcasting the games meant some quick lessons were learnt. A quota of microphone positions were tied in to recording channels in order that no future events would be missed and meant less switching within the control room between overseas broadcasters.

## The World Listens In

The planning and coordination of overseas broadcasts had been meticulous and jointly managed by Lobby and Konrad Syrop, Assistant Head of European Broadcasts within the BBC's Overseas Department. In a report of the broadcasting operation for the BBC Board of Governors the sheer scale of the operation became apparent: 1,545 transmissions from Wembley Stadium, 525 of which were to Europe and 225 to North and South America. There were 2,622 recordings of commentaries, interviews and eyewitness accounts, using 6,066 discs. The BBC dedicated 750 staff to the games, including 300 engineers, 250 commentators and 200 other staff whose 'devotion to duty', Lobby wrote, 'took no account of long hours and exacting work'.[42] Many staff worked double shifts to service the needs of the international visitors whose 35 daily broadcasts kept the BBC's lines open up to 15 hours a day. The BBC's General Overseas Service, operating outside Europe, produced five 15-minute 'Olympic Reports' each day and produced nearly 29 hours of programming for its international audience. North American broadcasts totalled 34 hours 25 minutes; South American nations received 30 hours of coverage.

The scale of the event and the international broadcasts had a dramatic effect on audiences around the world. The transmissions had included the first international broadcast to Korea and in the Olympic report by George Looter for the BBC's General Overseas Service he reprinted a translation of a letter sent to the Korean commentator Min Chai Ho of the Korean Broadcasting system from his wife. It read:

> I heard your voice from London last night. Before the broadcast started, I was very anxious because the test broadcast last Friday was not a success; and also it was very dark when I listened because the electricity was off. But at 11.45 when the electricity came on, all the town was filled with your voice and I could not help crying. You are a very long way away, many thousands of miles over land and sea, but still I can hear your voice just as though you were sitting beside me.[43]

There is pathos within this simple letter from a wife to her husband working thousands of miles away. It reveals the unstable first steps of a new, increasingly global, communications technology. The world was being connected in new ways through the combined power of the internationalization of sport and broadcasting. It reveals the unstable nature of life still recovering from war. But most importantly, it reveals the power of the immediacy of broadcast sport, particularly international sport that is delivered from the other side of the world but in a familiar voice that connects with a national audience and culture.

## Television

The sense of experimentation and the constraints of resources were felt most strongly in the BBC's attempts to televise the Olympic Games. Before the war the BBC had rushed to introduce a public television service in 1936, not fully appreciating the lack of demand for the technology or the manufacturers' unwillingness to innovate new markets.[44] With barely 20,000 television sets sold, the service was suspended in 1939 at the outbreak of War. With the resumption of television in 1946 the BBC's approach to the medium remained one of managerial and financial restraint. There were only 80,000 television licences in 1948, with an estimated audience of half a million, most located in a 40-mile radius of London. As far as the BBC were concerned there could certainly be no grounds to fear that televising the games would affect attendances at Olympic venues.

### Television Access and Facility Fee

In 1948 television still played second fiddle to radio by some margin. It received only one-tenth of the budget that radio enjoyed, and even senior managers were not convinced of its strengths. Dimmock, who had joined the

BBC after a brief career as a racing correspondent with the Press Association, reflected on television's status at this time:

> It was very exciting. But of course we were totally looked down on by radio. Radio didn't give us any money. They thought we were just a stupid lot of peep show boys at Alexandra Palace. They thought of us as the film world, nothing at all to do with radio. Radio was respectable.[45]

The perception that television equated with film did pose problems for the BBC. Newsreel companies whose magazine approach to the coverage of sport had become very popular during the inter-war years now faced competition.[46] The Rank Organization had bought rights to film the games for £20,000 and was highly protective of its exclusive agreement. BBC Television outside broadcasts were managed by Ian Orr-Ewing (later Lord Orr-Ewing) and his initial meetings and reconnaissance of the stadium had been conducted in March 1947 when the thorny issue of rights fees had been raised. In the context of spiralling costs, Lobby was scathing of the idea. In a memo to Orr-Ewing he wrote: 'I said then that we were one organization and that if we were putting our hand deep into our pocket to provide broadcasting facilities for all-comers we might not wish to put it deeper still in order to pay a television fee as well'.[47]

The issue rumbled on and by November 1947 Nicolls reiterated the point that 'Wembley has no right in the image that appears on our television receivers' and that any payment would be for 'goodwill and access'.[48] The BBC had maintained the view that paying a facility fee was acceptable on the grounds of lost revenue from gate receipts. But a 'rights fee' suggested a different kind of commercial relationship and a grey area as far as the law of copyright was concerned.

The organizing committee had no objection to live television, but filmed material relayed by television was a different matter. For 'if the public can at their convenience see television versions of the Games', Holt wrote to Haley, 'they will not leave their homes and go to the cinema to see the feature film'.[49] The edict was perceived as damaging to a fledgling technology. The BBC had also made arrangements with NBC in the United States to distribute television newsreels across the Atlantic. The news of the rights wrangle had reached the Americans, who threatened to make a formal diplomatic protest against the exclusive deal. In a plea that made great play of the world's perception of Britain, the Head of Television Service, Norman Collins, drafted a response on behalf of the Director General that recognized some private sports events may wish to exclude BBC Television but submitted that 'the Olympic Games fall within a different category and, being international in character and representative of Britain by virtue of taking place within this country, should not become an exclusive commercial property'.[50]

The statement was a precedent to future arguments between the BBC and the governing bodies of sport over the coverage of major sports events that would ultimately lead to non-exclusivity clauses around a series of 'listed events' that would include the Olympic Games. Haley lobbied the Commonwealth Relations Office, laying emphasis on the importance of television newsreel to the BBC's 'social developments in the field of broadcasting'.[51] By the end of January 1948 the matter had been resolved in a meeting between Haley and Lord Portal, with the BBC agreeing to present newsreels simultaneously with Rank's cinematic release and a 'gentleman's agreement' that any recordings 'off tube' would remain private to the BBC and not publicly available. A fee of £3,000 was agreed but it is unclear from the archives whether or not this payment was made.

## Televising the Event

The games presented new challenges for the presentation of sport. Orr-Ewing had studied the camera positions of *Olympia* at the 1936 swimming events and noted the camera angles of the pool were too low to enable viewers to identify the swimmers. The camera at the pool was duly raised higher in the stands to capture the event properly. The BBC had bought new Marconi Emitron cameras and planned to have three cameras inside Wembley Stadium and the fourth positioned outside to capture the thousands of spectators as they walked along Wembley Way, giving a wider perspective of the event.

The BBC transmitted 64 hours of programming, including one seven-and-a-half-hour stretch on one day. In spite of a few words of encouragement from athletes, viewers and the press, the technology had its limitations. The CPS Emitron cameras were British and inferior to the technology developed through the war by the Americans. According to Dimmock this was one area where British wasn't best: 'I was fighting our engineers all the time, saying, "we've got to get rid of this British equipment. I'm sorry, I'm very British, I'm very loyal, but it doesn't bloody work!" The moment the light went down the picture would peel off from the left hand corner'.[52]

Knowledge of how the cameras worked and how to produce the best picture with the limited resources was key to the operation. For this reason the BBC devised a method of using producers as commentators, in order to both save money and have a skilled hand on site to manage a situation when things went wrong. Again, as Dimmock explains:

> It sounds ludicrous now. We couldn't have a camera more than 300ft from the control van because that was the length of the cable. We couldn't have a cable that was longer than that. So that made it very difficult with putting the camera positions in. We didn't have enough cameras, but we did the pool and the main stadium. What we did was we produced and commentated. I did a lot of swimming commentaries. I didn't know a lot about swimming, I knew a little bit about it. We alternated. Then I did some show jumping, and I'd produce and commentate. But we were real 'jacks of all trade' really.[53]

Television commentators and specialists had been trained for weeks. Jack Crump commentated and acted as athletics advisor; Peter Wilson, a sports journalist, covered boxing with Colonel Dudley Lister; Freddie Milton was the specialist on swimming alongside John Webb on diving; and former referee Jimmy Jewell did the football commentaries.

Three mobile units were in use coming from locations that demanded rapid inter-switching between Wembley Stadium and the Empire Pool. In all, 56 events totalling 34 hours were televised from the stadium and 52 events including swimming and boxing made up a further 26.5 hours of programming.

According to the BBC's own report, the highlights of its television coverage included the opening ceremony with commentary from the imperious Richard Dimbleby. However, according to the report the 'most poignant moment for viewers came at the end of the marathon' as telephoto lenses followed the three leaders round the track as the 'tottering' Belgian leader Etienne Gailly was passed by the Argentinean Delfo Cabrera and Tom Richards of Great Britain. Other drama included the Jamaican Arthur Wint who pulled up in the final stages of the 4 × 400 metres relay, which commentator Max Robertson remembered as a 'very painful and frightful moment'.[54] In the immediate post-war period the conditioning of athletes was clearly not as good as it might have been and led to Danish swimmer Greta Anderson catching cramp and 'rescued from drowning under the very eye of the camera'. Such live action and drama on screen was revelatory, as was the ability to pull athletes straight from their events in front of the cameras for an interview. Both British athletes Maureen Gardner and the Dutch sensation Fanny Blankers-Koen were brought to the cameras immediately after their duel in the 80 metres hurdles, both having broken the Olympic record. In the pool 40 swimmers faced the cameras including Britain's Cathy Gibson, 'who made an astonishing television picture in the 400 metre free-style race as she battled from seventh place to third'.[55] The BBC report makes great play of the fact that many of the swimmers 'were televised while still wet', a sign that the immediacy of television, to graphically reveal sporting events as they happened was revelatory, not only for the audience, but for the BBC too.

## Reactions to the BBC Coverage

The information on radio and television audiences for the 1948 Olympic Games is pretty thin. The BBC did record some reactions through its Audience Research Unit and there is anecdotal evidence from the correspondence of sports administrators such as Elvin that the BBC's coverage and organization 'did much to boost our Country throughout the World'.[56]

The BBC's Overseas Audience Research received 18 letters with reference to the games that suggested interest had 'been at a lower level than the Test Matches'.[57] Criticisms were scarce but the report highlights one complaint that the BBC's radio coverage of the opening ceremony had revealed an ideological bias by omitting to mention the Spanish team and it was hoped that 'the BBC broadcasters will on no occasion mar accounts of the proceedings by any discourtesy towards nations for whom they are in the habit of exhibiting a distaste'.[58]

Television monitors had been strategically placed in the Radio Centre and the athletes' village. This tactic appears to have paid off, certainly according to a glowing report in the BBC's *Radio Times* shortly after the games:

> There seems to be general agreement that it [BBC television] acquitted itself even better than had been expected. Everywhere we went during the period of the Olympiad we heard admiring comments on the technical excellence of the transmissions. Enthusiasm was perhaps greatest among the competitors and officials from overseas who were watching television programmes for the first time, but seasoned viewers were also astonished by the results achieved.[59]

Unfortunately, 1948 was too early for 'telerecording' and no footage of the televising of the games survives for historians to pass judgement. But clearly, even among a very modest audience, television left a lingering impression. Haley received letters commending the technical achievement of televising the games. F.C. How of the Ministry of Supply commented on the success of British television that 'I am not often moved to write to the BBC, but I feel that I must offer to you and all concerned my congratulations'.[60] Haley responded:

> I got some idea of the impact of this even in Devon where, at the hotel I was staying at, newcomers from London, not knowing who I was, were talking about little else except their excitement at having seen the Olympic Games on television in their own homes. Like you, I hope that people going back to their own countries will carry word of what British television has shown it can do.[61]

News of such complimentary words from London's 'chattering classes' would have impressed BBC senior management. Although television would not truly make its mark until the Coronation in 1953, the hegemonic grip of radio would have been loosened by such comments.

## Conclusion

The archival written evidence for the 1948 Olympics provides an insight into a seminal era of experimentation in sports broadcasting, particularly in television. De Lotbiniere, along with an emerging specialist team of broadcasters, guided the BBC to a memorable phase in its development as a public service broadcaster. The role of television in connecting the wider public to international sporting rituals such as the Olympics is now embedded in our popular culture. Today it is driven by commercial and entertainment concerns; in 1948 it was largely driven by the ideology of the games itself, a desire to prove Britain could host the games in spite of the austere environment and the public service ideology of the BBC – something it continues to draw upon in its rhetoric regarding the licence fee and its continuation as a part of British cultural life. In their social history of broadcasting Cardiff and Scannell argue that at times of public ritual, such as royal ceremonies or sporting occasions, television can 'provide a fragmented audience with a common culture, an image of the nation as a *knowable community*'.[62] In 1948 one could have certainly made this argument for radio but not television. The rehearsed ceremonial and ritualistic elements of the games combined with the wider post-war social and economic context of austerity to create a shared sense of achievement in hosting the games. This, at least, appears to be the aim of the organizing committee and also of the BBC's approach to covering the games and hosting international broadcasters. No matter that British athletes had failed to win any gold medals. Hosting the games and international broadcasting had shown Britain at a liminal point between the devastated world created by the war and the seeds of a materially new modern world, represented by television, globalization and the spectacle of modern sport.

The *esprit de corps* of wartime carried forward in the Outside Broadcasting Department's approach to managing the coverage of the games, both domestically and overseas. Britain's reputation, its very ability to look forward and 'be modern' were at stake and under inspection. The evidence from the BBC Written Archives suggest the coverage of the 1948 Olympic Games, although passed over in many histories of British broadcasting, was significant in showing the power of sports broadcasting to bring communities together, even under severe economic and social conditions.

## Notes

[1]　De Lotbiniere to Nicolls, 27 May 1947. BBC Written Archives Centre [hereafter WAC], R30/2,066/1.
[2]　See Hennessy, *Never Again*; and Kynaston, *Austerity Britain*.
[3]　Smith, 'The Struggle for Control of the Air-waves'.
[4]　Vaughan-Thomas, *Trust to Talk*, 145.
[5]　Cardiff and Scannell, 'Broadcasting and National Unity', 67.
[6]　Baker, 'A More Even Playing Field?', 134
[7]　Briggs, *A History of Broadcasting in the United Kingdom*, vol. 4, 97.
[8]　Ibid., 98
[9]　Booth, *Talking of Sport*.
[10]　Nicholas, 'The People's Radio', 63.
[11]　Vaughan-Thomas, *Trust to Talk*, 188.
[12]　Cardiff and Scannell, 'Broadcasting and National Unity', 66.
[13]　Hampton, *The Austerity Olympics*, 22.
[14]　Standing to Aberdare, 2 Feb. 1945. BBC WAC, R30/2,060/1.
[15]　De Lotbiniere to McGivern, 8 Feb. 1946. BBC WAC, R30/2,060/1.
[16]　Large, *Nazi Games*, 250–1.
[17]　Uricchio, 'Introduction to the History of German Television'.

[18] Large, *Nazi Games*, 204.

[19] 'Television of the Games Disappointing Result', *The Times*, 3 August 1936.

[20] Large, *Nazi Games*, 251.

[21] Riddell to de Lotbiniere, 24 Feb. 1947. BBC WAC, R30/2,056/1.

[22] Ibid.

[23] Berlin 1936 had 20 boxes, 15 open microphone positions and 77 seats; Helsinki 1940 planned to have 16 boxes, 12 open positions plus an unaccounted for number of seats; and London 1948 had 12 boxes, 12 open microphone positions and 100 seats in Wembley Stadium.

[24] De Lotbiniere to Riddell, 6 March 1947. BBC WAC, R30/2,056/1.

[25] Robertson, *Stop Talking and Give the Score*, 58–9.

[26] Syrop to Director of Overseas Service, 12 Feb. 1948. BBC WAC, R30/2, 046/2.

[27] De Reading to de Lotbiniere, 26 July 1948. BBC WAC, R30/2056/3.

[28] Cardiff and Scannell, 'Broadcasting and National Unity'.

[29] Cited in Coase, *British Broadcasting: A Study in Monopoly*, 175.

[30] Wood, *A World in Your Ear.*

[31] Howgill to de Lotbiniere, 8 Oct. 1946. BBC, WAC R30/2,066/1.

[32] De Lotbiniere to Howgill, 4 Dec. 1946. BBC WAC, R30/2,066/1.

[33] Assistant Chief Engineer to de Lotbiniere, 22 April 1947. BBC WAC, R30/2,066/1.

[34] Ibid.

[35] Nicolls to de Lotbiniere, 10 July 1947. BBC WAC, R30/2,046/1.

[36] Nicolls to Haley, 10 Oct. 1047. BBC WAC, R30/2,066/1.

[37] 'Olympic Games', BBC WAC. R30/2,056/2.

[38] 'First report on the BBC Olympic Games Broadcasting Organisation At Wembley', 16 Aug. 1948. BBC WAC, R30/2,046/1.

[39] Glanville, *Wembley 1923–1973*, 66.

[40] Interview with the author, 12 May 2008.

[41] 'Olympic Games Broadcasting Organisation at Wembley', 16 Aug. 1948. BBC WAC, R30/2056/3.

[42] De Lotbiniere, Report on Olympic Games Broadcasting Operation', 3 Sept. 1948. BBC WAC, R30/2056/3.

[43] Report of Overseas (Non-European) Coverage of the Olympic Games, 20 Aug. 1948. BBC WAC, R30/2046/1.

[44] Winston, *Media Technology and Society*, 113–14.

[45] Interview with author, 12 May 2008.

[46] Huggins, 'Projecting the Visual'.

[47] De Lotbiniere to Orr-Ewing, 18 March 1947. BBC WAC, R30/2,066/1.

[48] Nicolls to de Lotbiniere, 10 Nov. 1947. BBC WAC, R30/2,066/1.

[49] Holt to Haley, 30 Dec. 1947. BBC WAC, R30/2,066/1.

[50] Collins draft letter, 2 Jan. 1948. BBC WAC, R30/2,066/1.

[51] Haley to Noel-Baker MP, 7 Jan. 1948. BBC WAC R30/2,066/1.

[52] Interview with the author, 12 May 2008.

[53] Interview with author, 12 May 2008.

[54] Robertson, *Stop Talking and Give the Score*, 69.

[55] 'Television and the Olympiad'. BBC WAC, R30/2056/3.

[56] Elvin to de Lotbiniere, 20 Aug. 1948. BBC WAC, R30/2056/3.

[57] 'Audience Reaction to Olympic Games Broadcasts'. BBC WAC, R30/2056/3.

[58] 'Television and the Olympiad'. BBC WAC, R30/2056/3.

[59] *Radio Times*, 20 Aug. 1948.

[60] How to Haley, 9 Aug. 1948. BBC WAC, R30/2,066/1.

[61] Haley to How, 1 Sept. 1948. BBC WAC, R30/2,066/1.

[62] Cardiff and Scannell, 'Broadcasting and National Unity', 168–9.

# References

Baker, N. 'A More Even Playing Field? Sport During and After the War'. In *Millions Like Us? British Culture in the Second World War*, edited by N. Hayes and J. Hill. Liverpool: Liverpool University Press, 1999.

Briggs, A. *A History of Broadcasting in the United Kingdom, vol. 4: Sound and Vision.* Oxford: Oxford University Press, 1978.

Booth, D. *Talking of Sport: The Story of Radio Commentary.* London: SportsBooks, 2008.

Cardiff, D. and P. Scannell. 'Broadcasting and National Unity'. In *Impacts and Influences: Essays on Media Power in the Twentieth Century*, edited by J. Curran, A. Smith and P. Wingate. London: Routledge, 1987.

Coase, R.H. *British Broadcasting: A Study in Monopoly.* London: Longmans, 1950.

Glanville, B., ed. *Wembley 1923–1973.* London: Kelly, 1973.

Hampton, J. *The Austerity Olympics: When the Games Came to London in 1948.* London: Aurum Press, 2008.

Hennessy, P. *Never Again: Britain 1945–1951.* Harmondsworth: Penguin, 2006.

Huggins, M. 'Projecting the Visual: British Newsreels, Soccer and Popular Culture 1918–39'. *The International Journal of The History of Sport*, 24, no. 1 (2007): 80–102.

Kynaston, D. *Austerity Britain 1945–1951.* London: Bloomsbury, 2008.

Large, D.C. *Nazi Games: The Olympics of 1936.* New York: Norton and Company, 2007.

Nicholas, S. 'The People's Radio: The BBC and Its Audience 1939–1945'. In *Millions Like Us? British Culture in the Second World War*, edited by N. Hayes and J. Hill. Liverpool: Liverpool University Press, 1999.

Robertson, M. *Stop Talking and Give the Score.* London: Heinemann, 1987.

Smith, J.D. 'The Struggle for Control of the Air-waves: The Atlee Governments, the BBC and Industrial Unrest, 1945–51'. In *Postwar Britain 1945–64: Themes and Perspectives*, edited by T. Gorst, L. Johnman and W.S. Lucas. London: Pinter, 1989.

Vaughan-Thomas, W. *Trust to Talk.* London: Hutchinson, 1980.

Uricchio, W. 'Introduction to the History of German Television, 1935–1944'. *Historical Journal of Film, Radio and Television* 10, no. 2 (1990): 115–22.

Winston, B. *Media Technology and Society: A History: From the Telegraph to the Internet.* London: Routledge, 1998.

Wood, R. *A World in Your Ear: The Broadcasting of an Era, 1923–1965.* London: Macmillan, 1979.

# 14

# BBC Radio and Sport 1922–39

*Mike Huggins*

T he 1920s saw a global expansion of radio sport coverage. American stations were the first to broadcast sports results, reports and live commentary. On 11 April 1921, a lightweight boxing match was broadcast on KDKA. Games from World Series baseball and Davis Cup tennis, also broadcast in 1921, were groundbreaking experiments.[1] The Dempsey versus Carpentier boxing match, transmitted from New Jersey on 2 July 1921, was widely listened to in halls and theatres within 250 miles, as the commentator, J. Andrew White, attempted to 'convey pictures' to the studio.[2] America's commercial radio stations quickly used sport as a programming and revenue staple, increasing demand for radios, and attracting large audiences to baseball, American football and boxing commentaries. The USA was a state-regulated service, with private ownership of broadcasting facilities, financed through advertising. By 1924 there were 1,400 stations, 3 million sets and almost daily sports broadcasts. Telephone lines spread coverage, and on 1 January 1927 the Rose Bowl football game was heard from coast to coast on NBC, as was the memorable Dempsey versus Tunney fight later that year. Sports broadcasts quickly attracted sponsors, leading to increased commercial pressures on American sport between 1926 and 1933.[3]

Other former British colonies were early entrants into sports broadcasting. In Australia, with its mixture of public and commercial radio, a Sydney station broadcast a testimonial match for Charles Bannerman in 1922, and in July 1923 a Melbourne steeplechase was covered. In 1924 Radio 2BL Sydney provided coverage of a rugby league cup final and MCC tour games.[4] Canadian Toronto station CFCA covered the final period of a

**Source:** *Contemporary British History*, 21(4) (2007): 491–515.

hockey match between North Toronto and Midland in February 1923, and there were further commentaries that year. South Africa covered rugby in 1924, and by 1926 countries from New Zealand to Ireland were experimenting with sports broadcasts. A station in Christchurch, New Zealand, covered rugby that May and trotting and hockey were covered later in 1926. On 29 August 1926 Eire's 2RN station was probably the first in Europe to provide live commentary on a field game when broadcasting the All-Ireland hurling semi-final, an early indication of the support Irish broadcasting subsequently provided for GAA games.[5] 1927 saw further countries begin commentary.

While knowledge of *global* sports broadcasting between the wars, especially but not solely for the USA, is increasing, there has been little detailed exploration of early British sports broadcasting, with the exception of Hayes' study of football.[6] This is the more surprising given that radio's general social and cultural history has been well served. Nicholas has explored the relationship between the BBC and its audience between 1939 and 1945, while the overall relationship between sport and the inter-war media has recently been analysed by Huggins and Williams.[7] Scannell and Cardiff deliberately excluded sport from discussion, while McKibbin's important treatments of radio broadcasting and sport remained unlinked.[8] Even so, they, and media historians such as Briggs and Pegg accept that inter-war sports coverage was one of the BBC's most direct contributions to entertainment.[9] Indeed, Scannell and Cardiff argue that the BBC became *the* central organ of British national culture partly through its regular coverage of key sporting events.[10] Pegg claims that radio, alongside the press and newsreels, helped shape Britain's sporting culture and emphasise the 'national' character of particular sports.[11] It has also been suggested that radio widened general interest in sport while domesticating sport as a spectacle.[12]

However, while such widespread consensus may contain considerable truth, the substantive evidence either to support and clarify such assertions, or to critique an important but hitherto unexamined part of the story of sport and the media, has been largely lacking. This analysis exploits sources that include BBC promotional literature, especially its *Radio Times*, handbooks and year books, material that was often self-important, uncritical and ideologically biased, alongside press articles, biographical and autobiographical material. The article begins by examining the problematic beginnings of BBC sports broadcasting in 1927 as it established approach and direction. Second, it analyses the main patterns of coverage between 1927 and 1939, testing out earlier claims and exploring further key questions concerning the extent to which BBC coverage reflected sporting interests across different social classes and of women as well as men. How did the nuances and tensions of social exclusivity and inclusion, social unity and class rivalry work out in practice? What of different and distinctive national and regional sporting experiences and tastes? Changes in BBC domestic broadcasting coverage over time, the differing responses to BBC broadcasting made by sporting governing bodies and clubs, audience experiences and responses and the art of commentary all shed light on such questions.

This study in part clarifies the tentative findings of earlier studies, confirming that between the wars the BBC helped reshape the way sport was experienced. The BBC, with its broadcasting monopoly and public-service approach, created a limited number of 'national' British sporting events. It provided a national commonality of experience through a regular calendar of key outside sports broadcasts, fostering anticipation and future pleasure. By mediating such sporting events to a cross-class audience, the BBC promoted social unity rather than rivalry. It created new norms and expectations about commentaries alongside BBC cultural values and attitudes. Previously even if some people watched sporting events, most read about them or watched them on screen only afterwards. Radio now allowed listeners a new dimension, a vicarious presence as events unfolded. By 1939 a clear BBC sports broadcasting style had emerged, especially in its treatment of national sporting events, explaining the nation to the nation, and establishing a clearer sense of British sporting nationhood. More generally it widened knowledge of sport. In the 1930s radio introduced people to sports they had never seen before. Sport became 'respectable' as broadcasting raised the status of its key events. Radio made the University Boat Race a national event. It helped rugby grow in popularity. In part, BBC sports transmissions brought Britain closer together while also perpetuating persistent regional and national differences (amongst the Scots and Welsh) through its regional broadcasts.

But the BBC's impact can be over-stressed. Its coverage was selective and somewhat elitist in approach, biased towards more middle-class and metropolitan events. Football received few commentaries, greyhound racing none, even though they were the two most attended commercial sporting spectator events, highly popular with the working classes. The BBC's sport coverage attracted female listeners but its coverage of women's sports was poor, especially compared to that of the newsreels. Contemporary arguments that foregrounding nationally important events perhaps helped diminish spectator support for local games are not strongly backed by evidence. The extent to which sport was domesticated, supporting BBC discourses of neighbourliness and family life, with the whole family sitting together listening, is also debatable, although many letters in its favour were from the housebound or partially sighted, since communal outdoor listening survived in some places through the 1920s and much of the 1930s. And finally, it is worth noting that, despite Reith's opposition to gambling and the BBC's avoidance of betting news, gambling experienced major growth in popularity between the wars.

## The Beginnings of Outside Live Sports Broadcasts 1922–27

Sales of radios in Britain were initially slow. Only 36,000 licences were purchased in 1922, and Britain initially lagged well behind the USA in broadcasting sport. The Marconi 2LO Company attempted a running commentary of the Kid Lewis versus Carpentier fight at Olympia for London listeners in May 1922. However, the Newspaper Proprietors' Association argued that radio was a rival form of news reporting and was able to block subsequent attempts at commentary by the British Broadcasting Company, then run by leading wireless manufacturers. In 1923 the parliamentary Sykes Committee on Broadcasting was concerned that any broadcasting of sports results would harm newspaper sales, but felt it might be acceptable to broadcast some 'special' outside events.[13] The BBC was placed under the jurisdiction of the Post Office, whose Postmaster General was very clear that the interests of the press and news agencies should not be alienated or financially embarrassed. So the BBC was subjected to severe restrictions on the coverage of outside events. Any concessions had to be prised from the press. In February 1925 the BBC undertook abortive negotiations to broadcast the 'running story' of the first half of the England versus Scotland rugby match, a 'coded narrative' of the Boat race and Cup final (with the key to the code published in the papers on the day) and an 'impressionist' broadcast of the Epsom Derby. The press, concerned about the broadcasting 'menace', rejected these.[14] In 1926 the BBC were given permission for an 'experiment' to provide conversation between experts, and the sounds of horses' hooves, bookmakers' shouts and other 'atmosphere', after negotiations with Epsom's organisers. It was a critical failure. Heavy rain dampened hooves and spirits. The final part of the commentary painted a very restricted picture: 'Here they come – now they're getting down to it – he's drawing ahead – it's sure to be Lex – no – Harpagon'. Then a distant voice said 'It looks like 9–5–1', before they were returned to the studio.[15] Listeners had to wait until the first news bulletin, at 7 p.m., to find out the result.

In 1926 the Crawford Committee on Broadcasting recommended a national, public-service broadcasting, crown-chartered utility, and on 1 January 1927 the BBC became the British Broadcasting Corporation, the *sole* British broadcaster. Its Director-General, John Reith, was ethically committed to universal dissemination of its 'public service' approach: inclusive, but raising public taste and promoting 'correct' social attitudes while informing, educating and entertaining. He wanted to create a genuine sense of audience involvement in national public life and culture. Sport, whose key events supposedly consecrated national sentiment, could help. Audiences would learn its finer points. Sport was entertaining, understood, an everyday fundamental part of life, especially on Saturdays. Reith and the head of Outside Broadcasting, Gerald Cock, decided that commentaries on Britain's major national sporting events would create excitement, provide unique listening experiences and help unify Britain.

So as early as 31 December 1926, with negotiations with the various news agencies and the press finally and positively concluded, the *Radio Times* announced a 'considerable expansion' of news broadcasting, including 'descriptive eyewitness accounts' of 'important events'. The obvious success of American broadcasting exercised BBC minds and Cock appeared interested in emulating American sports broadcasting approaches. In early January 1927 a *Radio Times* article described American football broadcasts, explaining that USA newspapers often had their own stations and reported sport regularly, so 'more interest was taken in the football and baseball pages than ever before'.[16] This public relations discourse thus hinted that broadcasts would *aid* British newspaper sales. Its view of American commentaries was positive, concealing intra-BBC debates about radio's role and fears that the 'national outlook and, with it, character' was 'gradually being Americanised'.[17]

The BBC admired the speed, slickness, freshness and topicality of American sports coverage. When the first commentator, Capt. H. B. T. Wakelam, was recruited, by producer Lance Sieveking, he was told that 'it had been decided to follow a recent American innovation and to put out running commentaries'.[18] But there was some unwillingness to get too involved in mass culture or attract mass audiences. Cock was opposed to the monopolistic power of American sports and entertainment organisations, saw real dangers in such over-commercialised moves, and wanted to maintain the highest possible standards of entertainment.[19] So only sporting occasions that the BBC could define as *national events* were initially covered.

The BBC found many of the more traditionally 'amateur' sporting bodies happy to welcome the 'national' broadcaster. Following discussions with the Rugby Football Union, and trial exercises at Blackheath and Richmond, a game on January 15th between England and Wales at Twickenham became Wakelam's first broadcast. A motor van transported the complicated transmission apparatus. The BBC trumpeted it as 'one of the most important events since the inception of broadcasting . . . the beginning of a new era in wireless', announcing that they would henceforth cover sports as 'an integral part of the broadcast service'. The BBC's post-bag praised the 'crowded hour of glorious life', and the 'wild glorious cheering from 40,000 throats'. Some highbrow critics regarded it as a failure, but the London and provincial press was generally supportive.[20] The *Times* saw it as 'vivid' and impressive', and accepted that commentary had clearly 'come to stay'.[21] The *Field* praised Wakelam: '[nothing] could have filled the bill better than the delineations, running fire of comments and ejaculations'.[22] In the following weeks, listeners heard second-half commentary on a League match between Arsenal and Sheffield and a fourth-round Football Association (FA) Cup tie between Corinthians and Newcastle United.

February saw further rugby internationals and FA Cup matches broadcast. March saw just over an hour of racing commentary on the Grand National. *Radio Times*, still describing this as 'experimental', to forestall potential criticism, provided an entertaining plan of the Aintree course. Veteran *Sporting Life* journalist Meyrick Good, who usually 'read the race' for the King, provided commentary, with George V standing beside him. Good commentated in the open, close to the enclosures, so cheering drowned his voice towards the finish. With a rapid return to the studio placings were also left unclear. After his broadcast he claimed that 10,000,000 had listened, commenting (for the press's benefit?) that audiences had been 'worked up to a high pitch of curiosity and want to see in cold print the evidence of their own ears corroborated and amplified . . . the broadcasting of these great racing events is more of an asset to the newspapers than otherwise'.[23] Five fixed microphones were used, for Good, for crowd and betting noise, for the Paddock, where a second commentator described the preliminaries, for the unsaddling enclosure, and for interviewing the winning jockey and trainer. One trainer wrote from distant Coblenz to say the commentary was 'a great success . . . the next best thing to seeing the race'.[24]

The Boat Race was a bigger technical challenge. The BBC broadcast commentary from a launch, whose aerial sent a signal to receiving stations at Barnes, which then forwarded it. The press, yet again, were generally impressed. The *Times* believed that listeners were in a distinct advantage over those who saw the event, and were well served by the 'expert analysis'.[25] The FA Cup Final, on April 23rd, included pre-kick-off sound of the vast crowd singing, claimed as 'the largest demonstration of Community Singing this country has ever beheld'.[26] Like crowd noise, this gave armchair listeners something of the communal atmosphere. Transmitting such national sporting rituals, often foregrounding royalty's presence, consolidated the BBC's cultural role, celebrated national pride, and reinforced a sense that such events belonged to the nation, not just supporters.

Cricket was covered not by running commentary but by much more limited 'eyewitness accounts'. At the end of April listeners were given brief reports and summaries of play of Surrey versus Hampshire at the Oval by former test player P. F. Warner. In May a 'descriptive narrative' on the Essex versus New Zealand game was provided. There was a ten-minute first report, summarising play, followed by brief hourly summaries, with a message inserted into the studio music programme for any especially exciting event. That summer there were occasional eyewitness accounts of both county matches and the Oxford v. Cambridge and Gentlemen v. Players games, perhaps a reflection of the gentleman-amateur backgrounds of BBC and commentating staff. Golf reports from the Amateur and Open championships received similar coverage.

Commentary coverage of the Derby in May, with Good dropped in favour of Geoffrey Gilbey, included interviews amongst the crowds, and band music. In late June and early July Wimbledon was broadcast. The St Leger was covered in September. The editor of that year's *Bloodstock Breeders' Review*, who listened in Guernsey, believed that the 1927 experiments in race broadcasting had been 'an unqualified success'. During the year sports talks were also scheduled. In April, for example, these included a survey of the women's hockey season and the prospects for England's tour of Australia.

But right from the start there were counter-currents against 'national' sporting coverage, helping consolidate regional and local identity and partisanship. It is important to stress that the BBC also reflected long-standing and persistent regional and national differences in sporting preferences. As early as 1923 Birmingham, Manchester, Cardiff, Glasgow, Aberdeen and Bournemouth had local stations. Further relay stations were set up in 1924. In 1926, because of wavelength restrictions, these were replaced by regional stations which the new BBC inherited. All regional stations were anxious to offer their own Saturday commentaries or eyewitness accounts alongside relaying national programming, and so reflect the sometimes different sporting interests of their listeners. In early March 1927, for example, London got an 'important association match', Manchester had Burnley versus Blackburn Rovers, Yorkshire had Sheffield United versus Spurs, while in south Wales, where rugby was the dominant game, the rugby union match between Swansea and Cardiff was broadcast. Later in the spring the Rugby League Challenge Cup final, between Swinton and Oldham, was also broadcast, but only from Manchester. In the summer the Roses cricket matches were also solely a northern feature. By contrast only London got the Eton versus Harrow game, reflecting perhaps more elitist metropolitan views.

## Coverage of Sport 1928–39

After 1927 the BBC continued to stress 'national' British events, although, as we shall see, these were underlaid by continued tensions of class, gender and region. Desensitised microphones soon cut out over-obtrusive crowd noise. Events such as the Grand National, Epsom Derby and Doncaster St Leger, the Boat Race, football and rugby internationals, the FA Cup final, the Amateur Golf Championship and Wimbledon, quickly became what the 1930 *BBC Yearbook* already described as 'old favourites' with listeners, fostering national pride in British sporting achievements. Some were covered by 'running commentary', others by reported summaries ('eyewitness accounts'). With the partial exception of the FA Cup final, the Boat Race and horseracing, most events covered attracted largely middle-class crowds. The Boat Race, with its Oxbridge associations, was seen by the BBC as the most outstanding of all outside broadcasts. Even so, as part of an annual compendium of broadcast national rituals and ceremonies, sports coverage presented the BBC in a more democratic light than much BBC output, which maintained a partial focus on high culture, as did the columns of the *Listener* – the BBC's magazine for listeners – which almost entirely ignored sport, an indication that it was perceived as too 'lowbrow' for its readers.

Sport took some time to be a major BBC priority, but in the early 1930s coverage of 'national' sporting events was expanded, cumulatively creating the elements of what Scannell and Cardiff described as a 'unified national life available to all'.[27] Initially expansion was fairly slow but it gathered pace rapidly from 1933 (Table 1).

The two sports most often covered nationally in the mid-1930s were motor sports and rugby, both largely, though not entirely, middle-class in

**Table 1:** Numbers of BBC national commentaries on sport 1930–35

| | 1930 | 1931 | 1932 | 1933 | 1934 | 1935 |
|---|---|---|---|---|---|---|
| Rugby union | 6 | 9 | 9 | 7 | 7 | 14 |
| Car and motor-cycle races | 3 | 4 | 5 | 4 | 5 | 12 |
| Tennis | Wimbledon | Wimbledon | Wimbledon | Wimbledon Davis Cup | Wimbledon Davis Cup Wightman Cup | Wimbledon Davis Cup Wightman Cup |
| Soccer | 1 | 4 | 3 | 4 | 4 | 6 |
| Racing | 4 | 5 | 5 | 5 | 6 | 6 |
| Rowing, yachting etc | Boat race Cowes | 1 | 1 | 1 | 4 | 5 |
| Cricket | 0 (eyewitness accounts only) | 0 | 0 | 0 | 5 | 5 |
| Boxing | 2 | 1 | 0 | 1 | 3 | 2 |
| Athletics | 1 | 0 | 0 | 0 | 3 | 2 |
| Ice hockey | 0 | 0 | 0 | 0 | 0 | 2 |
| Highland sports | 0 | 0 | 1 | 1 | 1 | 1 |
| Rifle shooting | 1 (Bisley) | 0 | 0 | 1 | 1 | 1 |
| Snooker | 0 | 0 | 0 | 0 | 0 | 1 |
| Rugby league | 0 | 0 | 0 | 0 | 0 | 1 |
| Speedway | 1 | 0 | 1 | 1 | 4 | 0 |
| American football | 1 | 0 | 0 | 0 | 0 | 0 |
| Water polo | 0 | 1 | 1 | 0 | 0 | 0 |

*Source: BBC Handbooks and Annuals.*

terms of their participation and spectatorship, and thus socially exclusive rather than inclusive. Motor sports, like the BBC itself, were emblematic of modernity. Eyewitness accounts of the RAC Tourist Trophy Races at Ulster and the Isle of Man were broadcast in 1929 and proved very popular, as was the seaplane race for the Schneider Trophy on the Solent. Speedway coverage peaked in 1934. In 1935 the BBC covered motor-cycle speed championships at St Andrews, hill climbs at Red Marley and Shelsey Walsh, Grand Prix and other motor car races at Ulster, Donnington Park and the Isle of Man, and the TT races at Ards and the Isle of Man.

The positive reception given to sport by listeners encouraged a move beyond national events to a wider expansion of Saturday sports coverage in the 1930s. In June 1932 the BBC broadcast three and a quarter hours of running commentary, 'the first occasion a programme so ambitious has been undertaken'.[28] By 1934 the BBC regularly offered national listeners whole afternoons of organised sport, with rapid shifts from one sport to another, and further regional variations. Saturday 15 August 1936, for example, saw 35 minutes of commentary and summary on the England v. India test, then music, 15 minutes of athletics, the test match again, semi-final and final single-handed bowls from the National Championship, then the test match once more. During the week, sports talks were also increasingly provided by a varied range of speakers, especially as the BBC began to feature 'personalities' in its coverage.

The early selective middle-class bias in terms of coverage began to soften in the later 1930s. By then a majority of British families had a radio, although significant numbers of poor families were probably still excluded from access to a radio in 1939, even if the unknown number of unlicensed receivers is taken into account, so the BBC was still not available to all. The BBC's own Listener Research Committee, which produced its first report in 1937, soon identified sport as having an impact on viewers (Table 2).

Pegg has argued that radio helped shape Britain's sporting culture by emphasising the 'national' character of particular sports.[29] But this became less true in the later 1930s, when the BBC responded to listener demand by expanding its 'national' coverage to include some 'representative' examples of less participatory sports such as basketball, clay pigeon shooting, cross-country championships, darts, fencing, gliding, pigeon racing, point-to-points,

**Table 2:** Accessibility of radios in Britain 1925–39

| Year | Number of licences | Number of licences per 100 families |
|------|--------------------|--------------------------------------|
| 1925 | 1,645,207 | 15.4 |
| 1927 | 2,395,183 | 21.7 |
| 1929 | 2,956,736 | 26 |
| 1931 | 4,330,735 | 37.1 |
| 1933 | 5,973,758 | 50 |
| 1935 | 7,403,109 | 60.7 |
| 1937 | 8,479,600 | 68.3 |
| 1939 | 8,893,582 | 71 |

*Source: BBC Annual Report* 1938, p. 73. M. Pegg, *Broadcasting and Society 1918–1939* (1983), p. 7.
Reprinted with permission from BBC Written Archives Centre.

power-boat racing, racquets, real tennis, rifle shooting, speedway, table tennis and snooker. Village cricket was also occasionally covered. Commentary on a village match at Oxney in July 1937, for example, survives amongst other BBC material in the British Library sound archives.[30] Such changes introduced listeners to sports they might never previously considered watching or reading about and further widened the audience. Sports coverage was slowly becoming more cross-class.

But if the BBC partly aided a unified national life, it should also be stressed that regional sports commentary continued to cater for specific regional sporting interests. For example, Manchester, from its first year as the central northern England station in 1929–30, always provided coverage of cricket's Roses matches and rugby league games. Manchester listeners later also heard occasional England National Baseball League games. Regionalism was further fostered through more regional early-evening sports programmes, such as 'Midland Sport' (later 'Midland Sporting Diary') or the 'London Sports Bulletin'. BBC national coverage was, however, very Anglo-centric. The emphasis on 'national' events ensured a majority of outside broadcasts came from London and the South East. By contrast Scotland was poorly catered for on the national wavelength, apart from rugby internationals from Murrayfield, and one of the Highland Gatherings which featured annually as part of athletics coverage. The Scottish FA refused soccer coverage apart from internationals. So it was its own radio coverage which largely defined Scotland, as when its Glasgow station featured shinty in April 1939.

On the other hand, the BBC's national sports bulletins, which were slowly expanded, did foster a national view of what key events defined 'sport'. In 1926 the press concerns still forced news reportage, including sports, to be later that 7 p.m. to allow sales of evening sports papers, but by 1928 the first daily news report, which still had to be based on press agency material sent over by hand, was permitted after 6 p.m. This was initially the only one to include up to five minutes of sports results. In 1933 the Saturday 'newsreel' feature also got a similar bulletin at 9.30 p.m., which occasionally included recorded commentary, to round the programme off. In 1938 a survey was carried out by the BBC's listener Research Section. Fairly representative of the nation in terms of age, sex and location but over-representative of the middle classes, it showed that the BBC's Saturday sports results service, including soccer, then broadcast at 6.15 p.m., was listened to regularly by 58 per cent of correspondents regularly and 16 per cent occasionally.[31] This facility increasingly required specialist staff. Angus Mackay, formerly been in charge of the sports department of the *Scotsman*, joined in 1936 as a sports sub-editor. Sporting news became a regular feature, with further 'sports experts' soon added to make the sports service more 'efficient' and 'comprehensive'.[32] By 1939 there were four full-timers, responsible for two daily sports bulletins and a sports talk for the Saturday evening bulletin. But though the *Daily Sketch* complained that the BBC had 'a director of everything except sport' in

1937, there was still no sports editor at the BBC even in 1939, which suggests that sport was still regarded as of only limited broadcasting importance.[33]

## The BBC and the Sports Bodies

The relationship between the BBC and the varied sports bodies sheds further light on the debate over how far the BBC could promote a national sporting culture and demonstrates yet again that this was so only to an extent. The BBC's coverage of sport and its potential tensions were underpinned by class and cultural biases both within the BBC and the different sports bodies and clubs, while the inter-relationships caused clear consequences in terms of the nature and extent of broadcasting coverage, and of listener interest.

The survival of amateurism and emphasis on sportsmanship in much of British sport, and the cultural background shared by BBC officials, commentators and many of the organisational bodies with whom they dealt, meant that the BBC was largely, although not entirely, able to claim entitlement to cover events without payment. Indeed, the BBC and wider public assumed that coverage *should* be offered freely by sports organisations as the nation's right. As early as 1930 the *Times* argued that the basic principle was that 'no national event, if it is capable of being broadcast, should be barred to listeners'.[34]

In general the BBC had a strong relationship with Britain's amateur-governed sports, who were largely prepared to privilege BBC coverage, providing facilities free of charge. Other more commercially inclined sporting bodies, however, felt that broadcasting would impact detrimentally on attendance, and sometimes demanded money. This clashed directly with the BBC's 'public-service' broadcasting philosophy.

Coverage of amateur rugby union, which had its power base in the south, dominated early BBC sports broadcasting, and the English Rugby Football Union, consistently anxious to publicly preserve its strongly amateur tradition, was the most receptive to the BBC. Most rugby clubs were little concerned about 'gates' and any anxieties were probably balanced by recognition that coverage helped carry 'the story of the game wider' and collect 'new adherents to click the turnstiles of the future'.[35] So it was no coincidence that the BBC began its outside broadcasting with rugby commentary. At Twickenham, the RFU secretary was keen to increase spectator numbers, and ground capacity was regularly expanded. Broadcasting seemed to encourage attendance there. Twickenham's facilities, and the fact that Oxford v. Cambridge, the Navy v. the Army, and England internationals were all played there, ensured that regular broadcasting was in everybody's interest.

Here, to an extent, broadcasting perhaps reshaped national sporting culture through increased interest in rugby, which proved popular with listeners across Britain, perhaps simply through regular coverage. Broadcasts from Murrayfield coincided with increased crowds. The Welsh RFU proved initially reluctant, and refused broadcasting permission in 1928, but were soon persuaded. Certainly many grammar schools changed from soccer to rugby between the wars. But the argument is true only to an extent. Rugby remained a resolutely middle-class sport in many regions, and there was little or no increase in crowds at club games. Equally, the single annual broadcasting of the Rugby League Challenge Cup Final, a northern phenomenon, initially put out only as a northern regional broadcast, although relayed from Wembley from 1929, was not enough to encourage the southern rugby union-supporting middle classes to visit Wembley in numbers once it was put out nationally from 1935. London rugby league final crowds remained well below those for FA Cup finals.

The extent to which coverage of horseracing promoted a unified national culture is less clear still. Emphasis on social unity came unstuck when it came to betting, a major opposition cutting across communities and families, dividing Britain not by class but by cultural attitudes. Recent research has shown that credit betting and sweeps were both popular with sections of the middle classes, although a vociferous and powerful minority, drawn in part from the more evangelical sections of nonconformity and the Church of England, bitterly opposed betting, stressed its physical, social, moral and economic ill-effects, and supported strong state action against it, thus making it impossible to soften existing legislation.[36] While others occupied a neutral position, nationally betting was only exceeded by cinema-going as the leading leisure spending activity. Gambling as a proportion of total consumer spending rose from 1.3 per cent in 1920 to 5 per cent in 1938. Much of this was gambling on the horses, though greyhound racing and the football pools also took their share.

Reith himself was strongly opposed to all forms of gambling, for which he had strong moral disdain. There was thus never any live commentary on greyhound racing's leading events, even in the late 1930s. Their working-class gambling associations were too strong. Likewise, from the very start of racing broadcasts the BBC avoided any broadcasting of betting news, and made no mention of betting odds, starting prices or bookmakers during commentary, though bookmakers could sometimes be heard in the background. So commentary essentially screened out much that spectators would have seen and heard. The difficulty for many listeners was that the leading broadcast races always attracted huge betting interest, with the Derby, for example, a focus for hugely popular sweepstakes. The winners of the Stock Exchange, Baltic and Calcutta sweepstakes in the 1920s and the Irish Hospital sweep-stakes in the 1930s, with their huge prizes, were always publicised in the *Times* and other leading newspapers, and most pubs and social clubs ran sweeps, despite their technical illegality.[37] So broadcasts without reference to betting was not congenial to punters, even if commentary and scene-setting probably brought racing to new audiences, especially women. And race commentary not only lacked betting information, but also detail. Early broadcasters had to describe the full race from a distant vantage point in the stands, using large binoculars, which made it difficult to commentate. Races were not read in three or four commentary relays until the later 1950s. And print journalists sometimes complained that scenes and incidents were poorly conveyed.[38]

It is also worth noting the extent to which many British owners and race-course companies were also unhappy at radio coverage. In the USA and Australia there had been a decrease in 'gates' and a drop in totalisator receipts once racing was broadcast, although Australian attempts to stop coverage had been stymied when the ABC commentated from rooms or platforms outside the racecourses.[39] Owner Sir Abe Bailey regularly objected to the broadcasting of running commentaries on races. 'We have', he contended, 'only to wait for the development of television, and there will be no necessity for any one to go to a race meeting'.[40] Within racing's higher circles, the Jockey Club, although an amateur, upper-class body, was unenthusiastic about Newmarket cover-age given its fairly small crowds. Eventually the Cesarewitch (1937) and Two Thousand Guineas (1938) were broadcast, but not the Thousand Guineas. Gosforth's directors refused to allow broadcasting of the Northumberland Plate when first approached in 1927. Ascot was not broadcast until 1937.

The argument that the BBC helped to promote a unified national culture is even less supported by football, which despite being the leading winter working-class spectator sport attracted fairly few commentaries in the 1930s. In the 1920s good relationships with the FA allowed broadcasts of FA Cup matches, and some leading League clubs were positive.[41] Including regional broadcasts, over a hundred matches were covered in the period through to 1931, quite substantial coverage. But many football League clubs mirrored press concerns about loss of revenue, and the BBC was not prepared to provide financial compensation. Concerns began early. In March 1927 *All Sports Weekly* asked 'Shall the football matches be broadcast?', and reported that some clubs already had 'a bitter mind against the proposal'.[42] In May 1928 the members of the Third Division (North) put forward a resolution that the League Management Committee should ban broadcasts and put pressure on the FA to do likewise, claiming commentaries kept people away from other matches in the region, especially lower division games. Such views were paralleled in the USA, where sports promoters equally feared that radio broadcasting kept paying customers away. The New York Giants, Yankees and Brooklyn Dodgers all banned broadcasts between 1934 and 1939.[43]

Thereafter the BBC constantly grappled with club complaints. In March 1931 at an informal meeting at Manchester, Birmingham City and an unnamed London club suggested an anti-broadcasting resolution should be put to the League's AGM. Birmingham subsequently refused to allow their FA Cup match against Chelsea to be broadcast. Other clubs sounded out opinion through press leaks, again arguing that broadcasting supposedly had an adverse effect on the 'gates' of the broadcast match, on other important matches in the neighbourhood and on the 'gates' of smaller 'struggling' clubs.

The BBC countered this, arguing that the attack was 'based on a fallacy', and citing carefully selected crowd figures to demonstrate that crowds on the Saturday of 14 February 1931 were higher despite rugby international and soccer Cup commentaries than on February 21st which lacked commentaries. It also cited letters from those who for reasons of health or blindness saw a game through the commentators' eyes.[44] The arguments had little effect and, despite widespread public support for the BBC, League coverage ceased. Arguing from crowd figures in reality proved inconclusive. Those clubs who opposed broadcasting, often less successful ones, could always find examples of diminished gates near a broadcast match. On the other hand, intervening variables such as the intrinsic importance of the game, the proximity of other important games, the local economic situation or weather conditions could all equally affect attendance.

The FA had a less commercial approach, happily allowing coverage of English home internationals. But the FA Cup Final created tensions, given the pressure from League clubs and the substantial fee annually paid by news-reels for 'exclusive' film rights. In April 1929 the FA demanded a fee from the BBC as well. The BBC refused, despite its clear attachment to the Cup Final as one of the most important days in British sport, and instead broadcast eyewitness accounts. Eight different commentators entered the ground with purchased tickets, and then in turn rushed back to a nearby flat to report. Summaries interspersed with music were provided. The BBC later claimed that it was 'entirely successful'.[45] In reality breathless commentators talking without script and with minimal preparation for up to ten minutes proved unsatisfactory. One reporter even wrongly announced that Chelsea, not Portsmouth, had scored. Listener and press response varied. Most welcomed the attempt. But it was also later unkindly described as 'the most humorous item on the BBC programme of 1929'.[46]

In early 1930, following increased representation of professional clubs on its Council, the FA withdrew rights to all cup tie broadcasts without a compensatory fee. The BBC refused to pay but offered a payment to charity. It published the correspondence of its negotiations to demonstrate FA 'intransigence'. Cock argued that the BBC was 'analogous to a newspaper' and press reporters paid no fee. He complained that FA opposition stemmed from the League clubs, 'professionals whose whole interest apparently is commercial'. He appealed to leading FA officials' more amateur, conservative and insular mindset, inferring that the BBC was protecting its audience from 'commercial' exploitation. He claimed that the 'blind, the invalid and the poor' could listen, while broadcasts 'actually increase and spread interest in the sports described'.[47] Much of the resulting BBC post-bag unsurprisingly supported his position. A *Times* editorial, headlined 'Commercial Football', pointed out that the final was oversubscribed and saw the commentary as for football enthusiasts everywhere, including the 'halt, the maimed and the blind'. It saw the charity offer as 'a fair sporting one' and castigated the FA for showing 'an ungenerous and mercenary spirit, opposed to the interests of sport in general and damaging the reputation of the Council'.[48] Letters to the *Times* argued that the FA's outlook was over-narrow and out of touch with the majority of football enthusiasts. The FA responded by denying 'allegations' of their commercial and 'professional' approach, demanding a retraction of this, and saying that the only real issue was whether they or the BBC should decide on where the offered money should go. Faced by further adverse publicity the FA sought a get-out. During a speech at the FA Council luncheon two days later the Bishop of Buckingham helpfully described the BBC's attack as 'absolutely unjustifiable', but appealed to the FA to 'nobly and generously give the public what they want – a running commentary'. The following day the secretary of the FA, Sir Frederick Wall, responded by inviting the BBC to broadcast.

However, opposition to commentary amongst professional clubs was still strong. In April 1931 a resolution to the FA Council restricted broadcasting to the final two stages of the FA Cup and to internationals, arguing that broadcasting was not in the best interests of clubs or the game as a whole. A further resolution in June suggested that only the Cup Final should be allowed. Thereafter soccer broadcasts were largely limited to the internationals, the FA Cup Final, Oxford v. Cambridge or the Charity Shield.

The BBC's tacit acceptance of the League's attitude, and reluctance to challenge the FA, reflected a reluctance to get involved in commercial competition. Its approach contrasted strongly with that of the leading British newsreel companies. When access was denied to them they used a variety of strategies, including smuggled cameras and light aeroplanes, to gain coverage.[49] In Australia, where many football and racing companies opposed coverage, commercial radio stations tried to find rooms overlooking grounds. Commentators occasionally even climbed trees. But the FA did allow one innovation to be broadcast which helped consolidate the Cup's appeal. This was the third round draw, live from the FA Council Chamber. The scene was set by a commentator and then 'the proceedings were left to speak for themselves'.[50]

Cricket too proves problematic for arguments about how far BBC sport broadcasts created a national view of sport. Here however, it was the BBC who was reluctant to provide coverage. Between the wars cricket was perceived as the embodiment of Englishness, moral worth and social harmony despite being riddled with privilege and social distinction. Those social groups with economic and political power esteemed it highly. Matches against dominion sides, especially Australia, always attracted widespread cross-class interest.[51] But the BBC appears to have believed that only fast-moving sports made interesting running commentary. Up to 1934 cricket coverage was largely limited to occasional eyewitness accounts. Cricket's slower pace supposedly did not have sufficient domestic appeal. This contrasted with Australia, where there had been ball-by-ball coverage as early as December 1925. Interest in test matches there was huge. Over two million sets were sold in 1930 so Australians could listen to broadcast reports on the first test match of the series in England, many staying up until 3 a.m. The MCC 'bodyline' test tour of Australia in 1932–33 created huge interest amongst Australian listeners to ball-by-ball commentaries. When the Australians toured England again in 1934, the recently formed ABC introduced 'synthetic' coverage from a Sydney studio, using a succession of cablegrams as the basis for imaginative commentary, with sound effects such as crowd noise to complete the illusion, a technique already used by some commercial stations earlier in the 1930s. Test cricket commentaries significantly enlarged Australian radio audiences.[52]

By contrast BBC coverage only slowly increased from 1934, with regular summaries at the start, lunch, the tea interval and close of play, plus brief ball-by-ball commentaries when play got exciting. It was only when the BBC's own Listener Research Committee surveys found that cricket commentaries were popular, that actual commentary expanded in the later 1930s. In 1938 a scorer, Arthur Wrigley, was employed for the first time to assist with background material.

Tennis was largely seen in terms of middle-class Wimbledon, although Davis and Wightman Cup commentaries were added in 1934. The BBC enjoyed a good relationship with Wimbledon's amateur authorities but here there were technical scheduling problems. Times of matches varied with play and weather. The final might be broadcast in full, but other Wimbledon matches sometimes only got final set commentary, breaking into normal programming. Even so, these descriptions were, according to the *Daily Telegraph*, 'deservedly popular' even in the 1920s.[53] They became increasingly popular thereafter. Here it is undoubtedly true that broadcasting helped extend awareness of the sport, most especially amongst women and the home-based.

But if the BBC was trying to be more inclusive, it should be pointed out that women's sport apart from tennis received far less radio coverage than it did on the various cinema newsreels or in the print media. Commentary on women's hockey, billiards and figure skating only began in 1937, and BBC sport was dominated by male commentators and sportsmen, even if Marjorie Pollard, hockey and cricket international and journalist, provided commentary on the women's test between England and Australia in 1936. The BBC still reflected a gender divide in society.

## Audience Response

How far did radio, with its remote, indirect experience of sport, quite unlike that of direct experience, 'domesticate' sport as a spectacle? It did, but only to an extent. In the 1920s few had a radio, and its novelty and attraction ensured some early listening experiences were communal, since public houses, town halls, clubs and other organisations sometimes broadcast commentary over loudspeakers, to the huge annoyance of the evening press. At Oxford, mass listening in the street was initially 'a regular activity', especially of evening sports results and Saturday sporting events. There were still 'reasonable' crowds in the street for the Boat Race as late as 1937.[54] When the first rugby commentary was broadcast, Wakelam received a letter from the staff of a south Wales bank, unable to make the journey, saying that they had enjoyed themselves and learnt about the run of play as they gathered round a loud-speaker to 'support the National team'.[55] When Cardiff City reached the FA Cup final in 1927 thousands crammed the city centre to listen on specially erected loudspeakers, and others stood outside wireless shops.[56] Police some-times had to break up large crowds holding up traffic. In 1929 radio-engineers on board the Flying Scot were able to receive Derby commentary, letting travellers know the result as it happened. But such communal involvement in sport, whilst fairly common in the 1920s, declined with increased set owner-ship, and listening to sport became a more home and family-centred pursuit in the 1930s.

It is clear that radio opened up sport to the house-bound, supporters who could not afford or were otherwise unable to travel to national events and casual listeners. As Scannell and Cardiff have pointed out, radio 'admitted listeners to public events, to their live presence, in a way no previous technol-ogy had been able to do'.[57] Letters from the blind and infirm regularly thanked the BBC. A London listener wrote that 'an invalid blind boy whom we visit told us that he was able by listening to the running commentary to get a better idea of the football matches than seeing brothers who went in person'. A Stockport man suffering long-term ill-health wrote that 'to one who has played the game and taken a great interest in sport, you can quite understand the great pleasure your minute description of the games has given to me. May I just mention the Arsenal club and directors to thank them for allowing the broadcasting and I can tell them they have thousands of supporters and well-wishers in the north'.[58] Such letters showed how radio extended the fan base, predating the better-recognised impact of television in eroding local loyalties.

Certainly, by bringing together the classes to listen to commentary, the BBC aided the promotion of social unity rather than rivalry. But such arguments cannot be stretched too far. The BBC coverage of sport by no means fully overcame the persistent class, gender, regional and national differences which characterised inter-war Britain in terms of the nature and extent of sporting preferences.[59] It needs to be remembered that in 1937 London (73% of families), the West (76%) and the Midlands (76%) all had substantially larger proportions of licence payers than northern England (66%), Wales (58%), Scotland (59%) and Northern Ireland (37%).[60] It is also worth emphasising that while surveys and viewers' letters, especially amongst the working classes, were positive about BBC sports coverage, variety and concert parties, light orchestral, military and dance music were all far more popular amongst the *Daily Mail* listeners who voted in a 1927 survey.[61] By

1935–36 Seebohm Rowntree's survey of York found that variety shows and sports, especially racing, were the most popular of the programmes provided by the local Relay Company.[62] Listeners felt they were actually 'at' the event. Some women who had hitherto showed little interest in sport found commentaries interesting, and were 'thrilled' by them, whether or not they fully understood the rules. Listening to broadcasts, like watching sport on the newsreels, generally increased women's interest in sport. Boxing proved popular with women, but only to listen to, not to watch.[63] Middle-class women, who often listened to the radio, could have had their interest in some sports encouraged by radio discussions and commentary. The 1939 Bristol University survey also suggested keen working-class interest in radio sport, and many 'always listened' to sports they had never actually seen.[64] The BBC's own Listener Research Committee, which produced its first report in 1937, identified sport as having an impact on viewers. A 1938 random sample, for example, included some limited exploration of audience tastes. Correspondents were asked which they 'liked' of 21 categories of programmes, including cricket commentaries (the only sport featured). Variety, theatre and cinema organ, military and dance music were all more popular than cricket, which came exactly midway, chosen by 49 per cent of the sample, liked by about two-thirds of the men but only a third of women. Regional differences were also important. Cricket commentary was much less liked in Scotland and Northern Ireland.[65] A BBC 1939 questionnaire survey showed that the Boat Race, previously of interest mainly to Londoners and exuniversity students, was now liked by 70 per cent of the audience panel. 51 per cent liked boxing, and 50 per cent liked cricket and soccer. Lawn tennis and horseracing were only liked by 34 and 33 per cent respectively.[66] Even so the growing popularity of tennis is suggestive of a change of attitude, while all horseracing's leading events took place on weekdays, as did almost all of Wimbledon, so were less likely to have been heard by those in work. In general working-class sample members liked sport more than middle-class ones, especially soccer and boxing. There were regional differences too. The Welsh liked rugby union more than other areas, the North and Midlands liked soccer more than the average, while rugby league also had a hold on the North. The London region liked the boat race and speedway more than the average.

## The Art of Commentary

How far did the BBC succeed in being 'inclusive'? Here again, it was only partially, since commentators faced ambiguities and tensions in catering for different types of listener. H. B. Wakelam (an ex-Harlequins wing-forward who had umpired at Wimbledon), who broadcast *inter alia* on rugby, cricket and tennis from 1927 right through to 1939, and wrote widely on broadcasting, felt that while the more experienced wanted the 'finer and more intricate points', others merely wished 'to be entertained'.[67] BBC letters and interviews confirmed this. A woman told one interviewer that 'a fight is more exciting on the wireless than when you are actually there'; a blacksmith 'liked a good fight commentary'; but a Leeds advertising clerk believed that while more boxing match commentaries would please him, 'some of the commentators on the fights you do broadcast are not good enough – not detailed and not technical enough'.[68] Wakelam felt there were key 'techniques'. Firstly, commentary should use the plain, simple, everyday language of conversation. Some new listeners would need clarification and explanation of the game. Being too technical was a serious fault, as only about ten per cent would understand. Secondly, continuity should always be maintained. An early handbook described George Allison, a man whose dimensions extended 'chiefly sideways', at the 1927 Derby, leaning out from the roof and held by a burly BBC staffer. He continued commentating furiously about the reception of the winner while a colleague went to the unsaddling enclosure.[69]

If sports commentaries did unite Britain they did so largely on the BBC's terms, mediated through the subjective discourses of BBC commentators. The latter were largely male sports journalists, former top amateur players and administrators, a fairly homogeneous group, almost all 'gentlemen' in terms of education (generally public school and university), social background and attitudes. Any detailed sporting knowledge was derived from their fairly upper-middle-class backgrounds. So commentary generally put across norms of amateurism and sportsmanship through its subjects, presenters and comments. It reflected the sporting values more of the *Daily Mail, Times* or *Daily Express* than the *Sporting Life*. Harold Abrahams (the former Cambridge student and Olympic medal winner) was one of several successful commentators who survived through the 1930s. Others included Bernard Darwin (former leading amateur golfer), Geoffrey Gilbey (racing journalist), Col. R. H. Brand (a member of the BBC, but a tennis tournament player and umpire) and Lionel Seccombe (an ex-heavyweight boxer and Oxford blue). Thomas Woodrooffe, an experienced microphone speaker, and former naval officer, who began commentating on racing, soccer, and very occasionally, cricket in the later 1930s, became famous for supposedly eating his hat after claiming, during the 1938 Cup Final, 'If there's a goal scored now I'll eat my hat'. Women rarely broadcast on sport, although Vera Lennox contributed to the first ever 1926 Derby broadcast to add fashion colour, and there were similar contributions to some later races, especially once Ascot was covered. But in the 1930s a few female sports experts began to commentate. The former player Mrs Elizabeth Ryan, for example, commentated on a women's singles match at Wimbledon in 1935.

Commentary speech usually adopted 'received pronunciation', subtly reinforcing national norms and emphasising class structure, since such accents were not always popular with working-class listeners, reinforcing what the 1928 *BBC Handbook* called 'fluency and a good voice'. By 1938 the BBC consensus seemed to be that voices should be 'straightforward, class and accentless', as far as possible, although Wakelam felt that accurate facts, knowledge and coherent, comprehensive speech were far more important than purity of accent and cadence.[70]

A peculiarly British style of commentary also emerged. Unlike American broadcasts, there was rarely exaggeration, over-dramatisation or over-excitement. The predominant style was factual, realistic, un-heroic, and less noisy and fast paced than today. Accuracy and sportsmanship was seen as more important than dramatic enhancement. Raymond Glendenning, who commentated on sport from the mid-1930s, argued that reporters must talk about 300 words a minute, but 'convey only genuine excitement. For this the test is: does the pace and pitch of his delivery match the variation in the background of the roar of the crowd'.[71] A conversational style predominated, although the number of words a minute slowly increased. Right through the inter-war period hesitations were still quite common in commentaries even by 'leading' commentators, and individuals or horses were sometimes clearly confused and wrongly identified. Many mistakes were made, especially in fast-paced sports. Commentators generally praised play, and critical analysis was brief, found during summing up or half-time comments. Terse, literal descriptions as a game unfolded, delivered with an emphasis on fairness and good sportsmanship, were common features. Many commentators moved soberly between literal reporting and a momentary and hardly perceptible excitement, and cricket commentaries still had a somewhat cold-blooded neutrality in the late 1930s.

Nevertheless, commentators did sometimes sound excited. During one early commentary on the Grand National, the commentator reportedly had backed a strongly fancied runner, and as his horse entered the straight he shouted it home for all his worth. Listening millions heard only the commentator's frantic and repeated cries of 'Come on my beauty!' in the final seconds.[72] Harold Abrahams was so excited when his friend Jack Lovelock was winning the 1500 yards at the Berlin Olympics, that he forgot the microphone and shouted exhortations to 'Come on Jack', and 'My God, he's done it. . . . Hooray!' There were letters of abuse to the BBC, but many letters of appreciation too.[73] George Allison, the football commentator, succeeded in balancing reporting with unbridled enthusiasm, even if occasional cries from the heart alerted listeners to the side he was on.[74] Allison regularly reflected on his commentaries and felt he tried to keep 'a steely grip on his enthusiasm', while conveying excitement through his voice, in 'a way which conveys to the listener a mental photograph of what is taking place'.[75] But his commentaries were occasionally sprinkled with exhortations to players to shoot, pass or tackle, and cries of excitement, such as 'By Jove'. He occasionally drank port, to soothe his throat during commentary, and later even admitted that he sometimes invented action to keep the listener interested during boring games.[76]

## Conclusion

There is little debate about the fact that radio helped a handful of major sporting events to join the list of approved patriotic moments singled out as worthy of national broadcasting, creating an annual calendar of leading events for listeners to anticipate.[77] Many were keen to hear these, and listening conveyed a sense of immediacy, excitement and vicarious participation in what were powerfully symbolic spectacles, at some of which the royal family attended. Such events already generated widespread public interest even before the advent of radio, and the major example of an event boosted nationally by radio was the Boat Race, formerly most popular in London and the university towns. It became more widely popular as a spring listening occasion. Jennings and Gill quoted one informant as saying, 'We never used to hear anything about that, and now there's many wouldn't miss it'.[78]

Did broadcasting generate wider interest and attendance in sport, as some have claimed?[79] Certainly at least one sports historian has suggested that football and horseracing achieved 'enormous popularity between the wars, due in part to their promotion through the sporting press and increasingly through the medium of radio'.[80] There is little evidential support for such a position. Football received quite limited BBC coverage in the 1930s, and demands for FA Cup Final tickets were regularly substantially oversubscribed well before its first broadcast. In general, variations in football attendance merely mirrored teams' playing success and local economic conditions. Crowds at race-meetings in the 1930s were generally less, not more, than in the early 1920s. Any changes in attendance largely mirrored the national economy, not radio coverage.[81] Equally there was no firm evidence that broadcasting negatively affected attendance at sporting events elsewhere, while broadcasting the Rugby League Cup Final did not fill Wembley. In general, working-class support for horseracing in the summer and football in the winter was not adversely affected by BBC coverage of a wider range of Saturday sports, while betting on horseracing, the football pools and greyhounds significantly increased despite the BBC's aversion to betting information.

What does sports coverage say about the emergence of a common culture, or a middle-brow culture more generally, which D. L. LeMahieu has detected in several cultural institutions, including the BBC? While Ross McKibbin has argued that there was 'no common culture, but rather a series of overlapping cultures', McKibbin accepts LeMahieu's point in so far as if there was a democratic culture between the wars, it was the culture of the new middle class of London, its suburbs and their equivalents elsewhere.[82] The British as a whole, and particularly the middle classes, were regularly represented in contemporary discourse as an exceptionally sports-loving people. The breadth of BBC coverage in the 1930s reflects this. Outright condemnations of sport surfaced rarely, even amongst those writers, artists and intellectuals who loathed sport, although absence of *Listener* comment is almost certainly significant, and there was a more generalised, and somewhat ambiguous, intellectual contempt from F. R. Leavis and others for many of the new patterns of leisure consumption.[83] Sport was certainly not 'high-brow'. But given sport's popularity, it could be argued that BBC radio, a major cultural force, pursued British middle-brow culture and taste in difficult times by largely transmitting a middle-class vision of British sport, a vision which also shaped BBC commentaries. The most popular working-class spectator sports, league football and greyhound racing, were not covered in the 1930s, and betting was ignored. At the same time however, BBC broadcasts provided a hybrid discourse, catering for provincial as well as metropolitan listeners and so regularly covering some more working-class regional as well as 'national' sports events, although the nature of 'national' sports coverage, despite forays into home nation soccer and rugby internationals, largely remained resolutely Anglo- centred and indeed metropolitan-centred. Such potentially divisive strands might be seen as threatening middle-brow culture.

Finally, it is worth reminding ourselves of Alison Light's influential argument that national identity became more feminised and domesticated from the 1920s.[84] Did BBC sports coverage further this? If so it can only have been to a very limited extent. National sporting events remained hugely popular with spectators. Certainly people listened to Saturday sport more at home than communally by the 1930s, but the BBC broadcasts do not seem to have kept male spectators at home. Surveys suggest some increased interest from women listeners, but they largely listened to accounts of men playing. Sport remained firmly associated with masculinity between the wars.

## Notes

1.  Oriard, *King Football*, 39–49. McCoy, 'Radio Sports Broadcasting in the United States, Britain and Australia', 20.
2.  *The Wireless Age*, July 1921, 10; *The Wireless Age*, August 1921, 11–21 has a full account.
3.  Hilliard and Keith, *The Broadcast Century*, 26; Sies, *Encyclopaedia of American Radio*, 531–2. See also Holmes, *Only Connect*; Sterling and Kitross, *Stay Tuned*; Smith, *Voices of the Game*; Smith, *Voices of Summer*. Halberstam, *Sports on New York Radio*.
4.  McCoy, 'Radio sports broadcasting', 22.
5.  Pine, *2RN and the Origins of Irish Radio*.
6.  Hayes, 'There's many a slip', 143–156. For the links between Irish radio and sport see Boyle 'From our Gaelic fields' 623–636.
7.  Nicholas, 'The People's Radio'; Huggins and Williams, *Sport and the English 1918–1939*, 24–41.
8.  Scannell and Cardiff, *Serving the Nation*; McKibbin, *Classes and Cultures*. Hill, *Sport, Leisure and Culture* relies largely on secondary sources for radio sport.
9.  Briggs, *History of Broadcasting*, Vol. 2, 119; Pegg, *Broadcasting and Society* 1918–1939.
10. Scannell and Cardiff, *Serving the Nation*, 278.
11. Pegg, *Broadcasting and Society 1918–1939*, 214.
12. See Crisell, *An Introductory History of British Broadcasting*, 8.

13. Sir F Sykes (chair), *Report of the Broadcasting Committee*, Command Paper 1951 (London: HMSO, 1923). See Nicholas, 'All the News that Fit to Broadcast'.
14. Briggs, *The History of Broadcasting in the United Kingdom*, Vol. 1, .264.
15. Glendenning, 'Race broadcasting', 225.
16. Fyfe, 'The Way they Have in America II: Broadcasting Football', *Radio Times*, 7 January 1927.
17. Quoted in Scannell and Cardiff, 'Serving the nation', 180–81.
18. Wakelam, *Half Time*, 187.
19. Cardiff, 'Time, money and culture', 373–393.
20. The *Birmingham Weekly Post*, 29 January 1927 summarised the 'general opinion' as 'extremely favourable'. For listeners' letters see *Radio Times*, 28 January 1927.
21. *Times*, 17 January 1927.
22. *Field*, 20 January 1927.
23. *Radio Times*, 8 April 1927.
24. Good, *Good Days*, 176–183 describes his commentary.
25. *Times*, 4 April 1927.
26. *Radio Times*, 15 April 1927.
27. Scannell and Cardiff, *Serving the Nation*, 277.
28. *Manchester Guardian*, 27 June 1932.
29. Pegg, *Broadcasting and Society 1918–1939*, 214.
30. 'Oxney match', T8529WR R C9, British Library sound Archive.
31. Quoted in Pegg, *Broadcasting and Society*, 138.
32. Briggs, *History of Broadcasting in the United Kingdom*, Vol. 2, 158. Mackay and Andrews, eds, *Sports Report Number 2*.
33. *Daily Sketch*, 25 January 1937.
34. *The Times*, 28 April 1930.
35. Wakelam's view in *Rugby Football*, 212.
36. Huggins, *Horseracing and the British 1919–1939*, 69–125 provides the most recent and detailed treatment of racehorse betting during this period. Clapson, *A Bit of a Flutter* has useful chapters on the pools and greyhound racing.
37. Huggins, *Horseracing and the British*, 89–93.
38. E.G. Galtrey, *Memoirs of a Racing Journalist*, 296.
39. *The Times*, 24 April 1929.
40. *Bloodstock Breeders Review*, Vol. 24 (1937), 272.
41. See Fishwick, *English Football and Society 1910–1950*, Chapter 5 for detailed discussion.
42. *All Sports Weekly* 26 March 1927.
43. McCoy, 'Radio sports broadcasting', 23.
44. *Radio Times*, 17 April 1931.
45. *BBC Yearbook*, 1930, 143.
46. Wakelam, *Half Time*, 236.
47. *Radio Times*, 28 March 1930.
48. *The Times*, 2 April 1930.
49. See Huggins, 'Projecting the visual'.
50. *BBC Annual 1936*, 57.
51. Williams, *Cricket and the English*.
52. Sissons and Stoddart, *Cricket and Empire*, 114. Cassman, *Ave A Go Yer Mug*, provides a useful analysis of the relationship between crowds and radio. During the 1932/33 bodyline tour two Parisian stations broadcast a synthetic commentary on the tests to British listeners, one using former player Alan Fairfax as commentator, but reception in Britain was often poor.
53. *Daily Telegraph*, 25 June 1928.
54. Pegg, *Broadcasting and Society*, 175.

55. Wakelam, ed., *The Game Goes On*, 174.
56. *South Wales Echo*, 25 April 1927, quoted in Martin Johnes, *Soccer and Society: South Wales, 1900–1936*, 163.
57. Scanell and Cardiff, *Serving the Nation*, 278.
58. *Radio Times*, 17 April 1931.
59. See Huggins and Williams, *Sport and the English*.
60. *BBC Handbook, 1938*, 49. But not everybody bought a licence, and in Northern Ireland some Catholics refused to pay.
61. Quoted in Pegg, *Broadcasting and Society*, 108.
62. Rowntree, *Poverty and Progress*, 409–10.
63. Beddoe, *Back to Home and Duty*, 129–31.
64. Jennings and Gill, *Broadcasting in Everyday Life*, 33–38.
65. Quoted in Pegg, *Broadcasting and Society*, 139.
66. Interim report, 16 and 28 April 1939, quoted in Pegg, *Broadcasting and Society*, 128.
67. *Radio Times*, 10 April 1931.
68. *Radio Times*, 24 March 1939.
69. *The BBC Handbook 1928*, 144–5.
70. Smithers, *Broadcasting from Within*, 17. Wakelam, *Half Time*, 335.
71. Glendenning, 'Race broadcasting', 229.
72. Rickman, *Come Racing with Me*, 25.
73. Abrahams, 'Athletic roundup 1924–1954', 42.
74. Maine, *The BBC and its Audience*, 91.
75. *Radio Times*, 10 April 1931.
76. Allison, *Allison Calling*, 37–52.
77. See for example, Holt, *Sport and the British*, 311–4.
78. Jennings and Gill, *Broadcasting in Everyday Life*, 33.
79. Briggs, *Golden Age of Wireless*, 121; Jennings and Gill, *Broadcasting in Everyday Life*, 38; Pegg, *Broadcasting and Society*, 215.
80. Wigglesworth, *The Evolution of English Sport*, 40.
81. Huggins, *Horseracing and British Society 1919–1939*.
82. McKibbin, *Classes and Cultures*, 327. LeMahieu, *A Culture for Democracy.* 230–31.
83. Leavis, *Mass Civilisation and Minority Culture.* See Carey, *The Intellectual and the Masses.*
84. Light, Forever England.

## References

Abrahams, Harold. 'Athletic roundup 1924–1954'. In *Sports Report Number 2*, edited by Angus Mackay, and Eamonn Abrahams. London: William Heinemann, 1954.
Allison, George. *Allison Calling*. London: 1948.
Beddoe, Deirdre. *Back to Home and Duty: Women Between the Wars 1918–1939*. London: 1989.
Boyle, R. 'From our Gaelic Fields: Radio, Sport and Nationalism in Post-partition Ireland'. *Media, Culture and Society* 14 (1992): 623–636.
Briggs, Asa. *The History of Broadcasting in the United Kingdom*. Vol. 1, *The Birth of Broadcasting*. London: 1961.
———. *History of Broadcasting in the United Kingdom*. Vol. 2, *The Golden Age of Wireless*. London: Oxford University Press, 1965.
Cardiff, D. 'Time, Money and Culture: BBC Programme Finances 1927–1939'. *Media, Culture and Society* 5 (1983): 373–393.
Carey, Peter. *The Intellectual and the Masses: Pride and Prejudice amongst the Literary Intelligentsia 1880–1939*. London: Faber & Faber, 1992.

Cassman, Richard. *Ave A Go Yer Mug: Australian Cricket Crowds from Larrikin to Ocker.* Sydney: Collins, 1994.

Clapson, Mark. *A Bit of a Flutter: Popular Gambling in England 1823–1961.* Manchester: Manchester University Press, 1992.

Crisell, Andrew. *An Introductory History of British Broadcasting.* London: Routledge, 1997.

Fishwick, Nicholas. *English Football and Society 1910–1950.* Manchester: Manchester University Press, 1989.

Fyfe, Hamilton. 'The Way they Have in America II: Broadcasting Football'. *Radio Times,* 7 January 1927.

Galtrey, Sydney. *Memoirs of a Racing Journalist.* London: Hutchinson, 1934.

Glendenning, Raymond. 'Race Broadcasting'. In *Flat Racing Since 1900*, edited by Earnest Bland. London: Andrew Dakers, 1950.

Good, Meyrick. *Good Days.* London: Hutchinson, 1941.

Halberstam, David. *Sports on New York Radio.* New York: McGraw Hill, 1999.

Hayes, Richard. 'There's many a slip 'twixt the eye and the lip: An exploratory history of football broadcasting and running commentaries on BBC radio 1927–1939". *International Review for the Sociology of Sport* 34, no. 2 (1999): 143–56.

Hill, Jeffrey. *Sport, Leisure and Culture in Twentieth Century Britain.* Basingstoke: Palgrave, 2002.

Hilliard, R., and M. C. Keith. *The Broadcast Century and Beyond.* Boston: Focal Press, 2001.

Holmes, Michele. *Only Connect: A Cultural History of Broadcasting in the United States.* Belmont CA: Wadsworth, 2000.

Huggins, Mike. *Horseracing and the British 1919–1939.* Manchester: Manchester University Press, 2003.

———. *Williams Jack. Sport and the English 1918–1939.* London: Routledge, 2005.

———. 'Projecting the Visual: British Newsreels, Soccer and Popular Culture 1918–1939'. *International Journal of the History of Sport*, (forthcoming).

Jennings, H., and W. Gill. *Broadcasting in Everyday Life: A Study of the Social Effects of the Coming of Broadcasting.* London: BBC, 1939.

Leavis, F. R. *Mass Civilisation and Minority Culture.* Cambridge University Press, 1938.

LeMahieu, D. L. *A Culture for Democracy: Mass Communication and the Cultivated Mind in Britain Between the Wars.* Oxford: Clarendon Press, 1988.

Light, Alison. *Forever England: Femininity, Literature and Consumerism Between the Wars.* London: Routledge, 1991.

Mackay, Angus, and Eamonn Andrews, eds. *Sports Report Number 2.* London: William Heinemann, 1954.

Maine, Basil. *The BBC and its Audience.* London: Nelson, 1939.

McCoy, J. 'Radio Sports Broadcasting in the United States, Britain and Australia, 1920–1956 and its influence on the Olympic Games'. *Journal of Olympic History* 5 (1997): 20–25.

McKibbin, Ross. *Classes and Cultures: England 1918–1951.* Oxford: OUP, 1998.

Nicholas, Sian. 'The People's Radio: The BBC and its Audience 1939–45'. In *Millions Like Us? British Culture in the Second World War*, edited by Nick Hayes, and Jeff Hill. Liverpool: Liverpool University Press, 1999.

———. 'All the News that Fit to Broadcast: The Popular Press versus the BBC 1922–45'. In *Northcliffe's Legacy: Aspects of the British Popular Press 1896–1996*, edited by Catterall Peter, Seymour-Ure Colin, and Smith Adrian. Basingstoke: McMillan, 2000.

Oriard, Michael. *King Football: Sport and Spectacle in the Golden Age of Radio and Newsreels, Movies and Magazines, the Weekly and the Daily Press.* Chapel Hill, NC: The University of North Carolina Press, 2001.

Pegg, Mark. *Broadcasting and Society 1918–1939.* Beckenham: Croom Helm, 1983.

Pine, Richard. *2RN and the Origins of Irish Radio.* Dublin: Five Courts Press, 2002.

Rickman, Eric. *Come Racing with Me.* London: Chatto & Windus, 1951.

Rowntree, B. S. *Poverty and Progress: A Second Social Survey of York*. London: 1941.

Scannell, P., and D. Cardiff. 'Serving the nation: Public service broadcasting before the war'. In *Popular Culture Past and Present*, edited by B. Waites, A. Bennett, and G. Thompson. London: 1981.

———. Cardiff David. *Serving the Nation: A Social History of British Broadcasting*. Vol. I, *1922–1939*. Oxford: Basil Blackwell, 1991.

Sies, Luther F. *Encyclopaedia of American Radio 1920–1960*. Jefferson, NC: McFarland, 2000.

Sissons, R., and Brian Stoddart. *Cricket and Empire*. London: George Allen & Unwin, 1984.

Smith, Curt. *Voices of the Game*. New York: Simon & Schuster, 1992.

———. *Voices of Summer: Baseball's Greatest Announcers*. New York: Carroll and Grif, 2005.

Smithers, S. W. *Broadcasting from Within*. London: Isaac Pitman, 1938.

Sterling, S. H., and J. M. Kitross. *Stay Tuned: A History of American Broadcasting*. Mahwah, NJ: Lawrence Erlbaum, 2002.

Wakelam, Capt. H. R. B., ed. *The Game Goes On*. London: Arthur Barker, 1936.

Wakelam, Capt. H. R. B. *Rugby Football*. London: J.M. Dent, 1936.

———. *Half Time: The Mike and Me*. London: Thomas Nelson, 1938.

Wigglesworth, A. *The Evolution of English Sport*. London: Frank Cass, 1996.

Williams, Jack. *Cricket and the English*. London: Frank Cass, 1999.

# 15

# The Interdependence of Sport and Culture

*Günther Lüschen*

## Introduction

S port is a rational, playful activity in interaction, which is extrinsically rewarded. The more it is rewarded, the more it tends to be work; the less, the more it tends to be play[1]. If we describe it in an action system frame of reference, this activity depends on the organic, personality, social, and cultural systems. By tradition, physical education has tried to explain this action system largely on the grounds of the organic system, sometimes making references to the personality system. Only on rare occasions it has been approached systematically from the social and cultural systems as well Yet is seems obvious that any action going on in this system is to be explained with reference to all of the sub-systems of the action system.

Even such a simple motor activity as walking is more than a matter of organic processes initiated by the personality system. It is determined by the social and cultural systems as well as is most evident, in the way the Israelians from the Yemen walk. Since in their former society, in the Yemen, the Jews were the outcasts, and every Yemenite could feel free to hit a Jew (whenever he could get hold of one), the Yemenitic Jew would always run in order to escape this oppression. This way of walking finally became an integrated pattern of his culture. And though the environment in Israel no longer is hostile to him, the Yemenitic Israelite still carries this pattern with him as part of his culture and walks in a shy and hasty way.

**Source:** *International Review for the Sociology of Sport,* 2(1) (1967): 127–139.

This example shows in addition that the different subsystems of action are not independent from one another, they are structurally related. Thus, in dealing with the cultural system of sport and its interdependence with general culture, we will not always be able to explain the culture of sport and that of its environment in terms of the cultural system, and therefore should refer as well to the social and personality system to describe and explain what we call culture. It was Radcliffe-Brown who stressed the point that culture should be explained through its social structure. Furthermore, one should discuss the function of a unit within general culture, as well as cultural process and change[2].

## Concepts of Culture and Review of Results

Culture as a concept does not refer to behavior itself. It deals with those patterns and abstractions that underlie behavior or are the result of it. Thus culture exists of cognitive elements which grow out of every day or scientific experience. It consists of beliefs, values, norms, and of signs, that include symbols of verbal as well as non-verbal communication[3].

Anthropologists have sometimes held a broader view of culture and given more attention to the material results of human behavior. Leslie White in a critique of the above-stated concept of culture has called for more attention to "acts, thoughts and things dependent upon symboling". These would include not only the study of the above-mentioned elements, but also those of art, tools, machines, fetishes, etc.[4]. As attractive as White's critique may be, especially for cultural anthropology as an independent science, this approach as related to the cultural study of sports has led more to mere curiosity about things than to theoretical insights. This methodological approach has also dealt more with the cultural diffusion of sport and games than with the social structure of which they are a part. For decades we have learned about all types of games in all types of societies (especially primitive ones), which may well lead to the conclusion that we know more about the games and sports displayed by some Polynesian tribe than those of our own children and ancestors. For an understanding of sport it is less important to find the same games in different cultures as Tylor did[5]. It is more important to analyse for example the different meaning of baseball in the United States and Lybia, which in the one culture has ritualistic functions, while it has also economic functions in the other[6].

Another concept of culture, mainly held in Central Europe, has almost led to the same results for sport. In this concept "higher" culture was separated from civilization and expressed itself significantly in the arts and sciences. On the basis of values attributed to sport a priori, it was related either to "Zivilisation" or to "Kultur"[7]. Physical educationalists through Huizinga's theory on the origin of culture in play saw in the latter approach their main support[8]. Thus defining sport as a special form of play, physical educationalists felt safe in their implicit attempt to justify sport for educational purposes. Yet Huizinga's theory has not only been criticized on the basis of ethnological findings[9], but he himself was very critical about the play-element in sport[10]. Those that believed in the role of sport within higher culture were hardly able to prove their hypothesis. So, as recently René Maheu[11], they often expressed their hope that sport in the future would contribute to "Kultur".

One can hardly deny that sport has indeed some impact on "higher" culture, as may be shown by symbolic elements from sport to be found in script and language. In an analysis of the cultural meaning of the ball-game of the Aztecs and Maya, Krickeberg found that in their script there were elements related to this game. The symbol for movement, for example was identical with the I-shape of the ball-court[12]. "To get (take) a rain-check" refers to baseball, but has now become in American English symbolic for any situation where you get another chance. "That's not cricket" refers to a dishonest procedure in everyday life. And though German is not as idiomatic as English, it contains elements which originated in sport and games as well. "Katzbalgerei", and the phrase "sich gegenseitig die Bälle zuspielen", refer to a game which today is still known in the Netherlands as "Kaatsen" and perhaps appears in the New York children's game of one-o-cat. As did football in Shakespeare's *King Lear,* so appeared this game and its terminology in the 16th century poetry of J. G. Fischart[13].

How weak the relationships of sport to "higher" culture indeed are, may be shown by the relatively unsuccessful attempts to establish, through special contests in modern Olympics, a relationship between sport and the arts. Sport only rarely expresses itself in the material aspects of culture. It is, what I would like to call a momentary activity.

Just from a certain level on may an event have its appearance on such a short-range cultural element as the sports page of the next day's newspaper[14]. This appearance of sport in the media of mass communication, in language, poetry, and the arts is significant for the overall meaning of sport within society, but these manifestations tell us little about sport itself and its interdependence with general culture as we define it.

It may also be interesting to discuss cognitive elements such as scientific insight coming out of sport. Also religious beliefs and ritual found in sport would be an interesting point of analysis. Yet showing how sport is indeed bound to society and structured by general culture, we will mainly discuss our problem on the level of cultural values and their related social structure.

## Sport as Part of Culture and Society

That sport is structurally related to culture and society has sometimes been questioned. Yet it is quite easy to show how strong this relationship is. Sport is indeed an expression of that socio-cultural system in which it occurs. David Riesman and Reuel Denny describe how American Football was changed through the American culture from rugby to a completely different game. It is now well integrated and quite obviously shows in its vigor, its hard contact and greater centrality on the individual, the basic traits of the culture of American society[15].

On the level of the so-called primitive societies we see the same dependence of sport and games on culture and its underlying social structure. The Hopi Indians had 16 differents terms for foot races which nearly all referred to one aspect of the social organization of that tribe[16]. A recent socio-historical study on three Illinois subcultures finds the same close relationship between socio-cultural system and sport[17]. And Käte Hye-Kerkdal outlines the tight structural relation between the log-races of the tribe of the Timbira in Brazil and their socio-cultural system. This ritualistic competition between two teams has symbolic meaning for nearly every aspect of the dual-organization of this tribe. It refers to all kinds of religious and social polarities and is so strongly imbedded in this religious-dominated system that winning or losing does not have any effect on the status of the team or individual, nor are there any other extrinsic rewards. Yet these races are performed vigorously and with effort[18].

Now that we have proven that there is a structural relationship between sport and culture, the first question is that of sport's dependency on culture. What factors make for the appearance of sport? Or more specifically, what are the underlying cultural values?

## Cultural Values and Sport

By values we mean those general orientations in a socio-cultural system that are not always obvious to its members, but are implicit in actual behavior. On the level of the personality system they are expressed partly in attitudes. Values should be separated from, norms which are derived from values and are actual rules for behavior. For instance, health is a high value in the American culture as it seems to be in all young cultures, while death is higher in the hierarchy of values in old cultures like India[19]. On this continuum we may explain why sport as an expression of the evaluation of health is more important in American than Indian society. The whole emphasis on physical fitness in the United States may well be explained by this background, and the norm "run for your life" is directly related to it.

### Sport, Industrialization and Technology

In comparing the uneven distribution and performance level of sport all over the world, one widely accepted hypothesis is that sport is an offspring of technology and industrialization. The strong emphasis on sport in industrialized societies seems to show that industrialization and technology are indeed a basis for sport. This would be a late confirmation of Ogburn's theory of social change, as well as of the Marxian theory that society and its structure depend on its economic basis. However there are quite a number of inconsistencies. Not all sport-oriented societies or societal sub-systems show a relation to technology and industrialization, and historically games and sport have been shown to have existence prior to industrialization. Yet it can hardly be denied that certain conditions in the later process of industrialization have promoted sport; and technology has at least its parallels in modern sport. The above-stated hypothesis may, despite its obvious limitations ead us to the independent variable.

## Sport, a Protestant Sub-Culture?

In an investigation that because of its methodological procedure turned out to be a profound critique of Marxian materialism, Max Weber studied the interrelationship of what he called "The Protestant Ethic and the Spirit of Capitalism"[20]. This investigation about the underlying values of capitalism in Western societies quoted data on the overrepresentation of Protestants in institutions of higher learning, their preference for industrial and commercial occupations and professions, and the stronger trend towards capitalism in Protestant-dominated countries (most obvious in the United States). Weber found not the material basis but Protestant culture, with achievement of worldly success and asceticism held as the basic values, caused industrialization and capitalism. In accordance with the Calvinistic belief in predestination the Protestant felt that he was blessed by God once he had achieved success. Thus, need for achievement became an integrated part of his personality and a basic value in Protestantism. Together with the value of asceticism this led to the accumulation of wealth and to Western capitalism. If we turn to sport, we find the same values of achievement and asceticism. Even the Puritans, generally opposed to a leisure life, could therefore justify sport as physical activity that contributed to health[21].

Today we find significance for this relationship in the YMCA, in a group like the American Fellowship of Christian Athletes, and also in the Protestant minister who in Helsinki became an Olympic medal winner in the pole vault. He showed the consistency between Protestantism and sport in his prayer right after his Olympic winning vault. Max Weber's findings about the relationship between the Protestant ethic and the spirit of capitalism may thus well be extented to the "spirit" of sport. Not only Weber was aware of this relationship but also Thorstein Veblen who described the parallels in religious and sport ritual[22].

The relationship between sport and Protestantism is not only to be observed in the emphasis on sport in the Scandinavian and other Protestant countries. A rough compilation of the probable religious preference of Olympic medal winners on the basis of the percentage of different religious groups in their countries also shows the dominance of Protestantism up to 1960. Protestantism accounted for more than 50% of the medal winners, while its ratio among the world population is less than 8 per cent[23]. Furthermore, in 1958 a survey of young athletes in West Germany showed the following distribution according to religious preference (in %)[24]:

|  | Whole population West Germany | Sport Club-Members 15–25 | Track, Swimming | High Achievers Track/Swimming |
|---|---|---|---|---|
| Protestants | 52 | 60 | 67 | 73 |
| Catholics | 44 | 37 | 31 | 26 |
| Others | 4 | 3 | 2 | 1 |
| n = | universe | 1,880 | 366 | 111 |

These figures indicate the over-representation of Protestants in German sport. Moreover, they indicate a higher percentage in individual sports, and an even higher percentage of Protestants among those that have achieved a higher level of performance. Thus it may be concluded that there is a correlation between Protestantism and sport and the culture of both. This was obvious for individual sports, but less for team sports where in the German sample Catholics appeared quite often. Since in Catholicism collectivity is highly regarded, this inconsistency is to be explained by the value of collectivity in team sports. It is consistent with this hypothesis that Catholic Notre Dame University has been one of the innovators of football in America. At present, it is a leading institution in this discipline. And internationally Catholic-dominated South America is overall rather poor in individual sports, but outstanding in team sports like soccer and basketball.

This result on the overall, strong relationship between sport and Protestantism is, despite support by data, theoretically insufficient. As was the case with sport in its relationship to industrialization, there are many exceptions.

The high achievement in sport of the Russians, the Poles, the Japanese, the Mandan Indians, the Sikhs in India, or the Watusi in Africa can not be related to Protestantism, though in Japanese Zen-Buddhism there are parallels.

## The Centrality of the Achievement-Value

Since again Protestantism can not be specifically identified as being the independent variable, we may hypothesize that there is a more general system of values as the basis for Protestantism, capitalism, and sport. In his critique of Max Weber, D. C. McClelland has considered the ethic of Protestantism as a special case of the general achievement orientation of a system, this being the independent variable. Achievement orientation (or, as he puts it on the personality-system-level, need achievement) precedes all periods of high cultural achievement in ancient Greece, in the Protestant Reformation, in modern industrialism[25] – and, as we may conclude in modern sport. He referred in his analysis also to the related social structure of the achievement value, (such as family organization), which should also be studied in its relation to sport.

If we turn again to the cross-cultural comparison of those systems that participate and perform strongly in sport, we find that in all of these societies achievement-orientation is basic. In Russia this value is expressed in the norm that social status should depend only on achievement. The Sikhs and the Watusi are both minority groups in their environment. In order to keep their position, they have to achieve more than the other members of the societies they live in. The Japanese[26] and the Mandan Indians[27] also place a heavy emphasis on achievement.

Similar results appear in cross-cultural investigations of different types of games as related to basic orientations in the process of socialization. Roberts and Sutton-Smith find in a secondary analysis of the Human Relation Area Files of G. P. Murdock that games of chance are related to societies that emphasize routine responsibility in the socialization process. Games of strategy are found in societies where obedience, games of physical skill in those where achievement is stressed[28]. Individual sports would mainly qualify as games of physical skill and again show achievement as their basic cultural value. Team sports as well are games of strategy. Their relation to training of obedience would support exactly what we called earlier the value of collectivity.

It remains an open question, for further research into the value structure of sport, as to which other values are related to this system. It is to be expected that the structure of values will be more complex than it appears on the basis of our limited insight now. Roberts and Sutton-Smith briefly remark that games of physical skill are related to occupational groups that exert power over others[29]. Thus, power orientation may be another value supporting sport. This would cross-culturally be consistent with power oriented political systems that strongly emphasize sport. Here we could refer to countries like Russia or the United States, as well as to tribes like the Mandan Indians.

## The Culture of Societal Sub-Systems and Its Relation to Sport

Within a society we find sub-systems that have their own sub-culture, which will be another influence on sport. The female role in modern societies still depends on a culture that stresses obedience as the main value-orientation, while the male culture is strongly oriented towards achievement. Thus we find a disproportionately high participation of men in sport which in most of the disciplines is a male-culture. One of the most male-oriented sports however is pool, a game supported mainly by the subculture of the bachelor; it has, with the general change in the number of people marrying lost its main supporting culture[30].

Another subsystem which in its culture shows a strong relationship to sport is that of the adolescent age-group[31]. Sport is dependent more on the culture of the adolescent than on that of any other age-group. Helanko raises the point, referring to his studies of boys gangs in Turku, that sport has its origin in the gang-age and boys' gangs. The fact that there are no rules for early sports to be found is seen as one of the supporting factors[32]. Generally speaking, achievement is again more central as a value in adolescence and early adulthood than later, where the main response to sport goes not so much towards achievement but towards values of health and fitness.

The different social classes have a culture of their own. The greatest emphasis on achievement and thus the highest sport participation, is to be found in the upper middle class. It is considerably less important in the lower class where routine responsibility is valued. The notion that there is no way to gain higher status accounts for the high regard for games of chance or those sports where one may just have a lucky punch, as in boxing[33]. Loy has related the different types of games and the passive and active participation in sport to different modes of adaptation and to the members of social classes[34]. His theoretical analysis as to "innovation" found in the lower class, ritualism in the lower-middle class, and conformity in the upper-middle class is supported by data, that show the same ways of adaptation in sport[35]. However, in responding to the social class system and its culture as related to sport one should have in mind that class determined behavior may not follow the traditional class lines in sport. Sport may indeed show or promote new orientations in the class system[36].

Finally sport is organized within, or relates to different institutions, whose cultures sometimes have a profound influence on sport itself. This is especially true for physical education in schools where, with the same skills and rules, we may find a completely different culture as compared to sport in the military establishment. And while intercollegiate and interscholastic athletics are overall a surprisingly well integrated subculture within American schools and universities, the different values held by an educational (the school or university) and a solely success-oriented unit (the team) may well lead to strong value-conflicts. This could result in a complete separation of school and athletics[37].

## Functions and Dysfunctions

### The Functions of Sport within Culture and Society

After we have found achievement, asceticism in individual sports, obedience (collectivity) in team sports, and exertion of power the basic value orientations that give structure to this activity, we may then proceed to the second question: How does sport influence the socio-cultural system at large? Though we have little evidence through research, we may on the basis of structural-functional methodology be able to outline the basic functions of sport for pattern maintenance, integration, adaptation and goal attainment.

As in the case of the Timbira, Hye-Kerkdal states that through the log-race the basic values of that culture were learned. Furthermore, the participants were functionally integrated into the social system[38]. Thus we may hypothesize that the main functions of sport are for pattern maintenance and integration.

Since sport implies (as we saw) basic cultural values, it has the potential to pass these values on to its participants. We know at least from studies of the process of socialization that the exposure of children to competitive sport will cause these children to become achievement-motivated; the earlier this exposure occurs, the more achievement-motivated they become[39]. And the child's moral judgment may for instance, be influenced through games such as marbles. Again, according to Piaget, the child not only becomes socialized to the rules but he at a later age also gets an insight into the underlying structure and the function of the rules of a game, and thus into the structure and function of social norms and values as such[40]. Overall from the level of primitive societies to modern societies sport does not only socialize to the system of values and norms. In primitive societies it socializes towards adult and warfare skills as well[41].

Since we mentioned that sport is also structured along such societal subsystems as different classes, males, urban areas, schools, and communities, it functions for integration as well. This is obvious also in spectator sport, where the whole country or community identifies with its representatives in a contest. Thus, sport functions as a mean of integration, not only for the actual participants, but also for the represented members of such a system.

Sport in modern societies may as well function for goal-attainment on the national polity level. Sport in primitive societies functions besides for goal-attainment also for adaptation, since the sport skills of swimming, hunting, and fishing are used for the supply of food and mere survival.

## Possible Dysfunctions of Sport and Social Control

A question that should be raised at this point is whether sport is dysfunctional for culture and society as well. Th. W. Adorno has called sport an area of unfreedom ("ein Bereich der Unfreiheit")[42], by which he obviously referred to the differentiated code of rules which earlier led Huizinga to his statement that excluded sport from play[43]. Both seem to overlook what Piaget called the reciprocity and mutual agreement on which such rules rest[44]. And they may also be considered as an expression of a highly structured system.

Another dysfunctional element for culture and for the system of sport itself could be the centrality of achievement. It has such a high rank in the hierarchy of values of sport that, by definition, the actual objective performance of a member of this system will decide the status he gets. In the core of sport, in the contest on the sports-field there only is achieved status. It seems that there is no other system or any societal subsystem with the exception of combat where achievement ranks that high. It may create conflict once this value-orientation is imposed on the whole culture, and it may create conflict within the system of sport itself since its members bring other values into this system as well.

M. Mead in an investigation of competition and co-operation (the first concept of which is related to achievement) of primitive peoples, however, finds that there seems to be no society where one of these principles existed alone[45]. And on the micro-sociological level, small groups seem to control this value by discrimination against those that deviate from the group norm of a fair performance[46]. Thus one would notify some kind of a mechanism built into a social system that keeps it in a state of balance. Exactly this seems to happen within sport where the sporting groups themselves and their differentiated organizational and institutional environment perform social control in regard to those participants whose achievements surpass a certain level.

In a survey of sport club members in Germany, it was found that the norms expressed for the behavior of an athlete referred surprisingly less to the achievement-value, but very often to a value of affiliation, which is to be defined as a positive orientation towards other group members or opponents. Fair play was the one mentioned most frequently. The value of affiliation expressed by the respondents was found the more in normative statements the higher their level of performance. On the basis of the hypothesized mechanism of social control they are under stronger pressure to affiliate with others[47]. Similar results were found in a field experiment with two school classes[48]. This may explain (on the basis of this structural relationship) why in the culture of sport, we find not only the value of achievement but also that of fair play and other affiliative orientations.

However, achievement and affiliation may not necessarily be related. It depends on the amount of social control imposed on sport from the internal as well as external system, whether this relationship will be strong or weak. In professional boxing these controls are very weak, while in golf with the handicap-rule they seem to be comparatively strong.

How much this pattern would influence the culture as such is an open question. Yet it seems not so mis-oriented as Litt and Weniger thought when Oetinger stated that sport would provide a good model for political partnership[49]. We may on the basis of our findings hypothesize that also on the political level the amount of social control will decide whether two or more systems will co-exist or not.

## Change and Evolution

### Sport and Socio-Cultural Change

After we have discussed the culture and underlying social structure of sport and its function, we are left with Radcliff-Brown's third programmatic point – that of social and cultural change. We know little about the role of sport in socio-cultural change, though we hypothesized earlier that it may have a function of innovation, or at least structural relationship to changes in the system of social classes. Sport has also functioned as an initiator for the diffusion of technical inventions, such as the bicycle or the automobile[50]. The same holds true to a degree for conduct in regard to fashion and a healthy life. Typically, this question of change has been highly neglected so far.

## Sport and Cultural Evolution

If we finally try to explain the different cross-cultural appearance of sport on the basis of an evolutionary theory it is hard to justify on the basis of our present knowledge, about the appearance of sport that there are such things as primitive and developed cultures of sport. The Mandan Indians had a highly developed sport culture, the Australian aboriginals as perhaps the most primitive people known to us today knew quite a variety of recreational activities and physical skills, and the variety of competitive games in Europe and America in the past was probably richer than today.

An evolution can only be seen on a vertical level which on the one hand shows in a state of mechanic solidarity rather simple rules in sport and games, while in a state of organic solidarity as in modern industrialized societies the code of rules and the structure of games get more differentiated.

What we may furthermore state is, that on the level of primitive cultures sport's function is universal, often religious, collectivity oriented, and in the training of skills representative and related to adult and warfare skills, while modern sport's function may be called specific for pattern maintenance and integration, is individual oriented and in the training of skills non-representative. The rewards are more in-strinsic in primitive cultures, while they are more extrinsic in the sport of modern cultures. Thus, referring to our definition at the beginning, one may well differentiate between physical and recreational activities of primitive cultures and sport in modern cultures[51].

## Notes

1. I owe much of this definition to a discussion with my colleague, G. P. Stone, University of Minnesota.
2. A. R. Radcliffe-Brown, *Structure and Function in Primitive Society*, III, The Free Press, Glencoe, 1952.
3. This refers to a concept held by Kluckhohn/Kroeber and Talcott Parsons. For a general reference as to culture and the action frame of reference within structural-functionalism see H. M. Johnson, *Sociology: A Systematic Introduction.* Harcourt, Brace and World, New York 1960.
4. L. White, *The Concept of Culture.* In: "American Anthropologist". 61, 1959, p. 227–251.
5. Cf. E. B. Tylor, *On American Lot-Games.* In: "Internationales Archiv für Ethnographie" supplement 9. Leiden 1896, p. 55–67.
6. C. Gini, *Rural Ritual Games in Lybia.* In: "Rural Sociology", 4, 1939, p. 283–299.
7. Most significantly to be found in an unpublished lecture of C. Diem *Sport und Kultur*, 1942 at the University of Halle.

8. J. Huizinga, *Homo Ludens*. The Beacon Press, Boston 1955.

9. Cf. A. E. Jensen, *Spiel und Ergriffenheit*, "Paideuma", 3, 1942, p. 124–139.

10. J. Huizinga, *op. cit.* p. 196.

11. R. Maheu, *Sport and Culture*. In: "International Journal of Adult and Youth Education" 14, 1962, 4, p. 169–178.

12. W. Krickeberg, *Das mittelamerikanische Ballspiel und seine religiöse Symbolik*. In: "Paideuma", 3, 1944.

13. Cf. articles *Katzball* and *Katzenspiel*. In: J. Grimm and W. Grimm, *Deutsches Wörterbuch* 5. Hirtz, Leipzig 1873, p. 279 and 302.

14. For one of the few content-analyses of the special jargon of sport-language see P. H. Tannenbaum, and J. E. Noah, *Sportugese: A study of Sports Page Communication*. In: Journalism Quarterly 36, 1959, 2, p. 163–170.

15. D. Riesman and R. Denney. *Football in America*. In: D. Riesman, *Individualism Reconsidered*, III, Glencoe 1954, p. 242–251.

16. S. Culin, *Games of the North American Indians. 24th Annual Report*. Bureau of American Ethnology. Washington D. C. 1907, p. 801.

17. Ph. J. Hill, *A Cultural History of Frontier Sport in Illinois 1673–1820*. Unpl. PhD-Thesis. University of Illinois, 1966.

18. K. K. Hye-Kerkdal, *Wettkampfspiel und Dualorganisation bei den Timbira Brasiliens*. In: J. Haekel (ed.). *Die Wiener Schule der Völkerkunde*. Wien 1956, p. 504–533.

19. Cf. T. Parsons, *Toward a Healthy Maturity*. In: "Journal of Health and Human Behavior" 1, 1960, 3, p. 163–173.

20. M. Weber, *Die protestantische Ethik und der Geist des Kapitalismus*. Gesammelte Aufsätze zur Religionssoziologie. Tübingen 1920, 1.

21. Cf. P. C. McIntosh, *Sport and Society*. Watts, London 1963, p. 35–45.

22. Th. Veblen, *The Theory of the Leisure Class*. University of Chicago Press, Chicago 1899.

23. G. Lüschen, *Der Leistungssport in seiner Abhängigkeit vom sozio-kulturellen System*. In: "Zentralblatt für Arbeitswissenschaft". 16, 1962, 12, p. 186–190.

24. Unpublished, investigation of German Sport's Youth by Lüschen 1958. Data obtained by random-sample of sportsclub members 15–25 in West Germany and West Berlin.

25. D. C. McClelland, *The Achieving Society*. Van Nostrand, New York 1961.

26. R. N. Bellah, *Tokugawa Religion: The Values of Pre-Industrial Japan*, Ill, Free Press, Glencoe, 1957, p. 57.

27. D. C. McClelland, *op. cit.* p. 491.

28. J. M. Roberts and B. Sutton-Smith, *Child Training and Game Involvement*. In: "Ethnology". 1, 1962, 2; p. 166–185.

29. B. Sutton-Smith, J. M. Roberts, R. M. Kozelka, *Game Involvement in Adults*. In: "Journal of Social Psychology" 60, 1963, 1, p. 15–30.

30. N. Polsky, *Poolrooms and Poolplayers*. In: "Trans-action" 1967, 4, p. 32–40.

31. J. S. Coleman, *The Adolescent Society*, Ill.: The Free Press, Glencoe, 1961.

32. R. Helanko, *Sports and Socialization*. In: "Acta Sociologica" 2, 1957, 4, p. 229–240.

33. S. K. Weinberg and R. Arond, *The Occupational Culture of the Boxer*. In: "American Journal of Sociology" 57, 1952, 5, p. 460–463.

34. J. W. Loy, *Sport and Social Structure*, Paper at the AAHPER Convention. Chicago 1966.

35. G. Lüschen, *Soziale Schichtung und soziale Mobilität*. In: "Kölner Zeitschrift für Soziologie und Sozialpsychologie" 15, 1963, 1, p. 74–93.

36. G. Kunz und G. Lüschen, *Leisure and Social Stratification*. Paper at International Congress for Sociology, Evian/France 1966.

37. This institutional influence is so strong that it may well be advisable to treat informal (recreational), formal (organized for sport purpose only) and institutional sport (physical education and athletics in school) separately.

38. K. K. Hye-Kerkdal, *op. ext.*

39. M. R. Winterbottem, *The Relation of Childhood Training in Independence to Achievement Motivation.* Unpl. PhD-Thesis. University of Michigan, 1953.
40. J. Piaget, *The Moral Judgement of the Child.* The Free Press, New York 1965.
41. F. Stumpf, F. W. Cozens, *Some Aspects of the Role of Games, Sports and Recreational Activities in the Culture of Primitive Peoples.* In: "Research Quarterly", 18, 1947, 3, p. 198–218 and 20, 1949, p. 7–30.
42. Th. W. Adorno, *Prismen*, Suhrkamp, Frankfurt 1957.
43. J. Huizinga, *op. cit.*
44. J. Piaget, *op. cit.*
45. M. Mead, *Competition and Co-operation Among Primitive Peoples.* University of California Press, Berkeley 1946.
46. F. J. Roethlisberger, W. J. Dickson, *Management and the Worker.* Mass: Harvard University Press, Cambridge 1939.
47. G. Lüschen, *Soziale Schichtung . . ., op. cit.*
48. G. Lüschen, *Leistungsorientierung und ihr Einfluß auf das soziale und personale System.* G. Lüschen (ed.) *Kleingruppenforschung und Gruppe im Sport.* Köln und Opladen: Westdeutscher Verlag, 1966: 209–223.
49. Oetinger, F. Partnerschaft. Stuttgart 1954. Litt and Weniger in "Die Sammlung", Göttingen 1952 attacked the concept of partnership as a mode of political conduct which would not provide a way of socialization towards political power.
50. A. L. Kroeber, *Anthropology.* Harcourt, Brace and World, New York 1963, p. 163–165.
51. Cf. H. Damm, *Vom Wesen sogenannter Leibesübungen bei Naturvölkern.* In: "Studium Generale". 13, 1960, p. 3–10.

# 16

# Hero Crafting in *Sporting Life,* an Early Baseball Journal

*Lori Amber Roessner*

"Next to religion, baseball has furnished a greater impact on American life than any other institution."

–President Herbert Hoover

By the turn of the twentieth century, organized baseball, which originated in the late 1830s, was firmly entrenched as America's national pastime, heaped in mythic legend and lore.[1] Early baseball journalists, a number of whom were former amateur players, made a significant impact on the game's success, acting as promoters, advisors, and record keepers.[2] These journalists functioned as an "intricate system of supportive personnel" surrounding baseball, according to sports historian and sociologist Allen Guttmann.[3] Their work came at just the right time.

As the game's popularity soared, fans eagerly sought news about favorite players, the most notable of whom included Christy Mathewson (New York, Cincinnati) and Ty Cobb (Detroit, Philadelphia). The nation's sports writers, numbering into the thousands by 1912, were only too happy to oblige, churning out column after column, story after story about baseball's cast of heroes.[4] Treatment in the popular press, alongside alternative media such as radio, movies, vaudeville shows, and songs, served to mythologize baseball players by touting their "super-human" speed, strength, and agility.[5]

Early sports writers engaged in a symbiotic relationship with organized baseball, serving to promote the game and its players while commodifying

---

**Source:** *American Journalism,* 26(2) (2009): 39–65.

heroes to sell more newspapers.[6] From 1871 until the early 1900s, early sports magazines and newspapers helped promote baseball to the level of the national pastime; sports writers then began crafting heroes that exemplified the embodiment of America's democratic ideals from mostly working class players.[7]

In the last half of the twentieth century, sports media historians have focused much scholarly attention on the examination of sports writing in the Jazz Age, duly documenting the journalist's role in mythologizing sports heroes.[8] In doing so, they have largely neglected the role of the sports writer in prior decades, as well as created a doctrine, which suggests that the manufacture of sports heroes originated in the 1920s.[9] This article provides evidence that hero crafting was not a phenomenon unique to the Jazz Age, but was alive and well in prior eras. In addition, the study explores the techniques and devices sports writers employed to craft heroes in *Sporting Life*, a prominent yet understudied journal, from 1912–1917.[10] Through a textual analysis, it examines how writers mythologized professional baseball stars and prominent leaders using devices such as box scores, sayings, poems, adages, short biographies, obituaries, photographs, and full-length features. As historian Barry Schwartz notes, "like truth, the great man is created, not discovered,"[11] and this article is but a beginning step in identifying commonly used mechanisms of hero crafting in the print media. Whether conscious of it or not, the newspaper industry including sports writers and editors often employ many of these hero-crafting techniques in contemporary society.

In addition to exploring the devices that sports journalists used to manufacture turn-of-the-twentieth-century heroes, this article provides a glimpse into the American psyche. According to social historian Harold Perkins, "The history of societies is reflected more vividly in the way they spend their leisure than in their politics or their work . . . It is an integral part of a society's culture and gives a unique insight into the way a society changes and impacts other societies."[12] Exploring the myths entrenched in early sports writing helps one to gain a greater understanding of American mores, values, and beliefs in the early twentieth century.[13]

## America and Baseball in the Industrial Age

From 1880 until 1920, America's second industrial revolution vastly transformed the country's landscape, creating large metropolitan cities with skyscrapers and a mounting mass workforce. During this era, local economies became increasingly tied to a national economy that engaged in the selling of goods and services both locally and abroad. Answering the call for a mass labor force, millions of Americans migrated from rural to urban areas with the promise of economic prosperity in factories.[14] The onslaught of urbanization brought higher standards of living and increased leisure time for some and provided a new market of middle- and upper-class individuals with discretionary time and spending money for the newly-formed professional baseball league.[15]

By the early twentieth century, professional baseball had emerged from numerous league and player wars that plagued its formative years as a successful enterprise that sparked the American imagination.[16] Perhaps, sports historian David Voigt best sums up why baseball so resonated with the American public:

> It was as if Americans needed new rituals to unify and sustain themselves in a new world of city and factory . . . baseball met both challenges by providing fans with a tension-relieving spectacle . . . played by skilled new heroes. Beyond this, hope of becoming a player offered poor boys a bit of the American dream of cash and glory.[17]

As baseball's position as the national pastime became cemented into American culture, sports journalists began touting stars as heroes.[18]

## Sports Media in the Industrial Age

Sports journalism dates back to the 1820s, when newspapers provided accounts of certain events such as cricket, horse racing, and prize fighting.[19] John Stuart Skinner's *American Turf Register* (1829, monthly) and William Trotter Porter's *The Spirit of the Times* (1831, weekly) were the first two journals devoted exclusively to sport.[20] These two early sports magazines relied on their readers for much of the copy.[21] Despite the presence of these early sports publications and short newspaper accounts, not until the advent of the penny press did newspapers begin devoting any lengthy coverage to sport.[22]

America's fascination with baseball was both reflected in and perpetuated by widespread press coverage.[23] By the 1880s, the leading daily newspapers had sports departments,[24] providing Americans with "a steady diet of (sports) information."[25] The emergence of sports beats led to more colorful accounts about every aspect of baseball from training camps to player profiles. During the 1880s, several mass-circulating sports magazines such as *Sporting Life* and *Sporting News* were created by business-savvy individuals who saw that the public was primed for constant, in-depth coverage.[26] The prevalence of sports coverage emerged as editors saw that sport "was good copy."[27] More importantly, it boosted circulation, attracting a large male readership that craved sports news.[28]

Early sports journalists enjoyed a mutually beneficial relationship with magnates and players in the newly emerging sports world. The coverage provided developing leagues with publicity, and the copy sold newspapers and created lucrative careers for journalists.[29] As Charles Ponce de Leon notes:

Sportswriters recognized that heightened public interest in sports was good for them too, creating a huge audience of people who had no choice but to turn to the daily press for coverage of events that they were unable to attend in person. Accordingly, many journalists joined forces with athletes and promoters, producing articles that were vital to the fortunes of the industry.[30]

According to Richard Seymour, sports writers "spread the cult of baseball among the masses" and contributed to the establishment of "the business as a commercialized entertainment" converting it "into an integral part of the American social scene."[31]

During this era, sports writing emerged as a distinct form of journalism with original illustrations, box scores, and a unique writing style.[32] As other sports media historians have argued, at the turn of the twentieth century two styles of sports writing were emerging – the overly-optimistic, sentimental "gee whiz," and the cynical, "aw nuts" models; however, early in the century, the sentimental, optimistic accounts were in heavy supply as sports writers emphasized the virtuous aspects of baseball.[33] As Richard Orodenker argues, several common myth-narratives were prevalent in the writing of this era including that of the sports hero.[34]

## Heroes in the Industrial Age

Since the days of the ancient Olympic athlete, a hero was perceived as "a god-like creature with superhuman ability or strength."[35] These great men served as exemplars for the masses, evolved through abstraction into the perfect model.[36] According to Thomas Carlyle, one of the first historians to explore the hero in the mid-nineteenth century, heroes reflect sociocultural values and norms.[37] Although the conception of what type of person is deemed to be heroic has transformed since the ancient times, the form has remained relatively unchanged (nearly always including reference to a humble birth, demanding quest, decisive victory, and triumphant return), Joseph Campbell asserts.[38]

By the turn of the twentieth century, the American conception of great man had evolved, as the Victorian hero, someone who exemplified admirable qualities, became infused with the notion of celebrity, a renowned person.[39] Thanks in part to a changing nineteenth-century press, the twentieth-century hero transformed into a mass-circulated and produced celebrity in many respects.[40] As Robert Cathcart asserts, "all Americans, no matter how humble their origins, how lacking in physical and intellectual qualities, could aspire to notoriety and fame. . . ."[41]

While Hollywood starlets and popular personalities were, as Daniel Boorstin would say, simply "known for being known," media depictions of sports celebrities retained a modicum of traditional heroic flair in the early twentieth century.[42] As Robert Mandell argued, "the sports pages regularly produced heroes for a society that seemed unable to produce many heroes in other areas of public life."[43] Sports heroes, after all, were known for their brute strength and speed, which were touted by era journalists as comparable to that of Greek heroes and warriors. Early sports writers argued that athletes had natural ability that they refined for hours on end.[44] These journalists often emphasized athletes' heroic journeys complete with a story of separation, initiation, and return, in addition to touting their mental and moral attributes. However, according to sports scholar Donald Mrozek, the twentieth-century sports journalist emphasized the "primacy of deeds over virtues."[45] Although era sports writers emphasized heroic actions, they made sure to note that the sports hero played baseball not for glory or monetary rewards but for the love of the game.[46] Thus, sports stars enjoyed traditional heroic portrayals mixed with celebrity-style coverage, becoming what Susan Drucker terms as pseudo-heroes.[47]

A number of media scholars have explored the role of the press in providing society with heroic narratives. For instance, Janice Hume explores the media's role in defining, redefining, and perpetuating the conception of the American hero in a series of studies on the press and public memory.[48] Hume argues that the portrayal of heroes in the press not only reflects but also shapes societal norms and values. Similarly, in *Daily News, Eternal Stories*, Jack Lule argues that journalists utilize mythical heroic archetypes to instruct and inform society.[49] More recently, Brian Carroll has explored the role of the press in mythologizing the twentieth-century African American sports hero.[50] Although each of these scholars has examined the role of journalists as public storytellers with the power to define the American hero, they have not emphasized the techniques that early journalists used to craft heroes.

## Methodology

Although scholars like Bruce Evensen, Mark Inabinett, and Orodenker have documented how journalists of the Golden Era of sports writing mytholo gized baseball stars, the research about earlier sports writers remains scant.[51] This study will illuminate the role of a prominent, yet under-researched, sports journal and its influential editor Francis Richter in mythologizing sports stars at the turn of the twentieth century.[52] In addition to providing evidence that *Sporting Life* sports writers assisted in the manufacturing of cultural heroes prior to the Jazz Age, this study seeks to explore the mechanisms employed in mythologizing prominent baseball stars and leaders within the pages of *Sporting Life*. One question served to guide the narrative: what techniques did *Sporting Life* writers employ to mythologize – that is, to construct and interpret mythic narratives about – prominent professional baseball stars and leaders from 1912 to 1917?

A five-year time frame was selected to explore how *Sporting Life* crafted heroes from Dead Ball Era stars such as Ty Cobb and Christy Mathewson in the decade preceding what is commonly referred to as the Golden Age of sports writing. After a broad reading of issues of *Sporting Life* from 1910 to 1920, the researcher systematically selected twenty-five issues, averaging twenty-five pages in length, from 1912 to 1917 in order to ensure a manageable sample size. Using a constructed year and month, issues from each quarter, as well as issues following the World Series for each of the seasons from 1912 to 1916, were selected, and more than 205 *Sporting Life* articles were examined through an in-depth textual analysis.

Textual analyses attempt to delve below the surface of a text – in this case, twenty-five issues of *Sporting Life* – to unearth rich meanings. According to cultural studies scholar Stuart Hall, textual analyses require "a long preliminary soak" which determines "representative examples which can be more intensively analyzed."[53] The analysis in this article is rooted in James Carey's ritual view of communication. Under this theoretical paradigm, communication is a "symbolic process whereby reality is produced, maintained, repaired, and transformed," and journalism is a ritualistic cultural production that assists in the "construction and maintenance of an ordered, meaningful cultural world. . . ."[54]

Though *Sporting Life* never acquired the circulation base of a major newspaper such as the *New York World*, it is important to examine its content because it was one of the most influential sport journals of its day with a prominent editor who impacted baseball's development.[55] This research will add to the scholarship on the theoretical concept of heroism by exploring the devices or mechanisms used to manufacture sports heroes at the turn of the century. It will also add to our understanding of the relationship between journalism and baseball at the turn of the twentieth century, which has long been neglected in favor of studies of the Golden Age of sports writing. In addition, it will provide context about a prominent sports editor and publication that has been overlooked by many scholars.

Based on the in-depth textual analysis, three distinct forms of hero crafting emerged: the numerical, the narrative and the image. These forms will serve as a framework for further discussion about the mechanisms and techniques employed by *Sporting Life* to mythologize prominent professional baseball stars and leaders. In addition to illustrating the techniques of hero crafting, the examples within these sections serve as evidence that prior to the Jazz Age journalists were mythologizing professional baseball stars and prominent leaders.

## The Numerical

This section examines the mechanisms of hero crafting which appeared in numerical form within the pages of *Sporting Life* such as box scores and records. The numerical form was operationalized as any content that emphasized statistical information or records. Statistics played an integral role in baseball and the promotion of stars to the status of heroes. According to Mrozek, baseball's status as the national pastime is intricately tied to the scientific complexity entrenched in statistics.[56] In 1886, an English sports historian,

Montague Sherman, remarked that the pursuit of statistical records was an American obsession.[57] This section explores how the statistics prevalent in box scores and records serve as a gauge of greatness to contextualize heroic on-the-field feats.

Each of the issues sampled contained box scores and brief game recaps, as well as descriptions of record-breaking feats, similar to what one might find on any contemporary sports page. Due to meticulous record keeping initiated during the 1870s by Henry Chadwick, baseball writers also kept fans abreast of baseball records in pitching, fielding, and hitting. For instance, during this era, *Sporting Life*, along with other publications, devoted a great deal of attention to the batting average of Ty Cobb, who strung together nine consecutive batting titles from 1907 until 1915.

*Sporting Life* also ran articles on pitching records during the height of the Dead Ball Era (1900–19), known for low batting averages and impressive pitching. On May 24, 1913, a *Sporting Life* writer noted Washington pitcher Walter Johnson's 56 shutout innings from April to May 10, a major-league record.[58] On July 20, 1912, the journal published several articles about New York Giants' pitcher Rube Marquard's nineteen consecutive victories during the season, which tied a major league record set in 1888,[59] and in June 1916, *Sporting Life* touted New York pitcher Charley Radbourne, who won eighteen games in a month as "beyond all competition."[60]

Through the mechanism of box scores and game recaps, *Sporting Life*, like other journals of the day, emphasized that a sports hero gains legendary status by record-breaking deeds on the diamond. Statistical references such as box scores and records provided a framework to compare athletic feats – a contextual marker of greatness. Through numerical mechanisms of hero crafting, the feats of baseball stars and legends from a bygone era could be compared to the feats of modern-day heroes. As several scholars have pointed out, the early twentieth-century hero became well known more for his deeds than virtues; thus, box scores and records became the primary vehicle to measure sports stars' heroic deeds. In the twentieth century, according to Drucker, "a hero's deeds, in the record book, might be enough to create a hero."[61] And, as Mandell notes, "In no other sport are the notorious American yearnings for clean heroes and verifiable achievements made more manifest by acknowledged statistical records."[62]

## The Narrative

This section examines the mechanisms of hero crafting which appeared in narrative form within the pages of *Sporting Life* including short biographies, poems and adages, obituaries, and full-length feature articles. The narrative form was operationalized as any editorial content that appeared in print form with the exception of the written recaps following statistical break-downs in box scores, commonly referred to as agate copy. It is also important to note that descriptions of talented African American baseball stars, who were barred from the professional ranks and systematically ignored by the popular press, and women, who were relegated to support roles in sport, are excluded from the narrative within *Sporting Life.*

## Short Biographies

*Sporting Life* ran short biographies, ranging from 75 to 200 words, about prominent baseball players and managers on every cover in the sample from March 1912 to February 1915. Alongside large mugshots, these short biographies provided readers with brief descriptions of a player's physique, career, and records. Mirroring the form and style of era baseball cards, heroic accolades often accompanied informational descriptions. For instance, below a headline heralding Henry Gowdy as the "hero of the World's Series," one *Sporting Life* writer credited "the remarkable young catcher . . . and the star of the World's Series in every department . . . with being responsible for the great success of the Braves' pitchers."[63] In another example, a *Sporting Life* writer describes the "brilliant" Detroit first baseman Del Gainor, whose "dashing all-around work made him a mighty factor in the Detroit team's record-breaking pace in the . . . 1911 race."[64]

Ty Cobb and Rube Marquard were the two most prominent baseball stars profiled in biographies within the sample. Described as "the most sensational player of the age," Cobb's biography told of his youth and minor league background, culminating in describing Cobb as "one of the great stars of the American League," "a mainstay of the Detroit team," and "the most sensational performer of this generation" with "apparently no limit to his ability and endurance."[65] Heralding Marquard as the "sensation of the 1912 season," his biography chronicles his heroic journey. After a promising career in the minors, Marquard struggled in his first two seasons with the New York Giants, winning only five out of 18 games in the 1909 season; according to the biography, "McGraw, however, never lost faith in Marquard, and last year he reaped the reward as Marquard suddenly developed into the star pitcher of the National League," climaxing with nineteen consecutive wins in 1912.[66]

While these short biographies do not use the flowery language that would later be made well-known by what Orodenker refers to as the "Mattie, Gee Whiz" writers of the 1920s, short biographies, alongside other hero-crafting mechanisms in *Sporting Life* and other publications, served to mythologize baseball stars by chronicling their heroic journeys, as well as providing detailed informational accounts about their physique and playing careers.[67] According to Orodenker, baseball cards, guides, and, in this case, press accounts not only provided evidence of baseball's numerology but also provided detailed informational accounts that fed baseball's muse – memory. By emphasizing the players' extraordinary athletic feats and moral virtues, writers of *Sporting*

*Life* created a model to which young boys could aspire. Like baseball cards, these narrative descriptions, positioned under a large headshot of the player and separated from other editorial content, could be clipped from the pages of *Sporting Life* and included in the home shrines of adoring fans.

Although these brief biographies often focused on the primacy of action over virtues, they did emphasize moral virtues identified in the baseball creed such as determination and hard work. For instance, in a biography of Lee Magee, the player-manager of the Brooklyn Federal League Club, a *Sporting Life* journalist wrote that "the smart ball player . . . was the one man in the Cardinal ranks who stood out as a persevering player, no matter what the score, or standing of that team. . . ."[68] In addition to emphasizing virtues aligned with the baseball creed, biographies, which emphasized physical size, strength, and speed, helped shape American values and conceptions about masculinity and gender identity.[69]

## Poems and Adages

*Sporting Life*, like other era publications, often included poetry about baseball and its players. New York Giants pitcher Christy "Matty" Mathewson, one of the era's most famous stars, was often lauded in poetry. In "Spring Has Almost 'Came,'" William F. Kirk touted Mathewson's hurling ability, calling his pitching a sign of spring's approach,[70] while in another poem titled "When 'Matty' Was a Boy," Kirk wrote:

> Of course you kids love Matty and the deeds that he can do:
> He's just your big blond idol, and your father's idol, too.
> Long years of brilliant triumphs gave this athlete real renown,
> And so today "Our Matty" is a pet in New York Town.
> You think your chance of winning fame is far away and slight,
> And so you envy him by day and dream of him by night.
> But when you think life's battle hard, let this thought bring you joy:
> Success was just as hard to win when Matty was a boy.[71]

Likewise, in a poem titled "The Ultimate in Pitching," Grantland Rice argues that Mathewson is one of the greatest pitchers, noting that "as one would say the 'fadeaway' which Matty shoots is most bewitching . . ."[72]

On March 25, 1916, *Sporting Life* waxed poetic about another Dead Ball Era star, John Henry "Hans" Wagner, a famous Pittsburgh short-stop more commonly known as Honus Wagner.[73] In a poem fittingly entitled "Here's to Hans," H.J. Flatley wrote:

> Long ago we were told that old Hans was declining,
> That his speed and his cunning were things of the past . . .
> We read with a sigh that the Dutchman was slipping
> And sadly thought over the fame that was his
> For it's tough to believe that a hero is tripping

And yielding his perch on the crest of the biz.
But Hans comes back with each passing season . . .

In his heroic tribute, Flatley argues that Wagner's heart separates him from the "brilliant and fast" youth of the game.

*Sporting Life* also published "Sayings of Great Men," a series of baseball adages, on its editorial page. These adages put prominent baseball players and managers on a pedestal, making them appear wise beyond their years. For instance, notable baseball legend Ty Cobb was quoted as saying: "If you would get there with both feet use your head."[74] Other baseball legends such as Connie Mack, former major league player and manager of the Philadelphia Athletics, were often quoted in these sections. A *Sporting Life* writer attributed the following quote to Mack: "intuition is merely a remarkable faculty possessed by a good guesser."[75]

The use of poetic devices has been integral in the creation of heroes throughout history. As Tristram Coffin and Hennig Cohen argue, heroes of popular lore are symbolic exaggerations "distinguished from ordinary men and women by such qualities as their unusual strength, skills, morality, guile or kindness to others."[76] In *Touching Base*, Steven Riess notes that at the turn of the twentieth century, sports journalists attempted to satisfy the public's insatiable appetite for baseball heroes through feature stories, fiction, and poetry.[77] Through poetic mechanisms, writers for *Sporting Life* served to mythologize stars by tying their athletic prowess to the archetypal hero myth through the use of metaphor and symbolism. Poems and adages served to elevate talented individual players to a heroic celebrity status.

## Obituaries

On 37 occasions in the sample from 1912–1917, recently deceased players, managers, writers, and magnates were eulogized in *Sporting Life*. Often times, these eulogies were short announcements listed in the "Latest News By Telegraph Briefly Told." For instance, on October 23, 1915, an article and accompanying photograph about Federal League financial backer Robert Ward's death appeared nearby a tribute to deceased manager Fred Clarke.[78] According to the tribute, Clarke "was highly esteemed . . . an ideal character (who) was pleasant yet a fighter on the field." The journalist went on to note that his passing was a "hard blow to the sport."[79] When team owner John T. Brush died in 1912, *Sporting Life* emphasized his contributions to the game.[80] But, it was Albert Spalding's death in September 1915 that garnered by far the most coverage of any death in the sample. A death announcement, full-length article written by *Sporting Life* editor Francis Richter, large mug photograph, and editorial followed a front-page banner headline which read "Heroic Figure Passes from the Stage."[81] The article described Spalding as someone who did more for baseball than "any other man living or dead." He was said to be a "potent figure in every department of the game by reason of his skill as a player and manager, his judgment and force as executive, his power as a financial genius, and his resourcefulness in the business and political end."[82]

The following editorial emphasized the loss: "when the grim reaper took Albert G. Spalding he removed forever from the domain of sport an heroic figure . . ." that "wrote his name large and indelibly upon every page of its history."[83] The editorial went on to argue that Spalding was

> a big man, mentally, morally, and physically, and he did things in such a broad, generous, and efficient way that he produced colossal and permanent results. He possessed all the elements of true greatness – the vision to conceive, the capacity to execute, the courage to defend, the sagacity to guide and preserve, and the resourcefulness to control, great projects.

In addition, the editorial chronicled his heroic journey from his "humble start" to his playing career as the "greatest pitcher of his generation" to his management skills in "winning the first pennant of the National League" to his position in the sporting goods industry to his role as the "first power" in the National League and savior of baseball.[84] The editorial emphasized his heroic attributes such as his work ethic, genial attitude, and personal integrity, culminating by espousing Spalding "as the game's chief constructive genius and as its greatest missionary."

Serving as a mechanism of hero crafting, obituaries within the pages of *Sporting Life* posthumously chronicled the on- and off-the-field deeds and virtues of players, coaches, managers, owners, and influential leaders in professional baseball. Like short biographies, these narrative devices provide detailed and, at times, inflated accounts that serve to manufacture heroes from prominent players. While Coffin does not mention obituaries directly, he does argue that the legend and folklore found within baseball narratives – in this case obituaries – "re-writes the past into a drama to fit its own purposes."[85] More recently, Hume has examined how nineteenth-century obituaries reflect the dominant cultural values as placed within the context of collective memory.[86] Based on this argument, obituaries play a prominent role as a contextual marker of greatness.

## Full-Length Feature Articles

Throughout the 1910s, *Sporting Life* increasingly relied on the full-length feature article, ranging from 500 to more than 1,000 words, to inform its readers about the latest news on their favorite stars. During the era sampled, these features transitioned from articles that focused primarily on a particular team or group of players to ones that focused primarily on one individual star.[87] These early features contained few, if any, quotations from professional baseball players or leaders and were based primarily in the opinion of the writer. By the end of the 1910s, however, the writing had evolved to mirror modern-day features with attributed quotations from baseball stars interspersed throughout the pieces. During the era, *Sporting Life*, like other publications of the day, devoted considerable full-length feature coverage to two era stars – Ty Cobb and Christy Mathewson. The remainder of this section will focus on how the journal mythologized the two most prominent sports stars of the era.

*Sporting Life* journalists portrayed Detroit outfielder Ty Cobb as a cross between a full-fledged hero and trickster. For instance, in a front-page article which appeared on May 25, 1912, *Sporting Life* presented Cobb in a balanced light providing an account of his run-in with an angry fan.[88] The article explored how Claude Lueker, a Highlander fan, insulted Cobb with a racial slur. Cobb in a column-length statement explained, "The man who attacked me in New York is the same one who has made it unpleasant for me on other trips . . . I lost my temper, jumped into the stand and let him have it. I am sorry for the effect which such an incident has on the game." Within the remainder of the article, the journalist provided a balanced account of the player strike that followed Cobb's suspension for the incident; the editorial, however, called the players' strike, "a woeful blunder . . . (an) unprecendented, regrettable, and utterly useless revolt" admitting that the incident would "only serve to strip Cobb of whatever sympathy his suspension had evoked."[89]

In subsequent articles, Cobb is portrayed in less balanced lights – as a villainous trickster for holding out for larger salaries or a hero. For instance, on February 1, 1913, under the headline "Ty Cobb Chided: the Harm Caused by His Salary 'Hold-Out,'" the sports writer presents the comments of Detroit President Fred Navin, who blames Cobb for additional players demanding larger salaries. In an editorial that follows, the journal writes, "if Cobb won even a partial victory in his salary argument . . . it was dearly bought by appreciable loss in prestige, reputation, and public sympathy."[90] According to Coffin, Cobb's trickster image "symbolizes the days before the slugger Ruth when baseball was played close to the vest."[91] After press coverage of violent incidents, like the run-in with Luecker, "legends begin to grow, creating Cobb as a man never to be aroused, never to be crossed, a man made up of only fury, ice-blood, and a thousand devices. Cobb thus becomes a creature without normal motivation, a ballplayer, like some primitive trickster, who goes about his business of victory oblivious to the laws and customs of the society in which he lives."[92] However, on July 24, 1915, a *Sporting Life* journalist attributes Cobb's success as a "tribute to a man's resourcefulness." According to the article, Cobb was "a baseball genius," not only because of his "natural gifts, not only his speed and eye . . . (and) his brain," but also because of "his careful application to his work."[93] But, no matter what the situation, the journal depicted him as one of the generation's greatest ball players. In an article on July 8, 1916, Sid Keener argued that Cobb was the best "batsman" in the game's history.[94]

While *Sporting Life* often portrayed Cobb as a mix of trickster and hero, no one player enjoyed more heroic praise than New York Giant pitcher Christy Mathewson. For instance, in a front-page article, which appeared on July 27, 1912, the journal argued that after allowing "only one clean hit . . . in eight innings . . . 'Matty' (was) never better."[95] Later in the article, the journalist offered "a few more works of well-deserved praise of . . . 'the peerless pitcher.'" The article chronicles the heroic journey of Mathewson, who walked Joe Kelley, the first batter that he faced as a Giants pitcher. Mathewson, "carved his name in baseball history" with his "wonderful arm and head (which) have carried him through thrilling campaigns," according to the article. As Orodenker notes, based on coverage in the popular press, iconic hero Christy Mathewson occupies a place, alongside the fictional dime-novel character Frank Merriwell, as a flawless hero.[96]

Through full-length feature articles, *Sporting Life* not only provided its readers with informational accounts about star players of the Dead Ball Era, it also provided narratives that served to mythologize era players. Full-length feature articles, emphasizing the heroic archetype – a player's rise to greatness, decisive victory, and triumphant return – served to manufacture heroes and villains out of star ball players. Infused with the descriptions of athletic feats and character traits emphasized in the baseball creed, the articles within *Sporting Life* often provided personal details about athletes' lives that the public had begun to demand as their appetite for the "inside dope" was whetted by the popular press of the day.

## The Image

Photography was utilized in every issue of *Sporting Life* sampled. Often mug shots of star players accompanied articles, numbering four or five per page. From 1912 to 1915, *Sporting Life* published large photos of uniformed players such as Ty Cobb, Christy Mathewson, and Rube Marquard alongside short biographies featured in the middle of the front page.[97] Later, from mid-1915 to 1917, the sporting journal used a mix of action and still-life portraits on their covers.[98] Action photos often featured players throwing, fielding, and batting. In addition, in the weeks following the World Series, *Sporting Life* published large team photos of the champion squads and large portraits of the series' heroes.[99] The mugs of players often featured cutlines such as "Arthur Fletcher: the Infielder Who Alone Starred For Giants" and the covers of these issues often featured cutlines such as "Duffy Lewis and Harry Hooper: Batting Heroes of the 1915 World Series."[100] Several issues sampled featured opportunities for readers to purchase team and individual pictures of championship teams and rising heroes.[101] For instance, the March 16, 1912, issue of *Sporting Life* contained a coupon that allowed readers to purchase a

12-card series of "picture cards" of baseball players from prominent teams such as the Philadelphia Athletics, the Detroit Tigers, the Chicago Cubs, and the New York Giants for four cents.[102]

Photographs within *Sporting Life* provided readers with a vehicle for memorializing and idolizing sports stars. The portraits of favorite sports heroes could be easily clipped directly from the journal pages or purchased at a minimal cost by admiring fans, who might then post the images onto the wall of a home shrine. Media scholar Carolyn Kitch has done a great deal of research into the role of magazine images and collective memory. According to Kitch, popular magazines, in this case *Sporting Life*, serve as cultural artifacts – as "memory objects."[103]

## Conclusions

At the turn of the twentieth century, journalists began actively manufacturing heroes as opposed to simply discovering them.[104] According to Riess and Orodenker, era sports journalists served as promoters engaged in a public-relations campaign with league owners to extol baseball's virtues.[105] This study provides evidence that *Sporting Life* journalists mythologized sports stars prior to the Jazz Age through hero-crafting mechanisms such as box scores and records, short biographies, poems and adages, obituaries, full-length feature articles, and photography. According to Coffin and Cohen, heroes owe their fame to professional writers, whose work is "designed in advance for calculated purposes, to publicize a cause or to turn a profit."[106]

This study highlights how each of the forms of hero crafting – the numerical, the narrative, and the image – worked in tangent to mythologize Dead Ball Era athletes. Numerical forms like box scores and records served as a contextual marker of greatness. According to Mandell, at the turn of the twentieth century, Americans became increasingly obsessed with quantifiable records and statistical achievements.[107] These numerical forms allowed writers to compare the feats of present-day heroes with those of a by-gone era.

Although *Sporting Life* journalists gauged a player's status through quantifiable deeds entrenched in the narrative of short biographies, within other narrative forms, sports writers mythologized the deeds, physique, including the intellect, and the virtues of era stars. These writers at times emphasized heroic virtues like perseverance and hard work that coincided with the baseball creed, which according to Riess, aligned with the dominant white Anglo-Saxon Protestant value system and "contributed to both individual and public welfare."[108] However, as Mrozek noted, the press accounts of this era did come to focus more on deeds that emphasized prowess rather than on moral virtues.

*Sporting Life* crafted heroes from mostly working class young men who in reality at times exhibited a lack of moral character on the field of play.[109]

Despite these real-life character flaws, the sports hero in the pages of *Sporting Life* came from humble origins but was a "bright" Caucasian young male who played "smart" ball with his hard hitting and fast fielding. The mythic, metaphorical, and symbolic language found within short biographies, poems and adages, obituaries, and full-length feature stories cast era middle-class Caucasian stars into the molds of heroes and villains. According to Peterson, baseball and its stars have been "transformed by the words of novelists, historians, biographers, and journalists into narratives of magical dreams, moral romances, romantic tragedies, and aesthetic delights."[110]

However, mirroring the trend in the popular press, *Sporting Life* began focusing on the personal lives of baseball players in the mid-1910s as distinctions between public and private personas blurred.[111] Full-length feature articles provided the "inside dope" on the private lives of baseball players, alongside heroic accolades. This served to obscure the traditional heroic molds creating what Drucker terms as pseudo-heroes.

In concert with the narrative and numerical forms, the widespread appearance of images of era stars allowed *Sporting Life* readers to memorialize their favorite heroes in personal shrines. These cultural artifacts allowed sports heroes to step off the pages of the journal and onto the walls – and quite possibly into the dreams – of admiring fans. As Carolyn Kitch notes, images within popular magazines, in this case *Sporting Life*, play a significant role in public or collective memory.[112]

One can only speculate that era sports writers, including those employed at *Sporting Life*, mythologized baseball stars because they realized that it was good for business. Some writers too may have bought into the pervasive ideologies of regeneration and nationalization that promoted sport as a beneficial activity at the end of the nineteenth century. While their colleagues engaged in muckracking, they provided meta-narratives that fed the American imagination, actively churning out heroes through numerical, narrative, and pictorial forms, which evolved as they honed their sports writing techniques.

This study adds to the theoretical scholarship of heroism by analyzing how *Sporting Life* crafted heroes in the mid-1910s, before the rise of noted mythmakers of the 1920s. In addition to providing evidence of the sports writer's role in mythologizing era stars, it also explores mechanisms of hero crafting, many of which are still in practice by modern journalists. This study also reveals whom *Sporting Life* did not craft as a hero. *Sporting Life* only depicted white men as heroic. Minorities such as women and African Americans were not crafted in this mold. This may be due in part to the lack of involvement of women and African Americans in major league baseball.

Finally, the study serves as a commentary on early twentieth-century American society. As Riess asserts, "the study of professional baseball's myths, realities, symbols, and rituals provides a means to better understand American mores, values, and beliefs."[113] Baseball coverage served to teach Americans dominant Victorian values. The rise of the sports hero, according to Mrozek, "exemplified the growing fixation on action and experience."[114] In addition, the sports star embodied the shifting fascination from character to deeds that was an overarching symptom of the twentieth-century trend toward secularization.[115] "The moral range among stars underscores this shift," Mrozek notes, "a Christy Mathewson revered for his upstanding personal life, and a Ty Cobb admired despite his seeming indifference to humane concerns. Their common ground was a scientific attitude toward baseball, along with their success in translating knowledge into victory on the playing field."[116] According to Orodenker, heroes, largely the product of sports journalists, are baseball's most pervasive myth.[117] At the turn of the twentieth century, sports writers claimed a monopolistic role of interpreting societies myths, which according to Susman, are "sufficient to unify the whole, to answer the largely emotional needs of the members of the community and to provide, when necessary, the collective dreams of the society about the past, present and the future in the same instant."[118]

## Notes

1.  David Block, *Baseball Before We Knew It* (Lincoln: University of Nebraska Press, 2005); Richard Peterson, *Extra Innings: Writing on Baseball* (Urbana: University of Illinois Press, 2001), 39–47; David Voigt, *American Baseball: From Gentleman's Sport to the Commissioner System* (Norman: University of Oklahoma Press, 1966), 5–7, 278. The development of baseball provides a prime example of such lore. Henry Chadwick, known as the "Father of Base Ball," had long asserted that baseball emerged from a number of English folk games including cricket, rounders, and a children's game called One Old Cat. After more than a half a century of debates surrounding the authenticity of baseball's American origin, in 1908, sporting goods manufacturer Albert Spalding organized a panel to derive the inventor of America's national pastime. The panel found that Abner Doubleday invented the game and devised the rules in Cooperstown, N.Y., in 1839. In subsequent years, journalists and historians continued to debate the origin of the sport. According to Block, baseball developed from a myriad of English games such as tut-ball, stool-ball, cat and dog, munshets, trap-ball, hand-in, and hand-out. Block argues that journalists, and baseball owners, promoted the Doubleday myth to support the ideology that baseball is uniquely American; another example of such mythic lore is the fact that Moses Fleetwood Walker, not Jackie Robinson, was the first African American to play major league baseball. From 1883–84, Walker played for the Toledo Blue Stockings. After a run-in with one of the National League's most influential players Cap Anson and a subsequent decision by the American Associations to uphold the National League's unwritten rule banning black players, Walker was released from the club at the end of the 1884 season.
2.  Richard Orodenker, *The Writers' Game: Baseball Writing in America* (New York: Twayne Publishers, 1996), 31; Steven A. Riess, *Touching Base: Professional Baseball and American Culture in the Progressive Era* (Urbana: University of Illinois Press, 1981), 15; Harold Seymour, *Baseball: The Early Years* (New York: Oxford University Press, 1960), 69.
3.  Allen Guttmann. *From Ritual to Record: The Nature of Modern Sports* (New York: Columbia University Press, 1978), 38.
4.  Francis C. Richter, *The History and Records of Base Ball: The American Nation's Chief Sport* (Jefferson, N.C.: McFarland & Co., 1912), 428.

5. Mark Inabinett, *Grantland Rice and His Heroes: the Sportswriter as a Mythmaker in the 1920s* (Knoxville: University of Tennessee Press, 1994), 1–130; David McGimpsey, *Imagining Baseball: America's Pastime and Popular Culture* (Bloomington: Indiana University Press, 2000), 89–128; Orodenker, *The Writers' Game*, 16–24.

6. Bruce Evensen, *When Dempsey Fought Tunney* (Knoxville, The University of Tennessee Press, 1996), X–XV; Inabinett, *Grantland Rice and His Heroes*, 1–130; Orodenker, *The Writers' Game*, 16–24; William A. Harper, *How You Played the Game: The Life of Grantland Rice* (Columbia: University of Missouri Press, 1999), 9; Reiss, *Touching Base*, 22.

7. Ibid.

8. Robert H. Boyle, *Sport: Mirror of American Life* (Boston: Little, Brown and Co., 1963), 241–47; Tristram Coffin, *The Old Ball Game: Baseball in Folklore and Fiction* (New York: Herder and Herder, 1971), 76–91; Evensen, *When Dempsey Fought Tunney*, X–XV; Inabinett, *Grantland Rice and his Heroes*, 1–130; Orodenker, *The Writers' Game*, 1–248.

9. Evensen, *When Dempsey Fought Tunney*, 1–214; Inabinett, *Grantland Rice and His Heroes;* Orodenker, *The Writers' Game*, 1–248.

10. Seymour, *Baseball*, 69; Orodenker, *The Writers' Game*, 30; Riess, *Touching Base*, Lori Amber Shaw-Roessner, "The Impact of Francis Richter on the Development of Baseball," JURO, Retrieved at http://www.uga.edu/juro/2003/shaw.htm; David Voigt, *American Baseball*, 7. Although many sports media historians cursorily explore *Sporting Life* (i.e. David Voigt, Harold Seymour, Steven Riess, and Richard Orodenker, among others), little research exists about the role of the publication or its long-time editor Francis Richter. This article attempts to build on the previous work of Shaw-Roessner, who attempted to provide a foundational account of the journal in 2003.

11. Barry Schwartz, "Emerson, Cooley, and the American Heroic Vision," *Symbolic Interaction VII* (Spring 1985), 110.

12. Mike Huggins, *The Victorians and Sport* (London: Hambledon, 2004), X.

13. Riess, *Touching Base*, 4.

14. Guttmann, *From Ritual to Record*, 98; Harper, *How You Played the Game*, 1–10; Steven Riess, *City Games: The Evolution of American Urban Society and the Rise of Sports* (Urbana: University of Illinois Press, 1989), 34.; Riess, *Touching Base*; Riess, "Sports and the Redefinition of American Middle-Class Masculinity," *International Journal of the History of Sport*, 6. In fact, sports historian Steven Reiss attributes the evolution of the city, accompanied by mass transit and communication, directly to the rise of baseball (and other professional sports) in the waning decades of the nineteenth century. Improvements in transportation allowed professional baseball teams to tour the country, while breakthroughs in communication such as the telegraph and the rotary press allowed the newly-acquired fan base to follow every inning through magazines and newspapers. In addition to technological innovations in transportation and communication, social developments also impacted the soaring popularity of baseball. As pollution and health problems arose in burgeoning cities, men of the Victorian era began to actively promote sport as a healthy activity. The press promoted baseball as in tune with middle-class values entrenched in the new sports creed, which emphasized sportsmanship, and as a source of regeneration for male workers concerned with the crisis of masculinity.

15. Boyle, *Sport*, 4, 32; Harper, *How You Played the Game*, 4; Glenn Moore, "Ideology on the Sports Page: Newspapers, Baseball and the Ideological Conflict in the Gilded Age," *Journal of Sport History* (1996), 239; Seymour, *Baseball*, 23–35; Voigt, *American Baseball*, 35. According to Boyle, "American interest in sport . . . is in large measure the end product of a number of impersonal factors: industrialization, immigration, urbanization, increased leisure time and income, commercial promotion and upper-class patronage." In 1871, the National Association of Professional Baseball Players

(the forerunner of the National League) was formed in New York City. For a decade, the National League – composed of eight teams – controlled organized baseball, establishing territorial rights to curtail rival clubs and creating a reservation clause to mandate that players were property of a club until traded, sold, or released. During the ensuing decade, the American Association, which introduced Sunday games and more affordable gate prices, posed the first sustained threat to the National Association, luring away star talent and cutting into the older league's gate receipts. In 1883, delegates from the National League and the American Association formulated the National Agreement, which promised mutual respect of all rosters and minimum player salaries. For nearly a decade, the two leagues co-existed, despite several player wars such as the Player Revolt of 1889, in which a group of players, led by former second baseman of the New York Giants and Columbia law graduate John M. Ward, denounced the reserve contract. In 1891, the embattled American Association merged with the National League, forming one unified league composed of twelve clubs.

16. Harper, *How You Played the Game*, 4; Riess, *Touching Base*, 7. According to Riess, "Professional baseball's ideology spoke directly to white Anglo-Saxon Americans and their need to secure order. According to the baseball creed, the sport was one of our finest national institutions whose latent functions contributed to both individual and public welfare."

17. Voigt, *American Baseball*, 4.

18. Charles Alexander, *Baseball Feudalism and the Rise of the American League* (New York: Henry Holt and Co., 1991), 81, 39. Seymour, *Baseball*, 23–35; Voigt, *American Baseball*, 4. By 1900, after an era of unprecedented growth, organized baseball had evolved into its current form. "Ban" Johnson formed the American League, offering more lucrative salaries and better playing conditions. And, in 1903, the newly-elected National League president Harry Pulliam granted the American League's status as an equal institution. Pulliam formed a three-man National Commission, composed of the two league presidents and one chairman, to rule professional baseball. With the formation of two, eight-club leagues, organized baseball prospered in its "Silver Age" (1900–1920).

19. John Rickards Betts, "Sporting Journalism in Nineteenth-Century America," *American Quarterly* (1953), (5)1, 54; Harper, *How You Played the Game*, 2–7; Orodenker, *The Writers' Game*.

20. Ibid.

21. Ibid., 6–7.

22. Joshua Gamson, "The Assembly Line of Greatness: Celebrity in 20th Century America," *Critical Studies in Mass Communication 9* (1992), 3; Harper, *How You Played the Game*, 11; Orodenker, *The Writers' Game*, 27–33; Ponce de Leon, *Self Exposure*, 242. By the mid-nineteenth century, new technologies such as the telegraph and the rotary press helped transform communication and the press. These technological innovations created a cheaper means of production and accelerated the growth of mass-circulating dailies. During this era, the cheap, mass-circulating dailies and magazines began publishing human-interest stories with more traditional interviews. The development of the news wire and the professionalization of reporting changed the concept of news, and by the 1870s, the modern interview format with the interspersing of direct quotes became employed at most major newspapers. Between 1880 and 1900, the number of dailies rose from 850 to nearly 2,000 newspapers. New developments in photography led to the inclusion of photographs in many newspapers and magazines. Also, during this era, the newspaper circulation wars between Joseph Pulitzer (the *New York World*) and William Randolph Hearst (the *San Francisco Examiner*) gave rise to yellow journalism, the name given to sensationalistic news accounts. It was within this context that sports journalism emerged. According to Orodenker, the mid-nineteenth century also marks the apex of the career of one of baseball's original scribes, Henry Chadwick, often referred to as the "Father of Baseball."

23. Reiss, *Touching Base*, 15. According to Riess, the amount of space devoted to sports coverage increase from four to seventeen percent between 1890 and 1923.
24. Betts, "Sporting Journalism in Nineteenth-Century America," 54; Orodenker, *The Writers 'Game*, 27–33; Ponce de Leon, *Self Exposure;* Riess, *Touching Base;* Seymour, *Baseball*, 69.
25. Ponce de Leon, *Self Exposure*, 242.
26. Betts, "Sporting Journalism in Nineteenth-Century America," 54; Orodenker, *The Writers' Game*, 27–33; Ponce de Leon, *Self Exposure;* Riess, *Touching Base;* Seymour, *Baseball*, 69; Voigt, *American Baseball*, 194–5. As Riess notes, magazine coverage peaked between 1910 and 1914, when 249 baseball publications existed, according to the Reader's Guide to Periodical Literature.
27. Harper, *How You Played the Game*, 8.
28. Betts, "Sporting Journalism in Nineteenth-Century America," 54; Orodenker, *The Writers 'Game*, 27–33; Ponce de Leon, *Self Exposure;* Riess, *Touching Base;* Seymour, *Baseball*, 69.Voigt, *American Baseball*, 194–5.
29. Orodenker, *The Writers' Game*, 31; Inabinett, *Grantland Rice and His Heroes*, 29–51; Riess, *Touching Base*, 5–15; Voigt, *American Baseball*, 244. Often providing sports writers with a means of transportation, lavish accommodations and an adequate working space in press boxes, teams, Orodenker notes, expected favorable press coverage. "The quid pro quo," he writes, "which lasted well into the next few generations of baseball writers, eventually became part of the game's early lore. . . . Writers traveled with the players almost on a daily basis and soon became part of the game – several of them served as official scorekeepers."
30. Ponce de Leon, *Self Exposure*, 244.
31. Seymour, *Baseball*, 351.
32. Orodenker, *The Writers' Game*, 2–24; Inabinett, *Grantland Rice and His Heroes*.
33. Ibid.
34. Orodenker, *The Writers' Game*, 16–24. Orodenker argues for the existence of five prevalent myth-narratives that abound in sports writing – the myth of America, the myth of the hero, the myth of timelessness, baseball as literature, and the myth of memory. According to Orodenker, sports writers often draw on "the imaginative, symbolic, allegorical, or metaphorical functions" of these myths within baseball prose (p. 16).
35. Betty Houchin Winfield and Janice Hume, "The American Hero and the Evolution of the Human Interest Story," *American Journalism* 15:2, (1998), 79.
36. Orin Klapp, *Heroes, Villains and Fools: The Changing American Character* (Englewood, NJ: Prentice-Hall, 1962).
37. Thomas Carlyle, *The Complete Works of Thomas Carlyle* (New York: P.F. Collier, 1897).
38. Joseph Campbell, *The Hero with a Thousand Faces* (Princeton, NJ: Princeton University Press, 1949), 30.
39. Susan Drucker and Robert Cathcart, eds., *American Heroes in a Media Age* (New York: Hampton Press, 1994), 83, 85.
40. Joshua Gamson, "The Assembly Line of Greatness: Celebrity in 20th Century America," *Critical Studies in Mass Communication 9* (1992), 1–24; Jack Lule, *Daily News, Eternal Stories: The Mythological Role of Journalism* (New York: Guilford Press, 2001), 1–27; Tristram Potter Coffin and Hennig Cohen, eds., *The Parade of Heroes: Legendary Figures in American Lore*, (Garden City, N.Y.: Anchor Press/Doubleday, 1978), XXI. Coffin and Cohen support Lule's thesis, arguing that professional writers manufacture heroes for the purpose of turning a profit.
41. Drucker and Cathcart, *American Heroes in a Media Age*, 43.
42. Ibid, 83, 85. Daniel Boorstin defined celebrity as being known for being well-known.
43. Richard D. Mandell, *Sport: A Cultural History* (New York: Columbia University Press, 1984), 185.
44. Ponce de Leon, *Self Exposure*, 252.

45. Donald Mrozek, *Sport and American Mentality, 1880–1910* (Knoxville: University of Tennessee Press, 1983), 128.
46. Ponce de Leon, *Self Exposure*, 252.
47. Drucker and Cathcart, *American Heroes in a Media Age*, 80–85. According to Susan Drucker, the press constructs myths, heroic illusions, about modern athletes. Instead of exemplars of virtue, sports heroes are media constructs, well-known for their athletic deeds.
48. Janice Hume, "Press, Published History, Regional Lore: Shaping the Public Memory of a Revolutionary War Heroine," *Journalism History* 30:4 (2005), 200–209; Janice Hume, "Changing Characteristics of Heroic Women in Mid-Century Mainstream Media," *Journal of Popular Culture* 34:1 (2000), 9–29; Hume, "Defining the Historic American Heroine: Changing Characteristics of Heroic Women in Nineteenth-Century Media," *Journal of Popular Culture*, 31:1 (1997), 1–21. Hume and other scholars have defined public memory as the manner in which a group of individuals share stories about the past.
49. Lule, *Daily News, Eternal Stories*, 2001.
50. Brian Carroll, "Early Twentieth Century Heores: Coverage of Negro League Baseball History in the *Pittsburgh Courier* and the *Chicago Defender*" *Journalism History* 32:1 (2006), 34–42.
51. Betts, "Sporting Journalism in Nineteenth-Century America"; Orodenker, *The Writers' Game*, 16–24; Andrew Schiff, *The Father of Baseball: A Biography of Henry Chadwick* (Jefferson, N.C.: McFarland, 2008), 1–262. Although Betts and Orodenker provide a chronicle of the first generation of baseball scribes in their studies, they do not explore the role of these early sports journalists as mythmakers. Schiff's biography of Chadwick primarily examines his role in the development of baseball.
52. Francis C. Richter, *The History and Records of Base Ball: The American Nation's Chief Sport* (Jefferson, N.C.: McFarland & Co., 1912), 156; Thomas Richter, "Obituary of Francis C. Richter," *The Reach Official American League Guide*, 244; "Obituary of Francis C. Richter" *Philadelphia Inquirer*, February 13, 1926; Lori Amber Shaw-Roessner, "The Impact of Francis Richter on the Development of Baseball" JURO, Retrieved at http://www.uga.edu/juro/2003/shaw.htm. According to research conducted by Shaw-Roessner, in 1883 Francis C. Richter established *Sporting Life*, a weekly sports journal that covered trap shooting and baseball initially before expanding coverage to all sports in the early twentieth century. By 1890, *Sporting Life*, which retailed for a dime per issue, averaged sixteen pages in length and proclaimed that its circulation (of approximately 40,000) was the largest of any sports journal. A former amateur baseball player, Richter began his journalism career in Philadelphia after a brief stint as a shirt maker. In the 1870s, Richter served as a managing editor for the *Philadelphia Day*, before a brief career at the *Sunday World and Public Ledger*, where he was purported to have started the nation's first sports department. As the editor of *Sporting Life*, Richter played a prominent role in the development of baseball. Richter advocated rule changes and plans to end league wars. Most notably, Richter argued for the lengthening of the pitcher's mound to 60-feet, 6-inches in order to balance offense and defense. In 1893, the rule was enacted after much lobbying from Richter. However, Richter is best remembered for advocating the Millennium Plan. The plan sought to change the reservation and drafting system employed in the minors and was finally adopted by the National League and American Association in 1888. Subsequently, Richter was offered the presidency of the National League in 1907, but turned it down because of his work with *Sporting Life*. In addition to his work with *Sporting Life*, Richter served as the official scorer for the World Series for twenty years and edited *Reach Guide*, an annual baseball guide featuring stats and player profiles, from its inception in 1901 until 1926.
53. Stuart Hall, *Paper Voices: The Popular Press and Social Change, 1935–1965*, (London: Chatto and Windus, 1975), 15.

54. James Carey, *Communication as Culture: Essays on Media and Society* (Boston: Uwin Hymann, 1989), 23, 18.

55. Orodenker, *The Writers' Game;* Riess, *Touching Base.* In 1886, when the Spink brothers established the *Sporting News* in St. Louis, *Sporting Life* had a circulation base of 40,000 subscribers. The *Sporting News*, which along with *Baseball Magazine* (1908–1957) became the journal's greatest competitors, gained a large circulation-base during the 1910s. The *Sporting Life*, however, remained a prominent journal until it ceased production in 1917 due to wartime material and personnel shortages. At this juncture, Francis C. Richter sold his holdings of *Sporting Life* to his partners Thomas Dando and August Rudolph. After the war, the *Sporting Life* was briefly published from 1922 to 1926.

56. Mrozek, *Sport and American Mentality*, 172.

57. Mandell, *Sport*, 192.

58. *Sporting Life*, May 24, 1913, 7.

59. *Sporting Life*, July 20, 1912, 9.

60. *Sporting Life*, June 24, 1916, 27–31.

61. Drucker and Cathcart, *American Heroes in a Media Age*, 89.

62. Mandell, *Sport*, 193.

63. *Sporting Life*, October 17, 1912, 1.

64. *Sporting Life*, March 9, 1912, 1.

65. *Sporting Life*, May 25, 1912, 1.

66. *Sporting Life*, July 20, 1912, 1.

67. Orodenker, *The Writers' Game*, 9.

68. *Sporting Life*, February 27, 1915, 1.

69. Mrozek, *Sport and American Mentality*, 176; Riess, *Touching Base*, 23.

70. *Sporting Life*, March 9, 1912, 3.

71. *Sporting Life*, December 14, 1912, 2.

72. *Sporting Life*, June 20, 1914, 5.

73. *Sporting Life*, March 25, 1916, 16.

74. *Sporting Life*, March 9, 1912, 3.

75. *Sporting Life*, July 20, 1912, 6.

76. Coffin and Cohen, eds., *The Parade of Heroes*, xxiii.

77. Riess, *Touching Base*, 5.

78. *Sporting Life*, October 23, 1915, 8, 12.

79. Ibid., 12.

80. *Sporting Life*, December 14, 1912, 9.

81. *Sporting Life*, September 18, 1915, 1.

82. Ibid., 1.

83. Ibid., 4.

84. Ibid., 4.

85. Coffin, *The Old Ball Game*, 76.

86. Janice Hume, *Obituaries in American Culture* (Jackson: University Press of Mississippi, 2000), 1–204.

87. *Sporting Life*, March 9, 1912, 8, 13. Many early full-length feature articles that centered solely on athletes in *Sporting Life* focused on whether Dead Ball Era players were greater than the first generation of major leaguers. For instance, an article that appeared on March 9, 1912, argued that in the past five years "big men" were better hitters than "men of small stature," citing batting averages of players like Nap Lajoie and Hans Wagner that were over .300. Another article in the same issue argued that Charles Comiskey, owner of the Chicago White Sox, was the best first baseman to have ever played the game.

88. *Sporting Life*, May 25, 1912, 1.

89. *Sporting Life*, May 25, 1912, 6.

90. *Sporting Life*, February 1, 1913, 1, 4.

91. Coffin, *The Old Ball Game*, 89.
92. Ibid., 91.
93. *Sporting Life*, July 24, 1915, 2.
94. *Sporting Life*. July 8, 1916, 4.
95. *Sporting Life*. July 27, 1912, 1.
96. Orodenker, *The Writer's Game*, 23.
97. *Sporting Life*, March 9, 1912, 1; May 25, 1912, 1; December 14, 1912, 1; September 6, 1913, 1; January 17, 1914, 1; June 6, 1914, 1; August 15, 1914, 1; October 17, 1914, 1; October 31, 1914; February 27, 1915, 15.
98. *Sporting Life*, October 23, 1915, 1; March 25, 1916, 1; June 24, 1916, 1; July 8, 1916, 1, 1; October 21, 1916, 1; December 2, 1916, 1.
99. *Sporting Life*, October 18, 1913, 1; November 22, 1913, 4; October 23, 1915, 4; October 21, 1916, 4–5.
100. *Sporting Life*, October 18, 1913,1; October 23, 1915, 1.
101. *Sporting Life*, March 9, 1912, 15.
102. *Sporting Life*, March 16, 1912, 12.
103. Carolyn Kitch, "Anniversary Journalism, Collective Memory, and the Cultural Authority to Tell the Story of the American Past," *Journal of Popular Culture* (2003), 44–67.
104. Winfield and Hume, "The American Hero and the Evolution of the Human Interest Story," 88.
105. Orodenker, *The Writer's Game*, 31; Riess, *Touching Base*, 54.
106. Coffin and Cohen, *The Parade of Heroes*, xxi.
107. Mandell, *Sport*, 192.
108. Riess, *Touching Base*, 8.
109. Voigt, *American Baseball*; Seymour, *Baseball*.
110. Peterson, *Extra Innings*, 37.
111. Drucker and Cathcart, *American Heroes in a Media Age*, 37.
112. Carolyn Kitch, "Anniversary Journalism, Collective Memory, and the Cultural Authority to Tell the Story of the American Past," 44–67.
113. Riess, *Touching Base*, 4.
114. Mrozek, *Sport and American Mentality*, 176.
115. Riess, *Touching Base*.
116. Mrozek, *Sport and American Mentality*, 176.
117. Orodenker, *The Writer's Game*, 24.
118. Warren Susman, *Culture as History: The Transformation of American Society in the Twentieth Century*, (New York: Pantheon Books, 1984), 8.

# 17

# Making Soccer a 'Kick in the Grass': The Media's Role in Promoting a Marginal Sport, 1975–1977

*Thom Satterlee*

S uppose you are a journalist assigned to write a story about a sport that is unfamiliar to most of your readers. The readers who know something about this sport know it by its reputation for being low-scoring, unmanly, and working class. Moreover, they think that this sport goes against their national identity and really belongs on foreign soil, where it began in the first place. Under such conditions you probably would not expect your story to be aided by the announcement that a new player – a foreigner who grew up in rural poverty and is best known for his finesse rather than his strength – has been recruited. And yet 25 years after soccer promoter Clive Toye brought the Brazilian soccer star Pelé to play in the North American Soccer League (NASL), no event has had a more significant effect in bringing attention to the sport of soccer in the United States.[1]

Pelé's three-season stint with the New York Cosmos, 1975–7, has become part of soccer legend in the USA. Sports writers and soccer historians regard his NASL tenure as the main cause for the sport's current popularity. In good American sports fashion, they quote statistics, such as the rise in the Cosmos's average home attendance from 3578 in 1974 to 34,142 in 1977, when Pelé played his last season (Eskenazi, 1980: 18). Pelé is also given credit for the boom in youth soccer. In a country where the sport largely had been relegated to PE classes and Ivy League colleges, the current number of youth soccer

**Source:** *International Review for the Sociology of Sport*, 36(3) (2001): 305–317.

players has reached close to 20 million (Glenn, 2000). If asked to explain this number, most people would point to one person: Pelé.

Indeed, Pelé's three years with the Cosmos may seem to represent a revolution in US soccer, with Pelé himself as the main revolutionary. In order to keep things in perspective, however, two qualifications should be mentioned. The first concerns the scope of the changes that Pelé's playing brought to the status of soccer in the USA. If the goal of soccer promoters in the 1970s was to, in Pelé's words, 'bring soccer alongside baseball and basketball and football' (1976), then clearly their success was incomplete, at least to date. Even though soccer has moved closer to the mainstream and shows promise of gaining more ground, especially with the recent establishment of a women's professional league, it still trails far behind the three major sports. This gap, in fact, is considerable and can best be understood through a distinction made by Andrei Markovits and Steven Hellerman in their recent book *Offside: Soccer and American Exceptionalism* (2001).

These authors make the useful distinction between sport as 'activity' and sport as 'culture'. Activity, they state, is 'what people do'; so the fact that a large number of Americans (even 20 million) play an organized sport simply means that it is a popular activity. Meanwhile the sport itself may fail to be a dominant force in the culture. The term 'sports culture', on the other hand, refers not to what people do, but to what they follow, what they 'breathe, read, discuss, analyze, compare, and historicize; what they talk about at length before and after games on sports radio; what they discuss at the office water cooler; and what comprises a significant quantity of barroom (or pub) talk' (Markovits and Hellerman, 2001: 9).

Although soccer in the USA does have its ardent fans and has in recent years held the nation's momentary interest (such as during the 1994 World Cup and the 2000 Women's World Cup, both played in the USA), the sport has failed to penetrate what Markovits and Hellerman call the 'hegemonic sports culture' and which they measure by a sport's representation in popular media (movies, novels), its TV viewership, and the extent to which the sport's language has become common idiom (Markovits and Hellerman, 2001). Using these barometers of cultural influence, soccer remains a relatively marginal sport in the USA.

The second qualification I wish to make is related to the first and leads to the focus of this article. Just as Pelé's influence on the status of soccer must be seen as limited – helping it become a more popular activity and bringing it closer to the mainstream, but not making soccer equal in status to football, basketball, and baseball – so too was Pelé's *ability to influence* limited. My basic contention is that Pelé's presence in US soccer, as important as it was in bringing attention to the sport, should be viewed as a catalyst. I would, therefore, have to disagree with soccer historian and commentator Paul Gardner when he refers to Pelé as 'the *deus* who had been summoned to solve all the problems of American soccer', comparing his entry into US soccer with that of a Greek god descending from the sky (1976: 197–8). The point I wish to make is that Gardner and the many other journalists, writers, and sports commentators who took up the Pelé story were the real *dei ex machina* in promoting US soccer. Granted, without Pelé they may not have had an audience to listen to them, but they certainly deserve credit for the way they presented soccer to their American audience – an audience they had reason to assume would be ignorant, apathetic, and even somewhat hostile toward their subject matter.

In order to explore the media's contribution in promoting soccer, I have surveyed articles published in the *New York Times* and in several popular magazines; trade books; and, finally, a televised soccer game, Pelé's last in the NASL. All of these sources appeared during or shortly after the time when Pelé played soccer in the USA. With little exception, soccer is portrayed in a positive light, and very often the authors or commentators make remarks that undermine the stereotyped view of soccer as an unexciting sport played by poor immigrants or schoolgirls.[2] Although some of the authors appear unversed in soccer and occasionally misinform their audience, the work of these journalists and writers is generally helpful in promoting soccer because they balance education and excitement, two necessary elements in moving a sport closer to the mainstream. In the conclusion of this article, I explore some reasons for the media's promotion of soccer and speculate on the comparatively negative press that the sport received during the 1994 World Cup.

## 'Threading a Lateral': The Mainstream Press Picks up the Pelé Story

It is unlikely that many Americans knew about Pelé before 1975, even though his fame elsewhere in the world was already well established by 1958 when, as a 17-year-old, Pelé starred in the World Cup in Sweden. The *New York Times*, for instance, printed no articles about Pelé until 1962, when one appeared. Between 1963 and 1968, the country's foremost newspaper again fell silent about the world's most popular athlete. Between 1968 and 1975 (the year Pelé signed with the Cosmos), the *Times* printed a scant six articles.

Meager as this may seem, the major American magazines were just as stingy and proved somewhat slower than the *Times* in giving space to the Pelé story, with the first magazine article about Pelé appearing in *Time Magazine* in 1963. Considering the hundreds of magazines published in this country, the figure of seven articles published between 1964 and 1975 is hardly more impressive than the half dozen in the *New York Times*. The number of books that American publishers devoted to Pelé before 1975 is easily counted: zero.

These figures suggest that in 1975 most Americans would have had little knowledge of Pelé. Moreover, assuming that the editors of national periodicals make choices that reflect the interests of their readers, these figures suggest that most Americans did not care to read about Pelé or the sport he represented.

Ignorant, apathetic, carrying decades-old stereotypes about soccer as unmanly, foreign, and lower class, the American audience for mainstream publications would have seemed a forbidding one for writers in 1975.

And yet an explosion of publications about Pelé appeared in mainstream presses during the years he played with the New York Cosmos. Between 1975 and 1977 at least 12 books were published by presses such as Harcourt Brace Jovanovich, Harper & Row, and Norton, with titles such as *Pelé: Soccer Superstar* (Sabin, 1976), *Pelé: Soccer's King in America,* and *Man with a Mission* (Adler, 1976). Magazines and newspapers likewise picked up their pace and in three years more than doubled the number of articles published over the previous 17 years of Pelé's career. Publications as diverse as *Sports Illustrated, Ebony, Reader's Digest,* and the *New Yorker* all published feature articles about Pelé. As former publicity director for the New York Cosmos John O'Reilly recalls sarcastically, 'All of a sudden, everybody felt that they were the top soccer sympathizers in the nation. Everybody wanted the first interview with Pelé because they had done so much for soccer' (quoted in Bodo and Hirshey, 1977: 123).

Also recalling the abrupt interest in soccer caused by Pelé's beginning to play for the Cosmos, writer Paul Gardner echoes a similar 'insider's' frustration:

> Suddenly the press box at the Cosmos games was jammed, full of people who could not pronounce Pelé's name, whose conversation made it painfully clear that they knew nothing of soccer, but well-heeled people who moved with a swagger not seen before in soccer press boxes, and who made a fuss if they didn't get a good seat. (1976: 199)

One of the earliest articles about Pelé certainly bears witness to Gardner's observations that some of the sport's new writers 'knew nothing of soccer' but were 'well-heeled people'. In 'Pelé Olé', part of the *New Yorker's* 'Talk of the Town' column for 30 June 1975, the writer describes a trip out to Downing Stadium to watch Pelé's first game with the Cosmos. In prose more suited to a John Cheever short story than to a sports column, the writer describes walking 'across fields of white clover' to join the 'fourth-largest metropolitan Father's day crowd' and watch the 'superbly muscled, hugely smiling, and completely relaxed thirty-four-year-old Pelé'. Clearly, this writer saw the 'quaint New Deal Downing Stadium' as the place to be.

But the writer's enthusiasm for the event does not translate into a keen understanding of what happens on the field. More importantly, without a common language to speak about the sport to others who share that language, the writer comes up with blunders like the following: 'With twelve minutes gone, Pelé brought the ball deftly up field and threaded a lateral to Mordechai Shpigler, an Israeli playing his fifth game for the Cosmos, who then kicked a dribbler past Cooper . . .' (*New Yorker*, 1975: 24). It would be difficult for a reader to imagine this play without first knowing what it means to 'thread a lateral' or to kick a 'dribbler'. But the writer is not making use of common soccer jargon so much as making up a vocabulary on the spot. 'Thread a lateral', for instance, would make no sense to soccer insiders; the phrase, in fact, seems borrowed from the language of American football – thus, if a reader unfamiliar with soccer's rules but familiar with American football pictures anything, it's likely to be a false picture of Pelé heaving an underhanded throw to Shpigler.

Although the author of the *New Yorker* article fails to communicate the intricacies of the game of soccer, the article is in several other ways ideally suited to its audience and makes a strong case for exactly what NASL promoter Clive Toye wanted: to bring more people out to future games by appealing to a wider audience. The target readers for the *New Yorker* – cosmopolitan, sophisticated, intellectual – might be assumed unlikely to attend soccer matches at run-down stadiums. And the Downing Stadium where Pelé played his first match for the Cosmos was hardly a family-friendly environment. Paul Gardner recalls that among the 'regular' press Downing Stadium on Randall's Island was known as 'Drowning Stadium' located on 'Vandal's Island' (1976: 197), while Don Kowet, author of *Pelé*, describes the stadium as 'dingy, dimly lit' and 'dismal' (1976: 27, 29). Yet the writer of 'Pelé Olé' turns the otherwise unseemly surroundings into the perfect setting for an adventure. Forced by a traffic jam to leave a cab and walk to the stadium, the writer nevertheless sounds as excited as a tourist visiting an exotic country:

> Abandoning our cab to a previously unheard-of traffic jam at the Randall's Island exit of the Triborough Bridge, we clambered over a guardrail and joined a steady stream of eager aficionados heel and toeing it over the bridge from Harlem. Across fields of white clover, past chuck wagons vending *comidas criollas* whose proprietors were tuning in the Bronx Bombers on the radio, around Cosmos ticket booths doing brisk business in six-dollar reserved and four-dollar general admission seats, to our own concrete perch, atop the only New York stadium adorned in fading stencil with the legend 'ΚΑΤΩ; Η ΧΟΥΝΤΑ,' which means 'BOO JUNTA' in Greek. (*New Yorker*, 1975: 23)

Not an ordeal, but an adventure. Not a seedy stadium filled with immigrant workers, but a kind of international bazaar with occasional linguistic riddles to test one's Greek. A description like the above appeals to the readers of the *New Yorker* by tapping into their sense of *wanderlust* and promising them a way to satisfy their curiosity without ever having to leave home. In spite of its surface errors, 'Pelé Olé,' from a soccer promoter's point of view, represents good press.

Two other articles that appeared during the early part of Pelé's first season demonstrate, again, the problem of communicating the game of soccer to an audience that knows little about the game. Unlike 'Pelé Olé', 'Curtain Call for a Legend' (Kirshenbaum, 1975) and 'Can Pelé Bring the Big Pay Day to U.S. Soccer?' (*Ebony*, 1975) avoid outright mistakes when describing soccer to their audiences. Nevertheless, the authors run into problems when they cannot assume the kind of soccer short-hand that insiders would use with one another. Consider these two descriptions of a play during one of Pelé's first practice sessions with the Cosmos. First the description in *Sports Illustrated:*

> . . . any pretense that Pelé was among peers was forever undermined when, positioned in front of the goal, he took a sharply angled, waist-high pass from Midfielder Johnny Kerr. Pelé bicycled himself into the air and sent an overhead kick screeching past second-string goalkeeper Kurt Kuykendall. Players on both sides cheered while Kuykendall asked, 'What happened?' (Kirshenbaum, 1975: 20)

And now from *Ebony:*

> At one of his first practice scrimmages with the Cosmos, the man Italians call // Re (The King) took a waist-high pass in front of the goal with his back to the goalkeeper. Instead of turning and firing, as many decent goalkeepers would have expected him to do, Pelé tumbled into his patented backward somersault and whistled the ball into the net with an *overhead* kick that left the defender muttering 'What happened?' and his teammates cheering. (*Ebony*, 1975: 138)

In soccer parlance, saying that Pelé scored on a bicycle kick would suffice; to make the story interesting, one might include the part about the shocked goal-keeper – but these authors had to do more than simply write an interesting story. They had the added burden of educating their readers about a common soccer term. Thus the *Sports Illustrated* author uses the phrase 'bicycled himself into the air', but realizing that this phrase was not enough to convey Pelé's move, adds an explanation that may help: 'an overhead kick'. Likewise, the *Ebony* author doesn't assume that 'patented backward somersault' conveys the entire picture, and so adds the same explanatory phrase that would not be needed for the audiences of most countries where soccer is a major sport.

To educate and at the same time to interest their audience became a common rhetorical predicament for authors who wrote about Pelé in the mid-1970s. As the two authors quoted above illustrate, it certainly was possible to manage these dual purposes. One strategy was to focus on spectacular moments, such as a bicycle kick, that lent themselves to vivid description and allowed the writers to entertain and educate at the same time. Another technique that other writers chose emphasized the 'exotic' nature of soccer. The fact that the average American knew little about the sport was turned to advantage by writers like Lowell Miller, whose *New York Times Magazine* article clearly assumed a soccer illiterate audience, but employed a style and strategy that made it a pleasure for that audience to learn more about soccer (1977: 12+). Miller begins his article by writing in the second person, a style that naturally draws in the reader. In addition, Miller's description of soccer emphasizes the newness and uniqueness of the game:

> On the soccer field, your light cleated shoes are really the only piece of equipment. The wind blows through your shirt and around your legs as you run. And you're running all the time, constantly moving, constantly alert. There's an open space. You run into it, creating an outlet for a pass. The ball comes to you. You control it, keep it close, using only your feet, perhaps your chest, never your hands. Hard-running defenders rush upon you and the field becomes a mass of enemy jerseys. (1977: 12)

Although his assumed audience needs to be told such basic information as the customary footwear for soccer players and the fundamental rule that players cannot use their hands, Miller's journalistic instincts tell him that his story must also interest. Thus he deploys the information in an appealing way. His risk, of course, is alienating another segment of his readers – those even marginally aware of the game's rules who might feel insulted by Miller's soccer primer. From a promoter's point of view, however, those knowledgeable readers are not as urgently needed as the prospective converts.

Like the *New Yorker* article, Miller's piece wittingly or unwittingly breaks down the stereotype of soccer as a game for foreigners. Miller does this by putting a positive spin on the 'foreign' aspects of soccer. Throughout his article, without ever seeming heavy-handed, Miller chooses key words such as 'chic' and 'international', appealing to his readers' value of global awareness (1977: 13). Toward the end of his article, Miller comes directly to the point: 'As the global village becomes a reality, it seems fitting that we join the rest of the villagers in their free-flowing, non-linear game' (1977: 38). Soccer, argues Miller's article, gives the USA an opportunity to broaden its horizons.

Another soccer stereotype that Miller's article undermines is the notion of soccer as a working class sport. Miller makes frequent mention of the business side of the game, assuring his readers that 'Madison Avenue is now following [soccer's] progress quite seriously' (1977: 13). The message that soccer is not a working class sport appears in several other articles at the time. Writers devoted ample space to discussing Pelé's (at the time) astronomical salary (*Ebony*, 1975: 138; Kirshenbaum, 1975: 21; Kowet, 1976: 5–6; *Time Magazine*, 1975: 56). Given that the world's highest-paid athlete played soccer, regardless of his humble beginnings, made it difficult for Americans to view the sport in the old way. Pointing out this fact in mainstream magazines was an expedient way to change views about a game that many Americans seldom even thought about.

Perhaps the most common way that writers helped change soccer's image and raise its status was through emphasizing Pelé's superstardom. To make Pelé's accomplishments understandable to their audience, writers routinely compared him to American athletes.[3] Often writers selected the names of athletes that their readers would hold in the highest esteem. The *Ebony* article, for instance, uses African-American athletes Wilt Chamberlain, Kareem Abdul-Jabbar, and Hank Aaron as points of comparison (1975: 136–8). Invariably, writers drew athletes from America's top three sports of football, baseball, and basketball (Kirshenbaum, 1975: 20; Kowet, 1976: 22–3).

Writers sometimes used another method to describe Pelé's unique talents. Instead of comparing Pelé to well-known American athletes, they described the soccer star as being nearly superhuman. Pelé, we learn, has a drastically slower heart rate than the average performing athlete, his vision is '30 percent better than most other athletes', and Pelé runs faster and jumps higher than other players (Kowet, 1976: 86–7). Most extraordinarily, as author Don Kowet reveals, Pelé's genius is both multipurpose and clinically proven:

> While the Brazilian national team was preparing for the 1966 World Cup, Pelé was miles away, in a university laboratory. His legs, arms and head were wrapped in wires, in a series of tests that were repeated off and on for three weeks. The results never varied. 'They showed,' said Dr. Hilton Gosling, an eminent Brazilian psychologist, 'that whatever field of endeavor this man entered – physical or mental – he would be a genius.' (1976: 87)[4]

Other articles that emphasize Pelé's unparalleled athleticism include 'Peerless Pelé: Rebirth of a Superstar' (Young, 1976), and the *Ebony* article mentioned earlier in which the author points out that Pelé's 'thighs look bigger than his waist' (1975: 138).

Presenting Pelé as an athlete of superior physical attributes went against the stereotype of soccer as 'unmasculine' and may have increased the average American's interest in the game. Another common feature of articles written about Pelé was a subtle attack on the stereotype of soccer as an 'immigrant' sport. Gone unchecked, such a perception may have prevented middle and upper class Americans from becoming fans. But the books and articles written about Pelé present him in a different light. He was not another immigrant seeking his own self-interest in the United States, but a missionary bringing soccer – arguably the world's strongest religion – to us. From his first press conference in a crowded New York City club to his final farewell in a self-authored article in the *New York Times* (1977: D2), Pelé maintained that 'everyone in life has a mission, and [his] dream is that one day the United States will know soccer like the rest of the world' (quoted in Kowet, 1976: 8). Articles such as 'Pelé's Mission Accomplished' (1977: 62–3) and books such as *Man with a Mission* (Adler, 1976) give prominence to this view. Pelé, such publications suggest, was not here to take anything, but to give the gift of soccer.

Although most articles present Pelé as a missionary loved by both fans and the press, a few sources point out the disgruntlement of a minority – chiefly American-born soccer players – at Pelé's dominating presence in the NASL. Kyle Rote, Jr., son of the famous American football player, played for the Dallas Tornado at the time when Pelé played for the Cosmos. Commenting on the amount of press Pelé received, Rote said,

> Now that we've gone from the era of the slaves to the era of the King, I don't want anyone to forget the slaves. They were the ones who built the pyramids for the King. I don't want anyone to forget all our free clinics and low wages. (Quoted in Kowet, 1976: 36)[5]

The resentment among American players towards their foreign counterparts began well before Pelé joined the team, however. Although the American players may have wanted to star in the league, few saw much game time. Some, like Stan Startzell and Joey Fink, felt that they were promised a more involved role with the Cosmos, only to find that their main usefulness to the team came off the field during press conferences and public relations spots. When first drafted to play for the Cosmos, Startzell touted the need for American players like himself because, as he put it, 'whoever heard of a mother telling her son to eat his Wheaties so he can grow up to be like Abaddia El Mostofa?' (quoted in Bodo and Hirshey, 1977: 71).[6] Startzell soon lost his flair when he realized how little playing time he would have. Defeated, he admitted that 'You've heard of token blacks. We'll, we were token Americans' (quoted in Bodo and Hirshey, 1977: 72).

The voice of opposition was, nevertheless, a fairly muted one. Overwhelmingly, the writers who picked up the Pelé story were exceedingly positive and frequently adept at undercutting the stereotypes that traditionally plagued the sport of soccer and stood in its way of becoming a more popular sport on US soil.

## 'Into the Danger Zone He Creeps': Sports Broadcasters Bring Soccer to National Television

Unlike sports writers who have the advantage of weighing and changing their words before they become print, TV sportscasters had to make on-the-spot decisions in how they called a game of soccer to their American audience.[7] Like sports writers, though, sportscasters found themselves in the same rhetorical landscape where they had to simultaneously educate and entertain. One example of the soccer sportscasters' situation and their role in reshaping American views about soccer can be seen in the 1977 NASL Soccer Bowl Championship between the Seattle Sounders and the New York Cosmos, which was Pelé's last professional game (NASL, 1998). Throughout the game, sportscasters Jon Miller and Paul Gardner make interesting choices that seem chiefly motivated by their assumption of an audience that needs almost constant education about the game of soccer. In only the first half of play, the two clarify who 'world-famous' soccer star Carlos Alberto is; the number of World Cups Pelé and the Brazilians have won; what a 'chest trap' is; the fact that the referee keeps time on the field rather than relying on a stadium clock; and numerous fouls and infractions specific to soccer. Had they been addressing a British audience, such remarks would have come as an annoyance.

The two announcers also appear sensitive to the possibility that their audience may become bored while watching a game of soccer. Jon Miller, for instance, invents the hyped-up phrase 'danger zone' to describe goal-scoring opportunities when one team brings the ball within yards of the other team's penalty box. Aware, perhaps, that Americans think of soccer as a slow game,

Miller underscores the game's 'lightning pace' and 'end to end action'. Paul Gardner, understanding his audience's frame of reference, explains the game's tension by describing the Sounders' defense as being like 'a full-court press in basketball . . . always trying to double team the man with the ball'. When the game's second goal is scored within five minutes of the first one, Jon Miller points out this fact, almost proudly, as if to tell his American viewers, 'See, soccer isn't such a boring, low-scoring game after all.'

Gardner and Miller also find opportunities to comment on the American players in the game. Although the teams consisted predominately of foreign players, the announcers give disproportional airtime to the American 'stars'. Miller assures viewers that American player McCallister is 'the wave of the future of this league, born and raised in Seattle and now as good a fullback, a young fullback, as there is in the league. He's going to get a lot better. His first full year.' Likewise, Gardner reserves some of his highest praise for the Cosmos' American goalkeeper, Shep Messing. During a break in the game, viewers hear from Ron Newman, the league's coach of the year, who also praises the American players and asks the rhetorical question, 'Is anybody playing out there better than McCallister or both the goalkeepers, Americans?'

The announcers project a positive view of the sport as one that is fast-growing in the USA. Much of the commentary, in fact, represents a form of soccer boosterism that would be, at best, unnecessary in countries with a soccer heritage and, at worst, a distracting annoyance. At times, however, the curtain seems to lift and one sees that backstage the props are still being arranged for soccer's debut as a major sport in the USA. Would a *Monday Night Football* announcer ever mention, as Jon Miller does, the flight arrival times for the two teams when they return home after the league championship game, and invite fans to greet them at the airport? And what lies behind his suggestion that viewers call up their local television stations and 'tell them you appreciate soccer; they'll be glad to know'? Clearly soccer was, even in Pelé's last season, still a marginal sport that needed to overhaul its image in order to appeal to a wider audience.

## Conclusion: Understanding the Good Press and Weighing the Bad

While my survey of the media's representation of soccer in the 1970s reveals a surprisingly generous attitude toward a marginal sport, I can only speculate about why soccer received such a positive treatment. Of course, one reason for the 'good' press is that NASL promoters organized a viable league and signed the world's most famous player at a record salary, thus providing a story worth telling. Additionally, the story focused on a hero who lived in New York City, the media capital of the world, and played for a team owned by Warner Communications, a major media corporation. The story could hardly have been more accessible. It certainly helped, too, that the hero was Pelé – a superstar with a rags-to-riches story, boyish charm, and a missionary zeal to spread the soccer gospel.

Yet even these conditions, favorable as they were, did not guarantee a positive story. Many Brazilian newspapers, for instance, worked from the same raw materials as their American counterparts but told a very different story, emphasizing Pelé's betrayal of sport and country; instead of hailing him for his selfless desire to promote the game of soccer, these reporters referred to their country's best-loved hero as a 'mercenary' (Jenkins, 1998: 185). Looking back at this period, one British writer sees Pelé's decision to play in the NASL as 'his finest piece of political opportunism' (Jenkins, 1998: 185).[8] It is true that these writers probably knew some facts about Pelé's life that were not as readily available to the American media – for instance, that Pelé was experiencing financial hardship at the time, throwing into question his motives for signing a $4.5 million dollar contract and finishing his career in a foreign country – still, this negative slant could feasibly have entered into the US media's portrayal about soccer's star of the 1970s.

Such negative slants were absent from US reporting for perhaps two reasons. First, even if an American journalist had wanted to 'blow the lid' on the Pelé story, pointing out that the star was really after the money and turned his back on his country, it is unlikely that American readers would be indignant. Why would they be? Few things are more quintessentially 'American' than wanting financial success, and the story of immigrants coming over to seek their fortune is so common that American readers could not be expected to share the Brazilians' outrage over Pelé's 'defection'. A second reason for the lack of negative press has to do with timing. Had Pelé been born a half century earlier and entered American soccer in the 1920s, the attitude towards outsiders would not have been as inviting (Waldstein and Wagg, 1995: 78). By the 1970s, however, Americans had abandoned their tendencies toward isolationism and moved into an opposite era, one in which soccer served as 'some sort of conduit for "multiculturalism" by way of its international appeal' (Markovits and Hellerman, 2001: 172). Thus, the cultural climate of the day suggested that a foreigner like Pelé should be treated as a welcomed ambassador. Instead of resisting him as an outsider, Americans were more likely to thank Pelé for helping them become part of the global village by urging them to 'join the rest of the villagers in their free-flowing, non-linear game' (Miller, 1977:12).

Aside from the promotional brilliance of setting up the Pelé story for the media's easy use, and apart from distinctive qualities of the American audience, a third and far more ambiguous factor was the members of the media – the individual writers and sports announcers themselves. What motivated them to tell a positive story? I am tempted to make two broad categories based on possible intent. In one category we could place those who, like Paul Gardner, had been writing about soccer long before Pelé arrived on the scene. Besides the financial rewards of their work, they hoped to see soccer emerge as a major sport in the USA. In another category, we could put the people who knew little about the game, but were either asked or volunteered to report on Pelé and the growth of soccer. These people might be seen as 'venture journalists', motivated to tell a positive story in the hopes the sport would continue to grow and thus secure them a niche for future writing/announcing assignments. Admittedly, these categories are at best vague and rely on a great deal of 'mind reading'. In fact, the writers and announcers themselves might not be able to reconstruct their own motivations for reporting as they did 25 years ago.

Regardless of their motivations, however, the people who picked up the soccer story in the 1970s probably shared what I have called a common 'rhetorical landscape'. By this I mean that soccer writers and announcers, because they told about a sport that was new to much of their audience and told about it in a context where reader/viewer interest is an assumed imperative, had to be adept at mixing education and excitement.[9] Thus, sports writers in the 1970s were made to 'thread' a rhetorical 'lateral' when attempting to write interesting stories for an audience that expected excitement but needed exposition. Likewise, sports announcers on television crept into their own 'danger zone' because their job assumed that they would be skilled at 'embellishing the drama of the affair, thereby making it more palatable to the action-hungry audience' (Comisky et al., 1981: 343), but in the case of soccer they had to translate the drama as well as embellish it. This rhetorical landscape, then, may be the most convincing explanation for the absence of negative press: with the expectation on them to make the story interesting, and with the additional burden of explaining the story to their audience, writers and announcers simply had no room to add negative critique to their already complicated rhetorical package.

The situation changed, however, during the 1994 World Cup, hosted in the USA. Numerous examples of anti-soccer rhetoric have been noted and discussed by writers on both sides of the Atlantic (Lever, 1995; Markovits and Hellerman; 2001; Sugden and Tomlinson, 1994). The attacks occurred in major newspapers and on network television, including soccer 'slams' by late-night television icons Jay Leno and David Letterman. These instances of 'bad' press were so ubiquitous that a recent book about soccer in the USA can devote eight pages to a 'Sample of the Soccer Hostiles' published about the 1994 World Cup (Markovits and Hellerman, 2001: 286–93). One reason for this comparatively negative press (besides the age-old stereotypes, which have not vanished) may be that writers and commentators could now assume a soccer literate audience. The days of educating their audience were largely over, thus allowing the critics to step in with their words.

Ironically, this bad press tells a good story about the development of soccer in the USA. Whereas the media's overwhelmingly positive portrayal of soccer in the 1970s points to a public willing to fall in love with the new sport on the block, the more recent coverage shows a public that cannot ignore soccer, not even those members who would rather not be bothered by it. To return to the distinction mentioned earlier in this article, that of 'sport as activity' and 'sport as culture', soccer's penetration into American culture is visible not so much by the number of people who play the sport, but by the number who talk about it. These critics of soccer, then, with every bad word they had to say, nevertheless contributed to a conversation featuring a sport that 30 years ago would hardly have occurred to an earlier generation. I would add, too, that the attention (good or bad) that soccer now receives is due in large part to the media's coverage in the 1970s and to a rhetorical situation that turned writers and announcers into sport promoters.

## Notes

1. For detailed accounts of the events surrounding Toye's recruiting efforts, see Kowet (1976: especially chs 1 and 8); Bodo and Hirshey (1977); and Miller (1977).
2. Several authors have summarized and analyzed the history of soccer in the USA. Most point out that the popular view of soccer as a sport for immigrants or schoolgirls has hindered the sport's progression into the mainstream. Excellent accounts include Waldstein and Wagg (1995); Gardner (1976); and, most recently, Markovits and Hellerman (2001).
3. The practice of comparing Pelé to American athletes began early. In the first paragraph of the first US article about Pelé, author Juan de Onis compares Pelé to Mickey Mantle (1962: 7).
4. Unfortunately, Kowet provides no bibliographical reference for Dr Gosling's study.
5. Rote's mixture of allusions here is fascinating. 'King' naturally refers to Pelé's most common nickname; however, within the context of Rote's other allusions, Pelé the King becomes Pelé the Pharaoh of Egypt, while Rote and other NASL old-timers are the slaves. Given that Rote grew up in a middle class family while Pelé grew up in poverty, and given also that Rote is white and Pelé black, the references to slavery carry tremendous irony, even if unintended.
6. Abaddia El Mostofa played for the NASL's Montreal team in the early 1970s.
7. For the idea of examining the comments of sportscasters as a way to investigate their role in shaping Americans' perceptions of soccer, I am indebted to Richard Haynes (1999).
8. In *Soccer Madness*, Janet Lever notes that Brazilian sentiment towards Pelé changed for the positive as a result of 'a public relations campaign . . . [that] allowed the Brazilian people to share this mission and the glory that came with the successful completion of his final retirement in October, 1977' (1995: 143).
9. Such a rhetorical situation was by no means new. Tony Cirino finds a similar trend in news articles devoted to soccer in the 1890s, citing the example of a *New York Times* article called 'Football with the Feet', in which the author uses two columns 'not only explaining the rules of this new game, but also providing tips to pique the interest of prospective spectators' (1983: 7–8).

## References

Adler, L. (1976) *Man with a Mission: Pelé.* Chicago, IL: Raintree Editions.
Bodo, P. and Hirshey, D. (1977) *Pelé's New World.* New York: W.W. Norton.
Cirino, T. (1983) *US Soccer vs the World: The American National Team in the Olympic Games, the World Cup, and other International Competition.* Leonia, NJ: Damon Press.

Comisky, P., Bryant, J. and Zillman, D. (1981) 'Commentary as a Substitute for Action', in M. Hart and S. Birrell (eds) *Sport in the Sociocultural Process.* Dubuque, IA: Wm. C. Brown.

de Onis, J. (1962) 'Soccer Ace Brazil's National Idol', *New York Times* (2 Dec): 7.

*Ebony* (1975) 'Can Pelé Bring the Big Pay Day to U.S. Soccer?' (Sept.): 136–8.

Eskenazi, G. (1980) *A Thinking Man's Guide to Pro Soccer.* New York: Dutton.

Gardner, P. (1976) *The Simplest Game: The Intelligent American's Guide to the World of Soccer.* Boston, MA: Little, Brown.

Glenn, J. (2000) 'The Un-American Game: Our Soccerphobia has Political Roots', *Utne Reader Online.* 16 March. http://www.utne.com.

Haynes, R. (1999) '"There's Many a Slip 'Twixt the Eye and the Lip": An Exploratory History of Football Broadcasts and Running Commentaries on BBC Radio, 1927–1939', *International Review for the Sociology of Sport* 34(2): 143–56.

Jenkins, G. (1998) *The Beautiful Team: In Search of Pelé and the 1970 Brazilians.* Sydney: Simon & Schuster.

Kirshenbaum, J. (1975) 'Curtain Call for a Legend', *Sports Illustrated* (23 June): 8–21.

Kowet, D. (1976) *Pelé.* New York: Atheneum.

Lever, J. (1995) *Soccer Madness: Brazil's Passion for the World's Most Popular Sport.* Prospect Heights, IL: Waveland.

Markovits, A. and Hellerman, S. (2001) *Offside: Soccer and American Exceptionalism.* Princeton, NJ: Princeton University Press.

Miller, L. (1977) 'The Selling of Soccer Mania', *New York Times Magazine* (28 Aug.): 12+.

NASL (1998) *N.A.S.L. Final: New York Cosmos vs Seattle Sounders.* Natchez Trace, MS: Trace Video Sports Club.

*New Yorker* (1975) 'The Talk of the Town' (30 June): 23–4.

*New York Times* (1977) 'Pelé's Farewell: What Soccer has Meant' (2 Sept.): V2.

Pelé (1976) 'Foreword', in P. Gardner, *The Simplest Game: The Intelligent American's Guide to the World of Soccer.* Boston, MA: Little, Brown.

Sabin, L. (1976) *Pelé: Soccer Superstar.* New York: Putnam.

Sugden, J. and Tomlinson, A. (1994) 'Soccer Culture, National Identity, and the World Cup', in *Hosts and Champions: Soccer Cultures, National Identities and the USA World Cup.* Aldershot: Arena.

*Time Magazine* (1971) 'Pelé's Mission Accomplished' (12 Sept.): 62–3.

*Time Magazine* (1975) '4.5 Million Dollar Gamble' (30 June): 56.

Waldstein, D. and Wagg, S. (1995) 'Unamerican Activity? Football in US and Canadian Society', in S. Wagg (ed.) *Giving the Game Away.* London: Leicester University Press.

Young, W.R. (1976) 'Peerless Pelé: Rebirth of a Superstar', *Readers Digest* (Sept.): 113–17.

# 18

# Assessing the Sociology of Sport: On the Mediasport Interpellation and Commodity Narratives

*Lawrence A. Wenner*

Perhaps I wasn't an "accidental tourist" (Tyler, 1985). Still, mine was a side excursion when first visiting the sociology of sport early in the 1980s. Not trained in sociology or sport per se, I thought the field of communication and media studies needed to discover sport. Later I came to think that the sociology of sport needed to discover communication and media studies.

In unique ways the story of sport and media is about two disciplines getting to know each other and meeting occasionally in cultural studies (Whannel, 2013). For the sociologist of sport, it strikes me that studying how media has changed sport, and more importantly, plays in cultural, political, and economic relations, is unavoidable. Yet, even with increasing realization that there could be no big-time sport without big-time media and, in becoming a ubiquitous voice in telling the story of sport, media influenced the doing and meaning of sport at virtually every level, the study of mediated sport remained of peripheral interest in the field for a surprising while. Over time this changed and media became more central and considered in broad inquiries about how sport is framed, understood, enacted, and transacted.

## Trajectories

The early trajectories of media in sport studies and sport in media studies reveal a tale of two nascent and insecure disciplines, both encumbered by academic reputations that needed bolstering, reluctant to dip their toes in

**Source:** *International Review for the Sociology of Sport*, 50(4/5) (2015): 628–633.

the water of the other for fear of weakening their cases for legitimacy (Wenner, 1998b). The push for "scientization" in physical education and the preoccupation with measuring "serious" social effects (e.g., propaganda, violence, children) in media research stifled studying the popular – *media* in sport studies and *sport* in media studies – for some time.

With the rise of British cultural studies, sport and media studies gained "permission" to engage one other without apology. As the study of sport and media advanced, recognition of their symbiosis became so fundamental that neologisms such as "mediasport" (Wenner, 1998b) were created. In this fusion, many scholars saw a cultural power greater than the sum of its parts. Mediasport merges two of Althusser's (1971/2001) ideological state apparatuses in a way that wields considerable influence by masking its force in twin pleasures of sport and media consumption (Wenner, 2013b). Following Althusser, essential reasons for studying the dynamics of the mediasport mix are that (1) "in its contemporary hypercommodified form, the ideological contours and ethical sensibilities of the mediasportscape dominate the cultural meanings that are associated with sport," and (2) "as it fulfills its market roles, mediasport strategically reaches out to us to narrate understandings of sport in the context of broader social relations" (Wenner, 2013b: 83–84).

Indeed, concerns over cultural power undergird bottom line findings about sport and its "mediatization" (Frandsen, 2014). This preoccupation can be seen as study advanced in three core areas of communication inquiry: (1) senders/institutions/production/encoding; (2) messages/content/texts/ representation/signification; and (3) receivers/audiences/fandom/consumption/decoding. Further, as distilled in recent stocktakings (Rowe, 2014; Wenner, 2015) of mediasport research within the sociology of sport, one may synopsize the area's predominant concerns as (1) "money and power" (i.e., commercialization, advertising, mega-events/spectacle, globalization, celebrity) and (2) "framing and identities" (i.e., gender/sex, race/ethnicity, ability/ disability, national/local).

In considering the "power balance" in mediasport and its abilities to cast cultural shadows, we know that mediated sport consumption can bring abundant pleasure and significance for audiences. Here, there is considerable capacity to ignite resourcefulness, and to re-appropriate meaning, often in resistance to institutional narratives. Nonetheless, if one steps back to examine what underlies much mediasport research, concerns over the prospects for meaningful agency in the face of the mediasport cultural complex are considerable. Indeed, for many, the weight of findings about the sport – media nexus symbolize much about what is wrong with sport today: its globalization, corporatization, and commodification; its reliance on spectacle, mega-events, and celebrity; its tendencies to reinforce dominant cultural ideologies; and its powers to essentialize and naturalize difference through characterizations of nation, race, gender, and other identities.

## Challenges

I often make the case for studying mediasport within the sociology of sport by asserting "the frame is more important than the game" (Wenner, 2006: 55). This is part hyperbole designed to disrupt sport-centered thinking and advance media on the agenda of the sociology of sport. Still, there is much truth in the claim. The "story" of sport, the explanations of its meaning and importance, may be far more culturally significant than the mounting of sport or the results of competition. Admittedly, the story of sport is told in many quarters. The voices of participants, spectators, functionaries, and many others articulate stories. Still, the relevance of Gerbner's refrain that "those people who tell most of the stories most of the time control a culture" (see Morgan, 2002) is obvious for the meaningful study of sport in culture. The simple answer concerning who tells most of the stories most of the time about sport is the media. Accordingly, disproportionate amounts of mediasport inquiry have focused on messages, content, texts, representations, and signification.

A ready pragmatic force fuels this fire. We often do the "easy stuff" first in clearing pathways to expedite scholarly careers. Textual analysis avoids the challenges of gaining access to study the organizations and workers who produce mediasport and is less cumbersome than doing systematic audience study. Yet, this structural imbalance persists in mediasport inquiry. In some areas, we need to reassess our gains. For example, our often-reproduced findings about the constancy of gender and racial inequities in media coverage have reached a point where we need to better connect dots to other parts of the communicative process. We need to better understand the organizational and professional cultures as well as market pressures that produce systematic biases, stereotypes, and exclusion. We need more insight about how different kinds of audiences are reading, embracing, and resisting such entrenched tendencies.

Simply put, connecting the dots, always an underlying concern of Hall's (1973) encoding/decoding model, remains a central challenge in mediasport research. As well, often overlooked is an important "part of the story" about the "telling of the story" of sport as it has been institutionalized in embedded proclivities of media. We need to better contextualize our deconstructions of the stories being told with increased sophistication about the omnipresent commodity context (Wenner, 2013a). In tandem, we need to give more attention to the form of address that is being used – consistently, strategically, and powerfully – to hail us. I argue that there is a surprisingly constant character to the hailing in media that aids and abets telling, and naturalizing, the tale of sport (Wenner, 2013b).

Notably, mediated sport narratives are inherently "dirty" and commodified (Wenner, 2007, 2009, 2013a). They are dirty, invoking Douglas's (1966) seminal notion, because sporting logics, spread as contagion, wield influence by appending to other spheres of culture, naturalized but little recognized as "matter out of place" (p. 66). Communicative engagement with sports dirt, intertwined with fanship enthusiasm, may receive little resistance as it is ritualistic, compartmentalized, and aimed at pleasure. When one factors this in along with Bauman's (2007) observations about "consumer sociality" pervading in an obligatory "market-mediated mode of life" and Debord's (1967/2004) conclusion that today's lived world is anchored in a commodity logic, it is hard to see sport narratives on media's main stages as anything other than commodity narratives. While sport-related advertising narratives are most archetypal, sports reporting, commentary, and announcing across media platforms are necessarily set in the logics of consuming both sport and media.

Over time, main stage mediasport conventions have coalesced around a form of address, a way of "hailing" and anchoring subject position, in telling the tale of sport that I call the "mediasport interpellation" (Wenner, 2013b). Here, hailing us through a dominant, stable, and interlocked "holy trinity" of gender, fan, and consumer identities in relation to sport is foundational to mediasport power. While cognizant that hailing to other identities – such as race, ethnicity, class, and nation – factor into many mediasport ideological equations, the mediasport interpellation poses that assertions about gender, the workings of fanship, and assumptions about consumption undergird the ideological work of mediasport narratives.

Gender remains the great divide of sport. Privileging male sport with routine celebration on culture's main stages, mediasport expands that crevasse. Even with increased pressures for change in gender roles and power relations, men continue to largely "own" sport and its consumption, and mediasport enables celebrating a last bastion of "vestigial hypermasculinity" (Wenner, 1998a). Further, mediated sport's narrative spaces routinely engage in symbolic annihilation, trivialization, and ambivalence when characterizing women in relation to sport.

Mediated sport also helps construct and hail a particularlized fanship. Fanship norms, for female and male fans, disproportionately follow and celebrate male sporting performance. The naturalization of female fanship for male sport is well-entrenched and male (and even female) fanship for women's sport has been exceptional and elusive. When main media stages, such as Olympic Games coverage, focus on women's sport, much is "gender appropriate." Finally, media castings of sport fanship, from characterized fan-ship in advertising (Wenner, 2013b) to those highlighted in coverage of contests, rely on self-serving imagery celebrating diehard, animated, colorful fans who consume (male) sport with rabid commitment.

Through the constancy of such "imagined" fanship, media sport coverage and sport-anchored advertising have worked to align our fanship identities with our consumer identities. The hypercommodification that has infused our relations with both sport and media is now foundational. Following Bauman (2007), in an increasingly promotional mediasportscape, sport fans are both idealized as consumers and have become commodities themselves.

As a consequence, sport fans, in both "lived experience" and idealized narrative imaginings, have their agency increasingly defined and confined by the commodity context while cognizant of their own commodity value (Wenner, 2007). Through constant hailing, sport-related consumption has been established and experienced as pleasure. It is this seating in pleasure that enables the dirty entailments of mediasport to resonate with consumers and mobilize lasting ideological powers.

## Futures

Some suggest that with the advance of new digital and social media, much change is likely for mediasport. There is much fine work in this area (Hutchins and Rowe, 2013) and, I am afraid, some undue euphoria. Some portend that new media will bring meaningful new relations in how sport transacts culturally as more of us become "prosumers," producing media as well as consuming it.

My assessment, based on what I see as the "lasting power" of the mediasport interpellation, aligns with the French expression "the more things change, the more they stay the same" (Wenner, 2014). This is not meant to be flippant or disregard that new media may indeed bring new opportunities for the citizen-fan to interact in the mediasphere about sport. Rather, it is to say that the "mediatization" and "sportification" logics that are embedded in the mediasport interpellation are considerable. They are also enmeshed with pleasure and entrenched subject positions.

For the foreseeable future, dominant mediasport will remain the rock hitting the water, with ripples from its splash largely setting the terms and conditions of engagement for new and social media. After all, the fodder and cultural logic concerning sport that grounds social media and blogging has to emanate from somewhere. The sporting contest, the point of departure, still resides in the hands of institutionalized mediasport. Thus, new sport media will likely build from a reliance on the old.

Because of this, change, the need for which is embedded throughout the scholarly research agenda for mediasport, may be slower than anticipated. Still, the future for mediated sport research is bright. Concern over mediated sport has spread across a broad palette to color the sociology of sport. Mediasport, now with dedicated scholarly journals and fast increasing legitimacy in communication and media studies, has reached critical mass. One can only hope that, with this, the received logic and power of the mediasport interpellation will begin to give way.

## References

Althusser L (1971/2001) *Lenin and Philosophy and Other Essays* (trans. B Brewster). New York: Monthly Review Press.
Bauman Z (2007) *Consuming Life.* Cambridge: Polity.

Debord G (1967/2004) *The Society of the Spectacle* (trans. D Nicholson-Smith). New York: Zone Books.

Douglas M (1966) *Purity and Danger: An Analysis of Pollution and Taboo.* London: Routledge & Kegan Paul.

Frandsen K (2014) Mediatization of sports. In: Lundby K (ed.) *The Handbook of Mediatization of Communication.* Berlin: Mouton de Gruyter, pp. 525–543.

Hall S (1973) *Encoding and Decoding in the Television Discourse.* Birmingham: Center for Contemporary Cultural Studies.

Hutchins B and Rowe D (eds) (2013) *Digital Media Sport: Technology, Power and Culture in the Network Society.* New York: Routledge.

Morgan M (ed.) (2002) *Against the Mainstream: The Selected Works of George Gerbner.* New York: Peter Lang.

Rowe D (2014) Media studies and sport. In: Maguire J (ed.) *Social Sciences in Sport.* Champaign, IL: Human Kinetics, pp. 130–152.

Tyler A (1985) *The Accidental Tourist.* New York: Knopf.

Wenner LA (1998a) In search of the sports bar: Masculinity, alcohol, sports and the mediation of public space. In: Rail G (ed.) *Sport and Postmodern Times.* Albany, NY: SUNY Press, pp. 301–332.

Wenner LA (1998b) Playing mediasport. In: Wenner LA (ed.) *Mediasport.* London: Routledge, pp. 3–13.

Wenner LA (2006) Sport and media through the super glass mirror: Placing blame, breastbeating, and a gaze to the future. In: Raney AA and Bryant J (eds) *Handbook of Sports Media.* Hillsdale, NJ: Lawrence Erlbaum, pp. 45–60.

Wenner LA (2007) Towards a dirty theory of narrative ethics. Prolegomenon on media, sport and commodity value. *International Journal of Media and Cultural Politics* 3(2): 111–129.

Wenner LA (2009) The unbearable dirtiness of being: On the commodification of mediasport and the need for ethical criticism. *Journal of Sports Media* 4(1): 85–94.

Wenner LA (2013a) Media, sport, and consumer culture: The fan as consumer in television commercials. In: Pedersen PM (ed.) *Handbook of Sport Communication.* London: Routledge, pp. 410–420.

Wenner LA (2013b) The mediasport interpellation: Gender, fanship, and consumer culture. *Sociology of Sport Journal* 30(1): 83–103.

Wenner LA (2014) On the limits of the new and the lasting power of the mediasport interpellation. *Television and New Media.* Epub ahead of print 6 May. DOI:10.1177/1527476414532957.

Wenner LA (2015) Sport and media. In: Giulianotti R (ed.) *Routledge Handbook of the Sociology of Sport.* London: Routledge.

Whannel G (2013) Reflections on communication and sport: On mediatization and cultural analysis. *Communication & Sport* 1(1): 7–17.

# 19

# The Unholy Alliance: Notes on Television and the Remaking of British Sport 1965–85

*Garry Whannel*

'In the 1960s an unholy alliance was developing. Sport was helping to make television and television was helping to make sport' (McCormack, 1984).

In the last twenty years British sport has gone through a transformation as dramatic as its earlier formative period of 1875–1900. The driving force of this transformation has been the changing economic environment produced by the spread of television and the massive growth of sponsorship. These economic forces have in turn produced a cultural transformation. The desire of sponsors for television coverage has meant that television's own needs have become a crucial factor for sport organizations to consider when planning their strategies. Athletics, a sport in the process of professionalization, is taken as a case study.

## Introduction

The period from 1875 to 1900 saw a transformation of British sport that laid the foundations for the next 100 years. Many national governing bodies were founded, often rooted in and establishing the amateur/professional division. Large-scale professionalized spectator sport began to develop. New national

**Source:** *Leisure Studies*, 5(2) (1986): 129–145.

competitions like the Football League and cricket's County Championship emerged (see Whannel, 1983a). The last twenty years has seen a similar period of transformation which, it can be argued, constitutes a remaking of British sport. The growth of television and sponsorship have together constituted an economic force that has in turn generated a cultural transformation in an uneven and contradictory process that has affected different sports in different ways.

The 1950s and 1960s were a period of crisis for traditional forms of sport organization, a crisis which in Britain revolved around financial crisis and control, and concepts of the amateur and the professional. The traditional amateur, benevolent paternalism of sports organization came under pressure from entrepreneurial interests as the contradiction between sport's financially deprived organizations and its commercial potential widened.

The income for sports organizations came from a variety of sources, principally gate revenue, membership fees, grants, television fees and a fairly low level of sponsorship. But the expansion of television, the increase in sport coverage and the growth of an international market in televised sport were making television coverage a major factor in sport economics. It was not simply that television fees opened up a new source of revenue, but rather that television served as a great attraction to sponsors. The attraction was considerably heightened in 1965 when television advertising of cigarettes was banned. Consequently major tobacco firms, such as John Player, Benson and Hedges and Marlboro, chose to plough large sums into television sport.

A sponsorship explosion began in the mid-1960s and has not yet abated. It has transformed the face of British sport. Sports are increasingly prone to ensure that they meet the requirements of television by providing events in the form that television finds attractive. Minor sports unable to get television coverage have gone through extensive contortions in attempts to appeal to this medium. In short, television's own definitions as to what constitutes good television sport have come to be of great influence in the world of sport itself.

While sport has always been a form of entertainment, certainly since the growth of spectator sport in the nineteenth century, it has always been a very particular form of entertainment. Based on uncertainty, both of outcome and of quality of performance, it therefore does not offer the same guarantee of quality as a theatrical or variety performance. It can be argued that, traditionally, spectators have accepted that some matches will be good and some dull.

One of the characteristics of any form of capitalist entrepreneurship and rationalized production is the attempt to reduce the uncertainty of the commodity. The increased penetration of sport by capital and resultant infusion of spectacular, internationalized and glamourized forms of entertainment can be seen as an attempt to reduce the uncertainty of the sporting commodity, at least as far as its entertainment value is concerned. Hence television's tendency to try and ensure that even if the event is dull, by judicious highlights, action replays, interviews etc., the programme itself can be entertaining. But television's conventions as to what constitutes good entertainment have become a determining factor upon sporting cultures themselves.

## State of Sport in the 1950s and Early 1960s

British sport after the Second World War and into the 1950s was particularly vulnerable to the economic forces leading to a redefinition and transformation of the sporting scene. Most sports, dominated by traditionalist, amateur, paternalist, voluntary administration, were slow to see or exploit commercial potential and in many cases had a marked resistance to the world of commerce. They were also slow to respond to the effects of an expanding leisure market in creating greater competition, which was to have a depressant effect on many traditional sports.

Athletics and cricket began to suffer serious declines in crowd numbers during this period, as did football. In 1955, ten days of athletics drew 290 000 to the White City, but by 1961 this was down to 160 000 and this was only the start of a decline that took crowds at some meetings down to the hundreds. The 1959 AAA championship was watched by one of the smallest crowds for years and the AAA had a £6000 deficit. The next two years saw a slight improvement, but in 1962 crowds were at their lowest since the war and there was little improvement for the next four years. By 1967 the AAA Annual Report saw bankruptcy as a very real threat. In 1969 the Saturday attendance of 8000 at the AAA championships was the lowest since before the First World War (Lovesey, 1979).

Cricket, too, was suffering. The total gate at the County Championship games slumped from 2 126 000 in 1949 to 750 000 in 1965. A 1956 Report into the Cricket Industry (PEP) said cricket could not survive on its gate revenue alone. Many counties were heading for bankruptcy and secretaries were finding it harder than ever to attract enough money from private benefactors. The traditional structure of the game was close to collapse (Brookes, 1978). Football, because of its large following, had generally had greater financial security than many sports but its crowds, too, were falling. Annual football league gates dropped from a post-war boom peak of 41.2 million in 1948–9 to 28.6 million in 1960–1.

Many sports underwent significant changes. Football abolished the maximum wage in 1960. Cricket abolished the old distinction between gentlemen (amateurs) and players (professionals) in 1962. Tennis abandoned its amateur-only rules to go open in 1967. Athletics remained amateur, but the pressures that led to the changes in amateur status rules in the 1980s were already beginning to develop. Meanwhile, television sport was entering a period of development and expansion. Sponsorship, which was a relatively insignificant source of income until the 1960s, was about to take off into a period of rapid expansion.

In a whole series of sports the power and authority of traditional sports organizations was to be challenged and threatened by entrepreneurial interests. The traditional organizations were characterized by under-capitalization, voluntary management and an amateur paternal–benevolent ideology. The new entrepreneurs operated with market-place economic principles and the ideology of show business within the rapidly growing leisure industry. The possibilities opened up by television, sponsorship and a worldwide star system formed the basis of their emergent power. The contradiction between traditional authority and new entrepreneurship developed in different forms in different sports.

## Growth of Sponsorship

Two factors were of particular importance in the emergence of sport sponsorship as a major force: the development of televised sport in the 1950s and 1960s and the banning of cigarette advertising on television in 1965.

In 1950 there were just 343 882 TV licences, covering 2% of British households. By 1954 this figure was up tenfold to 3.2 million sets. The launch of ITV in 1955 gave a further boost and by 1960 82% of the population had access to television (Paulu, 1961). The launch of BBC2 in 1964 led to an increase in the amount (although not the percentage), of sport on TV, gave the BBC the means to increase the range of sports and provided space for Sunday cricket and extended coverage of cricket, tennis and golf (Bough, 1980). Just as the growth of jet travel in the 1960s was making sport more international, so the spread of communication satellites gave television live access to international events around the world. Telstar, launched in 1962, bridged the Atlantic; in 1964 the Tokyo Olympics were broadcast live to 39 countries; and the 1968 Olympics were the first to be seen in colour in Britain. Along with colour, other technological advances in video editing and slow motion action replay, gave a great boost to the spectacle of existing televised sports and led to the successful promotion of new ones, most notably snooker.

Meanwhile, in 1965, the British Government had banned the advertising of cigarettes on television. While not all sponsorship was from cigarette firms, it was firms like Rothmans, John Player and Benson and Hedges that led the way. Sport sponsorship in Britain grew from less than £1 million in 1966 to £2.5 million in 1970, and this was only the beginning. By 1976 it was £16 million, by 1980 around £46 million, and in 1983 it was thought to be topping £100 million (Howell, 1983). As sponsorship proved its worth as a device for marketing and for establishing a corporate image, tobacco and alcohol sponsors were joined in increasing numbers by financial institutions, in particular Cornhill with their highly successful sponsorship of Test cricket.

Sponsorship is sometimes portrayed as a new form of patronage, which to a certain extent it is. But it is also firmly driven by entrepreneurial interest. A 1977 survey by The Cranfield School of Management, found that 'There is very little evidence to support the view that sponsorship is an altruistic activity' (Waite, 1976). Sponsorship was being adopted for pragmatic and commercial reasons and the three main criteria were: the ability of a sport to attract media coverage; a link between the sponsor and sponsored regarding the product, the product image or the corporate image; and the demographic profile of participants or spectators of the activity. The report points out that 'media coverage may not be of the over-riding significance which it is believed to be. If all coverage by TV, radio and press were to be stopped only 12% of respondents indicate that they would definitely not continue to sponsor' (Waite, 1976). Although the respondents may indeed claim this, there is extensive evidence to point to the vital importance of television coverage in attracting sponsors. In 1981, Cornhill's banners at Test match cricket appeared 7459 times on television, and the awareness level (the number of people who mentioned Cornhill when asked to name all the insurance firms they could remember) shot up to 17% compared with 2% in 1977 (*Economist*, 22/5/82). Of the top nine sponsored sports in 1982, all but motor racing were also amongst the top nine most televised sports (Sportscan, 1982).

One major effect of the growth of televised sport has been the heightened visibility of star performers and the consequent boost to their access to fringe benefits. England footballer Kevin Keegan was reported to have earned well over £250 000 in 1978, only half of which came directly from football. The rest came from media fees, endorsements and promotion deals. He has had, at various times, contracts with Nabisco, Lyons Maid, Mitre Footballs, Arthur Barker publishers, British Export Fashions, Patrick UK (boots), Fabergé (Brut), Harry Fenton suits, BBC, London Weekend Television (LWT) and Heinz Beans. He has had three companies – Kevin Keegan Investments, Kevin Keegan Enterprises and Kevin Keegan Sports and Leisure – registered in the Isle of Man, where the tax is 21% (*Sunday Times*, 15/10/78 and 16/11/80).

In the late 1970s Bjorn Borg's promotional contracts brought him $50 000 a year to wear Tuborg handbands, $25 000 to wear a shoulder patch for Scandinavian Airlines, $200 000 for wearing Fila clothes, $50 000 for wearing Tretorn shoes, $20 000 for using VS gut, $100 000 for his US racket and about $100 000 for a different European racket (Kramer, 1979, p. 271). By the 1980s, these earnings were easily available even to those in supposedly amateur sports. In 1980, US marathon runner Bill Rodgers made between $200 000 and $250 000 selling his own brand of shoes and clothes, speaking, writing, giving clinics and from three Bill Rodgers Runner Center shops in Boston (*Sunday Times*, 12/7/81).

Along with the increased prominence of television sport, emergence of international stars and growth of sponsorship, came the growing power of a new role, the sport agent, a middle man who handled economic relations between individual sports stars, sports organizations, promoters, sponsors, advertisers and television companies. Such agents have become a major and powerful new feature of world sport. As they are often able to obtain commission from more than one of the parties to an agreement, it is sometimes hard to see in whose interest they are acting. Among the most powerful agencies are Mark McCormack's International Management Group (IMG), and West Nally.

McCormack first came to prominence as the agent of three golfers who dominated the game during the 1960s, Arnold Palmer, Gary Player and Jack Nicklaus. These three dominated two decades of golf. By 1969 they had won 20 of the major championships. From 1960 the American Masters was won successively by Palmer, Player, Palmer, Nicklaus, Palmer, Nicklaus and Nicklaus. Starting with these three was a lucky break and the foundation of McCormack's empire followed rapidly. 'By 1966 we had become a major presence in golf. We were organised, we had the right people in place and we knew where we were going. I thought we had better diversify' (McCormack, 1984, p. 163). He has gone on to represent, among others, Arnold Palmer, Jackie Stewart, Chris Evert, Jean Claude Killy, Billy Jean King, Michael Parkinson, Peter Alliss, Muhammad Ali, Angela Rippon and, in perhaps the ultimate triumph of diversification, the Pope. He has been reported to take an average of 25% and sometimes as much as 50% in commission. 'I always talk about winning. I'm very competitive and self confident – both inwardly and outwardly – and I don't mind showing it. I want to win more points than the next man' (McCormack, 1984).

McCormack became a pioneer in the field of made-for-TV events and in 1966 set up a subsidiary, Trans World International (TWI). McCormack had already sold *The Big Three play Britain* (featuring Palmer, Nicklaus and Player) to the BBC and TWI followed this with *International Golf*, which ran for years. His company was to develop the made-for-TV event with increasing sophistication, setting up the Legends men and womens tennis tours, the world championship of womens golf, the Pepsi Grand Slam and the World Triathlon Championship.

After acquiring a dominant position in golf by the early 1970s, IMG rapidly expanded its operation into tennis. 'Apart from Connors and Evert, virtually all the top talent in men's and women's tennis is controlled by Donald Dell or Mark McCormack' (Kramer, 1979, p. 273). TWI ran a tennis series in the 1970s for CBS, *Winner Take All*, which was criticized by Congress because, unknown to the public, appearance money was paid (*Evening Standard*, 18/9/80). IMG became a management consulting and marketing firm operating out of 15 offices around the world, whose work ranges from creating and implementing sports events for over 100 corporations to operating fashion modelling agencies out of New York and London. In 1984 gross revenues were expected to exceed $200 million (McCormack, 1984).

McCormack now claims that TWI is the world's leading independent producer of sports programming and the world's largest representative of television rights to international sporting events. The company produces or co-produces nearly 200 hours of sports programming each year, including *Superstars* for the BBC and *Battle of the Network Stars* for ABC, numerous skiing, track and field events for CBS, the World Professional Figure Skating championships and the Chevrolet World Championship of Women's Golf for NBC. It represents international television rights for Wimbledon, the US Tennis Open, the NFL, the National Basketball Association and most of the major golf championships. McCormack is quite clear about the importance of star personalities: 'If I were forced to repeat IMG's initial success today, I would have to wait for the right combination of factors – the connections – to come along; an emerging new participant sport; one with seeming whirlwind growth potential, and a superstar who embodied the essence of that sport' (McCormack, 1984).

McCormack is aware of his power to influence the direction that sport takes, but claims that he doesn't interfere: 'In a sport such as tennis, where we represent many of its corporate sponsors, all merchandising and TV rights to Wimbledon, the television rights to the US Open, 15 of the top 20 men and women players and run numerous events and series of events, I have no doubt, if we wanted to, we could make an impact on the way the sport is structured and the way it is governed. This would be very short sighted' (McCormack, 1984 p. 172). In the context of such accumulated power it is hard to take McCormack's claim of non-involvement with the policy of sport organizations seriously.

Another agent, West Nally, has concentrated its efforts in dealing with governing bodies rather than individuals. It has played a significant role in the gradual move to open professionalism in the athletics world. For instance, in 1980 West Nally paid International Amateur Athletic Federation (IAAF) $400 000 for a three-year deal to promote a series of Golden Events, which was to include a clash between Coe and Ovett. They make their money by finding sponsors and selling the TV rights and stadium advertising space. The Golden Mile was to be at Crystal Palace: the BBC could show it as part of their own deal, and many European countries could get it through the EBU, but West Nally sold the USA rights to NBC for about $50 000 (*Guardian*, 20/8/80). It also played a key role in the first World Athletic Championships in 1983. This event was expected to earn the IAAF between $20 million and $25 million. West Nally sold the television rights, film rights, sponsorship and ground advertising. As in the 1984 Olympics, sponsorship was sold to a small number of companies which West Nally said they hoped would bring 'dignity as well as profit to the event' (*Television Weekly*, 20/6/83). The European Broadcasting Union paid nearly $1 million for the television rights. Sponsors like Coca Cola, Iveco, Kodak, Canon and TDK paid around $1 million each, as well as presumably providing what they could in the way of 'dignity'. The audience was believed to have topped 1000 million.

Sports organizations increasingly came to identify sponsorship as crucial to survival. It was believed that television coverage was essential to attract the more lucrative sponsorship deals, so consequently sports have increasingly emphasized the need for coverage. Television's own practices, then, became particularly important. Sports were more eager than ever to ensure that they could provide what the television professionals wanted.

## Television Wants a Good Show

There is not the space for a detailed text analysis of television sport, or an extended discussion of its practices. In such work, the importance of stars and personalities, action and drama, spectacle and audience identification has often been emphasized (see Buscombe, 1975; Clarke and Clarke, 1982; Colley and Davies, 1982; Whannel, 1984). Clearly, television foregrounds stars, and in interviews and discussions begins to transform them into celebrities and personalities. Action is important to televised sport but certain sports (tennis, snooker, boxing) provide it in a way that seems to fit particularly neatly into the television frame. Such sports can be covered with very simple camera cutting patterns. By contrast, the coverage of golf or motor racing requires more visual work by television: note the large number of cameras and use of split screens in American golf coverage. Sports offer a narrative that promises to reveal an answer to the question 'who will win?' and the more dramatic the process of discovering the answer the better viewers are seen to like it by television authorities. (Note the preference for one-day cricket over the frequently less-conclusive five-day variety, and in American television the outlawing of the draw – drawn soccer games are settled with the infamous 'shoot-out'.) The spectacle of the Olympic Games and the World Cup obviously provides television with its largest audiences for sport, but even at less glamorous levels, the spectacle provided by a large visible and audible crowd is an important factor for television. Lastly, the ability to construct points of identification for the audience, either around star performers (tennis) or around national partisanship (football) and ideally both (most successful in the case of Torvill and Dean), is something in which television excels. In 1975, the head of sport for LWT, John Bromley, cited four basic conditions for good televised sport: the sport must have simple rules and be easily understood; it must be visual; it must be possible to televise it without involving too much extra work and expense, i.e. it must be practical to televise it; and the event must be capable of drawing a reasonable crowd at the venue (CCPR, 1975).

As well as having a clear idea about what it wants from sport, television also, by and large, gets it cheap. The occasional headlines about multi-million pound deals create a false impression. Early in 1985, the BBC and ITV were believed to be prepared to pay £19 million for four years of league football, but if one assumes a weekly football programme, plus all the clips needed for the Saturday lunch-time previews, this is possibly the equivalent of £50 000 per hour of television – certainly not cheap, but not extravagant for a sport that still, even after recent declines, commands a bigger audience than most sports. ITV captured athletics by offering £10 million for five years, which could be around £60 000 an hour, an expensive gamble on a sport with rising popularity in an effort by ITV to challenge the traditional BBC dominance of sport. Other popular sports like snooker and cricket are much cheaper for television, because of the large number of broadcast hours over which the payment for the rights can be defrayed, and, particularly for snooker, the production cost efficiency of having an outside broadcast unit in one site for a fortnight, providing several hours a day of television. The high fees paid for two or three major sports have to be set against the large number of hours devoted annually to television sport (generally over 1100 on BBC and over 600 on ITV and Channel Four). It is hard to put an exact cost-per-hour on television sport: it could be somewhere between £40 000 and £60 000. Tunstall's (1983) figures suggest it is around one third of the cost of major drama, and generally cheaper than documentary, current affairs and much light entertainment.

Indeed, while athletics and football can push for big fees, most minor sports are forced to compete with each other for the attentions of television, which, in a buyers market, can afford to play them off against each other. At the 1976 CCPR Conference, Alan Hart, head of BBC Sport, referred to the need to have long-term contracts, running for at least two to four years, and took a tough line over fees: 'An event which might cost £200 to buy and another £4000 to televise for a good but hardly world shattering 15 minutes was expensive by any standards' (CCPR, 1976). In fact television at £16 000 an hour was fairly cheap, and the amount actually paid to the sport (£200) was pitifully low. One theme of this conference was the advantage of two or three minority sports combining in one venue over 48 hours in order to fit the needs of television. The financial value of series like *Top Table* (table tennis) and *Jack High* (bowls) to television is that enough material for seven programmes can be recorded in 48 hours. Each of these series cost only twice as much as a single 30 minute slot of the same sport on *Grandstand*. The lure of sponsorship was often enough to encourage minor sports to accept low fees from television.

## Transformation in Sport

The importance of television coverage has in turn resulted in a whole series of transformations as sports try to ensure that their events are presented in forms suitable for television. One-day cricket is perhaps the most dramatic example. As a response to the financial crisis developing in the 1950s, the MCC were making cautious moves towards sponsorship and investigating the possibility of a one-day knockout cup. The following year, a Midlands experiment, inspired by Leicestershire and televised by ATV proved one-day limited overs competition to be practical. Meanwhile, the American company, Gillette, faced with competition from the new Wilkinson Sword blade, were looking for a truly English activity to help their image. By 1963, cautious overtures had led to Gillette providing a trophy and £6500 for the Gillette Cup, a small beginning for a cricket revolution.

Meanwhile the interests of television, professional cricketers and tobacco companies were about to combine in a dramatic fashion. Bryan Cowgill of the BBC wanted a regular cricket series, but one that could be televised start to finish, that would attract a new cricketing audience by offering a beginning, a middle and an end, but above all a definite result. He wanted a format that 'would encourage the players to be aggressive in their approach, where the hitting of sixes would bring rewards, where the scoring of the series' fastest fifty and the taking of wickets by bowlers rather than merely containing the run rate would put money in their pockets' (Bough, 1980, p. 19). Rothmans, anxious to retain a television visibility after the cigarette advertising ban, agreed to sponsor a series of televised Sunday cricket featuring the Rothmans International Cavaliers. The experiment was so successful, both in providing cheap Sunday afternoon programming for BBC2 and in pulling in crowds to cricket, that after a 1967 match had staggered the MCC by attracting 15 000 to Lords, the counties stepped in and set up their own Sunday League, sponsored by John Player. By 1972, West Nally had set up a third one-day competition sponsored by Benson and Hedges (see Ross, 1981; Laker, 1977; Willis, 1981; Bose, 1983).

The BBC and Bryan Cowgill also took a leading role in the introduction of open tennis. By the 1960s both Wimbledon and the BBC were becoming unhappy at the constant disappearance of top players into the professional circuits. Cowgill suggested an eight-man trial professional event to be staged at Wimbledon in August 1967. BBC provided $35 000 for the singles, and Wimbledon contributed $10 000 for the doubles. Once Herman David and Wimbledon became converted to the cause of open tennis, the rest of the tennis world rapidly followed suit and by 1968 tennis became open to professionals (Kramer, 1979, p. 259).

Football has always had a degree of resistance to the forces transforming British sport since the 1960s. Its substantial revenue from spectators, and status as the major national sport, gave it a greater negotiating power with television. The Football League resisted live football until 1983 and placed restrictions preventing any recorded football material being televised on Saturday afternoons. However, since the 1970s rising costs, escalating transfer fees and wage bills and declining gates have put pressure on the game, while the growing potential of sponsorship has become irresistable. The Football League finally agreed to live football in 1983 in exchange for which television allowed shirt advertisements, thus greatly increasing the sponsorship potential of major clubs. This turned out to be the first step towards the current stalemate, with the Football League locked into a conflict between the interests of the élite clubs who, in demanding a higher share of television and sponsorship revenue, are insisting on a rationalization (or pruning) of the League, and the second, third and fourth division clubs who are fighting a rearguard action to retain the Football League's distributive function, maintaining full-time football throughout the country.

Clearly, there is a host of sports whose popularity is largely due to television exposure. Television made show jumping a popular sport in the 1960s, did the same for snooker and darts in the 1970s, and some have high hopes that bowls can become the television sport of the 1980s. Increasingly, sports are prepared to devise made-for-TV events. Many of the proliferating snooker tournaments feature shorter matches than most professionals regard as a fair test of skill. The staging of basketball is noticeably aimed more at the camera than the live spectator, with individual introductions and microphones to catch the coaches' briefings. The Kellogs round-the-city cycling on Channel Four introduced a completely new mode of racing to Britain as a way of meeting television's requirements. The television professionals have been quite prepared to spell out the kind of changes they would like to see sports make. One sport with a large popular following, but persistent problems with television coverage, is badminton. People within the game resent the lack of coverage (South Western Sports Council, 1974) but Barry Davies argues that it does not easily fit the conventions of television, being a game with no natural pauses. 'The game's subtleties and disguise cry out for the use of slow motion but when could it be used?' Davies praises an experiment in different scoring methods during the Prudential mixed doubles (matches consisted of the best of five games, decided by nine points, with a clear break between games.) He claims that this increased the drama and excitement without falsifying the sport and goes on to describe some of the technical problems of camera placement and the need for careful use of close ups, 'a necessary part of the building of personalities on which any sport depends' ('TV's eye on Badminton', by Barry Davies, *Badminton*, October 1979).

During the 1970s, rowing, too, began to realize the importance of stars. The Amateur Rowing Association (ARA) made several attempts to obtain more television coverage between 1965 and 1970, but meetings with John Snagge and Alan Hart (then of *Sportsview*) brought no real change (ARA, 1969). The rowing authorities were concerned over the upper class image acquired by the exposure of Henley and the Boat Race to the exclusion of most other competitive rowing (ARA, 1971) and were worried at their lack of star personalities: 'What rowing needs even more than the drawing power of TV coverage, is a personality. We've not got a Georgie Best and that's part of the trouble when you seek sponsors. Nothing sells like success and had we won even a bronze medal at last year's Olympics it would have been a lot easier now' (Michael Stamford, Chair of the ARA sponsorship committee, in *Sportsworld*, June 1973).

By the mid-1970s they had quite clearly identified television as a pathway to sponsorship: 'The increase in public interests that would flow from additional television coverage and further international success, particularly if the ARA produced medal winning crews in the Olympics will give us a far stronger platform with which to seek sponsorship' (ARA, 1974).

Sponsors, too, are keen to promote change if it will lead to television coverage. Water polo had only had five events televised in 20 years, when they obtained their first sponsor, Aquafresh for a tournament played under amended rules. Further changes were discussed, 'to improve water polo's image, the rules should also be easily understood by the fans or potential fans, who will come in increased numbers to watch fast, exciting and well presented water polo'. The changes included a decreased playing area, to create the impression of a faster game, and additional balls and ballboys to save time and allow the game to flow more freely. (*Swimming Coach*, July 1975). One is tempted to add that removing the water might be worth trying too.

The Table Tennis authorities, together with their Coca Cola sponsors, commissioned a report in 1970, which offered extensive advice on how the game could improve its image. Suggestions included the need for a professional MC who would warm up audiences, teams to be introduced by a fanfare, instructed on how to time their entrances and exits, and to line up facing each other while anthems were played. It called for players 'to be encouraged to show by their bearing, much greater poise and sense of occasion', and called for development of the personality approach. It advocated a commentator with thorough knowledge of the sport but advised that he should 'sell the match as hard as he can'. It called for non-playing captains to be seated in positions where 'better pictures are obtained of them when they are giving instructions to their players between games' (Rawes and Partners, 1970).

Table tennis went actively touting for new sponsors, offering the English Open, shown in *Grandstand*, for £2500 and the English Closed, covered by *World of Sport*, for £1500, or as a job lot, the two for £4000 (ETTA, 1972). After extensive efforts in the build up to the 1977 World Championships, held in Britain, they eventually obtained a series of sponsorship deals with Norwich Union (*World Championship's 1977 Think Tank*, 21/9/73).

## The Case of Athletics

The recent history of athletics reveals graphically the way the interlocking forces of television and sponsorship are transforming sport. The turning point for athletics came at the start of the 1970s. Staff cutbacks and other stringent economies had pulled the AAA through its financial crisis, a move from the White City to Crystal Palace gave the sport a more modern, up-to-date appearance, and new stars, in particular David Bedford, began to catch the imagination (Lovesey, 1979).

By 1972, the AAA was solvent and had found a new sponsor in the Nationwide Building Society which was to support the AAA championships for the next 10 years. The move to Crystal Palace provided athletics with a new, growing audience. Athletics was becoming increasingly international as the development of more televised events and increased 'under-the-counter' money for the top 'amateurs' spawned a travelling athletics circus. With the emergence of a series of world class performers, Britain was particularly well placed to take advantage of this international growth.

Athletics had been televised by the BBC from the 1940s until 1985, but ITV finally won the exclusive contract away from BBC in 1984 after 12 years of trying. In 1972 John Bromley failed to convince the BAAB that ITV would give athletics adequate coverage, and the BBC kept the rights. In 1976 the BBC was able to renew its contract for another 4 years at a cost of just over £250 000. In 1980, the BBC renewed its athletics contract for another four years, at a cost of almost £2 million. It was bidding from ITV that helped to force the price up to eight times the 1976 level. BBC's first bid was £1.2 million, ITV bid £1.5 million just before the Moscow Olympics, and the BBC clinched the deal by offering £60 000 cash 'up front' to get the BAAB out of a cashflow problem (*Guardian*, 11/11/80).

At this time the Board felt unconvinced that ITV could give athletics adequate coverage and declined an ITV suggestion to just sign a two-year contract with BBC pending the arrival of Channel Four. One influence on the Board's attitude to ITV may have been the fate of gymnastics since Thames won the contract at the start of 1979. It was widely felt that the coverage was inferior, although Thames disputed this (*Time Out*, 15/8/80).

More than any other single factor, it was the emergence of Coe and Ovett and the rivalry between them, from 1979 onwards, that helped to transform British athletics. Their much publicized races have made athletics into a major television sport, contributing to the competitive bidding in 1984 which resulted in ITV's capture of the exclusive contract and a substantial increase in television revenue (see Whannel, 1982).

Athletics was at last beginning its slow move to open professionalism. Undercover payments to top athletes had been an accepted, although secret, part of the sport for a long time. But the challenge of Packer to the cricket authorities had alerted the athletics world to the danger of an outside entrepreneur establishing a rival professional branch of the sport (although previous attempts had foundered: see Krise and Squires, 1982). A change in IOC rules about broken time payments meant that athletes could now be paid training and other expenses, and compensated for lost wages (*Observer*, 12/8/79). The Sports Aid Foundation was established to provide training and living expenses for top British athletes. In 1980 an AAA sub-committee recommended cash prizes, appearance money and benefit from advertising to athletes (*The Times*, 3/10/80). On 15th December, 1981, the IAAF proposed the establishment of permit meetings, in which promoters could pay appearance money to particular athletes. The money could not go to the athlete but was held in a trust fund, administered by the national association, and could be used to provide the athlete's expenses. The fund would go to the athlete on retirement.

With the television contract up for renegotiation in 1984, ITV's bid of £10.5 million seemed likely to win the day. The one factor that looked as if it could sabotage ITV's chances was the sensational news that they were to withdraw from the 1984 Olympic Games coverage, having failed to come to an agreement with ACTT over pay and conditions.

Earlier on in the year, the IBA had changed the rules over advertising. Sponsors would now be allowed to advertise before, during and after the coverage of events they were sponsoring. IMG and other agents could see that sponsors were likely to favour ITV covered events in future. This now seems to have been an important factor in the decision to award ITV the contract.[1]

Athletics already had many successful sponsorship arrangements, but now the time was right to put the whole operation on a professionalized basis. The BAAB called for bids from sports agents to handle the sponsorship deals. IMG, West Nally, Keith Prowse and Alan Pascoe all put in bids (*Evening Standard*, 12/10/85). John Bromley warned the BAAB not to sign anything concerning sponsorship without making sure that ITV could deliver. To the surprise of many the contract went not to the established giants IMG or West Nally, but to ex-athlete Alan Pascoe. He won the right to sell athletics events to sponsors. Pascoe's first deal with Pearl Assurance put £1 million into the sport over 5 years. Deals with Kodak, Pearl and Peugot – Talbot meant that Pascoe rapidly reached his commitment to provide £600 000 per year. He commented that there were still events available 'but we are asking a lot of money to project athletics in its new image . . . Sports sponsorship is no longer a somewhat naive jab at name improvement or prestige getting. It is a very sophisticated marketing tool. You are aiming directly at potential customers and wholesalers. Sponsorship becomes an event in itself, with meetings, incentive promotions, point of sale stands and so on all at one specific time and place' (Alan Pascoe, *Sunday Times*, 3/2/85).

But the contractual arrangements have heightened the tensions inherent in the gradual professionalization of athletics. Injuries and the desire of athletes to avoid confrontations with rivals when not physically or psychologically prepared, limit the ability of promoters to guarantee the presence of stars. The desire of USA and British television to rematch Zola Budd and Mary Decker, leading to the extension of the Peugeot – Talbot Games into a two-day event produced a thin looking second day that failed to attract a full house. The resentment of many athletes at the handling of financial arrangements was heightened when it was revealed that Zola Budd had been paid £90 000. It is clear that athletics is still only at the beginning of a major transformation. Mark McCormack believes that athletics could be to the 1980s what golf was to the 1960s and tennis to the 1970s – the boom sport.

Arnold Palmer was the right person to represent at a time when the sport of golf was growing by leaps and bounds. A decade later with our representation of Laver, then Newcombe, and then Borg, we were able to repeat this success in tennis, and now, again ten years later, we are positioned to do the same thing in running, though no stratospheric superstar has yet emerged in this sport (McCormack, 1984, p. 237).

The traditional amateur paternal forms of sport organization were of course themselves always profoundly contradictory, containing both a class-ridden élitism, an uneven degree of semi-democratization, a commitment to voluntarism and service, and the economic function of distributing resources to the less commercially viable sectors of sport, and thus maintaining a broad base. The commercial challenge is equally contradictory in that, while providing the means of economic survival for many sports, and producing entertaining and pleasurable spectacles, it has concentrated resources at the élite levels, made sport a branch of the advertising industry, made sports overconscious of image and the needs of television, and heightened the tensions between the uncertainties inherent in sport and the need of entrepreneurs to offer guaranteed entertainment. This whole process, profoundly remaking Britain's sporting cultures, should lead us to ask the question 'who is sport for?'

## Note

1. A television programme about the televising of athletics will be screened on Channel Four in spring 1986, as part of the series *Open The Box*, produced by Beat Ltd.

## References

Amateur Rowing Association (1969) *1970–1975 Development Plan*, ARA.
Amateur Rowing Association (1971) *Sponsorship Opportunities in Rowing*, ARA.
Amateur Rowing Association (1974) *Five-year Plan 1975–1980*, ARA.
Bose, M. (1983) *All in a Day*, Robin Clarke, London.
Bough, F. (1980) *Cue Frank*, Futura Publications, London.
Brookes, C. (1978) *English Cricket*, Weidenfeld and Nicolson, London.
Buscombe, E. (ed) (1975) *Football on Television*, British Film Institute, London.
CCPR (1975) *Report of Conference of Sport Administrators*, CCPR, London.
CCPR (1976) *Report of Conference of Sport Administrators*, CCPR, London.
Clarke, A. and Clarke, J. (1982) Highlights and Action Replays, in *Sport Culture and Ideology*, (edited by J. Hargreaves), Routledge & Kegan Paul, London.
Colley, I. and Davies, G. (1982) Kissed by history: football as TV drama, *Sporting Fictions*, CCCS, University of Birmingham, pp. 189–208.
English Table Tennis Association (1972) *Sponsorship Presentation*, April.
Howell, D. (1983) *The Howell Report into Sports Sponsorship*, CCPR.
Kramer, J. (1979) *The Game: My Forty Years in Tennis*, André Deutsch, London.
Krise, R. and Squires, W. (1982) *Fast Tracks: The History of Distance Running*, Stephen Greene, Brattleboro, Vermont.
Laker, J. (1977) *One Day Cricket*, Batsford, London.

Lovesey, P. (1979) *The Official Centenary History of the AAA*, Guinness Superlatives, Enfield, Middlesex.

McCormack, M. (1984) *What They Don't Teach You At Harvard Business School*, Collins, London.

Paulu, B. (1961) *British Broadcasting in Transition*, Macmillan, London.

Political and Economic Planning (1956) *The Cricket Industry 22*, No. 401, PEP, London.

Rawes and Partners (1970) *Table Tennis 1970*, Rawes and Partners Ltd., London.

Ross, G. (1981) *The Gillette Cup*, Futura Publications, London.

South Western Sports Council (1974) *Sponsorship in Sport*, South Western Sports Council.

Sports Council (1971) *An Enquiry into Sponsorship*, Sports Council, London.

Sportscan (1982) *Sports Sponsorship Computer Analysis*, Sportscan.

Tunstall, J. (1983) *The Media in Britain*, Constable, London.

Waite, N. (1976) *Sponsorship in the United Kingdom*.

Whannel, G. (1982) Narrative and television sport: The Coe and Ovett story, *Sporting Fictions*, CCCS, University of Birmingham, pp. 209–30.

Whannel, G. (1983a) *Blowing The Whistle: The Politics of Sport*, Pluto Press, London.

Whannel, G. (1983b) Sit down with us: TV sport as armchair theatre, in *Leisure and the Media*, (edited by S. Glyptis), Leisure Studies Association, Conference Proceedings.

Whannel, G. (1984) Fields in vision: sport and representation, *Screen 25*, 97–107.

Willis, R.G.D. (1981) *The Cricket Revolution*, Sidgwick and Jackson, London.

# 20

# Pregnant with Anticipation: The Pre-History of Television Sport and the Politics of Recycling and Preservation

*Garry Whannel*

N ew media are rarely clearly understood when they first arrive. Indeed the early uses of new media are often, comically, at odds with the forms that they later assume – one only needs to recall the early development of the internet as a means for scientists to pool their data to illustrate this point.

Audiences and audience practices have to be produced, and a regularizing of the relationship between the production and consumption of a media's product has to be established. This is not a sudden invention, but a gradual process, involving technological refinement, state regulation, commercial investment and popular wants, needs and desires. It follows that a better understanding of this process can reveal much about the dynamic processes of popular culture.

Technological innovation is always embedded in social relations, of power and subordination; of production and consumption, of domination and resistance (see Thussu, 1998; Jansen, 2003). The new media and digitalization have produced a culture of replication, which is intensely reflexive and self-referential (see Kellner, 1995; Pellizzoni, 1999). The ways in which societies are able to communicate information and entertainment has been shaped by historical processes in which technology, regulation, commercial forces and popular desires interact (Maddox, 1972; Charon, 1987; Sardar, 1993;

**Source:** *International Journal of Cultural Studies*, 8(4) (2005): 405–426.

Winston, 1996; Butsch, 1998). The emergence of new media forms generally involve significant processes of social tension, and transformation (see for example Goodhart and Wintour, 1986; McNeil, 1991; Wollen and Hayward, 1993; Wise, 2001; Utterson, 2004). Technological innovation always provides new challenges for regulation – social forms have to be evolved that take account of changing circumstances (see Ferguson, 1987; Friedland, 1996; Kunneman, 1990, Broderick, 2000).

New technologies become the focus of the popular imagination, and our imagination concerns fears as well as hopes (see Gunning, 1991; Morley and Robins, 1992; Hanson, 1993; Ezrahi et al., 1994; Tester, 1995) for examples). Technological change opens up new possibilities, even as it reproduces old forms of dominance and exploitation. Fears of the greater availability of pornography are perfectly valid, as are concerns about the use of chat-rooms by paedophiles. Yet, as some feminists have argued, online interaction, providing a degree of anonymity, and flirtatious space, also contains progressive and transformative options for the exploration of sexual identities. The possibilities of virtual identity are seen by some as challenging established notions of body, space, identity and sexuality (see, Van Zoonen, 1992; Taylor et al., 1993; Balsamo, 1996; Springer, 1996; Ainley, 1998; Di Filippo, 2000).

The domestic location of much media technology since the rise of broadcasting has reshaped the internal dynamics of domestic organization and the social interactions of family life; and consumption has become a dominant mode of everyday life (see Mackay, 1997; Miller, 1997; Silverstone and Hirsch, 1992; Silverstone, 1994; Silva, 2000; Morley, 2003). The internet has produced a new rapid, global form of information exchange which in turn produces new modes of social interaction (see Dutton et al., 1986; Dery, 1994; Schroeder, 1995; Mansell and Silverstone, 1996; Sawhney, 1996; Munt, 2001). The dramatic pace of innovation in the era of the computer, the internet and digitalization has brought about more profound transformation, in which flow has superceded space, analysed in detail in the work of Castells (1978, 1980, 1983, 1989 and 1994, with Peter Hall).

The rise of modern sport has been both fueled and shaped by technological innovation (see Betts, 1969). Sport spectating is an ordered and regimented form of participative consumption in which pleasures are experienced in terms of drama uncertainty and intensity (see Bryant et al., 1994; Eastman and Riggs, 1994; Trujillo and Krizek, 1994; Wenner, 1994 and Zhang et al., 1996). The very role of spectator is a consequence of the earlier phase of the commodification and commercialization of sport in the late 19th century (see Guttmann, 1986; Vamplew, 1988; Edelman, 1993).

Television provided a distinctive re-representation of sport, which has been regarded, critically, as a re-ordering and, for some, a dilution of the spectator experience (for discussion of these issues see Wenner and Gantz, 1989; Whannel, 1983 and 1998; Rowe, 1995; Sandvoss, 2003). For some, one aspect of television's re-presentation of sport involves a significant emphasis on and dramatization of violent play (see Bryant and Zillmann, 1983; Bryant, 1989). The masculine-focused discourse of media sport has consequences for gender positionalities (see Bruce, 1998; Sargent et al., 1998).

Spectator perception of sport is strongly subjective as Hastorf and Cantril (1954) demonstrated in an influential paper. Media sport offers a variety of modes of viewing and of pleasure (see Sapolsky and Zillman, 1978; Zillman et al., 1979; Gantz, 1981; Duncan and Brummett, 1989; Eastman and Riggs, 1994; Eastman and Land, 1997). Youth audiences may be addressed in, and respond in, particular distinctive ways (Lines, 1998, 2000).

## News, Entertainment and the Emergence of Television Sport

The emergence of television sport has to be seen as part of the process whereby concepts of news and entertainment were shaped through a diverse set of institutions and practices. Regular newspapers had, in the UK, become well established by the end of the 18th century. However, the combination of an established, although still evolving technology – printing; and new modes of distribution and retail, was well in advance of the emergence of a literate reading public. The 18th-century coffee houses of London had to employ readers to read newspaper content aloud – partly for the illiterate and partly for those who would not wish to purchase the expensive newspapers. It took the growth of the railways between 1840–1860, the development of wireless telegraphy, and the 1870 Education Act to produce the substantial advances in transportation and literacy that contributed to the emergence of a modern mass circulation daily press.

Some of the earliest experiments with cinema constructed it as an individualized technology – the 'what the Butler saw' type of machine. When it developed as a projected technology it took some time for conventions of assemblage, camera position and angle to emerge. In the earliest narrative films, 'explainers' were often utilized to talk to the audience and explain the story to them. When sound arrived in the late 1920s many were convinced that it was a gimmick, and that it would never last. Radio was developed largely as a military technology, and it was only after the war that radio manufacturers began to encourage the development of broadcast services, often with very little conception of what a broadcast service might be. There was no specific reason that television had to be a domestic medium, rather than, as in Germany in 1936 for the Olympic Games, a means of live relay to public spaces. The BBC launched a television service in the mid-1930s, but many in the BBC continued to regard radio as the prime medium, and it was not until the 1960s that television began to be taken seriously by the radio old guard. The internet began as a mode of academic exchange, developed a bulletin board and interest group culture, spawned the web, with its abundance of free material, and has only in the last five years been thoroughly penetrated and re-shaped by commerce.

Raymond Williams has drawn attention to the tendency to draw on one of two models to explain the development of media. The first, technological determinism, regards advance as driven by new technological innovation; the second regards technological innovation as symptomatic of social changes. WIlliams proposes a more complex model in which social change and technological innovation interact; and suggests restoring the notion of intent to conceptualization of technological development (Williams, 1974: 9–32). In analysing the relation of culture and technology in society, Castells argued that

> there is a historically articulated complex of transformations which concerns simultaneously, capitalism as a social system, informationalism as a mode of development, and information technology as a powerful working instrument. It is this complex socio-economic-technical matrix that is transforming societies and thus cities and regions. (Castells, 1989: 3)

Applying the spirit of such analyses to television sport suggests linking the early development of television to its need to win audiences; to the need to spectacularize sport; and hence to the development of such devices as action replay, slow motion, and much later, tele-track. Our subsequent habituation to the presence of such devices contributes to the 'strange' and 'primitive' appearance of television sport in its emergent period.

One main area of technological innovation was concerned with the image itself. Peter Dimmock, Head of BBC Sport in the 1960s, said that the 'essence of a true "Outside Broadcast" is to report real happenings, while they happen and from where they happen' (Dimmock, 1968: 3). Much early innovation was associated with attempts to enhance this 'veracity' effect. Improvements to cameras and lenses made the image sharper, the introduction of colour enhanced its naturalism, and video, action replay and slow motion provided the ability to recompose time.

Equally important, though, was the development of satellite-based telecommunications that, by the mid-1970s, allowed the transmission and rebroadcast of live sport events around the globe. Such developments in media technology brought a new intimacy and closeness – that restructuring of cultural transactions that McLuhan famously dubbed 'the global village' (McLuhan, 1964). McLuhan's observation was prescient, although, like any village, it turns out to have a well-entrenched social hierarchy in which there are those who are information rich and information poor. The global reach of television, enabled by satellite technology, is part of that broader process analysed by Castells, in which the nature of place, space and distance are transformed by the informational age with its technological revolution and restructuring of capitalism (Castells, 1989).

So if television sport was emerging as a distinct cultural form in the 1950s, how might one understand it? Stuart Hall has argued that television is a hybrid medium that borrowed and adapted its distinctive forms from other media and thus evolved distinctive new forms – the magazine programme, the panel game, the sports broadcast (Hall, 1975). This process of hybridity continues to mark television, except now it borrows mainly from itself. The combination of elements of soap opera, fly-on-the-wall documentary and game show produces *Big Brother.* Combine *Big Brother* with the celebrity culture and the result is *I'm a Celebrity Get Me Out Of Here.* Television took the basic sport event; simulated the view of an ideal spectator, added the ability to manipulate time, gave it an entertainment format with presenters, and added the panel of experts, which combines the intense seriousness of *The Brains Trust* with the laddish comedy of male bar-room camaraderie. Television felt its way, tentatively at first, and then with increasing confidence, towards a routinized and conventionalized format. So *Television Sport Magazine* gave way to *Sportsview*, and irregular Saturday outside broadcasts spawned *Grandstand* (which has lasted almost 45 years so far). In America, ABC came up with the influential *Wide World of Sports,* with its guiding principles 'up close and personal', and 'the thrill of victory, the agony of defeat' (see Whannel, 1991, 1992). New media produce new ways of seeing – conventions have to be established by television institutions and learnt by audiences, in order that the encoding-decoding loop be completed.

## Neither Pre-Televisual Nor Fully Televisual

The core of this article concerns the nature of sporting events, subsequently mythologized, that took place during the dawn of the television age. Such events, it seems to me, have a particularity, borne out of their temporal location in relation to television as a social institution. They are not really fully of the television age – captured by the cameras before the establishment of firm conventions of sport coverage, and before the technological maturation of the medium, they appear strange in their black and white graininess. Neither are they truly pre-televisual – they exist in televisual form – indeed their very graininess distinguishes them from earlier moments preserved on newsreel film or in photographs. The Real Madrid vs. Eintracht Frankfurt European Cup Final in 1960 is a case in point. The only record of the game, as far as I know, is a tele-recording of the BBC live transmission; made by pointing a film camera at the television screen. This introduces a second level of degradation of quality. The original pictures would have been fairly grainy. The tele-recording may well have been obtained from images sent from Glasgow to London. This low-grade film version resurfaced in recent years on DVD, complete with a caption to acknowledge a four-minute gap when there was a technical fault during the live transmission.

Two aspects are striking. A limited number of cameras and, probably unwieldy lens systems, meant an almost complete absence of close ups. In comparison with today's coverage, the difference is so striking that even non-sport-fans spot the absence within seconds. Second, it includes action replay and slow motion repeats of goals and other incidents. Action replay was not introduced in the UK until 1966, with slow motion appearing a couple of years later. So, I assume, these inserts have been prepared for the DVD, by re-running the film version. However, as the whole match is rendered thoroughly authentic in its antique graininess, it would be easy to assume we were watching the original version. Conversely, and opposed to some other historical material, it appears that no attempt has been made to clean up or digitally enhance the original. Historical 'evidence' has always been tricky and potentially misleading but in an era of electronic preservation and digital enhancement the problematic areas multiply.

Which events constituted genuinely pre-televisual moments? The Berlin Olympics was extensively preserved in filmic form, but, as far as I know, there is no material preserving the television relays to local cinemas. The great Arsenal side of the 1930s established their glory largely without the benefit of television, although there is a famous picture of team members peering with fascination into the lens of an early BBC Camera at Highbury Stadium. The athletic feats of Jesse Owens, Sydney Wooderson, the tennis victories of Suzanne Lenglen and Fred Perry; the boxing of Joe Louis and Jack Dempsey, were all moments of pre-televisual stardom.[1]

If these moments are pre-televisual, when are we, without doubt, in the televisual era? Arguably, in the UK, with England winning the World Cup in 1966. The Chile World Cup of 1962 is, I would argue, definitely liminal – operating on the threshold of available technology, and still black and white, grainy and lacking close ups, but the Mexico World Cup of 1970, seen in Europe in full colour, was definitely fully televisual. Perhaps the birth of the established televisual era can be pinpointed more exactly and co-terminously with colour. The Manchester United victory in the European Cup in 1968 was in colour and part of an established televisual era. However, the Celtic victory in the European Cup of 1967 took place in Portugal, was transmitted in black and white, and belongs more properly to the threshold moment. There is a liminal moment in that period when the conventions and technological resources of television were still being formed (see Whannel, 1992).

Clearly, attempting to identify this liminal period too precisely takes one into the area of cultural specificities. Other countries which had developed television systems by the 1960s will have their own distinctive moments and chronologies, although I would suggest that all would have gone through a liminal period. In the USA, the period between the launch of ABC's *Wide World of Sports* (1964), and the introduction of *Monday Night Football* (1970) was a crucial formative period. Countries which developed television systems after 1970 tended to receive television from the start as a matured technology. Note that George Best and Muhammad Ali, despite appearing, in early parts of their career in black and white, are not really part of this liminal moment that constitutes the emergence of television – they were, eventually in colour, in close up, and definitely stars of television, whereas

Roger Bannister, Stirling Moss, Ferenc Puskacs, and Babe Ruth were not. Indeed, I argue in *Media Sport Stars*, that the ability of television as an intimate close up and domestic medium produced Best and Ali as two of the first television stars and as the beginning, at least implicitly, of modern celebrity culture (Whannel, 2002).

## Liminality and Communitas: The Construction of the Mass Television Audience

Liminality emerged as an anthropological concept, associated with rituals like pilgrimages and the Grand Tour. It concerned thresholds, rites of passage, and transitions. Carson starts his discussion of the concept by referring to the door, the ladder, the crossing, the maze, and the bridge (Carson, 1997: xiii). Moments of liminality – threshold moments – can be revealing about the nature of the transition that is occurring. The crossing of the liminal threshold involves the forging of a new communitas – can one speak of the creation of a television viewing public in this sense?

Acquisition and installation of new technology involves a form of rite of passage. With early television this involved the purchase or rental of a television, the installation of an aerial, and the tuning of a set – do these constitute rites of passage? Nowadays many of us are familiar with the process of installing software, configuring a television or a mobile phone, scanning for channels, initializing, and logging on, and these too constitute threshold moments in which we, sometimes uncomfortably, enter into new technological domains and into new relationships with technology.

New media have to construct audiences. There were no intrinsic reasons why television should necessarily have been primarily a domestic medium. In some of the earliest television sport coverage, at the Berlin Olympic Games of 1936, events were not broadcast, but relayed to local cinemas. Some of Muhammad Ali's fights, in the days before satellite television, and dedicated pay-per-channel sport channels, were relayed to cinema audiences around the world, seen as a more effective way of boosting revenue than selling the television rights to broadcasters. Initially, domestic sets were expensive, and the affluent middle-class seemed to share the cultural snobbery of the BBC radio elite that television was a vulgar gimmick.

Ironically, the early years of BBC television, following its re-launch in 1946, were marked, not by a vulgar descent into brash commercialism, but by a cautious approach and a sense of doubt as to who the audience might be and how they might be addressed. In the early days of television there was uncertainty about the process of promoting and selling programmes to an audience. The *Radio Times* entries are characterized by a prosaic factual accuracy with little of the Barnum-style showmanship more common in the commercial television broadcasting that is becoming established in the USA. In addition, the content of sport programmes was sometimes unclear when the *Radio Times* went to press. The European Cup Final of 1960 does not appear in the advance listings. On the evening Bannister broke the four-minute mile, film of the race was shown on *Sportsview*, first launched a month earlier. The *Radio Times* entry merely states, in its low key entirety:

> May 6 1954
> 8.20 Sportsview
> Introduced by Peter Dimmock
> Bringing to you from around the world of sport the latest news, views and personalities
> Edited by Paul Fox
> Presented by Dennis Monger

It was, famously, the Coronation in 1953 that helped to boost the popularity and acceptability of television, although in the UK it took the launch of Independent Television in 1955 to really make the television audience grow. Interestingly, there is no convincing evidence from the 1950s that sport was a big factor in the growth of an audience – only from the time of the 1966 World Cup, and then, with the introduction of colour, action replay, slow motion, and live satellite feeds does sport seem to become a more important factor in the appeal of TV.

Peter Dimmock, BBC Head of Sport, commented, 'our constant aim is to reflect the event to the viewer at home with the best possible pictures and informed commentary from an acknowledged expert who will add to the picture and not talk too much' (Dimmock, 1964). Television executives knew that sport fans would watch its coverage, and it was concerned to win the marginal viewer, and to address the family audience. So from an early point styles of presentation and commentary were sought to avoid adopting a discourse of expertise (see Whannel, 1991). In the mid-1960s, television sport began to move from its formative to its maturing period.

## Senses of Place: The Stadium, the Living Room, the Sports Bar and the City Centre

The sport spectacle, as it developed in the early 20th century, was a ritual of place and space, in which the enclosed space of the stadium and the mythologized significance of the great stadia – Yankee Stadium, Soldiers Field, Wembley, Bernabeu, Sydney Cricket Ground, Lords, the Maracana, the Aztec played an important role (see Bale, 1992; Vertinsky and Bale, 2003). Whereas the classic sport spectacle took place only in the stadium, television added the living room, and by the 1960s far more people consumed sport spectacle from the living room than would ever visit, or could ever be accommodated by, even the largest stadium. Crawford discusses the Real Madrid and Eintracht Frankfurt European Cup Final of 1960, arguing that this was one of the first televisual sport spectacles. The game was transmitted across Europe via the Eurovision link. Crawford reports that by 1968, the European Cup Final was being watched in at least 30 countries (Crawford, 1992: 436). Already, then the embedded place of the stadium was being displaced, as the spectacle began to be consumed in far larger numbers through television.

Cardiff and Scannell (1981) argue that radio helped produce shared national corporate rituals – the Christmas Message and other royal occasions, but also the Derby, the Grand National, the Boat Race and Cup Final Day. Television built on and extended this sense of a significant proportion of the nation sitting down at the same moment to consume the same images. Having gone through the liminal process of entry into the television age, a new communitas had emerged, the communitas of the collective television audience. A period was inaugurated in which people shared the experience of being an audience, an experience typically marked by conversations at the work-place, at school gates and in shop queues about the previous night's television. These forms of cultural exchange eventually became dubbed 'water-cooler' moments. In the de-regulated, digitalized multi-channel era, sport is one of the few cultural forms left that regularly provides such moments.

The pre-televisual spectacle took place in and only in the arena. The televisual spectacle constructed a unilinear donor recipient relation (see Whannel, 1992) between the institution of television and the individual subject viewer in domestic contexts. Having learned to be an audience, we then learned to experience intensity. As television developed the conventions of sport presentation, it registered the unrivalled ability of some major sport to hold huge audiences at unsocial hours. Such events, like the musicals discussed by Richard Dyer, have a utopian element – they offer abundance, energy, and intensity to set against the weary routines of everyday lives (see Dyer, 1978).

But, where does the modern sport event now take place? Is it at the stadium, in the town centre, in all public spaces, in the living room, in the pub or sports bar? The modern sport spectacle has become de-centered – its audiences and rituals are dispersed across the nation, and sometimes, around the world. However, this spectacle is forged and held together by television, which unites its various audiences. During the 1990s the culture of collective viewing in public places, long common in continental Europe, became a more significant phenomenon around the world. In the UK, the emergence of public and collective viewing has been particularly dramatic. It has been driven by the combination of a whole set of factors – the proliferation of television channels, the emergence of dedicated sport channels, the commodification of television, the establishment of pay-per-channel and pay-per-view, the de-regulation of television, the growth in numbers of major sport events, the expansion in scope of those events, and the liberalization of licensing laws governing the opening hours of bars.

The dramatic growth in the viewing of football and other sports in bars during the 1990s has produced a whole new context for the consumption of the sports spectacle. The communal public viewing experience is, in its sense of shared collective ritual, closer to the stadium experience than to the domestic one. Indeed, now that football stadia are generally all seated, and dominated by surveillance, the bar, which facilitates movement, interaction, and profanity, is arguably closer to the traditional football audience experience than is the modern stadium (see Brick, 2001). The work of Castells suggests that we conceptualize such developments as part of a process he characterizes as:

> . . . the emergence of a space of flows which dominates the historically constructed space of places, as the logic of dominant organisations detaches itself from the social constraints of cultural identities and local societies through the powerful medium of information technologies. (Castells, 1989: 6)

However, a different way of understanding this process would emphasize the productive tensions and contradictions that continue to exist in the relation between the lived experience of viewing and the mediated production of the image. The modern sport spectacle though, has undoubtedly become de-centered. Not only is it consumed in diverse spaces and contexts (the stadium, public squares around the world, bars, cafes and restaurants, as well as homes), not only does television link these sites together (note the placing of cameras in public spaces like squares and bars to catch celebration and despair) but it is no longer so easy to attribute primacy to any of these viewing contexts. Can one really argue that the stadium is more or less significant than the accumulated bars and homes around the globe?

But if the modern sports spectacle is de-centered, it is heavily television dependent – indeed it is now hard to have a spectacle of sport that does not have a televisual dimension – the very absence of cameras shrieks that this event is really not that important; just as the global audience legitimizes the stadium audience's sense of the importance of occasion.

## The Construction of Moments as Iconic

The full emergence of television in its mature form, with live colour pictures from around the world, up close and personal, with big close ups, was an important stage in the generation of a celebrity culture and subsequent commodification of the star image. First because the up close and personal high quality framing of shots produces identification, and second because it produces familiarization with key stars.

The constant compression of the story into key iconic moments, in highlights, encapsulate great moments, end sequences and title sequences – these combined with the production of metonymic images in the press and magazines mean that there is a routinized reduction of events to single iconic moment (e.g. Gazza's tears).[2] Bannister's four-minute mile, for example, is almost always represented by him crossing the finishing line and then breasting the tape. It is hard, however, for moments to emerge as iconic without the close up and its endless replication across media. Examination of star pictures over the last 30 years suggests a growing self-consciousness of the mythologization process – witness for example the prevalence amongst footballers of trademark modes of celebration – signature poses.

One of the most strongly established mythologies of sport concerns Real Madrid, and their consecutive victories in the first five European Cup Finals. This took place in the formative period of television, but produced the myth of Real Madrid as both reigning supreme and performing with a majestic grace – in short truly 'Real' – regal. The power of this myth has survived all the ups and downs between the Hampden Park triumph in 1960, and the failure of the Galacticos in 2004. An even more powerful club in commercial terms, Manchester United, also owe their fame in part to a mythologization – in this case of the Busby Babes, the team largely destroyed in the Munich Air crash of 1958. And as with Real Madrid, the myth has helped Manchester United retain their special 'aura' even through the long lean years between the European Cup win of 1968 and the period of Premier dominance that began in 1993.

The combination of mythology, global television and tabloid-style print journalism produces the celebrity culture and the commodification of star image. Warhol's famous edict that in the future everyone would be famous for 15 minutes was prescient, but star-celebrity has a longer shelf life. The departure of Beckham from Manchester United to go to Real Madrid illustrated these commercial processes at work. The 2002 World Cup made Beckham a huge and marketable star name in Asia, a market in which Real Madrid were lagging behind Manchester United. A large transfer fee and huge wages paid to Beckham were enabled by the increased income from replica shirt sales in the Asian market. None of this could happen without the ability of television to unite performance and image.

This ability is not a simple product of television as a technology, but grows out of television's development of distinct conventions of sport presentation, such as the use of the close up in gaps between action. So the sport events of television's liminal period generated few memorable iconic images, despite the talent and fame of performers such as Stanley Matthews, Alfredo Di Stefano and Ferenc Puskacs. Only as television entered its mature phase of development did it become a generator of iconic imagery – George Best, Muhammad Ali and Pele being among the first real television era stars.

## The Past Reconstructed in the Present

Television, having developed from its grainy black and white childhood into a colourful and sophisticated maturity as a medium, appears now to have entered a late middle age in which it exhibits a growing tendency to live, not in the past, but off its past. List programmes, nostalgia television, 'where are they now?', 'who were they then?' formats, are among the pretexts for archive clip-based television. In part of course, this is driven by the economic need to find cheap ways of living off the back catalogue. Short clips do not involve the complex apparatus of rights clearance and repeat fees that full scale repeats do. It is also a significant part of the popular culture equivalent of that process that Raymond Williams dubbed the 'selective tradition' (Williams, 1961). Television's periodic capsule reviews of the history of sport mark a constant setting in place of performer, event and significance (Whannel, 1989).

In what contexts do we see the past of sport now? There are serious television histories of sport, although rarely. There are histories of the particular periods, though sport is usually just a quick aside. There are quiz questions and game shows, and programmes that focus on a particular period in time such as *This Week In 1960*. The past is constantly being reconstructed in the present. In the process all sorts of re-inventions take place – the sanctified images of the story of Muhammad Ali allude to but under-represent the depth of media hostility to him in the 1960s. The tale of sport and apartheid is now told with little attempt to interrogate those who argued so strongly that it was the Anti-Apartheid movement that was at fault for 'bringing politics into sport'. Capsule histories of baseball gloss over the colour bar that persisted into the 1940s. Our national heroes are revered, whilst our drug cheats are quietly forgotten. Dangerous processes are at work in this apparently innocent bricolage.

Transformations in modes of news and sport presentation have an influence on the representation of history. Watching the video versions of England vs. Hungary in 1954, Real Madrid vs. Eintracht Frankfurt in 1960, and the film record of Bannister's four-minute mile in 1954, and reading the contemporary press coverage highlights the dramatic changes in the nature of sport coverage. There is now far more dramatization, personalization and sensationalism. The dominant impression of the coverage of these events is how low key it was, in comparison with now. There was negligible build-up in advance, and precious little fuss afterwards. Even though it was the first Cup Final to be televised, the much mythologized Matthews final was given a low-key build up in the *Radio Times*. The programme announcement simply said:

> The Cup Final
> Blackpool v Bolton
> from Wembley Stadium
> at 2.30
> (*Radio Times* 24 April 1953)

The full details, below, were prosaic and dry, doing little to excite audience interest:

2.30–4.50pm The Cup Final
Blackpool v Bolton Wanderers
Played at the Wembley Stadium
2.30 Scenes outside the stadium
Community singing organised by the Daily Express
Conducted by Arthur Caiger D.C.M.
2.55 Presentation of teams to H.R.H. The Duke of Edinburgh
3.00 Kick Off
3.45 Half Time
3.55 Second Half
4.40 End of Match
4.45 Presentation of the Cup and Medals by H.M. The Queen and H.R.H.
The Duke of Edinburgh
Commentator Kenneth Wolstenholme
Scenes before the match described by Peter Dimmock
(*Radio Times* 24 April 1953)

The match was featured on the front cover but only in the form of a rather
formalized montage that showed the stadium, the trophy and the two captains. Just 13 years later, the World Cup got far more space and more
hyperbole. There was a big build-up with a two page spread in the *Radio
Times* (2 June 1966: 2–3) followed by the *Radio Times* World Cup Number
(7 July 1966), which devoted 12 pages to the event. Even this major event,
however, disappeared from the newspapers a couple of days after the final.
Bannister's four-minute mile was not mentioned in *The Times* until the middle column of page 8 and then with the extraordinarily low key and banal
headline:

4 MINUTE MILE
TRIUMPH OF R.G. BANNISTER
POOR CONDITIONS OVERCOME
(*The Times* 7 May 1954)

The Real Madrid vs. Eintracht Frankfurt match was not mentioned in the
*Radio Times*, and television coverage was only announced in the daily papers.
*The Times* reported the match in the sports section, but it was not even the
main story, pride of place going to Oxford University vs. Lancashire cricket.
Another low-key headline reported:

DOMINATION OF REAL MADRID
EINTRACHT RARELY IN THE PICTURE
(*The Times* 19 May 1960)

In other words, the reified and mythologized place some sport events occupy
in accounts of the past can mislead us as to the degree of public attention
they won at the time.

## Olden Days: The Coding of the Past

Thanks to television, 'the past' and 'black and white' are now firmly locked together. Note that modern drama, in attempting to represent the past sometimes resorts to a simulated sepia, and use of de-emphasized primary colours to reproduce a sense of the past. Accent, too is utilized as connoting the past – BBC voices from the 1950s and earlier often sound so impossibly 'plummy' and 'hoity toity' to modern ears that they are ripe for satire. A marked division now hangs between the 1970s and everything that came before, which, to young people, has become 'the olden days'.

So what are the 'olden days'? What has the past become? A set of raw ingredients to be used in cooking? A set of images to illustrate a story? A collection of tired journalistic clichés reinforced with mythologized moments and iconic images? Or is the past an open text, available for rewriting by a thousand authors with diverse perspectives?

In surviving and preserved television images from the 1950s, sports in representation have a very different appearance – football looks slow and full of open spaces, athletics looks poorly organized and slightly chaotic, motor racing seems archaic, tennis players appear slow, cricketers ponderous. More significant differences are embedded in the nature of the televisual image. Roland Barthes, in attempting to locate the extra dimension of singing performance not analysable by score or libretto, discussed the role of the grain of the voice (Barthes, 1977). The images of the formative period of television cannot be understood without consideration of the grain of the image. These pictures connote in the way they do partly because they are not sharp but grainy; not colour but black and white; not 'now' but 'then'.

It follows that the rise of electronic sources and subsequently digitalization techniques tend to destabilize history. There are now far greater resources to clean up, to tidy, to improve and to re-master the past. Both sound and picture can be made sharper and clearer. The cleaning process is both technical and ideological. There is a tendency for the contradictions, awkwardnesses and untidinesses of history to be swept away along with the grain of the image and the hiss of the sound. The past is so constantly being re-mastered for us, it becomes very difficult to access it un-re-mastered form.

The combination of archive sources, archive sources cleaned up and re-mastered, and re-enactments, simulations and modern material made to look old, dis-articulates the always tenuous link between artefact and time and place. For example, back in the 1980s, ITV showed a series on the history of television. The sport section included material on the World Cup Final of 1966, purporting to be the television coverage. But it was in colour and the broadcast had been in black and white. Unforgivably, this history of television offered film material not broadcast at the time. The technology of replication dissolves authenticity; the technology of alteration destroys the apparent 'truth' of image – the past becomes merely the raw material of bricolage. Reflecting on the impact of the recycling of the past, Baudrillard declared that 'the lips of protest are closed with the sugar of history' (Baudrillard, 1994) but this offers an excessively one-dimensional perspective even on television history, which is still a leaky and contradictory system. Of course all production of history takes place within the framework of the problematics of the present; but, as any court of law will understand, there remains a distinction between re-interpreting the evidence and tampering with the evidence.

## The Political Economy of Preservation

For us to have access to the past, it must be preserved. Preservation is not merely an intellectual, conceptual or representational issue, it has its physical dimension. The Bannister race was shot on film, which was then transmitted on television. Live televised events were, of course, captured by television cameras, and before the late 1950s and the arrival of the first video recorders, the only way televised events could be preserved was by telerecording – a rather crude process in which a film camera was pointed at a television monitor. This had to be pre-arranged – if unexpected drama occurred at an event, it was too late. The tele-recording process also produced considerable degradation of quality.

Early television football was either live or shot on film, and the cost of film stock meant that often cameras only had around 15 minutes of film to capture a whole game. Consequently, cameramen had to exercise caution and tended to turn cameras on only if a goal looked imminent. If Bannister had failed in his attempt on the world mile record, but earlier in the day another athlete had broken a world record for, say, the 100m sprint, it would have gone unrecorded by the cameras. One consequence is that the only sporting moments preserved prior to 1960 were those shot on film, and those transmitted live and tele-recorded. Either way, it had to be clear beforehand that the event was worth preserving. The unexpected generally went unrecorded. In the UK, the first football match shot on video and then edited for television was done by Anglia TV in 1962. In theory this opened up a new era in which television sport could be preserved in archives. However, the cost of video tape and limited resources for archiving meant that very little preservation of complete programmes took place. Generally only great events and great moments were saved.

There is a now a whole industry dedicated to the dissemination of video and dvd material on sport. But the prevalent practice of re-versioning for different contexts and different markets has dissolved the concept of authenticity – it is hard to be sure if one is viewing the film as originally edited. The casual attitude that sport videos and dvds often display towards accreditation and dating exacerbates the problem.

In the political economy of preservation, the dynamic force is with the process of re-mastering, repackaging, re-branding and commodifying the past.

In this process our ability to understand and comprehend, to analyse and learn from the past, is in grave danger of being dismantled brick by brick. Once we had a set of buildings with their own distinctive spaces, times and contexts; now we have a set of digitized elements available for re-combination, as if they were a box of brightly coloured Lego bricks that can be plugged together as and when required.

Just as television's version of the past can dissolve place, time and context, so it can also contribute to an exaggerated impression of the impact of events that, at the time they occurred may not have been given as dramatic a focus as subsequent reconstructions bestowed. Access to the formative periods of a medium is important not merely for archival and documentation purposes: analysis of how conventions became routinized, enables us to understand how things could have been different, which in turn enables us to understand how things can be changed.

## Notes

1. A book-length study of European sporting heroes deals largely with pre-televisual fame (Holt et al., 1996).
2. Paul Gascoigne was shown crying by television cameras during the interval before extra time in the semi-final of the 1990 World Cup between England and Italy, because, having been given a yellow card, he would miss the Final game if England managed to qualify. The moment, re-circulated by television and the press served to make Gascoigne a major star, and contributed to the re-emergence of British football from the dark days of the 1980s when crowd trouble and stadium disasters had harmed its public image.

## References

Ainley, Rosa, ed. (1998) *New Frontiers of Space, Bodies and Gender.* London: Routledge.

Bale, John (1992) *Sport, Space and Society.* London: Routledge.

Balsamo, Anne (1996) *Technologies of the Gendered Body: Reading Cyborg Women.* Durham, NC: Duke University Press.

Barthes, Roland (1977) *Image Music Text.* London: Fontana.

Baudrillard, Jean (1994) *The Illusion of the End.* Cambridge: Polity.

Betts, J. (1969) 'The Technological Revolution and the Rise of Sport 1850–90', in Loy and Kenyon (eds) *Sport Culture and Society.* London: Collier and Macmillan.

BBC (1976) 'Public Opinion about the Television and Radio Coverage of the 1974 World Cup', *Annual Review of Audience Research Findings N2.* London: BBC.

Brick, Carlton (2001) 'Anti-Consumption or "New" Consumption? Commodification, Identity and "New Football"' in J. Horne (ed.) *Leisure: Culture, Consumption and Commodification*, pp. 3–15. Eastbourne: Leisure Studies Journal.

Broderick, Terry R. (2000) *Regulation of Information Technology in the European Union.* The Hague: Kluwer Law International.

Bruce, Toni (1998) 'Audience Frustration and Pleasure: Women Viewers Confront Televised Women's Basketball', *Journal of Sport and Social Issues* 22(4): 373–97.

Bryant, J. and D. Zillmann (1983) 'Sports Violence and the Media', in J.H. Goldstein (ed.) *Sports Violence*, pp. 195–211. New York: Springer-Verlag.

Bryant, Jennings (1989) 'Viewers Enjoyment of Televised Sports Violence', in L. Wenner (ed.) *Media Sports and Society*. London: SAGE.

Bryant, Jennings, Steven C. Rockwell and John Wesley Owens (1994) '"Buzzer Beaters and Barn Burners": The Effects on Enjoyment of Watching the Game go Down to the Wire', *Journal of Sport and Social Issues* 18(4): 326–39.

Butsch, Richard (1998) 'Crystal Sets and Scarf-pin Radios: Gender, Technology and the Construction of American Radio Listening in the 1920s', *Media Culture and Society* 20(4): 557–72.

Cardiff, David and Paddy Scannell (1981) *The Social Foundations of British Broadcasting*. Milton Keynes: Open University Press.

Carson, Timothy L. (1997) *Liminal Reality and Transformational Power*. Lanham, NY and Oxford: Oxford University Press.

Castells, Manuel (1978) *City, Class and Power*. London: Macmillan.

Castells, Manuel (1980) *The Economic Crisis and American Society*. Oxford: Blackwell.

Castells, Manuel (1983) *The City and the Grassroots*. London: Edward Arnold.

Castells, Manuel (1989) *The Informational City*. Oxford: Blackwell.

Castells, Manuel and Peter Hall (1994) *Technopoles of the World: The Making of 21st Century Industrial Complexes*. London: Routledge.

Charon, Jean-Marie (1987) 'Videotex: From Interaction to Communication', *Media Culture and Society* 9(3): 301–32.

Crawford, Scott A.G.M. (1992) 'Birth of the Modern Sport Spectacular: The Real Madrid and Eintracht Frankfurt European Cup Final of 1960', *International Journal of the History of Sport* 9(3): 433–8.

Dery, Mark (1994) *Flame Wars: The Discourse of Cyber-culture*. Durham, NC: Duke University Press.

Di Filippo, JoAnn (2000) 'Pornography on the Web', in David Gauntlett (ed.) *Web.Studies: Rewiring Media Studies for the Digital Age*. London: Arnold.

Dimmock, Peter (1964) *Sports in View*. London: BBC.

Dimmock, Peter (1968) *Television Outside Broadcasts* (BBC Lunchtime Lecture) 2 October. London: BBC.

Duncan, Margaret Carlisle and Barry Brummett (1989) 'Types and Sources of Spectating Pleasure in Televised Sport', *Sociology of Sport* 6(3): 195–211.

Dutton, William, Jay Blumler and Kenneth Kramer, eds (1986) *Wired Cities*. Boston, MA: G K Hall and Co.

Dyer, Richard (1978) 'Entertainment and Utopia', *Movie* 24.

Eastman, Susan and Arthur M. Land (1997) 'The Best of Both Worlds: Sports Fans Find Good Seats at the Bar', *Journal of Sport and Social Issues* 21(2): 156–78.

Eastman, Susan and Karen E. Riggs (1994) 'Televised Sports and Ritual: Fan Experiences', *Sociology of Sport Journal* 11: 249–74.

Edelman, Robert (1993) *Serious Fun: A History of Spectators Sports in the USSR*. New York: Oxford University Press.

Ezrahi, Yaron, Everett Medelsohn and Howard P. Segal, eds (1994) *Technology, Pessimism and Postmodernism*. Amherst, MA: University of Massachusetts Press.

Ferguson, Marjorie, ed. (1987) *New Communication Technologies and the Public Interest*. London: SAGE.

Friedland, Lewis A. (1996) 'Electronic Democracy and the New Citizenship', *Media Culture and Society* 18(2): 185–212.

Gantz, W. (1981) 'An Explanation of Viewing Motives and Behaviours Associated with Television Sports', *Journal of Broadcasting* 25: 263–75.

Goodhart, D. and P. Wintour (1986) *Eddie Shah and the Newspaper Revolution*. London: Coronet.

Gunning, Tom (1991) 'Heard Over the Phone: The Lonely Villa and the de Lorde Tradition of the Terrors of Technology *Screen* 32(2): 184–96.

Guttmann, Allen (1986) *Sports Spectators*. New York: Columbia University Press.

Hall, Stuart (1975) 'TV as a Medium and its Relation to Culture', *CCCS Stencilled Paper.* Birmingham: CCCS.

Hanson, Ellis (1993) 'Technology, Paranoia and the Queer Voice', *Screen* 34(2): 131–61.

Hastorf, Albert H. and Hadley Cantril (1954) 'They Saw a Game: A Case Study', *Journal of Abnormal and Social Psychology* XLIX.

Holt, Richard, J.A. Mangan and Pierre Lanfranchi, eds (1996) *European Heroes: Myth, Identity and Sport*. London: Frank Cass.

Jansen, Sue Curry (2003) *Critical Communication Theory: Power, Media, Gender and Technology*. Brighton: LSA.

Kellner, Douglas (1995) 'Intellectuals and New Technologies', *Media Culture and Society* 17(3): 427–48.

Kunneman, Harry (1990) 'Some Critical Remarks on Habermas's Analysis of Science and Technology', *Theory Culture and Society* 7(4): 117–26.

Lines, Gill (1998) 'A Case Study of Adolescent Media Consumption During the Summer of Sport 1996', in U. Merkel, G. Lines and I. McDonald (eds) *The Production and Consumption of Sport Cultures: Leisure, Culture and Consumption*, pp. 111–32. Brighton: LSA.

Lines, Gill (2000) 'Media Sport Audiences – Young People and the Summer of Sport '96: Revisiting Frameworks for Analysis', in *Media Culture and Society* 22: 669–80.

Mackay, Hugh, ed. (1997) *Consumption and Everyday Life* (part of the Open University course D318, Culture, Media and Identities). London: SAGE.

McLuhan, Marshall (1964) *Understanding Media*. London: Routledge and Kegan Paul.

McNeil, Maureen (1991) 'The Old and the New Worlds of Information Technology in Britain', in J. Corner and S. Harvey *Enterprise and Heritage*. London: Routledge.

Maddox, Brenda (1972) *Beyond Babel*. London: Andre Deutsch.

Mansell, Roger and Roger Silverstone, eds (1996) *Communication by Design: The Poitics of Information and Communication Technologies*. Oxford: Oxford University Press.

Martin, Luther et al., eds (1988) *Technologies of the Self: A Seminar with Michel Foucault*. Amherst, MA: University of Massachusetts Press.

Miller, Daniel (1997) 'Consumption and its Consequences', in Hugh Mackay (ed.) *Consumption and Everyday Life*. London: SAGE.

Morley, David (2003) 'What's "Home" Got to Do With It? Contradictory Dynamics in the Domestication of Technology and the Dislocation of Domesticity', *European Journal of Cultural Studies* 6(4): 435–58.

Morley, David and Kevin Robins (1992) 'Techno-orientalism: Foreigners, Phobias and Futures', in *New Formations*, n16, London: Lawrence and Wishart.

Munt, Sally R., ed. (2001) *Technospaces: Inside the New Media*. London: Continuum.

Neale, Steve (1985) *Cinema and Technology*. London: BFI.

Pellizzoni, Luigi (1999) 'Reflexive Modernisation and Beyond: Knowledge and Value in the Politics of Environment and Technology', *Theory Culture and Society* 16(4): 99–126.

Rowe, David (1995) *Popular Cultures: Rock Music, Sport and the Politics of Pleasure*. London: SAGE.

Sandvoss, Cornell (2003) *A Game of Two Halves: Football, Television and Globalization*. London: Routledge.

Sapolsky, B.S. and D. Zillman (1978) 'Enjoyment of a Televised Sporting Contest Under Different Conditions of Viewing', *Perceptual and Motor Skills* 46(1): 29–30.

Sardar, Ziauddin (1993) 'Paper, Printing and Compact Disks: The Making and Un-making of Islamic Culture', *Media Culture and Society* 15(1): 43–60.

Sargent, Stephanie Lee, Dolf Zillmann and James B. Weaver III (1998) 'The Gender Gap in the Enjoyment of Televised Sports', *Journal of Sport and Social Issues*.

Sawhney, Harmeet (1996) 'Information Superhighway: Metaphors as Midwives', *Media Culture and Society* 18(2).

Schroeder, Ralph (1995) 'Virtual Environments and the Varieties of Interactive Experience in Information and Communication Technologies, *Convergence* 1(2): 45–55.

Silva, Elizabeth (2000) *The Politics of Consumption @ Home: Practices and Dispositions in the Uses of Technologies – Reports on an Ethnographic Study of the Uses of Technologies in Contemporary Family Life.* Milton Keynes: Pavis Centre for Social and Cultural Research at the Open University.

Silverstone, Roger (1994) *Television and Everday Life.* London: Routledge.

Silverstone, Roger and Eric Hirsch, eds (1992) *Consuming Technologies: Media and Information in Domestic Spaces.* London: Routledge.

Springer, Claudia (1996) *Electronic Eros: Bodies and Desire in the PostIndustrial Age.* London: Athlone.

Taylor, Jeanie, Cheris Kramarae and Maureen Ebben, eds (1993) *Women, Information Technology and Scholarship.* Urbana, IL: WITS, University of Illinois.

Tester, Keith (1995) 'Moral Solidarity and the Technological Reproduction of Images', *Media Culture and Society* 17(3): 469–82.

Thussu, Daya Kishan (1998) *Electronic Empires: Global Media and Local Resistance.* London: Arnold.

Trujillo, Nick and Bob Krizek (1994) 'Emotionality in the Stands and on the Field: Expressing Self Through Baseball', *Journal of Sport and Social Issues* 18(4): 303–25.

Utterson, Andrew, ed. (2004) *Technology, the Film Reader.* London: Routledge.

Vamplew, Wray (1988) *Pay up and Play the Game: Professional Sport in Britain 1875–1914.* Cambridge: Cambridge University Press.

Van Zoonen, Liesbet (1992) 'Feminist Theory and Information Technology', *Media Culture and Society* 14(1): 9–30.

Vertinsky, Patricia and John Bale, eds (2003) *Sites of Sport: Space, Place and Experience.* London: Frank Cass.

Wenner, Lawrence (1994) 'Loving the Game to Death: Heroes, Goals and Spectator Emotion', *Journal of Sport and Social Issues* 18(4): 299–302.

Wenner, Lawrence, and Walter Gantz (1989) 'The Audience Experience with Sports on Television', in L. Wenner (ed.) *Media Sports and Society.* London: SAGE.

Whannel, Garry (1983) 'Sit Down With Us: TV Sport as Armchair Theatre', in S. Glyptis (ed.) *Leisure and the Media* (Conference Papers N16). London: Leisure Studies Association.

Whannel, Garry (1989) 'History is Being Made: Television Sport and the Selective Tradition', in R. Jackson and T. McPhail *The Olympic Movement and the Mass Media.* Calgary: Hurford.

Whannel, Garry (1991) 'Grandstand, the Sports Fan and the Family Audience', in J. Corner (ed.) *Popular Television in Britain: Studies in Cultural History.* London: BFI.

Whannel, Garry (1992) *Fields in Vision: Television Sport and Cultural Transformation.* London: Routledge.

Whannel, Garry (1994) 'Sport and Popular Culture: The Temporary Triumph of Process over Product', *Innovations* 6(3): 341–50.

Whannel, Garry (1998) 'Reading the Media Sport Audience', in Lawrence Wenner (ed.) *MediaSport*, pp. 221–32. London: Routledge.

Whannel, Garry (2002) *Media Sport Stars, Masculinities and Moralities.* London: Routledge.

Williams, Raymond (1961) *The Long Revolution.* Harmondsworth: Penguin.

Williams, Raymond (1974) *TV Technology and Cultural Form.* London: Fontana.

Winston, Brian (1996) *Technologies of Seeing: Photography, Cinematography and Television.* London: BFI.

Wise, Richard (2001) 'New Technologies, Old Ideas', paper given at *American Popular Culture Association Conference*, 13 April, Philadelphia, PA.

Wollen, Tana and Philip Hayward, eds (1993) *Future Visions: New Technologies of the Screen*. London: BFI.

Zhang, James J., Dale G. Pease and Sai C. Hui (1996) 'Value Dimensions of Professional Sport as Viewed by Spectators', *Journal of Sport and Social Issues* 20(1): 79–84.

Zillmann, D., J. Bryant and B.S. Sapolsky (1979) 'The Enjoyment of Watching Sports Contests', in J.H. Goldstein (ed.) *Sports, Games and Play: Social and Psychological Viewpoints*. Hillsdale, NJ: Lawrence Erlbaum.

# 21

# From Plantation to Playing Field: Historical Writings on The Black Athlete in American Sport

*David K. Wiggins*

A significant development in the field of American history within the last few years has been the marked increase in the number of scholarly publications dealing with sport. While professional historians have been, to use Dale Somers' terminology, "laggard in investigating the rise of sports," more scholars are now paying closer attention to one of this country's most pervasive social institutions.[1] No less than eight historical surveys and monographs concerning American sport have been written within the last decade. A growing number of articles on the history of American sport regularly appear in some of the most prestigious journals and anthologies. Scholars in the field have touched upon almost every conceivable subject, covering topics ranging from social elites in sport to the politics surrounding the modern Olympic games.

One group that has received increasing attention from scholars in the field is black athletes. No one familiar with the literature can fail to notice the expanded coverage given to black athletes in the historical surveys on American sport or the growing number of articles about these athletes in various publications. The recent surge in the number of historical writings can be attributed primarily to the phenomenal increase in the number of blacks participating in contemporary sport and the vital part that they played in the athletic revolution. Academicians realize that to understand the history of

**Source:** *Research Quarterly for Exercise and Sport,* 57(2) (1986): 101–116.

sport in this country it is imperative that the role played by the black athlete also be examined. It is necessary not simply because of the tremendous athletic achievements made by blacks, but because people like James J. Corbett, Avery Brundage, and Branch Rickey lived in a world affected by them. Tellingly, the majority of writings on black athletes have been completed by white historians. For whatever reasons, black academicians have yet to concentrate their efforts on black athletes and their contributions to American sport.

This essay reviews the published material pertaining to the history of black athletes in American sport.[2] Considering the number of studies now being done, it is time to take a critical look at the historians' treatment of the black athlete. The study is not comprehensive, focusing instead on the most influential books and articles. In a few cases, important doctoral dissertations have been included in the review. The essay aims to assess only the quality and character of the research completed on the black athlete and implies no judgment of the motivation or personality of individual scholars working in the field. On the contrary, the hope is to make the field more accessible to the non-specialist and to encourage more scholars to examine the role played by black athletes in American sport.

The material is divided into two areas: (1) historical surveys, and (2) articles and monographs. Within the latter category, the material is further divided into pioneering works, popular literature of the 1960's, and studies dealing with the following: black baseball, biographies of black athletes, black involvement in intercollegiate sport, the part played by the black press in American sport, the role of sport in the black community, and the portrayal of black athletes from other disciplinary perspectives. The essay concludes with recommendations for further studies.

The earliest surveys of American sport history generally excluded the black athlete from their analyses. With the exception of a token sentence on such things as black jockeys or boxers, these studies are predictably restricted to the sporting experience of Anglo-Saxons and Northern Europeans. John A. Kraut's *Annals of American Sport*, Herbert Manchester's *Four Centuries of Sport* in *America, 1490–1890*, Robert Weaver's *Amusements and Sports in American Life*, and Foster Rhea Dulles' *America Learns to Play: A History of Recreation*, examine only those institutions dominated by or exclusively manned by whites.[3] None of these white academicians makes attempts to analyze such things as the rise of the black baseball leagues, the part played by blacks in professional boxing, and the type of black cultural institutions that sprang up behind the segregated walls. These early chroniclers of sport, presumably, did not consider black sporting activities to be important.

The white authors of recent surveys on American sport do recognize the important contributions made by black athletes. Unlike the early chroniclers of sport, these authors take notice of black athletes in a more extensive way. John Lucas and Ron Smith are quite innovative in their treatment of the black athlete in their 1978 survey *Saga of American Sport*.[4] While far from comprehensive, the authors provide an accurate portrayal of the black athlete's experiences in American sport. They examine such things as the Jackie Robinson-Paul Robeson political collision, the differing impacts that Jesse Owens and Joe Louis had on American sport, and the various forces that combined to lessen racial segregation in competitive athletics during and immediately following the Second World War.

A different type of historical survey that includes information on the black athlete is *Sports in Modern America,* a collection of fourteen original essays edited by William Baker and John Carroll.[5] William McDonald's "The Black Athlete in American Sports" is one essay in the collection that is of particular significance for this study. Unfortunately, McDonald's work does not add a great deal to our knowledge of the black athlete. A rather cursory examination, it draws heavily on standard secondary works dealing with the black experience in sport. Perhaps the most enlightening aspect of McDonald's essay is his coverage of the debate within academic circles over the alleged superiority of the black athlete. An expanded examination of this topic would be a welcome addition to the literature in the field. In fact, it might prove particularly insightful for someone to analyze the debate from a historical viewpoint rather from merely a contemporary perspective. The controversy goes back at least fifty years when W. Montague Cobb, the well-known physician and physical anthropologist from Howard University, took anthropometric measurements of Jesse Owens and other black American track and field stars. Fascinated by reports claiming that the successes of black athletes in the 1932 Olympic games and in the years immediately following were attributable to inherent racial characteristics, Cobb conducted a study that dismantled these assertions. He reported that the differences in performance of individual black and white sprinters were "insignificant from an anthropological standpoint." Physical characteristics simply did not account for the "dominance of negro athletes in national competition."[6]

An analysis of the debate from a historical perspective would, no doubt, confirm many of the conclusions reached by sociologists who have examined the topic. The apparent domination and over-representation of black athletes in such sports as basketball and track, for instance, is not a result of any inherent racial differences but is caused by a myriad of discrepancies in American society. Simply stated, the disproportionately large number of black athletes in certain sports seems to be accounted for by more than simply biological adaption or economic deprivation. The cultural setting in which black athletes find themselves, the information about particular sports which is available to black athletes, and the black community's attitude toward certain activities are perhaps the essential reasons for the preponderance of blacks in selected sports.[7]

More provocative in its treatment of black athletes is Benjamin Rader's recently published survey *American Sports: From, the Age of Folk Games to the Age of Spectators.*[8] Perhaps the best overall survey yet to appear on American sport history, Rader does a particularly good job in examining the relationship between sport and societal changes. Like Lucas and Smith, Rader details quite nicely the contributions made by blacks to American sport. His discussion of Muhammed Ali and the black athletes' revolt of the 1960's is particularly insightful. He accurately describes how Ali's opposition to the Vietnam War, his conversion to the black Muslim faith, and his pronouncements against liquor, drugs, and "race-mixing" disturbed many black athletes. Yet Ali's bravery instilled many others with the additional courage that helped spawn a black athletic revolt.

While recent historical surveys have added to our knowledge of the black athlete, it is the numerous articles and monographs that contribute most to our understanding of black participation in American sport. The scant attention paid to black athletes, for instance, in the earliest historical surveys is offset by two studies published in the late 1930's that deal exclusively with black athletes. In 1938, Nathaniel Fleischer's multivolume *Black Dynamite: The Story of the Negro in the Prize Ring from 1782 to 1938* appeared, a work recounting individual careers of America's leading black boxers.[9] Easily criticized for an encyclopedic approach which slights traditional historical technique, the book is, nevertheless, a valuable source of biographical data. Featured are such noted fighters as Bill Richmond, Tom Molineaux, George Dixon, Peter Jackson, and Joe Walcott.

Edwin Henderson's *The Negro in Sports*, published in 1939, resembles Fleischer's work in a number of ways, particularly in its emphasis on the star athlete.[10] But unlike Fleischer, Henderson does not confine his work to boxers. He discusses the exploits of top male and female athletes in a number of different sports at the professional, college, and high school levels. In fact, if there is one strength to Henderson's early work, it is the wealth of ideas and information he furnishes for possible later studies. His coverage of the color line in organized baseball and the involvement of black journalists in numerous crusades to integrate American sport specifically inspired two recent studies.[11]

Distinct from the books by Fleischer and Henderson are a small number of studies published in the 1950's which assert that there had been slow but steady progress in the elimination of racial discrimination in American sport. Appearing soon after such notable events as Robinson's entry into organized baseball and Althea Gibson's appearance at Forest Hills, these works claim that blacks were gaining the same opportunities for success on the playing fields as other groups in American society. The most famous study of this kind is John R. Betts' 1951 dissertation "Organized Sport in Industrial America."[12] Long recognized as one of the classics in American sport history, Betts believed that the growth of sport in this country resulted primarily from the advance of urbanization and industrialization within the context of America's democratic institutions. To Betts, the notion of an American "melting pot" was most evident on this country's playing fields. While freely admitting that discrimination against certain groups was all too prevalent in American athletics,

Betts believed that sport did much to acquaint minority groups "with their fellow men and to break through the shell of nationalistic animosity."[13] Different people had been brought closer together, had been united in a common purpose, and had experienced common loyalties through the medium of sport. The black athletes' past, in particular, had been an inexorable procession toward freedom and equality.

Betts' study is a reflection of the rather romantic view that many Americans, both black and white, had of American race relations in general and sport in particular during the decade of the 1950's. The booming economy in America during this period, the idealistic rhetoric of World War II, and the Cold War confrontation with the Soviet Union combined to create an atmosphere that envisioned black athletes fitting into the sport establishment free of any racial prejudice. Unfortunately, this notion of American sport never quite materialized. While the media was quick to point out the success stories of black athletes involved in professional and collegiate sport, most people overlooked the fact that the racial integration of sport during the 1950's was limited to the star athlete and that it was normally a one-way street in which black athletes found it imperative to demonstrate their ability to assimilate the white value system. In sum, the generation of the fifties mistook tokenism for racial integration.[14]

Not until the mid 1960's, nearly a decade and a half after Betts completed his study, was there a significant increase in the number of studies published on the history of black athletes. The sudden emergence of scholarly works resulted from the groundswell of interest in the history of black Americans that extended broadly throughout American society. In 1968, for instance, the National Endowment for the Humanities sponsored workshops on various college campuses to discuss materials for courses on blacks and their contributions to American society.[15] Several states passed legislation during this decade requiring public school instruction in black history.[16] Senate and House subcommittees passed bills to establish a national commission on black history and culture.[17] The result, not surprisingly, was the publication or reissuing of books on black American history.

Many of the works on the black athlete that came out of the black consciousness movement of the 1960's were intended for public rather than scholarly consumption and were designed primarily to create a more positive self-image for black Americans. Such books as Andrew Young's *Negro Firsts in Sports*, Arna Bontemp's *Famous Negro Athletes*, Edwin Henderson's *The Black Athlete: Emergence and Arrival*, and Jack Orr's *The Black Athlete: His Story in American History*, are popular pieces of literature intended to extol the accomplishments of black athletes.[18] Frustrated because history had been unwilling to give blacks significant forebears with whom to identify, and because even the most liberal-minded whites were inclined to prejudicial assumptions, these authors sought to honor black athletic achievements and to uncover the racial attitudes of the American sports establishment. Unfortunately, these works tend to recognize the feats of outstanding black athletes in a rather panegyric fashion. Instead of taking into account a black sporting past that had rogues as well as heroes, these writings were merely a procession of "sugar-coated" success stories.

Equally disconcerting about these studies is the fact they do not take into account black and white cultural differences and the possible effects these differences had on the sporting experience. This is rather surprising considering the decided emphasis that blacks placed on racial pride and cultural distinctiveness during this period. These authors would have contributed a great deal if they had examined the distinctiveness of black sporting patterns in the way that Thomas Kochman analyzed black languages and culture in his recent book *Black and White: Styles in Conflict.*[19] Kochman, a professor of communication and theatre, has provided a model that could be extremely valuable for historians interested in the black athlete. Building on the research that has established the integrity of black English vernacular as a dialect with its own distinctive pattern, Kochman moves beyond dialect and discusses what he terms communication style. In the process, Kochman convincingly illustrates the value, integrity, and aesthetic sensibility of black culture, and, moreover, the conflicts which surface when its values are considered deviant versions of majority ones. He asserts that blacks approach competitive sports in a much different way from their white counterparts. Black athletes attempt to go beyond the "mechanics or technical aspects of play," intending to perform not simply proficiently but with style. Black players place a great deal of emphasis on improvisation, contributing to the game some personal maneuver that will make their play more individually distinctive. White athletes, on the other hand, view competitive sports primarily in terms of winning and losing. The traditional white conception of sports is of a cohesive group working toward the goal of winning and to accomplish victory in the most efficient and cooperative manner possible.

Two studies in the 1960's that stand apart from the aforementioned books and foreshadow the lines of inquiry pursued in the following decade are Finis Farr's *Black Champion: The Life and Times of Jack Johnson* and John P. Davis' essay "The Negro in American Sports."[20] Although a lack of documentation distracts from Farr's work, it still outshines Danzil Batchelor's 1956 study *Jack Johnson and His Times,* adroitly chronicling the career of America's first black heavyweight boxing champion.[21] Farr accurately describes the white antagonisms sharpened by Johnson's victories and the champion's refusal to accept a Jim Crow position in American society. While most blacks of the period assumed a position of accommodation, Farr tells us that Johnson was his own man, frequently roaming outside the boundaries of expected behavior. The champion lived expensively, ignored traditional taboos by marrying two white women, and took enormous pleasure in aggravating and annoying whites. He was convicted for a violation of the Mann Act in 1912 and fled the United States the following year, becoming the world's most notorious fugitive, Johnson died in an automobile accident in 1946, a victim, as Farr describes it, of an "inborn genius for fast movement."[22]

Davis' essay on the black athlete is well researched and lucidly written. There is much to recommend in the essay, but Davis' discussion of the disappearance of black jockeys is probably the most interesting and thought-provoking. There is a need, however, to expand on Davis' examination of black jockeys in an attempt to more fully understand the process by which most blacks were excluded from white organized sport by the turn of the century. No scholar has adequately explained how blacks were virtually eliminated from American sport after having participated with such distinction in the years immediately following emancipation. An ideal way to understand this exclusion, at least in one sport, would be to conduct case studies of black jockeys who held sway over their profession in the 1870's and 1880's. This could be followed by studies that deal with the plight of black athletes in other sports during the last half of the nineteenth century. This systematic line of research would help explain the descent of black athletes to their nadir at the beginning of the twentieth century.[23]

Davis' essay was followed in 1970 by one of the truly important works on the history of the black athlete, Robert Peterson's *Only the Ball was White*.[24] Peterson gives a detailed and fascinating look into the lives of the players and teams that made up black baseball. In so doing, he forces whites to confront some of the more somber truths and parables associated with the "national game." He makes it clear that organized baseball was characterized by a persistent white racism that black athletes found virtually impossible to transcend. Despite arguments to the contrary, American baseball had not been a "melting pot" for diverse ethnic groups, nor had it eliminated the racial disparities that distinguished other phases of society.

Peterson also illustrates that the experience of black athletes was not all that dissimilar to that of their white counterparts. Since many of the earliest studies on American sport fail to recognize the presence of blacks there is always the temptation to believe that they were doing and saying something entirely different from whites. Peterson's work clearly shows that the experiences of black and white athletes, though admittedly different, have continually been intertwined and complementary, despite the fact that the latter have usually forestalled and dominated the relationship. He explains, for example, that whites initially tolerated some black participation in organized baseball. Black players were loudly applauded in such cities as Louisville, Baltimore, and Washington, D.C. Moses "Fleetwood" Walker and his brother Welday were both playing Major League baseball with the Toledo Mudhens of the American Association in the 1880's. Perhaps as many as twenty blacks were participating on minor league teams in 1887.[25]

The most important contributions of Peterson's study were the first-hand accounts of black players describing what life was like in the black leagues. In contrast to many works on the black athlete, Peterson gives a clear understanding of the meaning sport had for players in the black leagues. In the process, we learn a great deal about the image black players had of themselves, and conversely, the image society had of them.

It would have been beneficial if Peterson's much admired and frequently cited study would have been followed up by equally impressive works on the black leagues, but this is unfortunately not the case. Subsequent works on black baseball do not approach the standards of *Only the Ball was White* and can probably best be classified as "coffee table" histories.[26] More impressive are a number of recent articles that examine the events surrounding Jackie Robinson's entry into organized baseball. Lee Lowenfish examines the timing, strategy, and consequences of Branch Rickey's decision to sign Robinson to a Major League contract with the Brooklyn Dodgers.[27] Bill Weaver investigates the Robinson story from a different perspective. He looks at this country's leading black newspapers to determine how they treated the signing of Robinson and his subsequent rise to Major League success.[28] David Wiggins takes a different approach in his recent study "Wendell Smith, the *Pittsburgh Courier-Journal* and the Campaign to Include Blacks in Organized Baseball, 1933–1945."[29] While scholars have given much attention to the part played by Rickey and white sportscasters in ending discrimination in organized baseball, this article focuses on the heretofore untold role of Wendell Smith and the *Pittsburgh Courier-Journal* in seeing that blacks were allowed in the sport. Wiggins illustrates that although there were other black newspapers in the United States that participated in the campaign against lily-white baseball during the 1930's and first half of the 1940's, it was the *Courier-Journal* that proved most effective in seeing that the game's racial barrier was finally lifted.

Perhaps the most insightful article yet to appear on the Robinson story is Ron Smith's "The Paul Robeson-Jackie Robinson Saga and a Political Collision."[30] Smith takes a fascinating look at the political confrontation that took place between Robinson and the great athlete and outstanding singer-actor Paul Robeson during the tumultuous anti-communist days of the early cold war era. Particularly important is Smith's portrayal of the decided philosophical differences that existed between Robinson and Robeson. Too many sport historians have falsely seen black athletes as a homogeneous group, perceiving them not only as sharing physical characteristics but also as thinking and acting alike. This typecasting can perhaps be explained by the group solidarity and joint response that black athletes often exhibit when encountering racial discrimination. But among themselves they have always been distinguished by skin color, organized around particular class lines, connected with their own political parties, faithful to their special religious denominations, and characterized by particular mores and value schemes.

These facts are nowhere made more evident than in Smith's account of the Robeson-Robinson confrontation. Smith illustrates that both of these outstanding black performers were involved in racial reform in America, but they were approaching change from different perspectives. Robeson was not as willing to compromise with white society to accomplish his racial goals. Robinson was more inclined to accede to the wants of white society for a time to bring about positive racial reforms. Robeson was more idealistic and inflexible and, as a result, "was politically, economically, and socially alienated from the greater American society."[31] Robinson was more pragmatic, thus prospering far better socially and financially than did Robeson.

While the aforementioned articles contribute a great deal to our understanding of Robinson and the integration of organized baseball, no work covers the subject more thoroughly than Jules Tygiel's recent book *Baseball's Great Experiment: Jackie Robinson and His Legacy.*[32] Combining exhaustive research with lucid writing, Tygiel's work makes significant advances over any of the books written previously about the Robinson legacy, including Murray Polner's *Branch Rickey: A Biography*, and Harvey Frommer's *Rickey and Robinson: The Men Who Broke Baseball's Color Barrier.*[33] More than just a recapitulation of the Robinson story, Tygiel goes beyond the usual accounts of Rickey's search for a black player or of the trials and tribulations Robinson faced during his playing days with the Dodgers. He describes in vivid detail the vigorous campaign to integrate organized baseball waged by the American Communist Party and such prominent sportswriters as Wendell Smith, Joe Bostic, and Sam Lacy. He gives a most interesting account of racial developments in the minor leagues and the part that the desegregation of baseball in the South played in the struggle against Jim Crow. He also assesses the impact that the integration of organized baseball had on the black leagues and the ultimate fortunes of the heroes of that league. Lastly, and maybe most important, Tygiel carries the story of baseball integration through 1959, when the Boston Red Sox became the last Major League team to sign a black player. In the process, he describes the frequently neglected stories of such pioneers of baseball integration as Roy Campanella, Larry Doby, Satchel Paige, and Willie Mays.

One black athlete who has received almost as much attention from scholars as Robinson is Jack Johnson. Just five years after the publication of Finis Farr's aforementioned biography, Robert Decoy came out with a book on Johnson titled *The Big Black Fire.*[34] The most frequently cited biography of Johnson, however, is Al-Tony Gilmore's *Bad Nigger! The National Impact of Jack Johnson*, a study of public reaction that conveys the boxer's controversial importance.[35] Unfortunately, the material in Gilmore's study is liberally drawn from Farr's book and William Wiggins' article, "Jack Johnson as Bad Nigger: The Folklore of His Life."[36] Like Farr, Gilmore chooses to chronicle America's reaction to Johnson from the time he acquired the heavyweight championship in 1908, until his defeat at the hands of Jesse Willard in Havana, Cuba in 1915. Similar to Wiggins, Gilmore argues that many whites hated Johnson not only "because he was a black conqueror of white hopes (but) because of his obvious preference for white women." Johnson was a "bad nigger" to the delight of many blacks but to the chagrin of other blacks and whites because "he refused to accept the place given to blacks in American society."[37]

Besides his heavy dependency on other authors, many of Gilmore's conclusions are open to question. He tends to downplay the support that many whites showed toward Johnson. Gilmore's claim that Johnson was responsible for the introduction of local and federal legislation to prevent racial intermarriage is probably a little strong. His assertion that most of white America wished to have Johnson's title stripped away is an exaggeration, even after his conviction under the Mann Act. The one contribution that Gilmore does make is his unprecedented use of black and white newspapers to chart Johnson's influence while champion.

A biography of Johnson that outshines all the rest is Randy Roberts' *Papa Jack: Jack Johnson and the Era of White Hopes.*[38] Few, if any, sport historians today write with the flair of Roberts, and this study is ample testimony to that fact. He combines an energetic writing style with solid scholarship to produce a book that readers with only a limited interest in boxing or black sport history would find captivating. Roberts recounts the life of Johnson from his boyhood days in Galveston, Texas to the bars, brothels, and boxing arenas of Mexico, Australia, England, and America. One distinguishing feature of Roberts' study is the use of heretofore neglected sources that give more insight into why Johnson acted as he did and what major environmental forces shaped him. The canvassing of census records and government documents, plus the discriminating use of newspapers and Johnson's own autobiography, furnish an accurate account of Johnson's life.[39]

Roberts' study has all the ingredients of a good biography. He not only gives a great deal of emphasis to Johnson, but also to the atmosphere and environment in which he lived. Roberts' craftsmanship allows one to grasp more precisely the interrelationship of Johnson with early twentieth century American society. In addition, Roberts treats Johnson as a thinking man, explaining why this country's most famous black athlete defied racial conventions with a combatant attitude and extravagant lifestyle. Roberts explores Johnson's character, motivation, features and mannerisms strengths and weaknesses, and conflicts. More than the historical forces surrounding him, Johnson is exposed in totality to the study and comprehension of his mind as well as his activities.

Easily the most salient feature of Roberts' study is the fact that Johnson is not treated as a particularly nice man. Many scholars over the last two decades, in an effort to avoid the appearance of "blaming the victim" or to protect their work from charges of racism, simply ignored patterns of behavior that might be construed as stigmatizing to particular black athletes. Roberts does not make that mistake. While Johnson encountered abhorrent racial discrimination, he was not simply an innocent victim. He was often manipulative, frequently underhanded, and in many instances, the cause of his own problems.

Johnson is certainly not the only black boxer who has been thoroughly treated by academicians. Joe Louis, America's famous black heavyweight champion of the 1930's and early 1940's, also has received his share of attention. A most intriguing and thought-provoking study of Louis is Anthony Edmonds' slender biography *Joe Louis*, a volume in the Great Men of Michigan Series.[40] Unlike many sport biographies, it does more than bombard the reader with a factual account of an outstanding athletic figure. Edmonds focuses instead on the public image of Louis, seeking to determine the particular images that the champion portrayed. Edmonds illustrates that Louis was of crucial importance to the majority of black Americans. His impeccable behavior earned him the respect of most whites and therefore opened new avenues of mobility for blacks. At the same time, his symbolic defeats of white men in the ring engendered race pride and caused a heightening of racial consciousness in the black community. Perhaps even more insightful than Edmonds' book is Jeffrey T. Sammons' recent article "Boxing as a Reflection of Society: The Southern Reaction to Joe Louis" and the study by Dominic J. Capeci, Jr. and Martha Wilkerson, "Multifarious Hero: Joe Louis, American Society, and Race Relations During World Crisis, 1935–1945,"[41] Sammons relates how the Southern press demeaned the accomplishments of Louis, never acknowledging his contributions to the sport of boxing. Capeci and Wilkerson examine Louis' transition from race champion to national idol amidst both the Great Depression and Second World War. The study is distinguishable from many other works on the black athlete because it reveals changes that took place in Louis' career over a ten year period of time, combines insights from various disciplinary perspectives, and clearly shows the interplay between sport and society.

It is unfortunate that more scholarly biographies of less famous black athletes have not been written. Data can be found, however, on two of the more honored yet less recognizable black athletes in Alexander Young's examination of boxer Sam Langford and in David Wiggins' article on Isaac Murphy.[42] Young gives an interesting account of the career of one of the finest boxers of the early twentieth century, who fought in five different weight divisions during his twenty-one year career. Young skillfully delineates the major influences on Langford's life and places the sport of boxing in its broader social and cultural context. Wiggins' article traces the riding career of Isaac Murphy, perhaps late nineteenth century America's best jockey. Wiggins points out that Murphy rode nearly every famous horse in the land and won every major race except the Futurity, which always eluded him. He was the first jockey to win three Kentucky Derbies, was victorious in four American Derbies, and won the famous Latonia Derby five times. Unfortunately, like other black athletes of the period, Murphy was eventually phased out of horse racing. Continuing weight problems, chronic alcoholism, and the effects of racial segregation in sports during the late 1800's resulted in his ultimate demise as a jockey.

Wiggins' article on Murphy points out some of the problems inherent in conducting a biographical study of a black athlete. While Wiggins carefully narrates the significant events in Murphy's career, very little is said about the motives, desires, and fears of the famous black jockey. There is no indication of what sport, and specifically horse racing, meant to Murphy. Part of the reason for this omission was Wiggins' reluctance to be speculative beyond what is, in the words of W. F. Mandle, the "permitted range of historical connection-spinning."[43] The most obvious explanation, however, for the lack of more insight into Murphy's life was the fact that Wiggins was limited in the sources he could utilize for the study. The work is based primarily on newspapers and secondary accounts, sources that allow for only the most rudimentary explanations. Unavailable were such primary materials as an autobiography, diary, or personal letters. This problem is prevalent in other historical areas of course, but seems particularly acute in Afro-American studies. Black culture is, after all, based to a large extent on oral and folk traditions. In many instances, the black Americans' own written records of survival are not available or easily accessible to scholars.

Although biographical studies dominate the field, there have been a number of important works published within the last decade that deal with the black athletes' experiences in intercollegiate athletics. John Behee was one of the first researchers to analyze this subject seriously in his 1974 book *Hail to the Victors! Black Athletes at the University of Michigan.*[44] Using a collection of papers housed at the University of Michigan and by interviewing former athletes, coaches, and athletic directors, Behee studied the racial conflicts and ultimate integration of black athletes at the famous Big Ten University. The book has some limitations. Behee notes, for example, that blacks participated in several sports at Michigan, but he does not adequately explain why they were virtually excluded from a number of others sports at the school. He also fails to relate his study to the more fundamental questions of race and culture evident within the development of American sport, and therefore, cannot clearly detail the complex reasons for the black man's eventual acceptance into competitive athletics. Despite these failings, Behee's work remains the most thorough study yet done on black participation in intercollegiate athletics at a single institution.

Complementing Behee's path breaking study are a number of subsequent articles that contribute a great deal to our understanding of the black college athlete. In a 1975 study, Don Spivy and Tom Jones collected data on 227 black athletes who played at the University of Illinois from 1931 to 1967 and discovered that they had a higher academic attrition rate than their white counterparts. The authors attribute this to pervasive racial prejudice within the university's academic structure and to the fact that these black athletes were largely deficient in preparation for college.[45] In a 1981 article, Jack Berryman examines the leading role played by three blacks in predominantly white college football in the state of Massachusetts during the racially oppressive years of the late nineteenth century. Berryman suggests that William H. Lewis, William H. Craighead, and Matthew W. Bullock were able to assume leadership positions at their respective institutions primarily because Massachusetts was a pioneer in positive black-white relationships.[46] Adolf Grundman's study

"The Image of Intercollegiate Sports and the Civil Rights Movement: An Historian's View," illustrates that Harry Edwards, Jack Olsen, and other critics of American sport failed to examine the relationship of the premises of the civil rights movement and sport to the frustrations of the 1960's. These social commentators disapproved utterly of the racism in American sport, but did not adequately explore "the reasons for the failure of racial integration in sport." Grundman argues that the reason for this failure rests in the late 1940's and 1950's, when romanticized images of sport and the expectations of whites that successful blacks would acquiesce to white middle class standards did indeed hinder integration.[47]

Quite different from the research completed on intercollegiate athletics are a number of articles that examine the role of the black press in American sport. The study that makes most use of black newspapers is David Wiggins' recent article on the 1936 Olympic Games.[48] By examining the *Baltimore Afro-American, Pittsburgh Courier-Journal* and several other influential black newspapers, Wiggins sought to ascertain the black press' reaction to the victories garnered by Jesse Owens and other black athletes in Berlin, and to determine what effect their participation had on the rest of black America. Wiggins clearly shows that although they were terribly disturbed by Germany's racial policies, the black press seemingly welcomed the controversy that arose during the games over that country's treatment of minority groups. The Olympics of 1936 made thoughtful whites painfully aware of the contradiction in opposing Nazi racial philosophy while doing nothing about racism at home. In defending their right to host the games, the German press had raised the issue of American racism to embarrass the country in the eyes of the world. This did not resolve the contempt that people felt towards Germany's own racial policies, but did raise the consciousness of some whites who had heretofore not thought seriously about the plight of black Americans.

Wiggins takes a different approach in a series of articles on the recreational patterns of slaves living on Southern plantations.[49] Influenced by the recent works of John Blassingame and Eugene Genovese, Wiggins' articles make it clear that however dehumanizing the Southern plantation became for slaves, their struggle for survival never became so severe that it destroyed their creative instincts or prevented them from establishing their own personal way of life. The distinguishing elements of their culture – superstitions, religion, music, folktales, and recreation – allowed slaves a degree of individual autonomy and self-respect. While slaves recognized the superior power which whites held as a group, they resisted total assimilation into white culture.

This view of slave life is symptomatic of the growing trend among historians to recognize that black Americans have been able to create and sustain a viable culture, despite the years of racial oppression. Growing out of the black consciousness movement of the 1960's, this conceptualization of the black Americans' past has undergirded the new approach to black history.[50] Until recently, the majority of academicians either denied the existence of a consolidated black culture or reluctantly accepted the possibility, but viewed it as a subculture that was at best a spin-off from the dominant white society. In many cases, the story of blacks was simply an appendage to the main currents of American history.

It is significant that many of the studies currently being done on the black experience in sport are still inextricably bound to the growth of American society and do not recognize the presence of a unified black culture. A notable exception is Ralph Watkins' recent study of recreation and leisure in the black community of Buffalo, New York during the early 1920's,[51] Watkins points out that black leaders in Buffalo maintained a rather ambivalent attitude about the new found leisure their community enjoyed during the post World War I period. Apprehensive about its negative effects, yet aware of the potential for good, black leaders organized and supported a myriad of activities designed to improve the quality of life in black Buffalo. The city's black residents participated in plays and dramatic readings, sports, dances, travel, and picnics. These activities were primarily supported by the black church, social clubs, fraternities, charitable organizations, and various informal associations organized on the streets of the expanding black community. The chance to engage in different recreational pursuits allowed blacks in Buffalo an opportunity to be more than "a group of desperate souls driven toward the sanctuary of the black church in the hope of escaping the enduring ghetto."[52]

While no scholar has published a monograph on sport in the black urban community, two excellent books dealing with the rise of sport in New Orleans and Boston during the latter half of the nineteenth and early part of the twentieth centuries include the black athlete in their analysis. Both Dale Somers' work on New Orleans and Stephen Hardy's book on Boston offer information on the type of sport participated in by blacks in two of America's most historic cities.[53] Somers, in particular, devotes quite a bit of space to the black athlete. He takes an interesting look at the black athlete's involvement in such popular New Orleans sports as horse racing, prize fighting, baseball, and bicycling. He briefly discusses the attempts by blacks to break the color-line at summer resorts and to establish their own athletic clubs free from any association with the white clubs of the city. Perhaps most informative is Somers' concluding chapter, in which he discusses the cessation of black-white athletic contests in New Orleans during the 1890's. Somers asserts that the "Crescent City" sports provided an inadequate social safety valve in the field of race relations.

The elimination of interracial athletic contests in New Orleans and elsewhere in America, of course, was just one aspect of the discrimination faced by blacks following the Compromise of 1877. For a variety of reasons blacks found it increasingly more difficult to participate fully in American life towards the latter part of the nineteenth century. The mounting racism against blacks was expressed, first of all, in a succession of decisions by the United States Supreme Court between 1873 and 1898. In such decisions as the

*Slaughter House Cases* of 1873, *Civil Rights Cases* of 1883, and the famous *Plessy vs. Ferguson Case* of 1896, the court drastically curtailed the privileges of blacks recognized as being under federal protection. The rights of blacks were also negatively affected by the United States decisions to plunge into imperialistic adventure in 1898. As America shouldered the burden of caring for some eight million blacks suddenly brought under their jurisdiction, it took up at the same time many of the Southern attitudes on race. Lastly, at the very same time that imperialism was sweeping the country, the notion of racism was being enthusiastically supported by scholars from various disciplinary perspectives. Academicians from such areas as biology, sociology, anthropology, and history supported the theory that the races were separate entities and that the Anglo-Saxon was superior to them all.[54]

Steve Hardy does not spend as much time on the black athlete in his study of Boston. He does describe the mixed reactions that Boston's black community had towards Jack Johnson's boxing exploits. Hardy notes that while some members of the city's black community viewed Johnson's "life-style as an improper and challenging model," others saw him as an "important defender of black rights."[55] Hardy also briefly explains the types of sporting associations formed by the city's black population around the turn of the century. He states that elite black Bostonians imitated their white counterparts by organizing tennis clubs, West Indian immigrants established cricket clubs, and newly arrived immigrants from the South frequented local gymnasiums. The desire to maintain distinct sport organizations, Hardy concludes, stemmed largely "from the exclusionary practices of the native population, both black and white."[56]

Certainly one of the more encouraging trends within the last decade is the quality of research completed on black athletes from other disciplinary perspectives. Scholars from such areas as anthropology, economics, political science, and sociology, have complemented the historical works quite well by examining the part played by blacks in recent sporting developments. Perhaps no other area of sports in America has commanded so much attention from sociologists as race relations. Such well known academicians as Stanley Eitzen, Norman Yetman, Roscoe Brown, and Barry McPherson have spent a great deal of time analyzing the various forms of discrimination practiced in contemporary sport.[57] Tellingly, these scholars generally concluded that black athletes are disproportionately represented in certain playing positions, receive lower salaries than white athletes of comparable abilities, and have continually been passed over for front office positions after their playing days are over.[58]

It is clear that historians are now paying much more attention to black athletes and the numerous contributions they have made to American sport. Studies dealing with the history of the black athlete appear with regularity in the leading journals, anthologies, and surveys on American sport. While progress has been made, there is still much room for further studies. One topic that needs further examination is the type of recreational pursuits engaged in by slaves living on southern plantations. Scholars need to expand on the series of articles by Wiggins and answer the questions left unresolved from his work. For instance, what kinds of changes took place in slave recreations over a period of time? Were slave recreational patterns decidedly different in the lower South than the upper South? Were the patterns of recreation for house slaves unlike that of the field hands? Were any of the recreational activities participated in by slaves uniquely African in origin? What was the status of those athletically inclined slaves who participated for their masters in such sports as horse racing and boxing? To answer these types of questions scholars would do well to utilize the slave narrative collection, particularly those edited by George Rawick.[59] While these materials present some unique problems, there are no sources that better reflect the reality of slavery as experienced by slaves themselves. The collection should, of course, be used with materials such as travel accounts, plantation diaries and letters, and white autobiographies.

Regardless of the sources utilized, scholars should recognize that in the plantation community, slave and master were inextricably bound together. By viewing slavery as an "organic" relationship in which masters and slaves lived symbiotically, academicians can seek to describe not merely the coherence of slave recreational patterns, but also the manner in which it influenced and was influenced by white society. This is not a call for work that ignores the distinctive patterns of slave recreation. Slaves were certainly active participants in shaping their own culture and the types of recreational activities that sprang from it had their own distinguishing features independent of whites. Yet, there seems to be a danger in focusing so intensively on the slaves' world that one ignores, or at best minimizes, the ways in which slaves' recreational activities were influenced by the slave system. In short, the key to understanding slave recreation is to recognize that in the plantation community, whites and blacks were involved in a dynamic, but ambivalent, relationship involving reciprocal rights and obligations.

To fully grasp the role of sport in antebellum America scholars cannot focus exclusively on slaves but should also analyze the pattern of sport and recreation among free blacks who inhabited various sections of the country. No scholar has explored this topic in any depth and it is unfortunate because the sources are available to conduct small scale investigations or larger monographic works.[60] While much of what has been said about slaves can be applied to free blacks, the types of inquiry and methodology employed will vary considerably. Free blacks, of course, were not confined solely to farms and small towns, but lived close to whites of every nationality in most of the larger cities of America. Generally, no unitary black ghettos developed in the large metropolitan areas prior to the Civil War. The lack of urban transportation and the need for blacks to reside near their place of work scattered free blacks throughout American cities. Whites were reluctant to establish a single community which might unite blacks and serve as a breeding ground for insurrection. As a result, free black people could be found in almost every section of American cities, living side-by-side with Irish, German, and Scottish immigrants. Fraternization between whites and free blacks extended to all corners of working class life. Free blacks and poor whites often frequented the same gambling houses, tippling houses, and other places of entertainment. Warm friendships between free blacks and whites also flourished at the other end of the social spectrum. Shared styles of life and class interests sometimes pierced the walls of racial suspicion in the upper reaches of American society. These facts raise several intriguing questions about the pattern of recreation and sport among free blacks. For instance, what were the differences in sporting patterns between wealthy free blacks and their poorer brethren? Were the sporting patterns of free blacks decidedly different from those of slaves? What were the differences in sporting patterns among free blacks in New Orleans and those in such influential Northern cities as New York and Boston? Did the fraternal organizations, social groups, and sporting clubs of free blacks differ substantially from those of immigrant groups?

To answer the above questions, scholars should be aware that discrimination continually scarred the lives of free blacks. Yet racial antagonism varied in intensity over both place and time; its results were directed in unique ways in various kinds of communities; and it touched different segments of the free black community in a variety of ways. This points to the need for academicians to conduct studies that deal comprehensively with many aspects of free black sporting practices or, if they cannot be so comprehensive, cover a substantial time period or compare a number of different communities over a shorter period of time. While initial studies on the role of sport among free blacks will most likely deal with specific communities, scholars should resist the temptation to remain narrowly focused on a particular time period or subject matter. Academicians who have examined other aspects of free black cultural patterns have become more aware of the need to place the history of a particular community in a larger context by comparing it with other communities. They realize the danger in generalizing from too narrow a chronological framework or from only a single community.

One of the least understood periods in black sport history are those years from emancipation to the beginning of the twentieth century. To gain insight into this neglected area it is crucial that academicians examine how freedom from slavery affected black sporting patterns. Emancipation, of course, altered the context in which black thought and belief had traditionally been rooted. Black culture thus evolved in conjunction with transformations occurring in the larger society – increased mobility and communication, expanded industrialization, and urbanization – changes in which, in the words of Lawrence Levine, the "number of reference groups multiplied and life styles became segmentalized and shifting."[61] In this type of social milieu, what modifications occurred in black sporting patterns? How did the rise of a more individualized ethos among blacks during the latter half of the nineteenth century affect their sporting activities? To answer these questions scholars might find it particularly worthwhile to take an indepth look at the changing social structure of the black family. Perhaps there is no better way to view the forces of change and continuity that took place in black sporting activities following emancipation.[62] This type of approach might also furnish some much needed insight into how black athletes were socialized into sport during the latter half of the nineteenth century. There are no historical studies that systematically examine the influence that siblings, parents, and extended family members have had on black athletes' involvement in American sport.

While the literature makes it plain that black athletes were virtually eliminated from white organized sport by the last decade of the nineteenth century, very little is known about how that process came about and how individual black athletes reacted to it. To rectify this gap in the literature, scholars might find it profitable to conduct biographical studies on Marshall "Major" Taylor, Moses "Fleetwood" Walker, and other prominent black athletes affected by late nineteenth century discriminatory practices. It is crucial in these studies that academicians be innovative and expand on the types of sources used in earlier biographies of black athletes. Scholars should stop relying so heavily on newspapers and utilize, if possible, such materials as personal letters, diaries, autobiographies, club records, and census data. It is also extremely important in these studies that scholars do not consider black athletes as simply innocent victims. Academicians should be forthright and acknowledge that black athletes were sometimes just as guilty of discrimination and dishonest tactics as anyone else. White culture did not have a monopoly on racial prejudice. It might prove profitable, moreover, for academicians to employ the latest theories in psychohistory to expand on their analysis of individual black athletes.[63] While, this approach is thick with methodological problems, perhaps there is no better way to grasp the meaning sport had for black athletes.

Most of the work that has been done on black athletes in American sport has dealt with the twentieth century. Yet, in some ways, we know less about the black experience in sport during this time period than in the latter half of the nineteenth century. While there is a wealth of information on such prominent black athletes as Joe Louis, Jack Johnson, and Jackie Robinson, there is a paucity of data on the entrepreneurs and promoters of black sport, the role of sport in black colleges, and the pattern of sport among urban blacks. In fact, the latter topic is one of the most obvious voids in the literature on black sport history. With the exception of Pete Axthelm's popular study of New York City basketball, no one has examined in any depth the role of sport among blacks in American cities.[64] This is somewhat surprising when you consider that the social history of the city has received such an enormous amount of attention over the last few years.[65]

Scholars interested in the role of sport among urban blacks should keep several things in mind when embarking on their work. They should be cognizant, first of all, of the external and structural forces that have shaped the black historical experience in the urban community. Scholars have to take into account the degree of white hostility towards blacks, the limits which the white population set to acceptable social contact, and the existence or lack of violence directed against blacks in the urban setting. Academicians should also be aware of the type and quality of various housing stocks, the kinds of transportation and communication systems available in a particular city, and numerous other aspects of urban society that might impinge, at any given time, upon black sporting patterns. Second, scholars would profit by comparing the sporting patterns characteristics of blacks, native whites, and immigrants in the urban setting. It is crucial that academicians sort out the causes for black/white differences in adaption to urban life and the effect it had on the role of sport. Third, scholars should resist the tendency to present the adoption and lifestyles of black urbanites in negative terms. Many of the earliest studies of blacks in cities placed a decided emphasis upon the "pathological effects" of racism and the inability of blacks to successfully adapt to urban life.[66] While the debilitating effects of the urban environment should be acknowledged, scholars interested in sporting patterns should concentrate on the way black urbanites have responded to their circumstances, either by the retention or creation of institutions or cultural values that are indigenous to the black community. Lastly, scholars should utilize some of the sophisticated methodological approaches employed by previous researchers on black city life. For instance, among those scholars studying the nineteenth century city, use of manuscript census has become de rigueur. Theodore Hershberg, Oliver Zunz, and other scholars of black urban life now regularly use a social-scientific methodology in their work.[67] Peter Gottlieb utilized oral interviews in his study of black workers in Pittsburgh between 1916 and 1930.[68]

Rivaling the need for studies on the black urban experience are those works that examine the black athletes' revolt of the 1960's and early 1970's. Enough time has now elapsed to gain the perspective necessary for conducting a legitimate study of the famous movement for racial equality spearheaded by Harry Edwards.[69] The black athletes' revolt, of course, was part of the larger black power movement, the crusade that emerged out of a conviction that civil rights legislation and poverty programs were failing to erase inequality and poverty because they were part of the white power structure. Black Americans were in the midst of a cultural revolution that emphasized the distinctiveness of black culture, the merits of black life-styles, and the value of race pride. This celebration of black culture was seen as a way to liberate blacks psychologically, eliminate the negative self-image prevalent among many blacks, and encourage black consciousness as a necessary foundation for the promotion of black political and economic power. While generally a unique development in Afro-American history, the black power movement did, nonetheless, draw on past experience. Analogies can be drawn, for example, with the Garvey Movement which received such broad support in the black community following World War I.

Scholars interested in the black athletes' revolt might find it helpful to conduct studies on the major black protest organizations such as C.O.R.E., the Chicago Urban League, and the N.A.A.C.P., to determine their ideological position on the revolt. Academicians would also find it worthwhile to immerse themselves in the several autobiographies written by black athletes who were either directly or indirectly involved in the revolt.[70] There is no better way to gain intimate knowledge of the way blacks thought, acted, and viewed the American sport establishment during some of the most tumultuous years in our nation's history. The utilization of autobiographies would, furthermore, provide scholars with the perfect opportunity to explore both the complexities of the black athletes revolt and the concept of psychic duality or "double-consciousness" espoused by W. E. B. Dubois some eighty years ago. Dubois, the celebrated black intellectual from Harvard, wrote in his famous 1903 book *Souls of Black Folk* that blacks in this country have always felt a two-ness – "An American, a Negro; two soles [sic], two thoughts, two unreconciled strivings; two warring ideals in one dark body, whose dogged strength alone kept it from being torn asunder. The history: of the American Negro is the history of this strife."[71] This double-consciousness of being black and being American, of which Dubois spoke, came into sharp focus for American blacks involved in the athletic revolt. While the civil rights movement was sometimes responsible for the increased participation of blacks in American sport, the implications of this type of "participation" was greater than Harry Edwards and a growing number of black athletes were prepared to accept. It was apparent that participation in highly competitive sport implied only the supremacy of everything white and the inferiority of everything black. It was a one-way process in which black athletes sought access into the American sport establishment, but only at the expense of being denied their own identity and their African heritage. The involvement in American sport simply offered no effective solution to the whole problem of cultural marginality. It was, in other words, virtually impossible for the black athlete to be both black and American.

An obvious void in the literature is the lack of any research that examines the history of the black athlete from a comparative perspective. It would be beneficial for scholars, in much the same way as Frank Tannenbaum examined slavery,[72] to compare and contrast the plight of the black athlete in America with those in such countries as England, Australia, and the West Indies. This type of approach might furnish additional insights into the sporting patterns and racial realities of various cultures and subsequently raise important questions that would further illuminate the shared experience of black athletes.[73]

Many more suggestions could be made concerning future directions for writing about black sport history.[74] The relationship between black athletes and the American Communist Party, the role of black women in American sport, and the portrayal of black athletes in American literature are just a few topics that come to mind. Let it suffice to say, however, that the writings on the history of the black athlete have improved markedly in recent years. The relatively small number of scholars working in this area should take pride in what they have accomplished. The black athlete's past has been illuminated in a manner that has expanded our knowledge of both black and white people in this country. The one thing that can be hoped for is that researchers with the proper academic training and a genuine interest in the black athlete will continue to be attracted to this field. If not, a decided gap in the literature will exist and a thorough understanding of the history of American sport will be unattainable.

## References

1. Dale A. Somers, *The Rise of Sport in New Orleans, 1850–1900* (Baton Rouge: Louisiana State University Press, 1972).
2. There have been a number of review articles published on the history of American sport. See for example: Melvin L. Adelman, "Academicians and Athletics: Historians' Views of American Sport," *Maryland Historian* 4 (Fall 1973): 123–34; idem, "Academicians and American Athletics: A Decade of Progress," *Journal of Sport History* 10 (Spring 1983): 80–106; Benjamin Rader, "Modern Sports: In Search of Interpretations," *Journal of Social History* 13 (Winter 1979): 307–21; Allen Guttmann, "Commentary: Who's on First? or Books on the History of American Sports," *Journal of American History* 66 (Sept. 1979); 348–54; Stephen Hardy, "The City and the Rise of American Sport: 1820–1920," *Exercise and Sports Sciences Reviews* 9 (1981): 183–210; Steven A. Reiss, "Sport and the American Dream: A Review Essay," *Journal of Social History* 14 (Winter 1980): 295–301; W. Manning Marable, "Black Athletes in White Men's Games, 1880–1920," *Maryland Historian* 4 (Fall 1973): 143–149; David K. Wiggins, "Clio and the Black Athlete in America: Myths, Heroes and Realities," *Quest* 32 (1980): 217–25; Nancy L. Struna, "Beyond Mapping Experience: The Need for Understanding in the History of American Sporting Women," *Journal of Sport History* 11 (Spring 1984): 120–133; Roberta J. Park, "Research and Scholarship in the History of Physical Education and Sport: The Current State of Affairs," *Research Quarterly for Exercise and Sport* 54 (June 1983): 93–103.
3. John Allen Krout, *Annals of American Sport* (New Haven: Yale University Press, 1929); Herbert Manchester, *Four Centuries of Sport in America, 1490–1890* (New York: The Derrydale Press, 1931); Robert B. Weaver, *Amusements and Sports in American Life* (Chicago: University of Chicago Press, 1939); Foster Rhea Dulles, *America Learns to Play: A History of Recreation* (New York: D. Appleton-Century Company, 1940).
4. John Lucas and Ronald A. Smith, *Saga of American Sport* (Philadelphia: Lea and Febiger, 1978).
5. William J. Baker and John M. Carroll, eds., *Sports in Modern America* (St. Louis: River City Publishers, 1981). For another anthology that was published upon completion of this text, see Donald Spivey, ed., *Sport in America: New Historical Perspectives* (Westport, Conn.: Greenwood Press, 1985).
6. See W. Montague Cobb "Race and Runners," *Journal of Health and Physical Education* 7 (Jan. 1936): 3–7, 52–56.
7. Several scholars have examined the issue from a sociological perspective. See for example, Larry E. Jordan, "Black Markets and Future Superstars: An Instrumental Approach to Opportunity in Sport Forms," *Journal of Black Studies* 11 (March 1981): 289–306; James LeFlore, "Athleticism Among American Blacks," in *Social Approaches to Sport*,

ed. Robert M. Parkin (Toronto: Associated University Presses, 1982), 104–121; John G. Phillips, "Toward an Explanation of Racial Variations in Top-Level Sports Participation," *International Review of Sport Sociology* 11 (1976): 39–53.

8. Benjamin Rader, *American Sports: From the Age of Folk Games to the Age of Spectators* (Englewood Cliffs, N.J.: Prentice-Hall, 1983).

9. Nathaniel S. Fleischer, *Black Dynamite: The Story of the Negro in the Prize Ring from 1782 to 1938*, 3 vols. (New York: The Ring Book Shop, 1938).

10. Edwin B. Henderson, *The Negro in Sports* (Washington, D.C.: The Associated Publishers, 1939).

11. See David K. Wiggins, "Wendell Smith, the *Pittsburgh Courier-Journal* and the Campaign to Include Blacks in Organized Baseball, 1933–1945," *Journal of Sport History* 10 (Summer 1983): 5–29; idem, "The 1936 Olympic Games in Berlin: The Response of America's Black Press," *Research Quarterly For Exercise and Sport* 54 (September 1983): 278–92.

12. John R. Betts, "Organized Sport in Industrial America" (Ph.D. diss., Columbia University, 1951). Also see A. S. "Doc" Young, *Great Negro Baseball Stars and How They Made the Major Leagues* (New York: A. S. Barnes, 1953); Frederick M. Cozens and Florence S. Stumpf, *Sports in American Life* (New York: Arno Press, 1956).

13. Betts, "Organized Sport in Industrial America," 807.

14. For the racial realities of American culture in the 1950's, see Richard Polenberg, *One Nation Divisible: Class, Race and Ethnicity in the United States Since 1938* (New York: Viking Press, 1980); John Hope Franklin, *From Slavery to Freedom: A History of Negro Americans* (New York: Alfred A. Knopf, 1980); C. Vann Woodward, *The Strange Career of Jim Crow* (New York: Oxford University Press, 1974); August Meier and Elliott Rudwick, *From Plantation to Ghetto* (New York: Hill and Wang, 1976).

15. Herbert McArthur, "National Endowment for the Humanities Workshops in the Materials of Negro History and Culture," *Wilson Library Bulletin* 43 (December 1968): 353.

16. *Negro History Bulletin* 32 (May 1969): 21–22.

17. "To establish a National Commission on Negro History and Culture," Hearings before the Select Sub-Committee on Education and Labor, House of Representatives, Nineteenth Congress, Second Session, on House Resolution 12962, Hearing held in New York City, March 18, 1968 (Washington, D.C., 1968).

18. A. S. "Doc" Young, *Negro Firsts in Sports* (Chicago: Johnson Publishing Company, 1963); Arna Bontemps, *Famous Negro Athletes* (New York: Dodd, Mead, and Company, 1964); Edwin B. Henderson, *The Black Athlete: Emergence and Arrival* (New York: Publishers Company, 1968); Jack Orr, *The Black Athlete: His Story in American History* (New York: Lion Books, 1969). See also Edwin B. Henderson, "Physical Education and Athletics Among Negroes," in *The History of Physical Education and Sport*, ed. Bruce L. Bennett (Chicago: The Athletic Institute, 1972), 67–83.

19. See Thomas Kochman, *Black and White: Styles in Conflict* (Chicago: The University of Chicago Press, 1981).

20. Finis Farr, *Black Champion: The Life and Times of Jack Johnson* (New York: Charles Scribner's Sons, 1964); John P. Davis, "The Negro in American Sports," in *The American Negro Reference Book* ed. J. P. Davis (Englewood Cliffs, N.J.: Prentice-Hall, 1966), 775–825.

21. Danzil Batchelor, *Jack Johnson and His Times* (London: Phoenix Sports Books, 1956).

22. Farr, *Black Champion: The Life and Times of Jack Johnson*, 287.

23. Davis' essay was published in *The American Negro Reference Book*, a work sponsored by the Phelps-Stokes Fund. In 1976 the fund sponsored another reference book which included an essay on sport written by Edwin B. Henderson. See Edwin B. Henderson "The Black American in Sports," in *The Black American Reference Book*, ed. Mabel M. Smythe (Englewood Cliffs, N.J.: Prentice-Hall, 1976), 927–963.

24. Robert Peterson, *Only the Ball Was White* (Englewood Cliffs, N.J.: Prentice-Hall, 1970).

25. Ibid.

26. See John Holway, *Voices from the Great Black Baseball Leagues* (New York: Harper and Row, 1978); William Brashler, *Josh Gibson: A Life in the Negro Leagues* (New York: Harper and Row, 1978); William Brashler, *Bingo Long's Traveling All Stars and Motor Kings* (New York: Harper and Row, 1973); Donn Rogosin, *Invisible Men: Life in Baseball's Negro Leagues* (New York: Atheneum Publishers, 1983). For another book that touches upon black baseball, see Art Rust, Jr., *Get That Nigger off the Field: A Sparkling Informal History of the Black Man in Baseball* (New York: Delacorte, 1976): See also Rob Ruck "Black Sandlot Baseball: The Pittsburgh Crawfords," *Western Pennsylvania Historical Magazine* 66 (January 1983): 49–68.

27. Lee Lowenfish, "Sport, Race, and the Baseball Business; The Jackie Robinson Story Revisited," *Arena Review* 2 (Spring 1978): 2–16.

28. Bill L. Weaver, "The Black Press and the Assault on Professional Baseball's Color Line, October 1945–April 1947," *Phylon* 40 (Winter 1979): 303–317.

29. David K. Wiggins, "Wendell Smith, The *Pittsburgh Courier-Journal* and the Campaign to Include Blacks in Organized Baseball, 1933–1945," 5–29.

30. Ronald A. Smith, "The Paul Robeson – Jackie Robinson Saga and a Political Collision," *Journal of Sport History* 6 (Summer 1979): 5–27.

31. Ibid., 23.

32. Jules Tygiel, *Baseball's Great Experiment: Jackie Robinson and His Legacy* (New York: Oxford University Press, 1983).

33. Murray Polner, *Branch Rickey: A Biography* (New York: Atheneum Publishing, 1982); Harvey Frommer, *Rickey and Robinson: The Men Who Broke Baseball's Color Barrier* (New York: MacMillan Publishing Co., 1982). There have been a number of more popular books written on the Robinson story. See for example, Milton J. Shaprio, *Jackie Robinson of the Brooklyn Dodgers* (New York: Julian Messer, 1966); Arthur Mann, *The Jackie Robinson Story* (New York: Grosset and Dunlap, 1950); Bill Roeder, *Jackie Robinson Story* (Grosset and Dunlap, 1950); Carl T. Rowan, *Wait Till Next Year* (New York: Random House, 1960).

34. Robert H. Decoy, *The Big Black Fire* (Los Angeles: Holloway, 1969).

35. Al-Tony Gilmore, *Bad Nigger: The National Impact of Jack Johnson* (New York: Kennikat Press, 1975). Also see Gilmore's articles "Jack Johnson: A Magnificent Black Anachronism of the Early Twentieth Century," *Journal of Social and Behavioral Sciences* 19 (Winter 1973): 35–42; "Jack Johnson, The Man and His Times," *Journal of Popular Culture* 6 (Spring 1973): 496–506; "Jack Johnson and White Women: The National Impact, 1912–1913," *Journal of Negro History* 58 (January 1973): 18–38.

36. William H. Wiggins "Jack Johnson as Bad Nigger: The Folklore of His Life," *The Black Scholar* 2 (January 1971): 4–19.

37. Gilmore, *Bad Nigger: The National Impact of Jack Johnson*, 95.

38. Randy Roberts, *Papa Jack: Jack Johnson and the Era of White Hopes* (New York: The Free Press, 1983).

39. For other studies of Johnson, see idem, "Heavyweight Champion Jack Johnson: His Omaha Image, A Public Reaction Study," *Nebraska History* 57 (Summer 1976): 226–241; idem, "Galveston's Jack Johnson: Flourishing in the Dark," *Southwestern Historical Quarterly* 82 (July 1983): 37–56; Raymond Wilson, "Another White Hope Bites the Dust: The Jack Johnson – Jim Flynn Heavyweight Fight in 1912," *Montana, The Magazine of Western History* 29 (January 1979): 30–30; Richard Broome, "The Australian Reaction to Jack Johnson, Black Pugilist 1907–09, in *Sports in History: The Making of Modern Sporting History* eds. Richard Cashman and Michael McKerman (St. Lucia, Australia: University of Queensland Press, 1979); Stuart Mews "Puritanicalism,

Sport and Race: A Symbolic Crusade of 1911," in O. J. Cuming and Derek Baker, eds, *Studies in Church History*, Vol. 8 (Cambridge, England: Cambridge University Press, 1972).

40.  Anthony O. Edmonds, *Joe Louis* (Grand Rapids, Mich.: William B. Erdmans, 1976). Also see Edmonds' article "The Second Louis-Schmeling Fight: Sport, Symbol and Culture," *Journal of Popular Culture* 7 (Summer 1973): 42–50.

41.  Jeffrey T. Sammons, "Boxing as a Reflection of Society: The Southern Reaction to Joe Louis," *Journal of Popular Culture* 16 (Spring 1983): 23–33; Dominic J. Capeci Jr., and Martha Wilkerson, "Multifarious Hero: Joe Louis, American Society and Race Relations During World Crisis, 1935–1945," *Journal of Sport History* 10 (Winter 1983): 5–25. For other studies of Louis, see Al-Tony Gilmore, "The Myth, Legend, and Folklore of Joe Louis: The Impression of Sport on Society," *The South Atlantic Quarterly* 82 (Summer 1983): 256–268; Alexander J. Young, "Joe Louis: Symbol, 1933–1949," (Ph.D. diss., University of Maryland, 1968); Barney Nagler, *Brown Bomber* (New York: The World Publishing Company, 1972); Gerald Astor, ". . . And A Credit to His Race: The Hard Life and Times of Joseph Louis Barrow, A.K.A. Joe Louis* (New York: Saturday Review Press, 1974); Norman Bell, *The Fighting Life of a Fighter* (London: The War Fact Press, 1943); John G. Van Deusen, *Brown Bomber: The Story of Joe Louis* (Philadelphia: Dorrance & Co., 1940); Edward Van Every, *Joe Louis: Man and Super Fighter* (New York: Frederick A. Stokes, 1936).

42.  Alexander J. Young, "The Boston Tarbaby," *The Nova Scotia Historical Quarterly* 4 (September 1974): 277–293; David K. Wiggins, "Isaac Murphy: Black Hero in Nineteenth Century American Sport 1861–1896," *Canadian Journal of History of Sport and Physical Education* 10 (May 1979): 15–32. Three interesting articles on another famous black boxer. Tom Molineaux, can be found in Michael H. Goodman, "The Moor vs. Black Diamond," *Virginia Cavalcade* 29 (Spring 1980): 164–173; Carl B. Cone, "The Molineaux-Cribb Fight, 1810: Wuz Tom Molineaux Robbed?" *Journal of Sport History* 9 (Winter 1982): 83–91; Jack W. Rudolph, "Tom Molyneaux – America's 'Almost' Champion," *American History Illustrated* 14 (August 1979): 8–14. Also, see David K. Wiggins, "Peter Jackson and the Elusive Heavyweight Championship: A Black Athlete's Struggle Against the Late Nineteenth Century Color-Line," *Journal of Sport History* 12 (Summer 1985): 143–168.

43.  W. F. Mandle, "Sports History," in *New History: Studying Australia Today*, eds. G. Osborne and W. F. Mandle (Sydney: George Allen and Unwin, 1982), 82–93.

44.  John Behee, *Hail to the Victors! Black Athletes at the University of Michigan* (Ann Arbor, Michigan: Swink-Tuttle Press, 1974). For a rather romantic view of the black college athlete, see Oceania Chalk, *Black College Sport* (New York: Dodd and Mead, 1976).

45.  Don Spivy and Tom Jones, "Intercollegiate Athletic Servitude: A Case Study of the Black Illinois Student – Athletes, 1931–1967," *Social Science Quarterly* 55 (March 1975): 939–947. Also see Spivy's recent article "The Black Athlete in Big-Time Intercollegiate Sports, 1941–1968," *Phylon* 44 (June 1983): 116–125.

46.  Jack W. Berryman, "Early Black Leadership in Collegiate Football: Massachusetts as a Pioneer," *Historical Journal of Massachusetts* 9 (June 1981): 17–28.

47.  Adolf H. Grundman, "Image of Intercollegiate Sports' and the Civil Rights Movement: A Historian's View," *Arena Review* 3 (October 1979): 17–24.

48.  David K. Wiggins, "The 1936 Olympic Games in Berlin: The Response of America's Black Press," 278–292. See the previously mentioned articles idem, "Wendell Smith, the *Pittsburgh Courier-Journal* and the Campaign to Include Blacks in Organized Baseball, 1933–1945," 5–29; Weaver, "The Black Press and the Assault on Professional Baseball's Color Line, October 1945–April 1947," 303–317.

49.  David K. Wiggins, "Good Times on the Old Plantation: Popular Recreations of the Black Slave in Antebellum South, 1810–1860," *Journal of Sport History* 4 (Fall 1977): 260–284; idem, "The Play of Slave Children in the Plantation Communities of the Old

South, 1820–1860," *Journal of Sport History* 7 (Summer 1980): 21–39; idem. "Sport and Popular Pastimes: Shadow of the Slavequarter," *Canadian Journal of History of Sport and Physical Education* 11 (May 1980): 61–88.

50. See for example Lawrence W. Levine, *Black Culture and Black Consciousness: Afro-American Folk Thought From Slavery to Freedom* (New York: Oxford University Press, 1977); August Meier and Elliot M. Rudwick, *Along the Color Line: Explorations in the Black Experience* (Urbana, Illinois: University of Illinois Press, 1976); Herbert G. Gutman, *The Black Family in Slavery and Freedom, 1750–1978* (New York: Pantheon Books, 1976).

51. Ralph Watkins, "Recreation, Leisure, and Charity in the Afro-American Community of Buffalo, New York; 1920–1925," *Afro-Americans in New York Life and History* 6 (July 1982): 7–15.

52. Ibid., 15.

53. Somers, *The Rise of Sport in New Orleans, 1850–1900*, 1972; Stephen Hardy, *How Boston Played: Sport, Recreation, and Community, 1865–1915* (Boston: Northeastern University Press, 1982).

54. For insights into the deteriorating status of blacks in American society during the latter half of the nineteenth century see, George M. Fredrickson, *The Black Image in the White Mind: The Debate on Afro-American Character and Destiny, 1817–1914* (New York: Harper and Row, 1971); Rayford W. Logan, *The Betrayal of the Negro from Rutherford B. Hayes to Woodrow Wilson* (New York: Collier Books, 1965).

55. Hardy, *How Boston Played*, 178–179.

56. Ibid., 138.

57. "See for example, Stanley D. Eitzen and David C. Sanford, "The Segregation of Blacks by Playing Position in Football: Accident or Design?" *Social Science Quarterly* 55 (March 1975): 948–959; Norman R. Yetman, Forret J. Birghorn, and Floyd R. Thomas, Jr. "Racial Participation and Integration in Intercollegiate Basketball, 1958–1980," *Journal of Sport Behavior* 5 (March 1981): 44–56; Roscoe C. Brown, Jr., "A Commentary on Racial Myths and the Black Athlete," in *Social Problems in Athletics*, ed. Daniel M. Landers (Urbana, Illinois: University of Illinois Press, 1976), 168–173; Barry D. McPherson, "The Segregation by Playing Position Hypothesis in Sport: An Alternative Hypothesis," *Social Science Quarterly* 55 (March 1975): 960–966.

58. For examples of other articles from various disciplinary perspectives, including history, see Harry Edwards, "Sport Within the Veil: The Triumphs, Tragedies, and Challenges of Afro-American Involvement," *Annals of the American Academy of Political and Social Sciences* 445 (1979): 116–127; Ali A. Mazuri, "Boxer Muhammad Ali and Soldier Idi Amin as International Political Symbols: The Bioeconomics of Sports and War," *Comparative Studies in Society and History* 19 (April 1977): 189–215; Marvin E. Fletcher, "The Black Soldier Athlete in the United States Army, 1890–1916," *Canadian Journal of History of Sport and Physical Education* 3 (December 1971): 16–26; G. B. McKinney, "Negro Professional Baseball Players in the Upper South in the Gilded Age," *Journal of Sport History* 3 (Winter 1976): 273–280; John Dommissee, "The Psychology of Apartheid Sport," *Journal of Sport and Social Issues* 1 (Summer/ Fall 1977): 32–53; Gerald W. Scully, "Discrimination: The Case of Baseball," in *Government and the Sports Business*, ed. Roger G. Noll (Washington, D.C.: Brookings Institute, 1974), 221–247.

59. See George P. Rawick, ed., *The American Slave: A Composite Autobiography* 19 vols. (Westport, Conn.: Greenwood Publishing Company, 1972).

60. There has been a plethora of studies written on free blacks in antebellum America. See particularly, Ira Berlin, *Slaves Without Masters: The Free Negro in the Antebellum South* (New York: Random House, 1974); John Hope Franklin, *The Free Negro in North Carolina, 1790–1860* (Chapel Hill: University of North Carolina Press, 1943); Marina Wikramanayake, *A World in Shadow: The Free Black in Antebellum South*

*Carolina* (Columbia: University of South Carolina Press, 1973); Leon F. Litwack, *North of Slavery: The Negro in the Free States, 1790–1860* (Chicago: University of Chicago Press, 1961).

61. Levine, *Black Culture and Black Consciousness*, 140.

62. The most extensive work on the history of the black family is Herbert Gutman, *The Black Family in Slavery and Freedom* (New York: Oxford University Press, 1976).

63. For examples of studies that utilize psychohistorical techniques see Dorothy Ross, "Woodrow Wilson and the Case For Psychohistory," *American Historical Review* 69 (December 1982): 659–668; Richard L. Bushman, "On the Uses of Psychology: Conflict and Conciliation in Benjamin Franklin," *History and Theory* 5 (1966): 225–240.

64. See Peter Axthelm, *The City Game: Basketball in New York from the World Champion Knicks to the World of Playgrounds* (New York: Harper and Row, 1970).

65. John W. Blassingame, *Black New Orleans, 1860–1880* (Chicago: University of Chicago Press, 1973); Kenneth L. Kusmer, *A Ghetto Takes Shape: Black Cleveland, 1870–1930* (Urbana, Illinois: University of Illinois Press, 1976); Gilbert Osofsky, *Harlem, The Making of a Ghetto* (New York: Harper and Row, 1965); Seth M. Scheiner *Negro Mecca: A History of the Negro in New York City, 1865–1920* (New York: New York University Press, 1965); Allen H. Spear, *Black Chicago: The Making of a Ghetto, 1890–1920* (Chicago: University of Chicago Press, 1967).

66. The most noteworthy example is E. Franklin Frazier, *The Negro Family in Chicago* (Chicago: University of Chicago Press, 1932).

67. "See Theodore Hershberg, ed., *Philadelphia: Work, Space, Family, and Group Experience in the Nineteenth Century: Essays Toward an Interdisciplinary History of the City* (New York: Oxford University Press, 1981); Oliver Zunz, *The Changing Face of Inequality: Urbanization, Industrial Development, and Immigrants in Detroit, 1890–1920* (Chicago: University of Chicago Press, 1982).

68. Peter Gottlieb, "Migrants and Jobs: The New Black Worker in Pittsburg, 1916–1930," *Western Pennsylvania Historical Magazine* 61 (Summer 1978): 1–17.

69. For information on the black athletes' revolt, see Harry Edwards, *The Revolt of the Black Athlete* (New York: The Free Press, 1969); idem, "The Olympic Project for Human Rights: An Assessment Ten Years Later," *The Black Scholar* 10 (March/April 1979): 2–8. A well known book that touches upon the revolt is Jack Olsen, *The Black Athlete: A Shameful Story* (New York: Time-Life Books, 1968).

70. See Curt Flood, *The Way It Is* (New York: Trident Press, 1971); Jesse Owens, *Blackthink: My Life as Black Man and White Man* (New York: William Morrow and Company, 1970); Bernie Parish, *They Call It a Game* (New York: Dial, 1971); Bill Russell, *Go Up For Glory* (New York: Coward McCann, 1966); idem, *Second Wind: The Memoirs of an Opinionated Man* (New York: Random House, 1974). There have been a number of other interesting autobiographies written by famous black athletes. See for example, Jack A. Johnson, *Jack Johnson is a Dandy: An Autobiography* (New York: Chelsea House, 1969); Marshall W. "Major" Taylor, *The Fastest Bicycle Rider in the World* (Battleboro, Vermont: Green-Stephen Press, 1971); Jackie Robinson, *I Never Had It Made* (New York: G. P. Putnam's Sons, 1971); Paul Robeson, *Here I Stand* (London: Dennis Dobson, 1958); Joe Louis, *My Life Story* (New York: Duell, Sloan, and Pearce, 1947).

71. W. E. B. Dubois, *The Souls of Black Folk* (New York: Fawcett Books, 1961), p. 17.

72. Frank Tannenbaum, *Slave and Citizen: The Negro in the Americas* (New York: Vintage Books, 1946).

73. Two works that discuss the status of black athletes in Great Britain and the West Indies respectively are Ernest Cashmore's *Black Sportsman* (London: Routledge & Kegan Paul, 1982), and C. L. R. James' delightful book *Beyond A Boundary* (New York: Pantheon Books, 1983).

74. Scholars interested in doing research on the black athlete are fortunate in that there are a plethora of bibliographic works available that are devoted exclusively to the history of blacks. The only bibliography, however, that deals specifically with the black athlete is Lenwood G. Davis and Belinda Daniels, comp., *Black Athletes in the United States: A Bibliography of Books, Articles, Autobiographies, and Biographies on Professional Black Athletes, 1880–1981* (Westport, Connecticut: Greenwood Press, 1983. See also Bruce L. Bennet. "Bibliography on the Negro in Sports, *"Journal of Health, Physical Education, and Recreation* 41 (January 1970): 77–78; idem, "Supplement Selected Annotated Bibliography on the Negro Sports, *"Journal of Health, Physical Education and Recreation* 41 (September 1970): 71; Grant Henry, "A Bibliography Concerning Negroes in Physical Education, Athletics, and Related Fields," *Journal of Health, Physical Education and Recreation* 44 (May 1973): 65–70.

M